THE ISRAELI ECONOMY FROM THE FOUNDATION
OF THE STATE THROUGH THE 21ST CENTURY

This book analyzes the development of the Israeli economy in its historical context. It shows how the ideology of the dominant group in the Zionist movement led to the development of agriculture, thus meeting the preconditions for successful industrialization. Remarkable, if uneven, growth has taken place, with increasing allocations for defense. Regional isolation led to the emphasis on high-quality exports for developed markets that has stimulated the technological base. Israel has benefited from mass immigration and increased access to foreign capital – factors that have transformed the economy. The book includes chapters on the development of the Jewish community in Palestine during the British Mandate; macroeconomic developments and economic policy; globalization and high technology; defense; the economics of the Arab minority; Israeli settlements and relations with the Palestinians; and the role of religion. It concludes with an examination of the socioeconomic divisions that have widened as the economy has grown.

Paul Rivlin is the Sandra Glass Senior Fellow at the Moshe Dayan Center for Middle East and African Studies at Tel Aviv University. He is the author of four other books: *The Dynamics of Economic Policy Making in Egypt* (1985), *The Israeli Economy* (1992), *Economic Policy and Performance in the Arab World* (2001), and *Arab Economies in the Twenty-First Century* (2009), as well as numerous monographs, papers, contributed chapters, articles, and reports on economic development in the Middle East and on international energy markets, defense, and trade economics. Educated at Cambridge, Harvard, and London universities, he has taught undergraduate and graduate courses on Middle East economics at Tel Aviv University, Ben-Gurion University of the Negev, and London University, and he has been a visiting professor of economics at Emory University. He has lectured in the United States, China, Canada, Egypt, India, Japan, Turkey, and Europe.

T0323683

The Israeli Economy from the Foundation of the State through the 21st Century

PAUL RIVLIN

Tel Aviv University

CAMBRIDGE
UNIVERSITY PRESS

CAMBRIDGE UNIVERSITY PRESS
Cambridge, New York, Melbourne, Madrid, Cape Town, Singapore,
São Paulo, Delhi, Dubai, Tokyo, Mexico City

Cambridge University Press
32 Avenue of the Americas, New York, NY 10013-2473, USA

www.cambridge.org
Information on this title: www.cambridge.org/9780521150200

First published 2011

Printed in the United States of America

A catalog record for this publication is available from the British Library.

Library of Congress Cataloging in Publication data
Rivlin, Paul.
The Israeli economy from the foundation of the state through
the 21st century/Paul Rivlin.
p.   cm.
Includes bibliographical references and index.
ISBN 978-0-521-19037-4 (hardback)
1. Israel – Economic conditions.   I. Title.
HC415.25.R583   2010
330.95694–dc22   2010033392

ISBN 978-0-521-19037-4 Hardback
ISBN 978-0-521-15020-0 Paperback

This book is dedicated with love and thanks to my mother, Zena, and to the memory of my father, Michael. As a child, I learned to discuss and debate the issues of the day around their kitchen table, usually with clarity and sometimes with passion. They taught me to think critically, to express myself clearly, to be concerned about events outside the home, and much else. My debt to them is great.

אם אין אני לי, מי לי; וכשאני לעצמי, מה אני
מסכת אבות פרק א,יג

If I am not for myself, who is for me?
And if I am only for myself, what am I?
The Ethics of the Fathers

"The political problem of mankind is to combine three things: economic efficiency, social justice, and individual liberty."
John Maynard Keynes "Liberalism and Labour," The Collected Writings of John Maynard Keynes Vol. IX, Essays in Persuasion. 1926; London: Macmillan St. Martins for the Royal Economic Society, 1972.

Contents

List of Figures   *page* ix

List of Tables   xi

List of Appendices   xiii

Preface   xv

1. Introduction   1

2. The Economy of the Yishuv and Its Legacy   12

3. The Economy, 1948–1985   34

4. Macro-Economic Developments, Growth, and Policy   69

5. Globalization and High Technology   94

6. Defense: Service or Burden?   118

7. Israel and the Palestinians   143

8. The Economics of Religion   166

9. The Arab Minority   187

10. Demographic Developments and Socioeconomic Divisions   208

11. Conclusions   240

Appendices   251

References   271

Index   285

Figures

2.1 Jewish occupational structure, Eastern Europe, 1880s   *page*   14
2.2 Jewish occupational structure, Palestine, 1920s   15
3.1 Annual change in the consumer price index, 1970–2009   58
4.1 GDP annual growth rates, 1990–2009   70
4.2 Central government revenues and expenditure, 1980–2008   80
4.3 Total central government spending, defense, and interest,
1980–2008   80
4.4 The budget deficit, 1998–2008   81
4.5 Public debt as percentage of GDP, 1998–2008   82
4.6 The tax burden in Israel and the OECD, 1970–2007   84
4.7 National income per capita in Israel as a percentage
of that in the United States, 1995–2005   87
4.8 The balance of payments current account
and the GDP growth rate, 1980–2009   89
4.9 Investment in Israel by non-residents, 1998–2008   92
4.10 Investments by Israelis abroad, 1998–2008   92
5.1 The share of exports and imports in GDP, 1950–2009   96
5.2 Manufacturing employment by technological
intensity, 1995–2007   102
5.3 Average monthly wage per employee post, 1990–2007   107
5.4 The Israeli labor force, 1970–2007   111
5.5 Employment in construction, 1980–2008   113
6.1 The defense budget, 1996–2009   121
6.2 Defense consumption expenditure, 1960–2006   121
6.3 Defense consumption expenditure as a percentage of
GDP, 1950–2006   122
6.4 United States military and civilian aid to Israel, 1997–2007   127

7.1 Population of Jewish settlements in the West Bank and
     Gaza, 1972–2008   147
7.2 Employment of Palestinian West Bank and Gaza
     residents in Israel, 1968–2005   154
8.1 Number of religious seminary students, 1971–2007   172
8.2 Total cost of child allowances, 1970–2007   176
9.1 Total fertility rates, 1960–2008   192
9.2 Arab and Jewish household monthly income, 1997–2006   200
9.3 Average monthly earnings by type of settlement, 1995–2006   201
9.4 The rate of poverty among Arabs, 1997–2008   203
10.1 The Gini coefficient of income distribution of the whole
     population, 1980–2007   217
10.2 Unemployment rates by years of education, 1998–2008   221
10.3 Incidence of poverty among individuals according to
     different measures, 1997–2007   222
10.4 Poverty by population group, 1997–2008   225
10.5 Poverty rates in Israel and selected countries, 1998–2006   227
10.6 Transfer payments and general government services
     per capita, 1995–2008   229
10.7 The share of labor in GDP, 1970–2007   237

Tables

1.1 Israel: Population, national income, and national
income per capita, 1950–2009   *page* 3

2.1 The Palestinian economy: Shares in net national
product, 1922–1947   19

3.1 The balance of payments current account, 1952–1980   42

3.2 The budget deficit and its financing, 1980–2008   61

4.1 Business sector inputs and total factor
productivity, 1990–2008   73

4.2 Labor market indicators, 1998–2008   76

4.3 The net capital stock, 2000–2007   79

4.4 The 1999 and 2009 budget proposals: Main components   83

4.5 The structure of the business sector, 1998–2008   85

4.6 Manufacturing production by technological
intensity, 1995–2007   86

5.1 Manufactured exports by technology intensity, 1990–2008   101

7.1 Spending on settlements in the territories, 1967–2003   150

7.2 Israeli net exports to and imports of goods from the
West Bank and Gaza, 1967–2008   158

8.1 Output losses due to ultra-orthodox non-participation
in the labor market, 1998–2007   173

8.2 Fertility rates in selected communities with populations of
10,000 or more, 2007   173

8.3 Child allowances, 2000–2009   175

9.1 Demographic trends, 1919–1949   190

9.2 Employment by sector, 2007   199

9.3 Share of wage and salary earners earning up to the minimum
wage, by type of settlement, 1995–2006   202

9.4 Gross national income per capita in the Middle East, 2006   206

10.1 The sources of population growth, 1948–2008   209
10.2 The age structure of the population, 1960–2008   211
10.3 The ethnic origin of the population, 1948–2008   212
10.4 The Jewish population by origin, 1948–2008   213
10.5 Fertility rates (number of births per woman), 1960–2008   215
10.6 The distribution of income before and after taxes
      and benefits: The share of each decile in total income
      per standard person, 1995–2007   219
10.7 Population aged 15-plus by years of schooling, 1997–2007   232

Appendices

2.1 The Yishuv: Population, national income, and national income per capita, 1922–1948   *page* 251

2.2 Agricultural, manufacturing, and construction output during the mandate, 1922–1939   251

3.1 Basic data on the Israeli economy, 2000–2008   252

4.1 GDP, 1995–2009   253

4.2 Share of working-age population in the labor force, 1996–2007   254

4.3 The net capital stock, 2000–2007   255

4.4 Israel and the OECD: Gross domestic product and gross domestic product per capita, 2007   256

4.5 Israel and the OECD: Indices of gross domestic product in purchasing power parities, 2005–2008   257

4.6 Israel and the OECD: Average annual growth rates, 1998–2008   258

4.7 Israel and the OECD: Civilian research and development, 2007   259

5.1 The balance of payments, 1995–2009   260

5.2 Foreign trade by country of import or export destination, 1995–2008   262

5.3 Output in the information and communications technology sectors, 2000–2006   263

5.4 Output and employment in the construction sector, 1980–2008   264

6.1 Budgetary and extra-budgetary defense spending, 2000–2005   265

10.1 Crude birth rate and death rate, 1950–2010   266

10.2 Immigration by period and last place of residence, 1882–2007   267

10.3 Number of families, people, and children living in poverty
before and after tax and benefits, 2002–2008   268
10.4 Number and share of pupils entitled to a school leaving certificate
and meeting university entrance requirements, 2000–2006   269

Preface

In my book, *The Israeli Economy*, published in 1992, I called for extensive reforms – largely designed to reduce government intervention – many of which have since been implemented. I also suggested that Israel's political culture made it difficult to create consensus around economic and other objectives. Since then, Israel's political structure has become more fragmented. A debate about economic and socioeconomic strategy has not, however, occurred. Instead governments of all kinds have implemented neoliberal policies. Political choices have been made about economic issues, usually under the guise of stabilization policies or because of the requirements of globalization, often with severe social consequences. The public was offered no alternatives by any significant political party. Despite this, there have been many economic achievements, including the absorption of more than a million immigrants in the 1990s and early 2000s, mainly from the former Soviet Union and Ethiopia during a period of regional conflict. It is against this complex background that I decided to write this book, which expands on what I wrote nearly twenty years ago, develops new themes, and reaches different conclusions, as would be expected with the passage of time.

The central theme in this book is the clash between efficiency and growth on the one hand and equity on the other. Market economies produce many, but not all, of the goods and services that people want: State bureaucracies do not. Market economies do not coincide with the model of perfect competition so laboriously taught to economics students. The truth is rather the opposite: In market economies, there are, as Adam Smith suggested, constant attempts to undermine competition. Even more worrying is the collusion of governments in the negation of competition. Furthermore, in a globalized system, governments are under pressure to limit public spending in order to reduce taxation. This limits their ability to compensate for the inequalities that market forces produce. The other issue that plays an increasing role is market failure. We are rediscovering, at great cost, something that some – usually the so-called unorthodox – economists knew all the time: Markets do not always work. Global warming is perhaps the greatest of these failures, but the international financial collapse of the second half of 2008 also raised fundamental questions about unregulated or deregulated financial markets. These issues are present in Israel, sometimes in an acute form, although they are hidden behind the more immediate problems of defense and so are neglected even more than in other countries.

This book is also a modest plea for a more realistic economics than that which prevails today. We need to look at the relationships between economics, politics, and sociology, and possibly other disciplines. For that reason, this book examines the ideas, values, and traditions of the different groups that have made up the Israeli population and analyzes their political strength and role. This is how ideas are formed, institutions built, and culture is made. A historical setting or context is essential to understand peoples' actions and reactions. The lesson of the current international financial crisis is that unregulated markets do not produce economically optimal solutions, let alone socially optimal ones; the effects of globalization should have taught us that lesson years ago.

I would like to thank Shlomo Avineri and David Webb for very useful suggestions; Elias Kraushaar for his enthusiastic work on the text; William Gutterman and Daniel Maddy Weitzman for their help with references, and Evie Goldfarb for her assistance. Arie Arnon, Ruth Klinov, and Jacob Metzer kindly gave me permission to quote their publications, as did the Maurice Falk Institute for Economic Research in Israel. I am very grateful to Scott Parris, my editor at Cambridge University Press, and his colleagues for skillfully steering this project to completion. Three anonymous reviewers made numerous suggestions, many of which have been adopted.

My family – Rosemary, Ben, and Alex – is the sine qua non of all my work. They have accommodated a sometimes absent and often absentminded husband and father and have encouraged me to continue researching and writing. Rosemary, once again, improved drafts and produced the graphics. Finally and belatedly, thanks to my aunt, Miryam Zafran.

I am, of course, responsible for all errors and omissions.

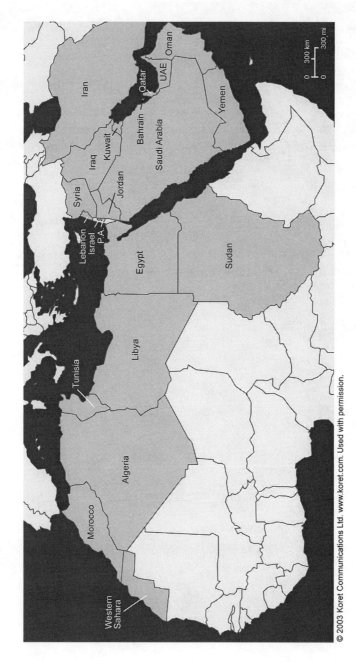

The Middle East

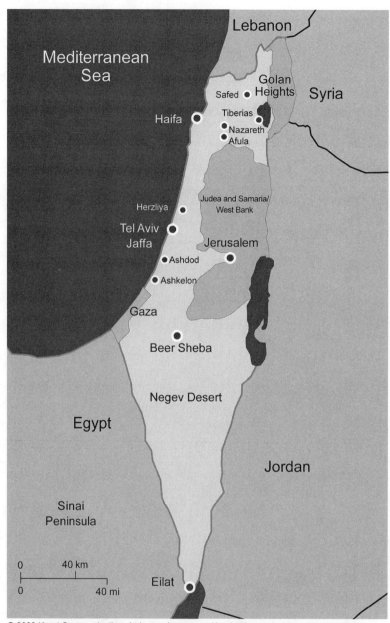

Mediterranean
Sea

Lebanon

Golan
Heights

Syria

Safed

Haifa

Tiberias

Nazareth

Afula

Herzliya

Judea and Samaria/
West Bank

Tel Aviv

Jaffa

Jerusalem

Ashdod

Ashkelon

Gaza

Beer Sheba

Negev Desert

Egypt

Jordan

Sinai
Peninsula

0   40 km

0   40 mi

Eilat

Israel

THE ISRAELI ECONOMY FROM THE FOUNDATION
OF THE STATE THROUGH THE 21ST CENTURY

ONE

Introduction

In 1882, when Zionist activity began, there were about 25,000 Jews in Palestine. By 1922, the Yishuv, or Jewish community in Palestine, had a population of 84,000. The national income was $8 million, or almost $1,500 per capita; by 1945, the Jewish population of Palestine was 550,000, and the national income had reached $147 million, or approximately $2,678 per capita, in constant prices and exchange rates. This was achieved under Ottoman and then British rule. In 1948, Israel declared its independence and was invaded by all of its neighbors. The war of independence left it without resources to absorb the huge immigration – its raison d'être – that arrived immediately following the war. Between 1950 and 2009, Israel's GDP[1] rose 34-fold, and its GDP per capita increased almost sixfold in real terms. By 2009, the population reached 7.4 million, the national income was almost $203 billion, and income per capita came to $27,275, using the 2008 prices and exchange rates.[2]

What explains the extraordinary eighteenfold growth of the Yishuv's economy? How can the growth of the Israeli economy be explained? The simple answer is population growth fed by immigration; imports of capital that permitted fast rates of investment; and successful organization and high levels of motivation. At a deeper level lie the issues of structural change, technological development, and economic policy making against a

---

[1] The terms gross national product (GNP) and gross domestic product (GDP) are used frequently in this book. Gross national product is total value of all final goods and services produced within a country in a particular year, plus income earned by its citizens (including those located abroad), minus income of non-residents located in that country. Gross domestic product is the total value of all final goods and services produced in a country in a given year, equal to total consumer, investment, and government spending, plus the value of exports, minus the value of imports. Where other definitions are used, they are explained in the text or in footnotes.

[2] Calculated using measuringworth.com

complex background of sociological and political change. Israel has capital-
ized on its disadvantages: It has always been at war and has lacked an economic hinterland in the Middle East. It therefore developed technologies
to provide its armed forces with "quality" to match Arab "quantity," which
were deliberately released for use in the civilian sector often great success.
It also orientated its exports to markets in developed countries. This was
both because nearby markets were closed and because the technological
nature of its production made it suitable for more sophisticated markets.
The benefits of this integration into the global economy have not been uni-
versally felt in Israel, and socioeconomic gaps have widened, fed in part by
ethnic and religious factors. It has also had to overcome, like many other
countries, many policy errors and other costs.

The Economy, 1948–2010

"As Israel's economy has strengthened, its society has weakened." This view,
widely held in Israel, is the main theme of this book. It examines the Israeli
economy at the beginning of the twenty-first century in its political, demographic, and social context. Emphasis is given to the links between economic growth and social policy, to the consequences of immigration, Israel's
defense effort, relations with the Palestinians, the economics of minorities,
and the role of religion. The scale of development over the last fifty years is
illustrated in Table 1.1. It shows that between 1950 and 2009, the population rose sixfold, the gross domestic product increased 34-fold, and gross
domestic product per capita went up eightfold.

On 14 May 1948, the state of Israel was declared; the next day, its Arab
neighbors and other Arab states declared war and invaded it. The immediate
economic problems were acute: War and mass immigration had to be
financed; the government was committed to provide basic commodities
to the existing population and to new immigrant. The creation of government administration was relatively easy, because semigovernmental Jewish
institutions that had developed during the Mandatory period became
government departments.

During 1949, cease-fire agreements were signed with the neighboring
Arab states, bringing to an end a year and a half of fighting. Between the
declaration of independence and the end of 1951, a total of almost 590,000
immigrants had arrived. Thus in its first three years, the Jewish population
of Israel doubled. From 1949, the majority of immigrants came from Middle
Eastern countries and most of them had much lower educational levels than
those who came from Europe or had been born in Palestine. Immediate

Table 1.1. *Israel: Population, national income, and national income per capita,*
1950–2009 (2005 prices and exchange rates)

	Population (million)	GDP ($ billions)	GDP change between dates (percent)	GDP per capita ($)	GDP per capita: change between dates (percent)
1950	1.27	4.49		3,546	
1960	2.19	12.90	187.3	5,896	66.3
1970	2.97	28.91	124.0	9,720	64.9
1980	3.88	48.53	67.9	12,516	28.7
1990	4.66	69.50	43.2	14,916	19.2
2000	6.30	119.47	71.9	18,966	26.7
2009	7.43	152.79	27.9	20,577	8.5

Sources: Central Bureau of Statistics, Statistical Abstract of Israel, 2009; Central Bureau of Statistics, First Annual Flash Estimates of the National Accounts for 2009 (Jerusalem: Central Bureau of Statistics, 2009).

needs were met by a policy of strict austerity based on the rationing of basic commodities: inflationary government finance accompanied by price controls. Housing and employment conditions for immigrants improved only gradually. In 1952, black markets and the inefficiency of the controlled economy resulted in the introduction of a so-called New Economic Policy. This included the devaluation of exchange rate, gradual relaxation of price controls and rationing, and temporary curbs on immigration to ease the absorption of new immigrants and reduce unemployment.

The first comprehensive data for the new state was published in 1950 and showed that the gross domestic product (GDP) was almost $4.5 billion and GDP per capita came to $3,546 in 2005 prices (see Table 1.1). Exports per capita were only $27 whereas imports were $237; the huge gap between exports and imports resulted in a shortage of foreign exchange and was an additional reason for the government to take control of foreign trade and payments.

From 1950 until 1965, Israel experienced a fast rate of growth: National income in real terms grew by an average annual rate of more than 11 percent, and per capita income by more than 6 percent. This was made possible by the combination of immigration and large capital inflows: United States aid, mainly in the form of loans; unilateral transfers from the Jewish community abroad; German reparation payments to the government of Israel; and restitutions to individuals and the sale of State of Israel Bonds abroad. Israel thus had resources for public and private consumption and investment that exceeded its national income by approximately 25 percent. This made possible a massive investment program, financed largely through the government budget.[3]

The scale of needs and the socialist, but pragmatic, philosophy of the main political party in the government coalitions both led to massive state intervention in the economy. Governmental budgets and strong protectionist measures to foster import substitution encouraged the development of new industries, especially textiles. Subsidies were given to help the development of new exports, beyond the traditional exports of citrus products and cut diamonds. By the early 1960s, the government realized that the growth of Israeli firms – and thus output and employment – was being restricted by the size of the local market. New markets were needed, and so Israel negotiated the first trade agreement with the then-European Community (EC). This provided nearly free access to EC markets for Israeli industrial products and limited access for agricultural ones. The agreement with the EC was expanded in 1975, and a more comprehensive free trade agreement was signed with the United States in 1985. The latter covered industry, agriculture, and services.

The balance of payments constraint remained and resulted in periodic deflationary policies designed to restrain domestic demand, reduce imports, and encourage exports. Once the balance of payments improved, the restraints were eased. In 1967, this occurred because the Six Day War boosted government spending on the military and led to a wave of almost euphoric confidence in Israel. The encouragement of domestic military industries led to the beginning of what has since been called the high technology revolution. Confidence in Israel and its new strategic position as a regional power in the Middle East also encouraged small but significant foreign investment in research and development of technology. Between 1967 and 1973, about 100,000 immigrants arrived from Western countries. Many of them had financial capital as well as higher education and were able to enter the labor market and finance their own immigration. There was also a small immigration from the Soviet Union, a result of the United States policy of détente. The feeling of security encouraged social unrest: The neglected second generation of immigrants from the Middle East and North Africa no longer deferred to the country's Labor leadership. The government responded to the demonstrations by developing social

---

[3] Halevi Nadav. A Brief Economic History of Modern Israel. *Economic History Net Encyclopedia*. http://eh.net/encyclopedia/article/halevi.israel

welfare programs. These were funded out of a growing budget deficit that did not seem to be a problem because the economy was growing.

Positive economic trends ended with the Yom Kippur War of 1973. This brought massive loss of life, injury, and huge military losses. Government spending on the military grew but tax revenues were affected by the reduced level of economic activity that resulted from the war. From 1975, when Israel returned the Sinai oilfields to Egypt, the balance of payments suffered from the increase in the oil import bill. This worsened when international oil prices rose sharply in 1979. The government tried to stabilize the economy and also introduced a major reform of the income tax system.

In 1977, the Labor Party lost power and for the first time, a right-wing Likud, government came to power. This change was the result of the alienation of many underprivileged Jewish voters from the community that had its origins in the Middle East, a more general rejection of an increasingly corrupt Labor Party, and a delayed protest against the conduct of the Yom Kippur War. The new government combined nationalists who wanted to expand Jewish settlement building in the West Bank, populists who wanted to increase benefits to the poorer section of the community, and liberals who wanted to reduce government interference in the economy. The economic policies followed were a combination of all of these, and the results were a rapid acceleration of inflation, larger budget and balance of payments deficits, and rising foreign debt. All this was accompanied by slow economic growth. The signing of the peace treaty with Egypt in 1979 transformed Israel's security position. The Lebanon War that began in 1982 compounded the economic problems, and by 1985, after a number of unsuccessful attempts to stabilize the economy, Israel was on the edge of economic catastrophe.

In July 1985, a comprehensive stabilization program was introduced that simultaneously dealt with all the aspects of the crisis: hyper-inflation, dollarization (the shekel had lost its function as a store of value), huge budget and balance of payments deficits, and a loss of international financial credibility that made borrowing abroad hard and very expensive. The program reduced inflation from an annual rate of approaching 500 percent in the first half of 1985 to 20 percent in the second half. The budget deficit was slashed and the balance of payments strengthened. The United States provided $1.5 billion in aid that gave the program credibility both inside Israel and abroad.

Israel has lived in the shadow of the 1980s economic crisis ever since. To prevent inflation, the exchange rate was kept stable for much of the period from 1985 to 1990. In the mid-1990s, the government and the Bank of Israel (the central bank) decided that inflation should be brought down to 2–3 percent annually: This was achieved with tight economic policies. Israel's economy was transformed. In 1986–1995, following the stabilization of the economy in 1985 and with mass immigration from 1990 onward, GDP increased by an annual average rate of 5.2 percent.

In the 1990s, one million immigrants arrived, largely from the former Soviet Union. They helped transform the economy by expanding the local market and thus creating economies of scale. From 1992, the availability of United States loan guarantees encouraged an inflow of capital to balance that of labor and thus provide the basis for economic growth.

The economic stabilization program of July 1985 began a major reduction in the role of the state and the introduction of a new, more liberalized economic order. The relationship between stabilization and liberalization is an important issue. The early 1990s brought significant moves to liberalize foreign trade and capital markets. In the years 1996–2003, economic growth decelerated to less than 3 percent, which, when population growth is taken into account, meant that GDP/capita was the same in 2003 as it had been in 1997. This is the main reason these years have been called the "second lost decade." The main reason for the lack of growth was the negative impact of monetary and fiscal policies designed to reduce inflation still further, the collapse of the hi-tech boom in 2001, and the Second *Intifada*, or Palestinian revolt. By 2004, economic growth had recovered and continued at a rapid rate until 2008. In 2004, the tax on income from investments at home and abroad was equalized. This encouraged Israelis to find higher returns abroad and contributed to a rise in investment income. The boom – centered on the high-technology sector – encouraged a huge increase in foreign investment and was largely export-based. This pushed the balance of payments current account into surplus, and as a result, the foreign debt became negative, meaning that Israel accumulated net foreign assets. The stream of income on these assets helped strengthen the current account of the balance of payments. In 2005, the Bank of Israel abolished the "exchange rate path" used to prevent excessive changes, but in 2009, it bought billions of dollars to limit the rise in the shekel against the dollar and other foreign currencies. Exports per capita reached $5,400 and imports $6,830. The 2009 current account of the balance of payments had a surplus of $7.3 billion; the foreign exchange reserves reached $60 billion, having doubled in two years, and since 2003, the exchange rate of the shekel had risen against the US dollar by 16 percent in nominal terms. At the end of 2008, the foreign debt was negative $55 billion, which meant that Israel had accumulated net foreign assets equal to about a quarter of its national income.[4] In 2010, Israel is expected to join the Organisation for Economic Cooperation and Development (OECD).

The strengthening of the economy while the society has become weaker is a reversal or a perceived reversal: For many years, Israelis felt that their society was strong but their economy weak. This seems paradoxical given that between 1948 and 2009, Israel attracted more than 3 million immigrants – a very large number for a country the population of which at the end of 2008 was 7.4 million. In 1948, when the state was created, two-thirds of the population was born abroad. In 2009, one-third of the population was made up of immigrants. The effects of immigration are central in Israel's economic history. Economic policy has been dominated by the search for capital that would permit the growth of employment and output, given the increase in the supply of labor made possible by immigration. In the last decade, this has increasingly come from foreign investment, something that has transformed Israel's economy, especially the balance of payments.

Israel has also experienced a profound change from a state-led economy to a much more liberalized and globalized one. It has developed a consumer society based on the Western model in which the satisfaction of individual wants rather than collective needs is paramount. Public spending on social programs has been reduced and the distribution of wealth has become more unequal. One of the main consequences has been an increase in poverty. The book analyzes trends that, though not unique to Israel, have had particularly severe effects due to the nature of Israeli society and the severe security problems that it faces.

Structure of The Book

Chapter 2 provides the historical background prior to the creation of the state. It examines the way in which the Jewish community in Palestine developed, combining a socialist ideology with a reliance on private capital. Both the effects of British rule (1917–1948) and the conflict with the Arabs are looked at as factors that help explain the structure of the economy and the ideological framework when the state of Israel came into being in 1948. This was the period in which three uniquely Israeli institutions were created: the Kibbutzim, or voluntary collectives; the Moshavim, or

---

[4] Bank of Israel. "Inflation Report." July-September 2009. no. 28. Table 7. Jerusalem: Bank of Israel. http://www.bankisrael.gov.il/deptdata/general/infrep/eng/inf-09-3e.pdf; Central Bureau of Statistics. Monthly Bulletin of Statistics. No. 10. 2009; Bank of Israel. Israel's External Financial Transactions. http://www.bankisrael.gov.il/deptdata/pik_mth/pikmth_e.htm

cooperative settlements; and the Histadrut, or General Federation of Labor. The Histadrut was not only a federation of trade or labor unions, but also an employer and provider of services on a scale that led it to be described as a state within a state; its headquarters in Tel Aviv were even nicknamed the "Kremlin" by Israelis. Another important institution that had its origins in the pre-state period was the public ownership of land.

Chapter 3 analyzes the development of the Israeli economy from 1948 to 1985. The economy passed through a number of distinct phases after independence. The first decade was dominated by the absorption of immigrants and state control of the economy. In the mid-1950s, the focus of economic policy moved away from agriculture to industry, within the framework of import substitution. The government encouraged Jewish entrepreneurs from abroad to invest in basic industries such as textiles and clothing. The economy grew rapidly in the 1950s and 1960s, although there were shortages of foreign exchange that necessitated deflation and periods of slower growth. These were years in which an egalitarian ethos prevailed and income inequality was much less than it is today. They were also years of austerity, at first so severe that many decided to emigrate. The share of government spending in GDP was much smaller than in recent years, partly because defense costs were lower and because the egalitarian income distribution limited the pressure for government intervention. Changes in government policy were generally pragmatic and were introduced when they would best serve the interests of the economy.

The Six Day War of 1967 was followed by a wave of optimism that resulted in high investment rates and rapid economic growth, but the Yom Kippur War in 1973 was a major blow to the economy. Apart from the loss of life and direct economic losses, it added to inflationary pressures and worsened the budget deficit and balance of payments. Although emergency steps were taken to stabilize the economy, the combination of economic liberalization and inflation led to severe instability in the late 1970s and early 1980s. Hyperinflation was the result, along with balance of payments and foreign debt servicing problems. The period 1974–1984 thus became known as the "lost decade." Numerous policy errors worsened the situation until, in July 1985, a radical and comprehensive stabilization program was introduced.

Chapter 4 examines macroeconomic developments, the sources of economic growth, and economic policy in recent years. It analyzes the development of the labor force, the capital stock, investment patterns, and the role of research and development, and then looks at the way in which the structure of the economy has changed and the mixed performance of productivity. It concludes with an examination of how the balance of payments and foreign debt have been transformed.

Chapter 5 deals with the globalization of the economy and the development of the high-technology sector. It emphasizes the role of foreign trade and its influence on economic growth and the labor market. Two sectors are compared: high technology that demonstrates the effects of globalization and the construction sector that has relied on cheap, imported labor and has, as a result, experienced very weak productivity growth. Conclusions are then drawn about the effects on economic growth and equity.

Israel's foreign trade relations were defined with the signing of free trade agreements with the European Community (EC) in 1965 and with the United States in 1975. Israel gained free access for its industrial goods and limited but adequate access for its agricultural products in EC markets. The EC agreement was later broadened by agreements to encourage joint technology development projects. The agreement with the United States was broader, covering industry, agriculture, and services. By the early 1990s, the government realized that free trade with rich countries only distorted trade and wasted foreign exchange because imports from cheaper sources were restricted whereas those from expensive countries were not. In the early 1990s, following the expansion of diplomatic and trading relations in Eastern Europe and Asia, Israel unilaterally eliminated quotas and reduced the taxes on imports from so-called third countries with which it did not have trade agreements. This led to a large increase in imports from India, China, and other countries; foreign trade had become liberalized to a great extent. The domestic effects were that consumers gained access to much lower-priced goods, and firms that could not compete reduced their activities or closed down.

One of the most important elements of Israel's economic structure is the very high level of defense expenditure that is examined in Chapter 6. Israel spends a larger share of its national income on defense than most developed countries and has done so for many years. The role of conscription and other hidden costs is detailed, as are economic aspects of Israel's defense relationship with the United States. The development of military industries and exports and the role of the military establishment in generating trained labor for the civilian high technology sector are also analyzed.

Chapter 7 examines Israel's relations with the Palestinians and the construction of Israeli settlements in the West Bank and Gaza. The economics of the relationship have been very one-sided: Israel was the industrial power and it imported unskilled or semiskilled Palestinian workers. The chapter suggests that apart from political consequences, many of Israel's policies have often been very damaging to its own economy.

The role of religion is the subject of Chapter 8, an issue that is almost unique to the Israeli economy: The Israeli government intervenes extensively in religious matters (and religious parties intervene extensively in politics) and allocates large resources for religious services and religious education. In fact, it goes much further and has subsidized the creation of a form of priesthood numbered in the thousands. This has had effects on the state budget, on the supply of labor, and on levels of poverty and on educational standards. Estimates of these costs are made.

The economics of Israel's Arab minority are examined in Chapter 9. After the creation of the state in 1948, the Arabs comprised about 20 percent of the population. This proportion remained constant throughout Israel's history, despite the large Jewish immigration. The economic and demographic factors affecting the Arab community are examined. In recent years, there have been changes in demographic patterns and in educational achievements that are of great potential significance.

Chapter 10 begins with an examination of demographic developments and changes in the ethnic composition of the population. The rapid increase in the population, largely the result of immigration, has been a major factor driving economic growth. Changes in the ethnic makeup of the Jewish population have had significant effects on Israeli politics and the values that dominate life in Israel. This took time to manifest itself: The children of immigrants who arrived in the 1950s helped alter the political course of direction from the 1970s. There is a paradox in Israel's political economy: Those who suffered most from economic liberalization often voted for the political parties that favored it. This can be explained in part by the ethnic element in voting patterns, a reflection of long-term social change. This was related to the waves of immigration that arrived in the country, each with a different background and values. It also reflects deep disillusionment with the strong state and trade union movement that dominated the economy until the 1970s. Although Israelis rejected the paternalism of these bodies, they have not totally abandoned the desire for a welfare state and other institutions that bind society together. The chapter then explores socioeconomic issues: income distribution, poverty, and welfare in the light of the globalization of the economy and government stabilization policies. The role of the Ultra-Orthodox and the Arab communities are also analyzed as explanations of income differentials and poverty levels. The role of the education system is examined.

Conclusions are drawn in Chapter 11. Given the burdens of defending the country and some self-inflicted costs, the performance of the economy has been remarkable. Pragmatic economic policy is a good thing as long as there is an overall aim. In the early stages of their development, economies that lack markets may find it hard to define their economic strategy. This suggests that governments can play a useful role in the early stages of development. Israel's very fast GDP and GDP/capita growth rates in the 1950s appear to validate this. Since then, it has moved broadly the way economists advocate and has benefited in terms of economic growth and rising living standards. In the last twenty years, wide gaps have opened in the distribution of income, wealth, and educational achievement. Poverty has become chronic and deep. There is a risk that these problems may become endemic and threaten the future of the economy because they remove significant numbers of people from the labor market and result in poverty being passed down from one generation to the next. Israel will have to find ways to combine elements of equity with economic growth if it wants to avoid major domestic tension.

TWO

The Economy of the Yishuv and Its Legacy

Institutions created by the Jewish community in Palestine (the Yishuv) from the early twentieth century until the creation of Israel played a major role in the state at least until the 1970s. This chapter examines the development of the Yishuv during the period of the British Mandate (1917–1948) and the institutions that had a lasting impact: the Kibbutz, the Moshav, the Histadrut, and the public ownership of land. The chapter begins by looking at the ideological motivation of the group of immigrants that played a dominant role in the creation of the state.

From Diaspora to Zion

Zionism, the movement that created the state of Israel, emerged in the nineteenth century. Although it had a religious impetus, based on biblical notions of the coming of the Messiah and the need to redeem the Holy Land, it was largely a secular response to the rising nationalism and anti-Semitism that prevailed in Eastern Europe, where most Jews lived. In the early 1880s, Tsar Alexander III issued a number of anti-Jewish decrees that drove hundreds of thousands of Jews from their homes. Between 1881 and 1914, as pogroms resulted in the massacres of thousands of Jews, some 2.6 million left Russia and the territories surrounding it.[1] The vast majority went to the United States and smaller numbers left for the United Kingdom and other Western countries. They did this along with millions of non-Jews who left Europe for economic as well as political reasons.

The numbers who went to Palestine were small: Between 1882 and 1903, some 25,000 Jews emigrated there. There was an increase after the turn of

---

[1] Mahler, Gregory S. 2004. *Politics and Government in Israel.* Lanham, Boulder, New York, Toronto, Oxford: Rowman & Littlefield Publishers Inc, 18.

the century, following the creation of the Zionist movement led by Theodor Herzl. In 1897, at its first congress held in Basle, Switzerland, the movement espoused the creation of a Jewish home in Palestine. The basic belief of the Zionist movement was that the Jews were a people like any other and as such had the right to a homeland, or what was later demanded: a country. The persecution of the Jews in Russia and Eastern Europe also demonstrated the need for a homeland. In the 1930s, as the persecution spread to Central and Western Europe, and as it took on the form of mass murder during the Holocaust, the pressure became even greater. Despite this, the emigration of Jews to Palestine remained small, especially compared with the number that emigrated to the United States and other Western countries.

In 1909, two landmark events occurred in the Yishuv. The first was the creation of Tel Aviv, the first Jewish city in the world. The second was the founding of Degania, the first kibbutz, or voluntary communal, agricultural settlement. These events were indicators of two significant trends in the Yishuv, namely the growth of the Jewish population as a result of immigration, something that necessitated the creation of new settlements, and the role of Labor Zionism.

Many of the Eastern European Jews were influenced not only by the idea of nationalism, but also by socialist ideas. They played a major role in the Russian revolution and the communist and socialist movements throughout Europe. Among the Zionists, there were socialists who believed that recreating a society such as existed in Europe was not in the Jewish interest. Only Labor-Zionism would, in their view, free the Jews not only from anti-Semitism but also from capitalist exploitation. Jewish capitalism existed in Palestine, partly as a result of the investments made, among others, by the French Baron Edmund de Rothschild who funded settlements that absorbed many immigrants. Rothschild and some of the socialists were to come into conflict later.

The aim of the Labor-Zionists was to "invert the pyramid" of Jewish employment and thus its social and economic structure. In nineteenth-century Eastern Europe, Jews were largely forbidden to own land. This had been true for all the centuries they had lived there. Most Jews lived in villages or small towns because there were restrictions on their movement to the cities. Although the economy was largely agricultural, there were no Jewish farmers because they were not allowed to own land, and therefore worked as traders and professionals. They were perceived as lacking roots and loyalty to the countries in which they lived because they often had more in common with fellow Jews abroad, something that encouraged feelings of separateness and anti-Semitism. This is illustrated in Figure 2.1.

Figure 2.1. Jewish occupational structure, Eastern Europe, 1880s.

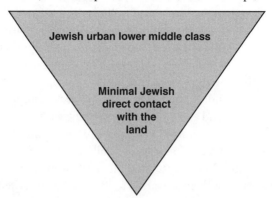

Inverting the pyramid meant creating a new socialist society with a large agricultural workforce that would also bring about the Biblical injunction of *Geulat Ha'aretz* (redeeming the land). The new occupational structure that was aimed at, and that to a certain extent emerged, is illustrated in Figure 2.2.

The Jewish agricultural workforce in Palestine became politically, if not numerically, dominant. The emphasis on agriculture made economic as well as ideological sense. The Zionist settlers created the first sector in a modern economy, one that would not only provide employment but also the inputs for industry. Wherever industrialization has been successful, it has been preceded or accompanied by an agricultural revolution. The Soviet Union was the best example of what happened when this combination did not occur; it never managed to generate agricultural surpluses large enough or for long enough to finance industrialization or feed the urban population with ease.

The socialist sector of the Yishuv began to develop when significant numbers of ideologically motivated immigrants came to Palestine during what was known as the *Second Aliya* (Second Immigrant Wave: 1904–1914) and *Third Aliya* (Third Immigrant Wave: 1919–1923). The total number of immigrants in these two waves was about 70,000, but their influence was far greater than their numbers suggest. It was during the 1920s that the *Histadrut*, or General Federation of Labor, was created. This organization, which was to become one of the most powerful bodies in the Yishuv and later in Israel, was not only a trade union but also an employer and provider of welfare services. The British adopted a policy of *laissez faire*: The Jews and Arabs were encouraged by the British to run their own affairs, and the former did so in a highly organized way. The Histadrut

Figure 2.2.　Jewish occupational structure, Palestine, 1920s.

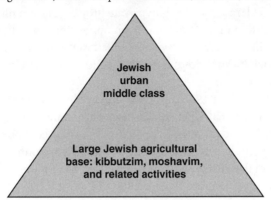

was set up primarily to serve the Jewish working class. It included the kibbutzim in its membership and was the backbone of a state within a state, providing services that the British did not, namely education, health, and welfare. Although most Jews lived in towns or villages outside the socialist settlements, many were employed by Histadrut-affiliated organizations. It served to protect Jewish workers' rights not only vis-à-vis their employers but also vis-à-vis cheaper Arab workers who were considered a threat to Jewish employment. In 1920, the Histadrut had nearly 5,000 members and in 1927, some 27,000, or about 75 percent of the Jewish workforce in the Yishuv.[2]

Immigration

Immigration into Palestine in the period of Ottoman and British rule has been classified chronologically. This has been a very useful division because the immigrants of the various *aliyot* (plural of the Hebrew word *aliya*, meaning immigration to the land of Israel) had significantly different characteristics. The First Aliya took place between 1882 and 1903 and followed the outbreak of pogroms of Jews in Russia. Some 30,000 Jewish immigrants arrived in Palestine as a result. The pogroms were organized or initiated by the state and marked the beginning of modern, political anti-Semitism. Most of the immigrants came from Eastern Europe, although there was a small immigration from Yemen as well. The early East European Zionists aimed to rebuild Jewish life politically and spiritually and chose an agricultural way of life as an example to others. They were not socialists, and the

---

[2]　The Jewish Virtual Library. http://www.jewishvirtuallibrary.org/jsource/History/histadrut.html

early agricultural settlements such as Rishon LeZion, Rosh Pina, Zikhron Ya'aqov, and Gedera were based on private property. Harsh physical conditions, heavy Ottoman taxation, and Arab opposition made life very tough, and many of the immigrants gave up and left the country. Assistance came from the French Baron Edmund de Rothschild who invested in settlements and provided employment.

The Second Aliya of 1904–1914 also followed continued anti-Semitism and pogroms in Russia. Some 40,000 Jews immigrated during this period, but absorption difficulties and the lack of a sound economy resulted in nearly half of them leaving. The Second Aliya had a profound impact on the development of the Yishuv. Most of its members were young and influenced by socialist ideals. During this period, the first kibbutz, Degania, was set up (in 1909); around the same time, Hashomer, the first Jewish self-defense organization in Palestine, came into being. The Ahuzat Bayit neighborhood, established as a suburb of Jaffa, became Tel Aviv, the first modern Jewish city, in 1909. The Hebrew language was revived by Eliezer Ben Yehuda who regarded Hebrew and Zionism to be symbiotic. Modern Hebrew was spoken by members of the Second Aliya, and Hebrew literature and Hebrew newspapers began to flourish at this time. Political parties were founded and workers' agricultural organizations began to form.

World War I interrupted immigration, and those that arrived after the war formed the Third Aliya. It was triggered by the October Revolution in Russia and the pogroms that followed it there, as well as in Poland and Hungary. In 1917, immigration was encouraged following the British conquest of Palestine and the Balfour Declaration that expressed Britain's support for the creation of a Jewish homeland in Palestine. Most members of the Third Aliya were young *halutzim* (Hebrew for pioneers) from Eastern Europe. Although the Mandatory government imposed quotas on immigration, in the 1920s, these did not cause significant tensions between the British and the Jews. By 1923, the population of the *yishuv* reached approximately 90,000. The new immigrants built roads and towns, and the marshes in the Jezreel Valley and the Hefer Plain were drained. The General Federation of Labor (Histadrut), the Elected Assembly, and the National Council – representative institutions of the *yishuv* – as well as the Haganah (the clandestine Jewish defense organization) were all established at this time.

The Fourth Aliya of 1924–1929 resulted from the international economic crisis and anti-Jewish policies in Poland, along with the introduction of quotas that restricted immigration to the United States. Most of the immigrants in this wave were middle class and brought modest sums of capital with which they established small businesses and workshops. They were much less socialist than those who arrived with the Third Aliya, and many settled in the towns. Notwithstanding the *yishuv*'s economic woes, including an economic crisis in 1926–1928, the Fourth Aliya did much to strengthen the towns, further industrial development, and increase the Jewish labor supply in the villages. Some 80,000 Jews came to Palestine during the Fourth Aliya; about a quarter of them left.

Up to the mid-1920s, most immigrants came from Eastern Europe, especially from areas that became part of the Soviet Union. From the mid-1920s, the majority came from Poland, and from the 1930s, from Germany and Central Europe. Immigrants from the West tended to have better education than those from the East for three reasons. First, until 1933, there were no restrictions in Western countries on the entry of Jewish students to universities, as there had been in Russia before the revolution. Second, average income levels in Central and Western Europe were higher than in Eastern Europe among both Jews and non-Jews. Third, the academic and technological standards of Central and West European universities were superior to those in the East. The Jews from Western Europe were, however, less infused with socialist ideas and tended to live in the towns and work in commerce or as professionals after their immigration to Palestine. They were looked down on by many of the socialists of the Third Aliya, who considered them to be landlords and profit-seeking bourgeoisie.[3]

During World War II, the immigration effort focused on rescuing Jews from Nazi-occupied Europe. Although some immigrants entered the country on visas issued under the British quota (18,000 per year), most of the new arrivals were illegal. Between 1919 and 1947, average annual immigration equaled 6.8 percent of the Jewish population of Palestine, and in 1919–1939, the annual average was 8.5 percent. These were very high shares compared with other countries receiving immigrants.[4]

Between 1919 and 1948, about 550,000 Jews and 67,000 non-Jews (mainly Arabs) immigrated into Palestine. Nearly 90 percent of the Jewish immigrants came from Europe and nearly 60 percent of those were from East Europe. Over 75 percent of the East Europeans were from Poland. In comparison, an estimated 3.3 million Jews left Europe between 1919 and 1939, and 2.6 million of them ended up in the United States.[5]

[3] Metzer, Jacob. 1998. *The Divided Economy of Mandatory Palestine.* Cambridge: Cambridge University Press, 77.
[4] Metzer, *The Divided Economy of Mandatory Palestine*, 70–72.
[5] Metzer, 59–83.

As a result of the immigration, the Yishuv not only benefited from rapid population growth but also from a rise in average educational levels. No records of the educational levels of immigrants were kept during the Mandate, but some useful calculations have been made. In 1931, the Jewish male population of Palestine had 7.6 median years of schooling and the female population had 5.6 years. About half of the population was born abroad; in 1926, about 47 percent of them stated they had learned Hebrew prior to their immigration. The acquisition of a second language and the ability to use it on arrival in Palestine were considerable economic assets for immigrants and for the Yishuv as a whole. (The multilingual background of immigrants and many of their children was to become an increasingly important asset as the Israeli economy opened up to foreign trade, as exports became more significant, and as globalization took place. This was another legacy of the Yishuv and one of the economic benefits of Zionism). Illiteracy declined from 14.1 percent of the Jewish population aged 14 years and older in 1931 to 6.3 percent in 1948. In 1940–1944, the share of adult males aged 25 and older who registered with recruitment committees (set up by the Yishuv to supply troops for the British army) was measured by educational level. The share of those born in Palestine with post-secondary education was 7.8 percent. Of those who immigrated between 1918 and 1932, it was 14 percent and of those who immigrated between 1933 and 1939, it was 25.6 percent.[6]

Economic Growth and Structural Change

Between 1922 and 1935, the economy of the Yishuv grew very rapidly (see Appendix 2.1). The late 1930s brought slower growth, the result of international economic conditions and conflict in Palestine. Growth was accompanied by structural change. Table 2.1 shows how the structures of the Jewish and Arab economies changed between 1922 and 1947. Appendix 2.2 shows that between 1921 and 1939 in the Jewish economy, output in agriculture increased nearly sixteen-fold, in manufacturing fourteen-fold and in construction more than threefold. As a result, the volume of output for these sectors in the Jewish economy overtook that of the Arab economy. In 1921, it was equal to 31 percent of Arab output; in 1939, it came to 141 percent.

Growth was made possible by the expansion of the labor force, the high average quality of human capital (measured by educational levels), and by imports of capital. Another significant factor was the economic policy of the Mandatory authorities. The British issued tenders for the development

---

[6]   Metzer, 80–82.

Table 2.1. *The Palestinian economy: Shares in net national product, 1922–1947*

	1922	1947
Arab Economy		
Agriculture	39.4	38.9
Manufacturing	5.2	2.3
Construction	1.8	2.4
Services	53.6	56.7
The Jewish Economy		
Agriculture	12.9	10.7
Manufacturing	19.7	33.1
Construction	12.5	6.0
Services	54.9	50.2

Source: Metzer, Jacob. *The Divided Economy of Palestine.*
Cambridge: Cambridge University Press, 1998.

of vital sectors of the economy, such as the Dead Sea minerals and generation and distribution of electricity. These were won by Jewish groups that proceeded to develop those sectors. Following the creation of the state of Israel, these enterprises became state-owned entities. The British also provided elements of protection for local industry in Palestine to encourage its development. During World War II, the British army increased its orders for goods and services from the Yishuv, which resulted in rapid growth of industrial production. In 1924, some protection was provided for the building, milling, distilling, match, and tobacco industries. In 1925, some imports were allowed in duty-free on condition that they were used in exports of finished products. Companies that benefited from these policies included the Nesher cement company, founded in 1925 by a Russian immigrant; it has retained a near-monopoly on cement production ever since.[7]

Capital Imports

The rate of investment in the Yishuv was very high: In the period between 1922 and 1947, it equaled 46 percent of the Yishuv's GDP, including

[7]   Smith, Barbara J. 1993. *The Roots of Separation in Palestine 1920–1929.* London and New York: I.B. Tauris & Co Ltd, 118, 165–166; Etzioni, Amir. 1998. "The Israeli Cement Industry." Institute for Advanced Strategic and Political Studies. 4. http://www.israeleconomy. org/cement.htmfile

investment in fixed assets, unimproved land, and the use of government investments. The share in total resources (that included the surplus of imports over exports), was lower, at approximately 24 percent. The high level of investment was made possible by large imports of capital from abroad. Most of these funds were private and included the unilateral transfers by immigrants, private investments made by Jews living abroad, and funds raised from the international Jewish community by the World Zionist Organization and its affiliated bodies.[8]

If socialist labor came from the East, financial capital came from the richer Jewish communities of the West, including the United States. The Yishuv, or later Israel, in its early years did not attract direct foreign investment. Few foreign Jews (and no non-Jews) were willing to set up businesses using their own funds. Jews were, however, willing to give money to help develop the Yishuv. They donated funds to quasi-governmental bodies of the Yishuv that had been set up by the Zionist movement.[9] This strengthened the quasi-state bodies vis-à-vis the private sector. As these bodies were dominated by the socialists, investment in agriculture was favored. Most Jewish capital, however, was brought by individuals. Between 1922 and 1947, net transfers by Jewish immigrants came to 110 million Palestine pounds; transfers by Jewish public institutions totaled 65 million Palestine pounds. These figures should be compared with total transfers by non-Jewish public institutions and the government of only 20 million Palestine pounds. In addition, private investment recorded in the capital account of the balance of payments came to 16 million Palestine pounds.[10]

The combination of immigration and capital imports was very successful in producing economic growth. Demand of immigrants for housing, consumer durables, and other services and their contribution to the labor force increased productivity of capital and the returns on it. In the case of the Yishuv, the immigrants brought their own capital – physical, financial, and human – so that supply of capital matched and sometimes even exceeded the rapid growth of the labor force.[11] In 1939, while the Jews constituted 31 percent of the population, they accounted for 88 percent of total industrial investment capital, 89 percent of net industrial output, 70 percent

[8]   Metzer, 105–106.
[9]   Kleiman, Ephraim. 1998. "The Waning of Israeli *Etatism.*" *Israel Studies*, Vol. 2 No. 2, 146–171.
[10] Halevi, Nadav and Ruth Klinov-Malul. 1968. *The Economic Development of Israel.* New York, Washington, London: Frederik A. Praeger Publishers, 19.
[11] Metzer, 106.

of the industrial labor force, 89 percent of the wage bill, and 90 percent of the installed horsepower employed in industry.[12]

The Arab Economy

Although it was often overshadowed by the Jewish economy, the Arab economy in Palestine experienced impressive growth during the Mandate. The population rose from 589,000 in 1919 to almost 1.3 million in 1947, largely the result of natural growth (see Table 9.1). This was made possible in part by improved health standards that reduced infant mortality and increased life expectancy. The economy, measured by net national product, rose nearly fivefold between 1922 and 1947, while on a per capita basis, the increase was 2.5-fold.

The Jewish and Arab economies in Palestine were largely separate. This was partly due to geography, but hostility between the two communities was the main cause. The Arab community was overwhelmingly rural whereas the Jewish community was mainly urban, and this was reflected in the pattern of employment and output. In the Arab economy, agriculture played a much bigger role in both of these parameters than in the Jewish one, despite the Zionist Socialist ideology of redeeming the land and developing agriculture. Notwithstanding their separation, there were significant links between the two economies, partially due to the differences between the two economies, which gave them different comparative advantages and thus incentives to trade. The Arab economy experienced little structural change as manifested in changes in the shares of individual economic sectors (see Table 2.1). The share of the manufacturing sector fell, even though its output rose more than twelvefold between 1922 and 1945.

Labor and capital inputs accounted for 75 percent of the growth of output in the Jewish sector, whereas in the Arab economy, total factor productivity may have accounted for half of the growth of output. This was the result of demand for its products, demand and demonstration effects of the Jewish economy, and the benefits of government-supplied services and infrastructure.[13]

1939–1945: The Economic Effects of World War II

The years 1939–1945 were ones of relative prosperity, mainly because the economy of the Yishuv had important markets in the British military

---

[12] Smith, *The Roots of Separation in Palestine 1920–1929*, 179.
[13] Metzer, 7–10, 17–18, 242.

establishment in the Middle East. This was despite the fact that the war disrupted the international citrus trade, something that helped turn many in the Yishuv against reliance on external trade. In the period between 1922 and 1939, the Yishuv exported 8 million Palestine pounds worth of goods and services to the British army in Palestine; in 1940–1947, the total exports reached 180 million.[14]

These pre-1948 experiences invoked an ideology of self-sufficiency that reinforced the socialist orientation of much of the society. After the Declaration of Independence in 1948, the leadership favored minimal reliance on foreign sources of capital and revenues from trade in order to build a self-sufficient economy. This was an ideology shared with other developing countries and had broad support from economists and international financial institutions.[15] It was not, however, the one that would permit economic growth in the 1950s, when Israel searched for sources of foreign capital (see Chapter 3).

The Legacy of the Yishuv

Many of the institutions that came to dominate Israel's economy and society, at least until the 1970s, had their origins in the activities of the Labor movement in the Yishuv. The Labor movement, which controlled the political and economic development of Israel from 1948 to 1977, consisted of the Histadrut with its affiliated bodies and, in various forms, the Labor Party. The Histadrut, both as a trade union organization and as one of the largest employers in the country, played a central role in the economy and in the provision of social services and had considerable political influence. Labor, therefore, was much more than a factor of production in the narrow economic sense.

The dominant version of Zionism, at least until 1977, was the state-led one that evolved out of European, left-wing ideologies at the end of the nineteenth and in early twentieth centuries. Collective action was regarded, at least until the early 1960s, as the most effective way to realize national interests. This ideology tended to view profits as parasitic and services as unproductive. Under conditions of war and mass immigration, such as those that existed in 1948, state dominance of the economy seemed appropriate to those who led the country.[16]

---

[14] Halevi and Klinov-Malul, *The Economic Development of Israel*, 19.
[15] Rivlin, Paul. 2001. *Economic Policy and Performance in the Arab World*. Boulder: Lynne Rienner, 3–8.
[16] Ben Porath, Yoram. 1986. *Patterns and Peculiarities of Economic Growth and Structure*. Jerusalem: Falk Institute, 4.

In the Yishuv, the Jewish leadership faced a formidable struggle to develop the economy. First, it was not in control of the territory, because the country was ruled by the Ottomans and then the British. Second, the local market was very small and the returns on investment were low compared with the risks and uncertainties involved. As a result, the Zionist project appealed more to the Jewish masses of Eastern Europe than to Jewish capitalists, and even less to non-Jewish ones. There were very few Jewish capitalists and most of them confined themselves to philanthropy. If the immigrants were to be absorbed, capital was needed. The solution was found in the formation of public bodies, controlled by the political leadership of the Yishuv and the international Zionist movement that raised funds in the Diaspora and invested them in the Yishuv. This was the logic behind the creation of the Jewish National Fund (see further in the chapter) and other bodies. Capital was raised from the more prosperous Jews in Central and Western Europe and in the Americas, whereas the immigrants came mainly from Eastern Europe. The Jews of Eastern European descent supplied the ideology based on the revolutionary ideas of Marxism, the Tolstoyan desire for a simple, rural way of life, and Anarchist notions of self-government. The fusion of these concepts led to the creation of the kibbutzim, the moshavim (villages with varying degrees of cooperation and communal ownership), and the Histadrut.[17]

In 1948, Israel was, in terms of the distribution of income and its social ethos, an egalitarian society. The Labor party and its left-wing allies dominated the life of the state, despite an early policy introduced by the first prime minister and Labor leader, David Ben Gurion, to build up state rather than party institutions. This policy meant that much of what was done by sectoral or political groups before independence (such as providing educational and employment services) was to be carried out by the government.

The effects of the Holocaust in Europe and the cost of the War of Independence (in which 1 percent of the entire Jewish population in Palestine was killed), were the background to a major effort of national renewal. There was little to buy and most of the population had a low standard of living, but there was a sense of mission. Following independence, the most significant changes were the welding of military groups into the Israel Defense Forces (IDF), the introduction of state education systems, and the government's increased responsibility for social welfare and employment.

---

[17] Kleiman, "The Waning of Israeli *Etatisme*," 146–171.

Labor Zionists came to Palestine in order to create a new type of Jewish society and a new type of Jew. They aspired to return to manual labor, particularly on the land, and to change the Jewish psyche and society by building a socialist economy in which people would be self-reliant and value work, in contrast to the Diaspora. In this sense, their mission was revolutionary. Unlike agriculture and industry, the service sector was considered parasitic, and intellectuals were viewed ambiguously by labor leaders. This ideology gave rise to many conflicts in the pre-independence period. The Socialist Zionists initially sought fraternal relations with Arab workers and peasants and wanted to include Arabs in the Histadrut, but at the same time opposed their employment by Jewish capitalists at lower wages than Jews would take. In the 1920s, as conflict between Jews and Arabs increased, the Labor movement created the Hagana, a defense force that became the basis of the Israeli army in 1948. With the creation of the state, many Labor leaders and activists took positions in government and ceased to provide the personal example of manual labor that had been the movement's ideology. Since 1948, events have also weakened the ideology of the Labor movement. After 1948, many relatively unskilled Jews from North Africa and the Middle East (known in Hebrew as Mizrachim) immigrated, and they were largely employed in low-status positions. They were often sent to developing towns in the periphery, where basic industries were set up to employ them. These industries were not established on a completely economic basis, and the immigrant workers were employed at low wages. With the education of the younger generation, productivity and real wages rose, but this generation of Mizrachim largely failed to take leading positions in the Labor-run economy and the Histadrut.

Attempts to prevent Arab employment in the Jewish economy continued until the early 1950s. The aim was to maintain employment and wages for the large numbers of largely unskilled Jewish immigrants. Gradually this broke down, and Arabs started to work in Jewish agriculture and in particular in construction. These patterns were reinforced after 1967, when Israel gained control of the West Bank and Gaza, with its Palestinian population numbering one million. Within a few years, Arabs from these areas began to supplant Israeli Arabs and Jews of Middle Eastern and North African origin in low-status occupations such as construction work. The latter moved up the ladder in terms of their work status, gaining jobs in the service and public sectors.

Since the 1960s, there has been a reversal of the Jewish work ethic as enunciated by the Socialist Zionists. The service sector grew; Israeli Arabs, Palestinians, and then other foreign workers were employed in the manual jobs that Jews did not want. The idea that manual labor would contribute to the redemption of the Jewish people also came into conflict with the desire, and the need, for higher education. In a country lacking raw materials and fuel deposits, it was quickly realized that the labor force was virtually the only economic resource. Increasing its skill level would, therefore, make an important contribution to economic development. Investment in education and training increased, which reduced the prestige of agriculture, construction, and other sectors reliant on manual labor. Government, with its large bureaucracy, became a growing source of employment in the service sector; inflation led to the growth of financial services, especially banking. These factors reinforced the movement away from manual and industrial employment.

The Histadrut

The Histadrut was founded in 1920 as a comprehensive organization for Jewish workers in the Yishuv. Its range of activities covered trade union matters, the development of new rural settlements, agriculture, industry, banking, insurance, housing, construction, transportation, social services, and cultural activities. The original and basic aim was to create employment for Jewish workers in Palestine. By generating full employment, high living standards, and job security, the organization aimed to help Jewish workers achieve personal dignity, all of which they had been denied in the Diaspora.

In 1921, to achieve these goals, the Histadrut set up Bank Hapoalim (the Workers' Bank). Two years later, Hevrat Ovdim (the Workers' Company, or Cooperative Federation) was created. By 1925, Hevrat Ovdim was acting as the holding company for all the communities' cooperatives. Cooperatives were organized for dairy production and for bus transportation. In 1927, when the Solel Boneh Construction Company went bankrupt, Histadrut leaders realized the importance of maintaining independent capital resources. Capital accumulation designed to meet the needs of its enterprises replaced job creation as the Histadrut's primary objective.[18] This practice limited the vulnerability and exposure of its companies and economic organizations to changes in the economy and government policy, but did not eliminate it. By 1930, Hamashbir, the retail cooperative, Hasneh, the insurance company, and others were incorporated into Hevrat Ovdim. Histadrut enterprises expanded their investments by reinvesting their profits.

Following Israel's independence, the Histadrut transferred some of its functions to the government. These included education, some labor

---

[18] Kleiman, Ephraim. 1987. "The Histadrut Economy of Israel: In Search of Criteria." Jerusalem Quarterly No. 41 (Winter), 77–78.

exchanges that had been under its control, social welfare services, housing, and assistance for new immigrants. It retained, however, its control over Kupat Holim Clalit, the health fund. Independence brought large government development budgets that financed much of the country's investment. Histadrut enterprises no longer needed to rely on their profits to maintain investment levels. They changed their focus to development of new plants in outlying regions of the country, in accordance with the government's population dispersal policy. As profitability was neglected for ideological reasons, Histradrut enterprises such as Koor, Solel Boneh, Kupat Holim Clalit, and the Egged Bus Cooperative were badly placed to deal with the radical changes in economic policy that came about in the late 1970s and 1980s. In that period, many Histadrut enterprises ceased to generate a profit. Solel Boneh suffered a second financial collapse and was merged with another Histadrut company in the construction sector.

The problems facing the Histadrut's industrial holding company, Koor, were partly the result of general trends in the economy affecting other industrial sectors. Owners of companies in all sectors did not fully understand that the government had largely ended its role as the financier of development. They suffered from huge increases in interest rates in 1985 and failed to realize that devaluations would not necessarily protect exports against rising costs at home. The problem was compounded in the Histadrut by the policy of avoiding redundancies and the fact that wage increases were not under the control of individual companies but were imposed from above. In the summer of 1988, reforms were announced reducing the power of the trade union department to force wage increases on Histadrut enterprises. Firms were to be sold or closed if they did not generate profits. This reform was an ideological shift of major significance because the Histadrut was bowing to market forces it unsuccessfully tried to resist. It returned to a policy adopted in the pre-state period, when emphasis was placed on maintaining financial independence rather than maximizing employment. A number of companies were sold, but worker resistance to the closing of others has brought delays in the implementation of the program

By 1989, the Koor group had accumulated losses of $854 million.[19] The political leadership of the Histadrut wanted both profits and higher wages, something that was only possible with higher productivity increases than those achieved. It also insisted that all workers be paid cost-of-living and other wage and salary increases regardless of the profitability of the company, a situation that in the late 1980s led to the resignation of Koor's

---

[19]　Schubert, Avi. 1990. "Koor Loses $303 million." *Haaretz* (21 June), S7.

managing director. As losses accumulated, the Histadrut's ability to finance them declined. The government, for both financial and political reasons, was unwilling to bail out bankrupt operations to the same extent it had in the past, and the trade union organization was unwilling to lay off workers.

Protection of Histadrut enterprises impinged on national wage negotiations. To obtain economic help for Kupat Holim and its pension funds, the Histadrut made concessions on other matters in its negotiations with the government and private sector employers. The involvement of health and pension fund considerations complicated negotiations that very often took place with the hidden agenda of maintaining Histradrut institutions. In the 1990s, one of the most important changes that took place was the collapse of the Histadrut as a body that did more than just represent workers. The origins of this lay in the separation of the Histadrut from the government in the early years of the state (in the Yishuv, it had been one of the "national institutions"). During the 1950s, the Labor party became less socialist and increasingly acted as the representative of the aristocracy of labor rather than that of all the workers.[20]

Eventually the problems faced in the cooperative sector resulted in the sale of most firms to the private sector, but there were virtually no experiments in terms of worker participation in management or direct ownership. Histadrut management was hierarchical, unimaginative, and conservative. This lack of innovation is perhaps surprising given the existence of kibbutz industries, with their egalitarian philosophy, within the same sector. Over time, the Histadrut lost control of most of its assets and became a federation of labor unions like others abroad.

The leadership of the Histadrut is elected by its members, and the Labor party had an absolute majority from its foundation until the 1990s. In the 1980s, there were about 1.6 million members and members' spouses in the Histadrut, including 165,000 Arabs and Druze. Elections to the Histadrut convention took place every four years, with lists of candidates being submitted by the political parties. The convention elected members to the council, which in turn elected the executive committee. The trade union department was also made up of political representatives in proportion to their representation in the convention. Workers' committees were elected on a nonpolitical basis at the place of employment. The Histadrut is now a federation of trade unions with the standard function of representing

---

[20] Khenen, Dov. 2000. "From 'Eretz Yisrael Haovedet' to 'Yisrael Hashniah': The Social Discourse and Social Policy of Mapai in the 1950s," in Shafir, Gershon and Yoav Peled, eds. *The New Israel*. Boulder: Westview, 71–100.

workers in negotiations with employers on wages, benefits, and conditions. There are also local labor councils that handle matters at the community level and act as a link with the leadership.

In October 1983, the Histadrut lost control of a key asset, Bank Hapoalim, following its nationalization along with other banks. The government took control of the banks as a result of their failed attempt to regulate the prices of their shares. Other major assets – Solel Boneh, the construction company, Koor, the industrial conglomerate, and Kupat Holim Clalit, the country's largest health fund – also went into severe financial crisis and had to be bailed out. This was largely done by ceding control over them, either to the government or to the private sector.

The policies of the Likud-led government that came to power in 1977 were hostile to the Histadrut that it considered a tool of the Labor establishment. The hyperinflation did not serve the interests of the Histadrut because, with the Likud in power, it no longer had access to government assistance. Finally, the 1985 economic stabilization program left it reeling, with many of its associates (such as kibbutz industries) and subsidiaries of Hevrat Ovdim bankrupt. These developments formed the background for changes that ended its economic empire and left it as a federation of trade unions. Even in that respect, it lost much of its influence.

In 1992, following the election of a Labor government, proposals were put forward for the creation of a national health service. This was done because the existing system of nongovernment health funds was not comprehensive, and despite the fact that Israel had been ruled by Labor for 29 years, some of its citizens lacked basic health insurance. The Histadrut opposed the plan that would have led to its loss of control over Kupat Holim Clalit. Given the close links between the Histadrut and the Labor Party, the government backed down. This led to the resignation of the health minister, Haim Ramon, who had been the main proponent of the plan. In the 1994 Histadrut elections, Ramon stood for the post of secretary general as an independent candidate. His victory meant that for the first time, a non-Labor member ran the Histadrut. The national health insurance bill was put forward again and gained a majority in the Knesset, becoming law in 1995. Ramon took over a bankrupt Histadrut and proceeded to sell off its assets.[21] By the 1990s, a new generation of college-trained workers was being absorbed in the nonunionized high-technology sector where American management systems were employed. The Histadrut remained

[21] Grinberg, Lev Luis and Gershon Shafir 2001. "Economic Liberalization and the Breakup of the Histadrut's Domain," in Shafir, Gershon and Yoav Peled, eds. *The New Israel*. Boulder, CO: Westriew, 103–127.

the coordinator of very powerful unions in public sector monopolies such as the airports, ports, the Israel Electric Corporation, the water sector, and, to a lesser extent, the education system.

Kibbutzim

The kibbutz (plural: kibbutzim), a phenomenon unique to Israel, is a community built on the basis of complete equality of all of its members and on the communal ownership and provision of all services. Members do not receive an income; they get all the services they require without charge and are given a small monetary allowance to spend outside the kibbutz. Most significant, from an economic point of view, is the fact that allowances are not, in any way, related to the individual's work effort. Only in extreme cases would a member be asked to leave the kibbutz if his or her efforts were considered unsatisfactory.

The lack of connection between effort and income (taken in the form of services and allowances) should, according to much conventional economic thinking, result in inefficiency and even financial collapse. By the 1960s, however, the kibbutzim had achieved relatively high living standards and impressive agricultural and industrial growth. They also resisted the trend toward urbanization; their population has not fallen as has that of other rural settlements. They have been successful innovators in agriculture and have undertaken a major industrialization in response to market forces. The marginal productivity of labor has been higher in kibbutz industry and agriculture than elsewhere in the economy, and, at least until recently, they were efficient in the use of capital.[22] While Labor was in power, they also had access to subsidized sources of capital. Since the mid-1980s, many kibbutzim have faced severe financial difficulties because of problems in agriculture and bad industrial and financial investments made prior to the large increases in interest rates in 1985. They have had to reduce living standards and cut back on investments while negotiating for government assistance in coping with their debts to the commercial banks.

One of the consequences was the transformation of many kibbutzim into non-socialist communities. They transferred their assets to their members, introduced wages partly, if not totally, determined by market forces, and charged members for goods and services provided to them. In 1996, there were 251 kibbutzim; in 241 of them, there was no link between what a

---

[22] Barkai, Haim. 1987. *Kibbutz Efficiency and the Incentive Conundrum*. Jerusalem: Falk Institute, 244–245.

member's work yielded and what he received as a living allowance from the kibbutz. This was pure socialism. In six kibbutzim, there was a partial link, and in four others, what a member's work yielded and what he received as a living allowance from the kibbutz (together with mutual aid) was fully linked. By 2005, a major change had occurred. In eighty-four kibbutzim, there was no link between what a member's work yielded and what he received as a living allowance from the kibbutz; in twenty-four, there was a partial link between the value of a member's work and what she/he received as a living allowance from the kibbutz, together with mutual aid.[23]

The kibbutzim have played an important role in Israel's development. They were the world's only movement of voluntary collectives and played a major role in the defense of the country, as well as in its agricultural and industrial development. They supplied military officers far beyond their share in the population and contributed to the absorption of tens of thousands of immigrants.

Moshavim

The moshav (plural: moshavim) is a farming community with individually owned and equal-sized holdings. The first moshavim were established by Labor Zionists during the Second Aliyah. There are two main kinds of moshav. The first is the Moshav Ovdim, or workers' moshav. Members produce individually and/or using pooled labor and other resources. Support of the community is carried out through a tax imposed by the moshav. This tax was equal for all households of the community, thus creating a system where successful farmers were better off than less successful ones. It contrasted with the kibbutzim where all members enjoyed the same living standard. The moshav relies on cooperative purchasing of supplies and marketing of produce; the family or household is, however, the basic unit of production. Moshavim are governed by elected councils.

The second kind is the Moshav Shitufi, a collective smallholder's settlement that combines the economic features of a kibbutz with the social features of a moshav. Farming is done collectively and profits are shared equally. It is similar to the kibbutz: Although consumption is family- or household-based, production and marketing are organized collectively. Unlike the Moshav Ovdim, land is not allotted to households or individuals but is worked collectively.

[23] Pavin, Avraham. 2006. "The Kibbutz Movement: Facts and Figures 2006." Ramat Efal: Yad Tabenkin: Research and Documentation Center of the Kibbutz Movement, 12 and 89.

Because the moshav retained the family as the center of social life and avoided experiments with communal childrearing or equality of the sexes, it was, in the 1950s and early 1960s, much more attractive to immigrants from the Middle East and North Africa than the kibbutz. For this reason, the kibbutz has remained largely an Ashkenazi institution whereas the moshav was not. On the contrary, the so-called immigrants' moshav provided one of the most successful forms of absorption and integration of Middle Eastern and North African immigrants, allowing some of them a much steadier ascent into the middle class than life in some development towns did.

Since 1967, the moshavim, like the kibbutzim, have relied increasingly on outside labor. Initially these were Israeli Arabs, then Palestinians from the West Bank and Gaza, and more recently, foreign workers have taken their place. Financial instabilities in the early 1980s hit many moshavim hard, as did the problem of absorbing all the children who wished to remain in the community. By the late 1980s, more and more moshav members were employed in nonagricultural sectors outside the community, so that some moshavim were coming to resemble suburban villages whose residents commuted to work. At the end of 2007, there were 401 moshavim with a population of 231,000 and 40 Moshav Shitufi with a population of 19,200.[24]

Land Ownership

Another enduring legacy of the Yishuv is the pattern of land ownership in Israel: Over 90 percent of land is owned by the state or parastatal bodies. From the beginning of the twentieth century, Jews bought land in Israel both privately and through the so-called national institutions. These institutions carried out the policies of the Zionist movement; their most important activity was to assist in bringing Jews to Palestine and in helping sustain themselves there. This meant that land had to be bought for both rural and urban use.

The Jewish National Fund (JNF) (in Hebrew: Keren Kayemet Le-Israel) was set up in 1901 as an auxiliary body to the Jewish Agency, under the framework of the World Zionist Organization. It raised (and continues to raise) money in the Diaspora. The land was purchased for the Jewish people worldwide rather than for the Jews in Palestine or in Israel. The assumption was that increasing numbers of Jews would immigrate to Israel, and thus

---

[24] Central Bureau of Statistics. 2009. *Statistical Abstract of Israel, 2008*. Table 2.12.

land should be acquired for their (future) use rather than just for the Jews already there.

The concept that land is a material asset with unique properties, which therefore should not be bought or sold like other commodities is biblical in origin. The forty-nine-year leases granted to leaseholders today are based on the biblical "Yovel," or jubilee. This is not a concept that modern economic theory accepts. Land, as a factor of production, should be tradable so that it can find its most efficient use. Over time, the JNF expanded its land holdings and functioned as an important link between the Jewish people in the Diaspora, the Yishuv, or pre-state Jewish community in Palestine, and the Land of Israel. Widespread, small-scale private donations made Jews feel that they were directly contributing to the attainment of the Zionist objective.

In 1948, when the state was created, there were four types of land ownership. The first, JNF land, represented most of the cultivated land in the country. Relatively little of this was located in the major urban centers. The second type was state land, inherited by the government of Israel from the British Mandate. The third was private land, and the fourth was land abandoned by fleeing Arab refugees. Between 1948 and 1960, three separate bodies – the government, the Development Authority, and the JNF – managed public land. In 1960–1961, the government and the JNF decided to unify the organizations involved, and the Israel Lands Authority (ILA) was created. Its task was to manage the land and its use; it did not and does not own it. Under the terms of the 1961 agreement with the JNF and the Basic Law of 1960 setting it up, the ILA does not sell land (except under special circumstances) but leases it. The Basic Law is the Israeli equivalent of a constitutional law: More than a simple majority in the Knesset is required for it to be changed. The agreement between the JNF and the government, under which a government body, the ILA, was to manage JNF lands, took the form of a contract in civil law.

The ILA, through its executive council, decides who is to have land, what price they will pay for it, and the conditions under which they can use it. The ILA therefore influences decisions regarding housing, office buildings, factories, farms, hotels, and other buildings on over 90 percent of the land in Israel. These enormous powers are not wielded within a clear, published legal framework. Many, if not all, of the decisions are made behind closed doors, despite calls from the State Comptroller for greater accountability. In 2009, the government proposed major reforms, some of which had been proposed by numerous committees set up to improve the functioning of the land market and privatize urban land ownership. Under these proposals, the JNF would swap land it owns in areas that are populated for largely unpopulated areas of the Negev that it would be given by the government. The government would then be able to sell land to homeowners without contravening the JNF's charter.

Conclusions

The economy of the Yishuv developed rapidly during the thirty-one years of British rule. Although the emphasis on agriculture had ideological causes, it successfully met a necessary precondition for industrialization. This was despite the political conflict that developed with the British in the 1930s and the military conflict with the Arabs in Palestine. The Yishuv absorbed nearly 500,000 immigrants, and living standards role considerably. The Yishuv also developed politically, creating governmental and parliamentary institutions under conditions of foreign occupation. Conflict with the Arabs did not break out with the declaration of independence in May 1948; it preceded it and was anticipated. This led to the creation in 1948 of the Hagana that became the main part of the Israeli army, and to the clandestine production of weapons. As a result, when the State of Israel was established, it had the institutions and economy with which to begin. Given the conditions that prevailed after the declaration of independence, this legacy was the most important ingredient in the survival of the new state.

THREE

The Economy, 1948–1985

Since independence, Israel's economy has moved steadily from state control toward a free-market regime. This chapter examines the main features of Israel's development in its first forty years. It shows how Labor Zionism gradually gave way to a much more capitalistic economy, partly through reforms in foreign trade policy from the 1960s to the 1990s, and also as a result of stabilization policies introduced in 1985.

The War of Independence, 1947–1949

In November 1947, fighting between Jews and Arabs broke out following the passing of a resolution in the UN General Assembly calling for the partition of Palestine into two states, one for the Arabs and one for the Jews. The Arabs rejected the resolution and the Jews accepted it. Against the background of this conflict, the British decided to abandon the Mandate, withdraw their armed forces, and leave Palestine. On 14 May 1948, the leadership of the Yishuv declared independence and the State of Israel came into being. One of the first acts of the new government was to open the country's borders to Jewish immigration.

In May 1948, following the declaration of independence, Israel's economic prospects were bleak; the country was at war with all of its neighbors. In addition, the war provoked an exodus of Arabs from Israel to the neighboring states. The reasons for this have been the subject of huge controversy, and a few points should be made about the implications for Israel's economic development. Although there was no plan to expel the Arabs, the fact that so many left made housing and land available for Jewish immigrants. A total of approximately 700,000 Arabs fled or were expelled, leaving an Arab population of over 150,000 in Israel, who became citizens of the new state.[1] After cease-fire agreements were signed in 1949, it was subject to terrorist attacks across its borders.

The war of independence also provoked a huge exodus of Jews from Arab countries to Israel (see Chapter 10, especially Tables 10.1, 10.4 and Appendix 10.2). In 1948–1951, some 300,000 immigrants arrived from the Middle East, with another 357,000 arriving between 1952 and 1964. Although the immigrants were welcomed and assisted, the flow was so large that only a bare minimum of support could be provided for them from public funds. Thousands were initially housed in tent encampments throughout the country before being moved into government-supplied huts. Some were housed in homes abandoned by the Arabs. Between 1948 and 1951, the Jewish population of Israel doubled.

1948–1952: Austerity

In the period immediately after the war, the government's economic priority was to create work, but it lacked the financial resources to achieve this objective. Loans were therefore taken from commercial banks through the sale of foreign exchange and government bonds. In addition, the money supply was increased, which resulted in inflation. These measures enabled the government to finance its basic activities and thus limited the rise in unemployment. In 1950, unemployment came to only 8.1 percent of the labor force (including the potential labor force in immigrant camps), a remarkably low figure given the large and sudden increase in the labor force.[2]

Influenced by the success of wartime Britain's planned and tightly controlled economy, the government instituted a policy of austerity. Basic goods and services were rationed and controls were placed on the production of nonessential items. These policies were in keeping with the egalitarian ideology that characterized the new state and its Labor-led government; they

---

[1] Morris, Benny. 2004. *Palestinian Refugee Problem Revisited*. Cambridge: Cambridge University Press. The issues arising from the loss of property of Jews who left Arab countries have been analyzed in Fishbach, Michael R. 2008. *Jewish Property Claims against Arab Countries*. New York: Columbia University Press. Jewish property losses were calculated at about $1.5 billion (calculated from Fishbach, pp. 103, 133, and 149). They, unlike the Arab estimates of Palestinian losses, were based on specific claims by a limited number of individuals. The highest Israeli estimate of Palestinian losses was about $5 billion in 2008 prices. The highest Arab estimate of Palestinian land and real estate losses was $69 billion (calculated from p. 122).

[2] Halevi, Nadav and Ruth Klinov-Malul. 1968. *The Economic Development of Israel*. New York, Washington, London: Frederik A. Praeger, 66.

also seemed to be the only way to manage the pressures caused by war and mass immigration. Despite these measures, during the first few years after independence, there were widespread shortages in official markets and rapidly rising prices on increasingly important black markets, with deleterious effects on morale. But there were also achievements: A network of roads and thousands of housing units were built, and the government began to develop basic services such as postal delivery, telecommunications, railways, airlines, and radio broadcasting. During the period before 1952, government policy attempted to achieve greater economic self-sufficiency. The emphasis of investment and settlement policy was agricultural; funds were channeled to new, rural, agriculturally-based communities. This policy was designed to provide employment, food, and raw materials; agricultural settlement was also seen as a means of dispersing the population throughout the country. Furthermore, by building settlements in outlying and border areas in the Galilee and the Negev, security was strengthened and the claim of the Jewish people to the land was enhanced. Because it was unlikely that the private sector would invest in remote areas of the country, the logic of government action was reinforced. In the area of foreign trade, government intervention was, by its very nature, better suited to preventing imports than encouraging exports. Imports could be easily controlled by administrative measures, whereas marketing exports abroad required the creation of companies with the necessary products and expertise, something that was beyond the government's capability. Hence, emphasis was placed on import substitution rather than exports as the driving force for growth in the economy.

The First Moves toward Liberalization

By 1952, the very tightly controlled economy was suffering serious shortages of foreign exchange and rising unemployment. To ease the foreign exchange constraint and provide funds for investment and thus employment, the first steps were taken toward economic liberalization. The government devalued the Israeli pound[3] and took other measures to reduce inflation, cut the budget deficit, and improve the balance of payments. Price controls were also relaxed. Financial pressures and a desire to increase the resources

---

[3] In 1948, Israel's currency was the Palestine Pound that had been in circulation since 1927 under the British Mandate and was equal in value to one pound sterling. In 1954, it was renamed the Israeli Lira, and the link to sterling was cancelled. In 1980, the Lira was replaced by the Shekel at a rate of ten Lira to one Shekel. In 1985, the Shekel was replaced by the New Israeli Shekel (NIS) at a rate of 1,000 Shekels to one New Shekel.

available for development were major factors leading to the decision to sign the Reparations Agreement with the Federal Republic of Germany in 1952. Designed to partially compensate Jews for the Holocaust, this arrangement provided for $800 million to be paid to the Israeli government and Jewish institutions over the following twelve years. Another source of foreign currency was the sale of State of Israel bonds, mainly in the United States, which began in 1951 and was very successful. The decision to raise capital abroad had significant ideological and practical implications. Orthodox economic theory might suggest that at least part of Israel's underemployed labor force would have been employed best in export industries set up by foreign investors. The investors would provide the technology, management, and marketing skills lacking in the economy. A deliberately undervalued exchange rate would encourage this development. However, policies of this kind ran counter to the political views of the government and the Histadrut, which together dominated the country's economic and political life. They wanted to create well-paid jobs that provided a high standard of living so as to attract new immigrants, in accordance with Zionist objectives. They did not favor reliance on the vagaries of foreign investors and international markets. By importing capital itself, the government was able to control a large part of the investment process and choose the sectors for development. It dominated the domestic capital market, borrowing from private savers to fund its deficit. This practice was not only a matter of financial necessity; it reflected an ideological preference for the centralized allocation of resources. It is also unlikely that foreigners would have invested directly in the Israeli economy given the risks involved at that time. In the mid-1950s, therefore, the government effectively became the guarantor of investments made by the private sector. The improvement in the capital account of the balance of payments, as a result of the reparations agreements and the sale of bonds, was the major factor behind an acceleration of the economic growth rate. GNP rose by an annual average of nearly 17 percent in the period 1954–1955, compared to 1.8 percent in the period 1952–1953[4] (see Table 1.1).

By 1954, the government concluded that economic growth could no longer be generated using agriculture as the leading sector. A new phase of industrialization was required to generate the jobs required for the growing population. Furthermore, the government decided that it could not carry this out alone: Private entrepreneurs would be needed. These were, however,

---

[4] Central Bureau of Statistics. 1986. *Statistical Abstract of Israel 1986.* Jerusalem: Central Bureau of Statistics, 171.

in short supply in Israel, and the willingness of foreigners to invest there was minimal. A search was made for Jewish businessmen who might be willing to come to Israel if conditions were right. This pragmatic approach was a significant feature of the policy of Mapai (the acronym for Mifleget Poalei Eretz Yisrael, or the Land of Israel Workers' Party), Israel's ruling party until it joined with another left-wing faction to become the Labor Party.

Foreign entrepreneurs were offered a package of incentives to come to Israel and set up new companies. The government supplied land, capital (including foreign exchange in order to buy machinery and other equipment abroad), and labor. The entrepreneurs were offered a market protected from competition by imports, and as the government restricted the number of investors in any industry, competition between local suppliers was limited. The aim of government policy was to generate employment and meet the basic needs of the local market. This was done within the framework of dispersing industry to the Negev and the Galilee where new development towns were created. On balance, the policy was successful even though it had to be adapted over time. The downside was that it created elements of dependency by the private sector on the government that lasted for many years.[5]

Immigration and Inequality

Following the declaration of independence, hundreds of thousands of immigrants arrived in Israel. Many were directed to rural areas and agricultural employment for which most of them had no relevant background. As a result, their productivity and earnings were low, resulting in a rise in inequality in the distribution of income. Veterans moved up the occupational ladder to take managerial and clerical posts that had higher earnings.[6] In 1948, 14 percent of veterans were employed in managerial and clerical posts; by 1954, the share was 21 percent. Their share in agriculture, industry, crafts, and construction fell from 53 percent to 42 percent.[7] The veterans were often of different ethnic origin from the newcomers of the 1950s, which created an ethnic-based earnings and status gap with long-term political consequences.

During the 1950s, the average educational levels fell due to the low level of schooling among many immigrants from the Middle East and North

---

[5]   Howard Pack. 1971. *Structural Change and Economic Policy in Israel*. New Haven: Yale University Press, 168.
[6]   Patinkin, Don. 1967. *The Israel Economy: The First Decade*. Jerusalem: Maurice Falk Institute for Economic Research in Israel, 66–69.
[7]   Halevi and Klinov-Malul, *The Economic Development of Israel*, 73.

Africa compared with that of the veteran population that included many who had arrived from Europe.[8] This was the opposite of what happened in the 1930s, when European immigration raised the average educational level of the population of the Yishuv (see Chapter 2).

Another factor that increased income inequality was the payment of restitution payments by the Länder (states) of the Federal Republic of Germany to European Jews. These increased nearly elevenfold between 1954 and 1958, from $6.1 million to $65.4 million.[9] Although immigrants from the Middle East and North Africa lost all their property, they were not compensated, and so restitution payments also increased ethnic income differentials.

Oil and Water

In addition to the problems of obtaining capital, Israel faced constraints obtaining two key inputs: water and oil. Dealing with both of these shortages involved government investments and much diplomacy.

During the 1950s and 1960s, Israel built the National Water Carrier (NWC), a pipeline from the Kinneret (Lake of Galilee) to the Northern Negev. This pipeline linked most of the regional water projects throughout the country, with a capacity of 450 million cubic meters of water per year. It was constructed by the national water company, Mekorot, in the 1950s and 1960s, with construction completed in 1964. The project was so large than when it was completed, a recession began because there were no other investment projects of that scale to maintain demand. The NWC was intended originally to supply water for irrigation to the central and southern regions of Israel, but since the early 1990s, it has supplied more than half of the country's drinking water. The aim was to combine Israel's four fresh water sources – the Sea of Galilee and its catchment basin, the NWC's main natural reservoir, the mountain aquifer, and the coastal aquifer – to provide water to the Negev, the arid southern region.[10]

Israel also faced serious problems obtaining oil, largely because of the Arab boycott. In 1952, the first year for which there is published data, Israel obtained 70 percent of its crude oil from Venezuela and 30 percent from Iran. By the mid-1950s, this had changed, and the majority – reaching 90 percent – came from Iran. The oil was shipped in tankers to Eilat and from

---

[8] Halevi and Klinov-Malul, 74.

[9] Patinkin, *The Israel Economy: The First Decade*, 52.

[10] Mekorot: Israel National Water Company. "Israel's Water Supply System." http://www.mekorot.co.il/Eng/Mekorot/Pages/IsraelsWaterSupplySystem.aspx

there was channeled north in a pipeline with a diameter of about 40 centimeters. The pipeline and its installation were funded by the Rothschild family, who were its owners. After the 1967 Six-Day War and the closing of the Suez Canal, Israel and Iran set up a company under joint ownership of the Israeli government and the Iranian National Oil Company. The Israeli government gave the company, called Trans-Asiatic, an exclusive franchise to transport and store the oil. Its subsidiary, the Eilat-Ashkelon Pipeline Company, acquired the pipeline to Be'er Sheva from the Rothschild family and laid a larger one, with a diameter of about one meter, alongside it, from Eilat to Ashkelon, where it also built terminals for loading and unloading the oil, completed in 1969. The closing of the Suez Canal made it difficult to supply oil to Europe from the Persian Gulf. The tankers were forced to sail on a long route around the Cape of Good Hope. The idea behind the establishment of the company was to shorten the sailing routes and the supply time, and thus, of course, earn more money. Tankers loaded oil in Iran, sailed to Eilat, where they unloaded the cargo at a special terminal, and the oil was then transported in the pipeline to Ashkelon. Most of it was loaded onto tankers bound for Europe, and a small percentage was used by Israel.

After ten years, a crisis developed. In 1979, the Iranian revolution resulted in the Iranian National Oil Company stopping oil sales to Trans-Asiatic, in effect paralyzing it. One of Ayatollah Khomeini's first acts, when he came to power, was to sever all links with Israel. The many Israeli companies and businessmen who had worked in Iran in construction, communications, infrastructure, drugs, and commerce had left already, during the last days of the Shah's rule, and Iran still owed money to some of them. All the joint initiatives in the areas of security and oil were discontinued.

Following the Iranian revolution, the Israeli managers of Trans-Asiatic tried to conduct secret talks with representatives of the Iranian National Oil Company to dismantle the partnership voluntarily and in an orderly manner, but the Iranians broke off all contact. Trans-Asiatic sold the oil tankers, dismissed dozens of employees, and closed operations and offices abroad. It was, however, saved from bankruptcy by the 1979 peace treaty with Egypt, under which Egypt promised to sell Israel oil as a substitute for the loss of the oil from the Sinai. The Egyptian oil arrived in tankers to Eilat, and from there it was transported via the pipeline to Ashkelon and then to refineries in Haifa and Ashdod.[11]

---

[11] Bialer, Uri. 2007. "Fuel Bridge across the Middle East-Israel, Iran, and the Eilat-Ashkelon Oil Pipeline." *Israel Studies*. Vol. 12. No. 3. 29–67; Melman, Yossi. 2006. "How Israel Lost to the Iranians." *Haaretz*, 7 December.

The Economy in the 1960s and Early 1970s

During the late 1950s and early 1960s, with full employment and rapid economic growth, domestic costs rose. Exports of goods and services grew more slowly in volume terms than they had in the early and mid-1950s; domestic demand squeezed them out. Imports rose more quickly, and in February 1962, the minister of finance Levi Eshkol announced an economic stabilization program that included devaluation and a reduction in protective measures. The current account of the balance of payments had deteriorated because of a large growth of imports. In 1964, the excess of imports over exports rose by 28 percent to higher level than had ever been experienced. Additional anxieties were generated by the facts that German reparations were due to end in 1966 and Israel's long expected associate membership of the European Economic Community (EEC) began to look uncertain because of French opposition.[12] In 1965, the government once again decided on a policy of reducing demand in the economy in order to increase exports and reduce imports. The improvement in the current account of the balance of payments in 1965 compared to the previous year is shown in Table 3.1. The table also illustrates the magnitude of the balance of payments problem and how it worsened in the 1970s.

By the early 1960s, reparations payments from Germany had declined, as had foreign investment and other capital transfers. The economy relied increasingly on short-term borrowing. Anxiety about the foreign trade account also increased as France adopted a hostile policy toward Israel in negotiations on associate membership in the European Community (EC). This hostility, it was felt, would threaten the development of trade links with Europe. These events led to a change in government policy that caused the economy to go into recession. The slowdown was deeper than originally contemplated: GDP growth slowed to about 2 percent a year in 1966 and 1967, compared with 10 percent annually in the previous five years. Growth of consumption and investment also decelerated, and between 1965 and 1967unemployment tripled.

The Six-Day War of June 1967, however, changed the picture dramatically: As public sector demand (mainly from the defense sector) rose sharply, economic activity took an upward turn. The dramatic military victory produced a wave of optimism throughout the country that lasted until 1973. The victory of 1967 encouraged foreign investment and capital inflows. The GDP growth rate jumped to 15.3 percent in 1968; during the

---

[12] Greenwald, C. S. 1972. *Recession as a Policy Instrument: Israel 1965–69*. London: C. Hurst & Co, 25.

Table 3.1. *The balance of payments current account, 1952–1980 ($ millions)*

	Exports	Imports total	of which defense	Transfers	Current Account	Current Account As share of GDP (%)
1952	69	287		191	−116	75
1955	127	300		210	−75	63
1960	323	490	28	311	−35	14
1965	680	847	111	329	−203	58
1970	1,334	1,932	624	658	−599	110
1975	3,686	5,521	1,774	2,089	−1,753	137
1980	9,856	8,977	1,655	3,021	−582	27

Source: Central Bureau of Statistics. Statistical Abstract of Israel. 1996. http://www.cbs.gov.il/archive/shnaton47/shnatone.htm#7

period 1969–1972, it averaged nearly 11 percent a year. This growth was made possible not only by an increased inflow of capital but also by a new supply of labor from the territories that had been captured in the war. In 1970, more than 20,000 Arabs from these areas were working in Israel; by 1973, the number exceeded 60,000. There was also a significant increase in immigration from the West: 123,000 arrived between 1969 and 1972.[13] Most of these immigrants brought both skills and capital and were rapidly integrated into the economy.

Factors behind Rapid Growth

The rapid growth of the economy between 1948 and 1972 was largely the result of inflows of labor and capital and appropriate economic policies. Between 1950 and 1960, the population increased by 61 percent; between 1960 and 1970, by 41 percent. Between 1950 and 1962, the civilian labor force more than doubled, from 450,000 to 927,000. In 1973, it reached 1.1 million. The skill and educational level of the labor force rose, despite large-scale immigration from the Middle East and North Africa, as a result of government training and educational programs. The growth of the other main factor of production, capital, was much greater. Between 1953 and 1965,

[13] Central Bureau of Statistics. 1974. *Statistical Abstract of Israel 1974*. Jerusalem: Central Bureau of Statistics, 109.

capital input, measured in constant prices, increased by an annual average of 10.8 percent; labor input rose by 3.8 percent and gross domestic product by 11.7 percent.[14] All of these factors contributed to the large increase in productivity. Almost all of the capital invested between 1948 and 1972 came from abroad; there was virtually no net domestic saving.[15] Although individuals and companies saved, the government borrowed from them in order to finance its deficit. The state's contribution was its organization of the inflow of capital from abroad. Capital and labor accounted for 30–45 percent of the increase in output, the rest coming from increased efficiency in production.[16] This situation was a function of the stage of development: Management and technological change became more important than increases in the supply of labor and capital as development proceeded and the economy matured.

The fast rate of growth and high levels of defense spending resulted in balance of payments problems, even though capital imports usually exceeded the growing current account deficit. These capital imports were mainly preferential forms of finance; the scale of expensive, short-term borrowing on international markets was limited before 1973. The structure of the economy, in terms of the share of the main sectors, changed little between 1950 and 1967, despite rapid growth.

In 1950, government expenditures accounted for 33 percent of GDP, in 1960 for 38 percent, but by 1970 they have risen to 65 percent.[17] The trend toward increased government spending mirrored that in the West: In the twenty-four Organisation for Economic Cooperation and Development (OECD) countries, government spending as a share of GDP rose from 29 percent in 1960 to 41 percent in 1988.[18] Despite many serious problems, the economic picture in the early 1970s was very bright. The success of government policy during this period has been summarized in the following way: The successful absorption of large numbers of immigrants, rapid growth of exports, extensive increase in education, and the application of technology in agriculture all indicated the effectiveness of economic policy.[19]

[14] Bruno, Michael. 1972. "Economic Development Problems of Israel," in Charles A. Cooper and S. A. Alexander, eds. *Economic Development and Population Growth in the Middle East*. New York: American Elsevier, 95.

[15] Bruno, "Economic Development Problems of Israel," 140.

[16] Bruno, 96.

[17] Arnon, Jacob. 1998. "Forty Years of the Israeli Economy." *Economic Quarterly*. Vol. 138. 251–268.

[18] *The Economist*. London. 7 January 1988.

[19] Bruno, 92.

The Debate about Economic Policy

In the early 1960s, a significant policy debate developed about the liberalization and decentralization of the economy, echoes of which could be heard for many years. As the 1950s passed, the degree of import substitution declined. Attention began to focus on resource misallocation and the costs of protection. The debate took place between a group of economists at the Hebrew University, the Bank of Israel, and the Ministry of Finance and a group at the Ministry of Industry and Trade. The former, adhering to what was becoming conventional economic thinking, believed that the price mechanism was the best way to allocate resources and that government controls could not improve on its results. The government decided to confine itself to creating a framework within which market forces would operate. The economic liberalizers advocated estimating a long-term equilibrium exchange rate by which the structure of production would be determined. The Ministry of Industry and Trade retained a state-centered view and contended, in broad terms, that ideas of equilibrium were applicable only in static situations and could not be applied to development problems, where structural changes were significant. With structural change, monopoly, and inevitable government involvement in the economy (if only because of the large defense budget), estimation of an equilibrium exchange rate was meaningless.

In 1962, the market-oriented proposals, comprising an end to administrative controls on imports and a unification of the multiple exchange rate system, were adopted, although their implementation took some years. Pressure from the Ministry of Agriculture delayed, and eventually reduced, the extent of liberalization in agriculture and food processing. Implementation of the strategy was placed in the hands of a public committee consisting of representatives of the Ministries of Finance and Industry, the Histadrut, and the Manufacturers' Association (the Federation of Employers). The Ministry of Industry often supported the arguments of those wanting continued protection. The result was that the costs and benefits of each case were analyzed separately, rather than on an overall basis, and by 1968, liberalization applied to only 50 percent of manufactured goods.[20]

Foreign Trade and Capital Imports

Between 1950 and 1960, the current account deficit fell sharply as a share of national income because exports increased more rapidly than imports. It

---

[20] Pomfret, 27–31.

rose again in the 1960s, partly because greater emphasis on exports increased their level of sophistication and also their import content. Exports, in current dollars, increased by a factor of sixteen between 1950 and 1967; their composition also changed because traditional commodities such as citrus and diamonds became less important, whereas those of other industries and services increased their share. They suffered for much of the period from an overvalued exchange rate and low standards of technology, especially ageing machinery. Costs were high because Israel was a long distance from its markets and sources of raw materials. Government assistance took the form of cheap credits for the purchase of capital equipment and export incentives. Although the volume of exports grew dramatically, it did so from a low base. The profitability of exports was often not high enough to persuade firms to sell abroad, as was especially true during the 1965–1967 recession. The economy became increasingly open to international trade: Imports tripled in dollar terms between 1950 and 1967, constituting 30 percent of GNP in 1950 and 35 percent in 1967.

Despite the fact that economic policy came under increasing criticism, the economy grew at rates achieved by few other countries, and the government succeeded in maintaining full employment. The protectionist policies of the 1950s did not harm the country's increased integration into the world economy during the following two decades. The economic policies adopted in the 1950s were successful because investment funds were usually allocated to sectors with growth potential and which were capable of providing employment in development areas. On the other hand, vested interests in the maintenance of industrial subsidies were created.[21] In its first twenty years, Israel imported about $7 billion in medium-term and long-term capital. Approximately 70 percent of this consisted of transfers, including German reparations, and personal and institutional remittances. The rest was loans and investments, including about 10 percent from the sale of Israeli government bonds abroad. Gradually the emphasis of policy changed: The import of capital, although still considered important, was set alongside the need to rationalize its use through greater reliance on market forces. As a result, by 1967, the economy had made the significant move from administrative protection (quantitative restrictions on imports) to tariffs (import duties). This change meant that prices, rather than the government, became the dominant influence on what could be imported. After 1975, in accordance with agreements with the EC, most of these tariffs on EC goods were reduced and at the end of 1988, they were abolished.

[21] Pomfret, 172–173.

Foreign trade liberalization moves did not resolve balance-of-payments problems. There was a current account deficit every year from 1948 to 1972; to finance this deficit, Israel had to obtain unilateral transfers (gifts) or borrow abroad. As a result, there were more resources available to the economy than those provided by GDP. The excess, when it was not provided by grants and gifts from abroad, was financed by debt. The extra resources borrowed in one year were paid for with interest payments in subsequent years. Although exports paid for an increasing share of the import bill, the absolute size of the trade gap grew. As a result of economic growth, however, the share of the deficit in GDP remained remarkably constant over a long period. During the 1960s, Israel's imports began to be partially financed by loans. The investments made possible by the import surplus were not profitable enough to fund repayment of the loans. As a result, the foreign debt grew faster than the economy's ability to finance it, and the import surplus became a burden on future generations.[22] These problems worsened in the 1970s and reached the breaking point in the 1980s.

1973: A Fateful Year

The Yom Kippur War, which broke out on October 6, 1973, resulted in the death of over 2,600 Israeli soldiers and over 7,000 wounded. It also marked a watershed in economic performance: Between 1973 and 1985, the economy was buffeted by a series of crises that lowered economic growth rates, worsened the balance of payments, and caused spiraling inflation. In 1973–1974, the increase in international oil prices and the international recession that followed it caused economic growth to falter and the balance of payments to deteriorate. Short-term, expensive loans were taken to finance the deficit, which in turn increased the foreign debt and interest payments abroad.

The cost of the Yom Kippur War exceeded 75 percent of that year's GNP of $9.2 billion, although it is impossible to specify the period over which this cost was borne. From October 1973, imports of defense goods increased sharply, as did public consumption. Defense expenditure increased in real terms by 66 percent compared with 1972. The disruption of the economy and the call-up of reservists (many of whom were still in uniform in the spring of 1974) affected exports and production. The United States assisted Israel with the foreign currency costs of the war (increased arms imports),

[22] Patinkin, 126–128.

but only from 1976 did this assistance fully cover the costs of direct defense imports.

Although in 1973 a secular decline occurred in the economic growth rate, it still remained higher than the average rate in member states of the OECD. In 1974 and 1975, this rate reflected in part the high levels of government expenditure on defense. There was a slowdown in 1976 and 1977 because economic policy became more deflationary, but Israel's adjustment to the era of high oil prices and international recession was belated and therefore costly.

The Increased Cost of Oil

Increases in the international price of oil had their effect on Israel soon after the war. At the end of 1973, the country was paying $130 per ton of oil on spot markets – a 40-percent increase in one year. As a result of the Arab boycott, Israel was unable to obtain supplies under contract and consequently had to pay double the price paid by those who had contracts with Middle Eastern oil suppliers. Under the terms of the Second Disengagement Agreement with Egypt, Israel evacuated most of the Sinai oil fields in 1976 and obtained a guarantee of oil supplies from the United States. Israel also received a large military assistance package from the United States to help finance its military withdrawal (see Chapter 6). Most of Israel's oil then had to be imported at high prices on international markets; the oil import bill rose from $98 million in 1972 to $628 million in 1975 and $1.8 billion in 1980. Between 1973 and 1982, the deterioration in the terms of trade, largely a result of the increase in the international price of oil, has been estimated to have cost $12 billion.[23]

Increases in oil prices were abrupt and caused inflationary pressures. Between mid-1973 and 1975, energy price increases accounted for about one-third of the acceleration in inflation; in 1980, inflation would have been 100 percent rather than 130 percent if oil prices had not risen on international markets. Israel's exposure to the effects of international oil price changes was intensified by the extent of the country's reliance on it as a source of energy. Only in 1974 was the decision made to construct the first power station that could use coal as well as oil. This station began operation in 1982, after Israel had withdrawn from the remaining oil fields in the Sinai that had since 1967

---

[23] Sussman, Zvi. 1986. *Israel's Economy: Performance, Problems and Policies*. London: Institute for Jewish Affairs and The Jacob Levinson Center of the Israel-Diaspora Institute for Jewish Affairs, 3.

supplied 25 percent of its oil needs. Higher oil consumption per unit of GNP and the factors described above combined to increase the ratio of energy imports to GNP from 1 percent in the 1950s and 1960s to 4.6 percent in 1974 and 12 percent in 1979. The development of the petrochemical industry increased demand for oil as a production input: The decision to develop this industry was made before 1973 and it contributed to a doubling of feedstock demand between 1974 and 1980. After 1980, the fuel bill fell as international prices came down. By 1985, the cost of fuel was $1.5 billion, 17 percent less in current dollar terms than in 1980.

The Yom Kippur War had important effects on Israeli society as well as on the economy; it also affected the country's politics. After public protests against the lack of preparedness for and the misconduct of the war, Prime Minister Golda Meir resigned. She was the last of the founding generation of the state to head the government. The new government formed by the Labor Party, led by Yitzhak Rabin, undertook the difficult task of adjusting the economy to the harsh realities of the post-Yom Kippur War period. Despite changes in the political leadership, the Labor Party had suffered a collapse in political power and vision. The government operated more on a day-to-day basis than before and tried to deal with crises in many sectors almost simultaneously. The sense of unity and purpose that had characterized Israel until the 1970s faded as domestic division increased and the founding fathers of the Labor movement died or retired (see further in this chapter).

1973–1976: Restraint and Reform

The period immediately after 1973 was an extremely difficult one for the economy. The war had caused massive disruption and consumed huge quantities of resources against a background of rapidly increasing oil costs. GDP per capita grew by only 1 percent a year between 1974 and 1977. Investment fell by an average of 4.7 percent a year and export growth slumped until 1976.

In November 1974, the lira was devalued by 43 percent, subsidies were cut, an import surcharge was imposed, and export subsidies were introduced. Fuel, water, and electricity prices were increased, all part of an austerity program. The government had to meet rising debt repayments and defense costs. Consumer prices rose by 40 percent in 1974, double their 1973 rate and more than triple their 1972 rate, far exceeding the inflation rate of countries with which Israel conducted most of its trade. Devaluations were therefore needed in order to maintain competitiveness. Anticipation of the

1974 devaluation led to capital inflows, which had inflationary effects. In June 1975, a system of so-called crawling peg devaluations was introduced with the aim of improving the balance of payments without causing the domestic instability induced by large devaluations.

In the period 1973–1976, private consumption grew much faster than GDP. This increase was also true on a per capita basis; it reflected the inability and unwillingness of the government to adopt even tougher measures. In 1975, the government implemented the recommendations of a commission on income tax reform. It indexed tax brackets to changes in the consumer price index and sharply increased their real value. A wide range of tax exemptions were abolished; nearly all wage earnings became subject to taxation at the same rate. These long overdue reforms constituted a major improvement in the tax system and were one of the major economic achievements of the period.

The 1977 General Elections

The general elections of 1977 marked a turning point in Israel's political history. Labor was defeated after twenty-nine years in power. The reasons for this included the shock of the 1973 war and resentment of Labor among many Sephardi Jews (of North African and Middle Eastern origin) because of their relatively low status and income compared to those of European origin. The Labor party had become divided and corrupt; its leadership no longer inspired the people. Also there had been a continuous shift to the right in some sections of public opinion on security and defense issues, which was reflected in the defection of the National Religious party from its traditional parliamentary alliance with Labor to the nationalist Likud. This move ultimately enabled Menachem Begin, the Likud leader, to form the new government.

The Likud comprised two sections. Herut was the main nationalist party whose major concerns lay in defense and foreign policy. The much smaller Liberal party was mainly interested in economic issues: It wanted to reduce both government control and the power of the Histadrut. Herut drew its support from the traditional nationalist section of the population and from Sephardi Jews who had become increasingly hostile to the Labor establishment. The interests of these two parts of Herut were different. Those favoring settlements in the West Bank and Gaza, which was to become the leitmotif of the new government, were ideologists who tended to be middle class and often, though not always, of European origin. The Sephardi working class lived in the development towns and the poorer sections of the main cities.

They were primarily interested in welfare and other programs that would benefit them directly. It was Begin's political achievement to bring these groups together in such a way that the latter group did not feel that settlements in the West Bank and Gaza were being built at their expense.

The liberals added a small middle-class constituency that supported the nationalist message of their senior partners in the Likud. After the election, their leader, Simcha Ehrlich, was appointed finance minister and started working on plans for economic reform. The concomitant of the Liberals' policies (which stressed efficiency, sale of public companies, and less government intervention) was a cut in government expenditure. This policy, however, came into conflict with the populist policies of the Herut, whose electoral strength lay in part with the underprivileged who would suffer from expenditure cuts. As will be seen, these tensions had profound effects on the economic policies of the Likud government between 1977 and 1984.

Budgetary restraint became very hard to achieve because of the commitment of the new government to expand Jewish settlement in the West Bank and Gaza. These settlements were the subject of intense international criticism and much domestic debate. From a narrow, economic point of view, they represented a spreading of the national development effort over a wider geographical area. Both the Galilee and the Negev continued to be underdeveloped, and their chances of receiving adequate funding receded during this period. The cost of the settlement program was high: In 1981–1982, it was estimated to have equaled 3 percent of GNP.[24] (The total cost of the settlement program between 1967 and 2008 was estimated at $28 billion. See Chapter 8)

1977–1980: Liberalization

Liberalizing the economy through exchange rate and foreign trade reform was not just a matter for the Liberal party and its finance minister. Many of the officials in the Ministry of Finance and the Bank of Israel, with whom the minister worked, had for years been associated with the Labor governments. They had formulated and implemented the liberalizations of that period and saw the 1977 reform as part of a comprehensive package of measures designed to make the economy more efficient. Hence the governor of the Bank of Israel, in his introduction to the Bank's 1977 Annual Report, stated that the foreign currency reform made economic policy more

[24] Arnon, Jacob. 1985. *Economy in Turmoil*. Tel Aviv: Kibbutz HaMeuchad, 182.

effective but that it was not a substitute for fiscal policies and other policies to control increases in prices and incomes.[25]

At the end of October 1977, the lira was devalued by 47 percent, travel taxes were abolished, foreign exchange controls were eased, customs duties were reduced, and other measures were introduced to liberalize the exchange and payments systems. One of the most important steps taken was to permit Israelis to buy assets linked to foreign currencies, which were thus protected against devaluations. Before the liberalization, only those involved in foreign trade, banking, recipients of foreign incomes, new immigrants, and non-residents could hold such assets. The October 1977 devaluation was not, however, accompanied by reductions in domestic expenditure. During 1978–1979, government expenditure increased by 1 percent compared with a decrease of 22 percent in 1976–1977. There was a similar pattern in investment, which rose by nearly 15 percent in 1978–1979 compared with a decrease of 18.6 percent in 1976–1977. In addition, in the two years after the October 1977 devaluation, private consumption rose by 16.5 percent in real terms, compared with 9.8 percent in 1976–1977.

In November 1977, President Anwar Sadat of Egypt made his historic journey to Jerusalem, and peace talks between Israel and Egypt began. In 1979, a peace treaty was signed and Israel began to withdraw its military installations and armed forces from the Sinai. The cost of moving hardware and equipment and building new military bases was considerable. It led to an increase in defense expenditures just when the defense burden needed to be substantially reduced to lower aggregate demand and make room for exports. The United States increased its assistance to Israel by about $1 billion in order to help fund the withdrawal from Sinai and the construction of new air bases in the Negev.

As a result of high domestic demand, exports rose in volume terms by only 8 percent in 1978–1979 compared with 29 percent in 1976–1977; imports, however, increased by 14 percent in 1978–1979 compared with a decrease of 5.5 percent during the preceding period. This pattern was exactly the opposite of what expected from a successful devaluation. Exchange rate and foreign trade liberalization is usually aimed, inter alia, at improving the trade balance. The gains achieved by deflationary policies between 1974 and 1977 were thus lost. A deficit on goods and services of $4 billion in 1975 had been reduced to $2.6 billion in 1977, but by 1979, it worsened to $3.9 billion.

The most dramatic effect of the 1977 policy changes was an upsurge in inflation that lasted until 1985. Consumer prices rose by 34.6 percent in 1977

---

[25] Bank of Israel. 1978. *Annual Report 1977*. Jerusalem: Bank of Israel, iii.

and 78.3 percent in 1978. The increase was in large part due to the devaluation, which increased import costs; these were easily passed on to consumers because of buoyant demand in the economy. The system of indexation, which linked increases in wages to those in the cost-of-living index, ensured that price rises were passed through the economy, with wages increasing in compensation. This situation made it difficult to reduce purchasing power. Domestic demand was not squeezed to make room for more exports and reduce imports. Growth of GDP accelerated from 2 percent in 1976–1977 to 4.5 percent in 1978–1979, but insofar as it was only a result of increased consumption, it was to be a temporary upswing. In 1980–1985, the annual average growth rate was 3.1 percent.

November 1979 to January 1981: Restraint Again

In November 1979, against a background of accelerating inflation, the finance minister Ehrlich was replaced by Yigal Horovitz. The new minister rapidly introduced a series of deflationary measures designed to improve balance of payments and reduce inflation. Consumer subsidies and allocations of interest-free credit were cut. Electricity prices and those of other public utilities rose, and import deposits were increased. Much construction activity was frozen, as was public service employee hiring. Income tax as a share of average salaries rose from 14 percent in 1978 to 19 percent in 1980. In 1979, revenues from income tax increased by 14.7 percent in real terms. While these were measures taken by the Finance Ministry, the Bank of Israel tightened monetary policy to reduce the inflationary effects of capital inflows attracted by high interest rates. Civilian public consumption was reduced by 1 percent in 1980, compared with an increase of 2 percent in 1979, but the effects of this change were undermined by increases in defense expenditures; as a result, total government consumption rose by 9 percent.

Horovitz's policies, which were accompanied by strong calls to the public to reduce its consumption and adopt a regime of austerity, helped improve the balance of payments. Private consumption fell by 2.7 percent in 1980 after an 8-percent rise in 1979; investment fell by 13.3 percent. These changes helped reduce imports and make room for exports. In 1979 and 1980, total exports of goods and services rose by 20 percent in dollar terms whereas imports rose by 8.5 percent. The civilian deficit fell from $1.9 billion to $1.2 billion; industrial exports rose by 25 percent. Balance-of-payments improvements were not, however, accompanied by slower inflation: The latter accelerated from 111 percent in 1979 to 133 percent in 1980. Accelerating inflation became a major cause of public anxiety and led to a change in economic policy. Horowitz also took one very significant step to weaken the Histadrut: He forbade its pension funds to finance Hevrat Ovdim, the Histadrut holding company.[26] This weakened Hevrat Ovdim financially and reduced the economic and political power of the Histradrut that had, up to then, in effect run its own internal capital market.

1981–1983: Populism and Crisis

Elections were due in the spring of 1981, and the finance minister wanted to maintain restrictive economic policies despite their lack of popularity. The Cabinet refused to back him and overturned his rejection of a proposed increase in teachers' pay. Yigal Horovitz resigned in January 1981. His successor, Yoram Aridor, immediately introduced radically different policies. He reduced taxes and increased subsidies in expectation of increased consumer expenditure that would yield higher tax revenues. The rate of devaluation of the shekel was also slowed.

The change of finance ministers represented the temporary triumph of populism over liberalism and austerity. The loosening of financial controls before the election was not without precedent, but the pre-election tax cuts and subsidy increases were on a scale never before experienced, and they continued after the election. The new minister's policies, which increased the public's purchasing power, helped bring about the reelection of the Likud government in June 1981 but were to have catastrophic economic effects.

The Acceleration of Inflation in the Late 1970s and Early 1980S

From 1979 until 1985, hyperinflation destroyed the normal operation of the price mechanism, and after 1980, it became the central issue in economic policy. The 1970s began with relatively low but accelerating inflation and ended with prices rising by more than 100 percent a year. By 1984, prices were rising at an annual rate of 445 percent. The origins of these problems can be found in the economic policy development of the 1970s. Between 1960–1961 and 1973–1974, as the economy moved from recession to boom,

---

[26] Grinberg, Lev Luis and Gershon Shafir. 2000. "Economic Liberalization and the Breakup of the Histadrut's Domain," in Gershon Shafir, and Yoav Peled, eds. *The New Israel*. Boulder: Westview, 119.

the government's budget deficit as a share of gross national product (GNP) rose from virtually zero to a peak of 16 percent. Between 1970 and 1972, the deficit averaged $1 billion, in 1973, it more than doubled to $2.3 billion, and by 1974, it had reached $3 billion. Until 1973, economic growth was strong and so these problems were not felt as constraints requiring changes in policy. After the Yom Kippur War, this changed because economic growth decelerated. In the period 1975–1985, the budget deficit averaged 13 percent of GNP. In 1984 it peaked at 17 percent.[27]

These massive increases had several causes; the main one was the rise in defense expenditure. There were also significant rises in social services spending, subsidies, transfers to individuals and firms, and interest payments. Between fiscal years 1977–1978 and 1984–1985, spending on these items rose by 110 percent, in dollar terms. As this spending was not matched by higher revenues, the deficit grew. Inflation in the mid-1970s was sustained by government deficits against a background of full employment.[28] Between 1973–1974 and 1978–1979, the deficit fell but inflation accelerated.

To improve the balance of payments, major devaluations had been carried out in 1971 (20 percent) and in 1974 (43 percent). The rate of exchange was then fixed, but the effect of the adjustment was transitory, and soon after the devaluation, inflation was back to its previous levels, wiping out the competitive gain. With the introduction of the so-called crawling peg exchange rate mechanism in June 1975, which took the form of a 2-percent monthly devaluation, inflation exceeded the rate of price rises in Israel's trading partners. In the years prior to 1975, expectations of price rises were influenced by events in the relatively distant past.[29] People reacted on the basis of what they remembered had happened in previous years. The crawling peg mechanism considerably reduced the lag in adjusting expectations, and so reactions to recent and more rapidly changing events now took place. Nominal changes in the economy occurred more rapidly, which caused the public to react with ever greater speed. The crawling peg was a mechanism that permitted inflation to continue: Everyone knew that wage and price rises would rapidly be followed by a devaluation that would restore the economy's competitiveness to the level that prevailed before domestic costs rose. The 1977 liberalization intensified this process by permitting the public to buy assets linked to the exchange rate for a number of foreign currencies. It was accompanied by a 47 percent devaluation, which increased the price

[27] Bank of Israel. 1975. *Annual Report 1974*. Jerusalem: Bank of Israel, Table V-1, 62.

[28] Bank of Israel. 1985. "Recent Economic Developments." Jerusalem: Bank of Israel, Publication No. 38, Table 16.

[29] Ministry of Finance. 1986. *The Budget 1986/87*. Jerusalem: Ministry of Finance.

level and the value, in local currency, of assets indexed to the consumer price index and the exchange rate.

In 1981, economic policy was reversed and measures were taken that increased the level of demand and added to inflationary pressures: Subsidies rose from $50 million in 1980 to $1.5 billion in 1981; indirect taxes, especially on imported consumer durables, were reduced; the lag in the adjustment of income tax brackets to inflation was eliminated; and transfer payments rose.[30] In addition to limiting devaluation of the shekel to 5 percent a month, the government restricted increases in prices of controlled commodities to the same rate, despite a much higher underlying rate of inflation. This meant that subsidies rose, increasing the budget deficit. The aim of this policy was to reduce inflationary expectations by reducing prices and thereby moderate wage demands. Implicit was the view that changing expectations would reduce inflation; increased spending on consumer durables would, the government believed, increase its revenues and thus help reduce the budget deficit. In fact, the opposite occurred: The deficit jumped from 8 percent of GNP in 1980 to 14 percent in 1981.

In June 1982, with the outbreak of the war in Lebanon, taxes were increased in an attempt to reduce the budget deficit, or at least slow its growth. The rise in taxation was only the first in a series of policy reversals that themselves increased uncertainty and instability. In the autumn of 1982, anxiety had mounted about the acceleration of inflation from an annual rate of 102 percent to 158 percent. There was a huge increase in the government's budget deficit due to higher defense spending and civilian consumption. This change had not been accompanied by a commensurate growth of net taxes, which led to both a higher rate of inflation and a large fall in public-sector saving.[31] By July 1983, the shekel had to be devalued by an extra 7 percent in addition to the regular adjustment. The public no longer believed that the government could maintain the artificially high exchange rate, which had brought about a cumulative deterioration in Israel's external competitiveness by 32 percent between 1981 and 1983. In May 1983, the Bank of Israel drew attention to the collapse of the economic policy and foreshadowed the crisis of October 1983, stating that the public did not believe that government policies would persist.[32]

In the period up to 1980, sales of foreign exchange to the public were used to stabilize the exchange rate rather than to control the money supply.

[30] The Bank of Israel. 1982. *Annual Report 1981*. Jerusalem: Bank of Israel, 5–6.
[31] The Bank of Israel. 1983. *Annual Report 1982*. Jerusalem: Bank of Israel, 6.
[32] Shiffer, Zalman. 1982. "Money and Inflation in Israel: The Transition of an Economy to High Inflation." *Federal Reserve Board of St. Louis Review*. Vol. 64. 33.

Exchange rate policy and open market operations in foreign exchange were instruments for reducing the import surplus.[33] From the period 1980–1982, policy changed: Sales of foreign exchange were made in order to cover the budget deficit and to maintain a stable exchange rate. Most public debt consisted of government bonds, linked to the consumer price index and sold in unlimited quantities at positive real rates of interest. Sales were used to stabilize the real rate of return on public debt, helping ensure that the government could meet its financing requirements. Some bonds were issued linked to the exchange rate; their volume depended on public demand. Their rate of return depended on the exchange rate and international interest rates, which could not be manipulated to control the money supply. In this situation, changes in the money supply magnified and prolonged price shocks in the system that affected inflationary expectations and were an important cause of devaluations. Indexation meant that price increases in one sector were transferred to others. Rapid inflation increased the speed of adjustment and shortened the lag between present price experience and changes in inflationary expectations. As a result, acceleration of price inflation preceded accelerations of monetary growth. During 1983, the public further increased its purchases of foreign currency. It was able to do this by selling bank shares, the values of which rose sharply as a result of the banks' support of their share prices. The banks bought their own shares using funds borrowed abroad. The public understood the implications of deteriorating balance-of-payments figures and acted to protect itself against a devaluation its very actions had helped make inevitable. In October 1983, the shekel was devalued by 23 percent and allowed to float on a daily basis. Finance Minister Yoram Aridor, who had proposed linking the shekel to the dollar as a means of simultaneously reducing inflation and improving the balance of payments, resigned. His so-called dollarization plan was seen as a gimmick that would bring to an end the country's economic independence. His resignation was a reflection of the disastrous consequences of the economic policies he had introduced. The government then took steps to protect the balance of payments and permitted inflation to increase.

With Aridor's resignation in October 1983, the fourth Likud finance minister, Yigal Cohen-Orgad, came to office. He introduced a program of deflationary measures and devalued the shekel, but as general elections were scheduled for the summer of 1984, economic policy was quickly reversed again. Taxes were cut, subsidies increased, and consequently, inflation accelerated.

---

[33] Bruno, Michael. 1985. "Economic Stabilization: The Emergency Plan in Its Early Phases." Economic Quarterly. Vol. 31. No. 124. 207–223.

During 1984, there was a major improvement in the balance of payments, largely due to a fast growth of exports, the result of a rapid but short-lived expansion of world trade. However, it was not large or rapid enough to prevent the foreign exchange reserves from falling in 1985, thus causing a major crisis. The elections of July 1984 resulted in a deadlock between the two major political parties and their allies in the Knesset. In September 1984, a government of National Unity was formed by Labor and the Likud along with some of their allies. The new government immediately devalued the shekel, reduced subsidies, and introduced restrictions on imports. Inflation accelerated from annual rates of 311 percent in the first quarter of 1984 to 496 percent in the second and 536 percent in the third (see Figure 3.1). In an attempt to reduce inflation, a three-month wage and price freeze was introduced from November 1984 to the end of January 1985. The Histadrut agreed to forgo compensation for wage erosion in return for a freeze on the prices of subsidized goods and on formerly uncontrolled goods and services. The freeze reduced the rate of inflation but not the underlying pressures, partly because the government had to increase its spending on subsidies. At the end of the freeze, prices rose sharply, and after subsidy cuts were implemented, another freeze was introduced at the beginning of February 1985. It was followed by a third freeze, which was supposed to last for six months. Producers were to absorb part of the increase in their costs; workers were to forgo part of the cost-of-living adjustments related to increases in the prices of subsidized goods. Reductions in subsidies were aimed at cutting the budget deficit. This was a voluntary package and that very fact helped undermine it. The underlying reason these measures failed was that they were supported by high levels of government expenditure, financed in large part by inflationary mechanisms. The floating exchange rate increased the price of imports and in turn contributed to inflationary pressures.

The Economic Stabilization Program of July 1985

By June 1985, it had become clear that inflation could not be reduced more than temporarily by wage and price freezes. Improvements in the trade deficit, which had occurred in 1984, faded in 1985. Most worrying was a decline in the foreign exchange reserves to what were considered dangerously low levels, which finally provoked major policy changes. At the beginning of July, at an all-night Cabinet meeting, the government adopted a comprehensive plan to stabilize the economy. Its aim was to improve the balance of payments and simultaneously reduce inflation. The program involved an immediate 18.8 percent devaluation of the shekel and a subsequent freezing of its

Figure 3.1. Annual change in the consumer price index, 1970–2009.

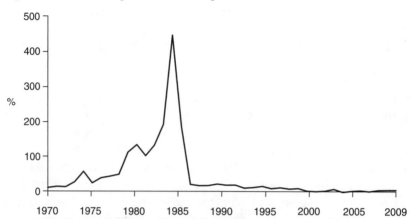

Source: Central Bureau of Statistics, "Statistical Abstract of Israel 2009." *Monthly Bulletin of Statistics*, February 2010.

rate against the dollar. (This freeze lasted until February 1987.) The prices of subsidized goods were increased by between 35 percent and 75 percent, whereas nonsubsidized items went up by 17 percent. This was followed by a freeze on prices. Employees were only to be partly compensated for the erosion of wages; an agreement to this effect was signed on July 15. The government, having unilaterally declared its intention of introducing a state of emergency, suspended cost-of-living allowance agreements. These would have brought an 18-percent increase in wages and salaries in August in order to compensate for 80 percent of the rise in prices that had occurred in May and June. Compensation for the July price rises (which came to 27.5 percent) would have been paid at the beginning of September under the old agreement. Instead, a 14-percent payment in August and a 12-percent payment in September were agreed to. This agreement followed pressure from the Histadrut, which declared a one-day national strike on July 2. Real gross wages at the beginning of August were 7 percent below their July 1 level, and at the beginning of September, they were 18 percent lower. During this period, tax thresholds increased sharply in real terms as a result of the slowdown in inflation. Income tax brackets were linked to the price index of the previous quarter; as inflation slowed in the autumn, taxpayers gained the benefit of linkage to the price rises of the early summer. The budgetary measures were designed to reduce the deficit by $1.5 billion, thus offsetting the increases that had occurred in the first three months of the 1985–1986 budget. The government proposed to cut $250 million from its expenditures on goods and services and to dismiss 10,000 public sector workers. Public spending would also be reduced by the erosion of gross wages. Other changes included a restriction on the purchase of foreign currency-linked assets to those with maturity of a year or more.

The most important aspects of the program were its comprehensiveness and the simultaneity of the measures. According to one of the authors of the plan, the most important single element was the cut in the budget deficit. Although the original proposals only pushed spending back to its March 1985 level, the measures actually taken resulted in fundamental changes.[34] The next item of importance was the freezing of the exchange rate at a competitive level. The exchange rate, in a small, open economy suffering from hyperinflation, was an important price "anchor." It affected inflation and was the basis for many asset prices in the linkage system. The public followed movements in the exchange rate as a guide to the value of its assets and as an indication of government policy and of the state of the economy. Freezing the exchange rate would provide a basis for holding down prices and nominal wages. Against this background, the system of indexation would be broken, granting only partial compensation for price rises and delaying payments for these purposes. These moves would lower wage costs and thus increase the economy's competitiveness in the face of lingering inflation and a frozen exchange rate. Monetary policy had to provide people with an incentive to hold on to local currency and assets denominated in shekels rather than to buy black-market dollars and assets denominated in foreign currency. This incentive was achieved with the aid of a very large increase in interest rates, which caused financial difficulties for the productive sectors of the economy. The government sought and received emergency aid from the United States in order to bolster the foreign exchange reserves. This aid improved the capital account of the balance of payments and reduced the need to borrow on expensive, short-term money markets abroad. It also sent a very powerful signal to the Israeli public and the international financial community that the measures were serious and credible. The program was very successful in reducing inflation. In the second month of its operation, prices were rising more slowly than they had for over three years. In September 1985, the New Shekel was introduced at a rate of one per one thousand Shekels. In the first half of 1985, prices rose by an average monthly rate of 12 percent and in the second half by 6.8 percent. By November 1985, the monthly inflation rate was less than one percent, and the price level actually fell in January 1986.

[34] Bruno, Michael. 1993. *Crisis, Stabilisation and Economic Reform: Therapy by Consensus.* Oxford: Clarendon Press, 108–155.

Reducing inflation was not the only aim of the program but it was the one that succeeded most. In 1985, there was also an improvement in the balance of payments, but this was partly due to a trend whose origins preceded the July program. The current account moved from deficits averaging $2 billion in 1983–1984 to a surplus of almost $1 billion in 1985.[35] The July measures were greatly assisted by the decline in the value of the dollar against the major European currencies in 1986, which lowered Israel's import costs while reducing its export prices in Europe. The fall in international oil prices also reduced costs and helped improve the current account of the balance of payments.

Major changes occurred in the state budget as a result of the July 1985 measures. Subsidies were drastically reduced, other expenditures were more modestly cut or frozen, and taxes were increased. The effect was to reduce the budget deficit (excluding interest payments) from 9 percent in 1984 to 2 percent in 1985. The reduction of subsidies to industry, agriculture, and parts of the service sector was of long-term significance. From 1985 on, many companies and economic entities such as cooperatives and kibbutzim began to suffer serious economic difficulties. They had relied on cheap government credits, which suddenly dried up or became much more expensive due to the sudden and massive rise in real interest rates. The real interest rate on nondirected, short-term local currency credits that financed production for the local market reached 100 percent in the second half of 1985. For nearly thirty years, reliance on the government, especially for cheap credit, was an accepted way of doing business: Suddenly the rules of the game had changed. It took years for this new reality to be absorbed by those concerned.

Table 3.2 shows the development of the budget deficit and its financing between 1980 and 2008. The period 1980–1984 reflects conditions before the stabilization program was introduced it contrasts strongly with the period 1985–1987. The stabilization program sharply reduced government spending and increased government revenues because tax revenues rose sharply. The effect of these two trends was a large decline in the deficit, excluding interest payments and a more modest but significant one in the deficit, including interest payments. Until 1985, the deficit had been largely financed by sales of foreign exchange. This had put downward pressure on the exchange rate of the shekel, with inflationary and other consequences. The ending of this fiscal pressure helped stabilize the balance of payments, the exchange rate, and thus the inflation rate. The table also shows two

---

[35] Central Bureau of Statistics. 2008. Statistical Abstract of Israel 2007. http://www.cbs.gov.il/shnaton59/download/st15_01x.xls

Table 3.2. *The budget deficit and its financing, 1980–2008 (percent of GDP)*

	1980–84	1985–87	1996–2000	2008
Total public expenditure	72.5	66.2	50.0	43.3
–Domestic expenditure	60.3	54.3		
–Interest	3.3	6.6	5.8	3.7
Total revenue	58.5	66.4	45.6	41.2
–Local revenue	48.3	50.8		
–Foreign revenue	10.2	15.6		
Total deficit*	13.9	–0.2	4.4	2.0
–Domestic	12.0	3.3		
–Foreign	1.9	3.5		
Deficit financing				
Foreign loans	6.6	–0.6		
Net printing of money	1.7	2.3		
Domestic borrowing	4.5	0.2		
Other	1.2	–2.1		

* minus=surplus

Source: Bank of Israel. "Annual Report 1987." Jerusalem: Bank of Israel, 1988; "Annual Report 2008." Jerusalem: Bank of Israel, 2009.

long-term trends. The first was the decline in public spending as a share of national income until 2008, and the second was the decline in public revenues after 1985–1987. The implications of these changes are analyzed in Chapters 4, 5, 6, and 11.

In 1987, fiscal restraint was reinforced by the cancellation of the Lavi fighter aircraft project (see Chapter 7). This enabled the defense industry to restructure along more economic lines and sent a clear signal that even in the area of defense, economic considerations would play a role in official decision making. The reduction in the deficit reduced government borrowing needs and freed more capital for the private sector. Before 1985, 70 percent of all outstanding credit was government-directed. As a result of these fiscal changes and a series of reforms in capital market regulations, the system of directed credit was abolished in 1990, and in the following year 70 percent of credit was undirected. Between 1985 and the early 1990s, the liberalization of capital movements in and out of the economy was implemented.[36]

[36] Bruno, *Crisis, Stabilisation and Economic Reform: Therapy by Consensus*, 76–87, 267–283.

Economic Analysis behind The 1985 Program

From the early 1970s until 1985, the government attempted to achieve real devaluations in order to improve the balance of payments and increase economic growth. The theory behind these policies was that a devaluation of the shekel in excess of local inflation would lower the price abroad of Israeli exports in relation to nontraded goods in the economy. It would also reduce the demand for imports by increasing their relative price. In order for such a policy to succeed, the government had to control or, if possible, reduce spending and wages in the economy to make room for exports. It had to strengthen incentives to sell abroad rather than at home. If local demand was relatively weak (because of deflationary policies accompanying a devaluation), then the likelihood of an increase in exports was greater than if local demand was strong. These policies did not work during this period, however. Exports increased in 1980 and 1984, partly because of reductions in domestic demand in 1979 and 1983, but in the first half of the decade, the export growth rate was weak. Economic growth was not sustained and the improvement in the payments in 1980 and 1984 was accompanied by accelerating inflation. Another approach was needed.

The policies introduced in 1981 were based on the theory that inflation was not related to real factors in the economy, such as the budget deficit, but was caused by the spiral of indexed wages, prices, and the exchange rate. The implication was that inflation had to be dealt with by "nominal" rather than "real" policy changes. These changes included the rate of devaluation and price rises; the latter was affected by the subsidy and indirect tax levels. If the government reduced the rate of increase in prices, inflationary expectations would be reduced, thus lowering future wage and price increases. In the past, inflation had been dealt with by managing the exchange rate, changing the prices of goods and services controlled by the government, and setting monetary targets. When balance of payments crises developed, the government devalued and increased the prices of controlled commodities. Its aim was to protect the foreign exchange reserves and implement a real devaluation. Indexation and a feeling that balance of payments problems were a more serious threat to the economy than inflation permitted the cost-push effect of the rise in controlled prices to increase the general level of prices. This occurred within the context of accommodating monetary policy and was designed to protect the private sector from the effects of cuts in public sector expenditure. The underlying notion was that the problems in the economy stemmed from an excessive level of government spending. Some influential economists began to believe that a significant link existed between the government deficit and the current account of the balance of payments. Excessive spending, financed by borrowing or printing money, increased the public's liquid assets. To protect the value of these assets against inflation and devaluation, the public bought foreign currency or assets linked to foreign currency, thus worsening the balance of payments. This forced further devaluation, with the resulting inflation increasing government spending in nominal terms, borrowing and printing money, and so the spiral went on. The speed with which this inflationary spiral occurred was a function of the linkage system. In the second half of 1985, a reduction of the budget deficit made it much less necessary to sell foreign currency to the public that helped bring about an improvement in the balance of payments. In the late 1970s, some Israeli economists began to understand that the inflationary problem was not just a matter of excess demand that needed to be restrained by cutting the budget deficit. The wage indexation system gave the inflationary process an element of inertia. According to Bruno, when indexation failed to compensate workers for price increases, other, endogenous and forward-looking forms of indexation provided part of the lubrication for an inflationary spiral.[37] The move from a semifixed pegged exchange rate to a crawling peg in 1975 meant that the economy lost a monetary "anchor." The introduction of foreign exchange-linked bank deposits made the monetary system much more accommodating. The money supply thus became increasingly endogenous. Reducing the budget deficit was still considered crucial, but a series of accompanying measures were also deemed necessary.

As a result of this new analysis, the comprehensive stabilization program was developed. To tackle the real fundamentals, orthodox measures included a large and permanent reduction in the budget deficit, an immediate devaluation, measures to increase the independence of the central bank, United States' aid, as well as the maintenance of the social safety net. The unorthodox measures included nominal anchors: a temporary exchange rate freeze, monetary controls, a wage freeze and temporary price controls.[38]

The Political Economy of Inflation
Control in Israel

In the period 1967–1973, warnings about dangers of accelerating inflation were ignored because economy was growing and the government had a very

---

[37] Bruno, 128–155.
[38] Bruno, 269.

full agenda between defense and social pressures. There was no immediate or serious balance of payments problem that forced reconsideration.[39] The economy was very exposed to the OPEC oil shock of 1973 because inflation was already high and because of the effects of the Yom Kippur War. The post-war Labor Government (1975–1977) headed by Yitzhak Rabin began a series of reforms designed to stabilize the economy and improve its growth prospects. It reduced government spending, devalued the shekel, and introduced a major reform of the income tax system. The stabilization measures helped reduce the current account deficit from $1.8 billion in 1975 to $680 million in 1976 and $350 million in 1977. Inflation declined from 39 percent in 1975 to 31 percent in 1976, but accelerated again in 1977, reaching 35 percent.

As a result of reforms and the fiscal policies adopted in 1977, inflation accelerated to 50.6 percent in 1978, 78.3 percent in 1979, and following the second oil shock, it reached 133 percent in 1980. The Likud governments were never able to conquer inflation and in 1984, following inconclusive general elections, a Labor-Likud coalition was elected. The new government introduced three wage-price freezes, each of which collapsed and then on July 1, 1985, it introduced the comprehensive program. There were several reasons for the delay in introducing measures that included both a freeze (an unorthodox policy measure) and budget cuts (an orthodox policy measure). The government was not persuaded of the seriousness of the situation until June 1985, when the external liquidity situation became critical and inflation accelerated. The foreign exchange reserves of the central bank fell from $3.1 billion at the end of 1984 to $2.5 billion at the end of the second quarter of 1985, when they were sufficient to cover only two months' imports. Inflation, measured by the rise in the CPI, increased from an annual rate of 221 percent in the first quarter of 1985 to 361 percent in the second quarter.[40]

There were also political factors that influenced the timing of the program. According to Michael Bruno, one of the main architects of the stabilization program, the first objective of the National Unity Government was a successful withdrawal of the army from much of the territory occupied in Lebanon. By May 1985, the Histadrut elections were over and Labor politicians felt fewer constraints about making tough economic decisions. The most relevant fact, however, was that, with the badly deteriorating economy, Prime Minister Peres' credibility, both internally and in the eyes of the U.S. administration, was at very low ebb. Only then, after all partial policy alternatives had been exhausted – and with some pressure from the visiting

---

[39] Haim, Barkai. 1995. *The Lessons of Israel's Great Inflation*, Boulder: Praeger, 91–104.
[40] Bruno, 100; Bank of Israel. 1986. *Annual Report 1985*. Jerusalem: Bank of Israel, 191.

Joint American-Israeli Economic Development Government Committee and with his back to the wall – was the prime minister ready to give the alternative, twice rejected route a fair chance.[41]

Indexation of Assets

The system of indexation was a major cause of accelerating inflation. The linkage of government bonds and other assets to the foreign rate, which began in 1977, reduced the length of lags in the linkage to the consumer price index meant adjustment on a basis, with a two-week lag: The increase in the index for any month was announced in the middle of the following month. Foreign exchange indexation increased liquidity because the exchange rate altered on a daily basis. Linkage of this kind prevented large shifts from financial to real assets. With the bulk of the public's savings linked, monetary accommodation inflation was almost automatic. The government could not obtain resources from an inflation tax; in fact, it lost them as a result of the inflation. Daily changes in the exchange rate were a more important transmitter of inflation than monthly or quarterly linkage of wages. Government policies designed to reduce or contain real wages were apparently intended to reduce private consumption rather than to lower labor costs. As a result, prices were increased in order to reduce purchasing power rather than relying on income tax changes and policies to control increases in wages and salaries.[42] The measures taken prior to July 1985 pushed up all costs.

Inflation at levels of over 100 percent a year was largely self-inflicted; it resulted mainly from economic mismanagement. The circumstances in which the economy found itself after the Yom Kippur War were extremely harsh, but it is significant that hyperinflation began in 1979 as the peace process with Egypt developed, rather than just after the Yom Kippur War. Those were years of rising oil prices and a lack of consensus, even within the government, on economic policy. The system of linkage, perfected by the introduction of foreign currency-linked assets, transmitted inflation and inflationary expectations throughout the economy with great efficiency. The costs of hyperinflation were much greater than was realized at the time, and those incurred in bringing it to an end in 1985 continued to be felt in the 1990s.

---

[41] Bruno, 100.
[42] Kleiman, Ephraim. 1985. The *Indexation of Public Sector Debt in Israel*. Jerusalem: Falk Institute, 11–13.

The Role of the United States

The United States took a much closer interest in Israeli economic policy beginning in 1984. Stanley Fischer of the Massachusetts Institute of Technology, who had conducted research at the Bank of Israel on the use of monetary policy in reducing inflation, became adviser on Israeli economic affairs to the United States' Secretary of State. Herbert Stein, also an economic adviser to the secretary of state, worked with Fischer on Israeli issues. During 1985, a team of Israeli government officials and economists met with Fischer, Stein, and a group of U.S. government officials in connection with Israel's emergency economic program and increased U.S. assistance. They formed the joint Economic Development Group headed on the Israeli side by the director-general of the Ministry of Finance Emmanuel Sharon. Other members included economics professors Michael Bruno and Eitan Berglas; Amnon Neubach, economic adviser to the prime minister; and Mordecai Frenkel, head of the Bank of Israel's Research Department. The U.S. side was headed by Deputy Secretary of State Allan Wells and included Fischer, Stein, and representatives of the Pentagon, the State Department, and the U.S. Embassy in Israel. The Americans advocated reductions in public expenditure, government use of and control over the capital market, freezing the rate, and lowering taxes. In this respect, they were in agreement with the consensus among Israeli economists, including in the government. The points made by Fischer were developed in the Research Department of the Bank of Israel and in the Economics Department of Hebrew University. They were made in a number of letters, made public, including one from the U.S. secretary of state to the Israeli prime minister in August 1986, and in a series of newspaper articles. They formed the basis of the economic program. During 1985, the idea of publishing economic advice to the prime minister in the Israeli press may have originated in Israel: If the government was perceived by the public to be under pressure from the United States, reforms might be more acceptable. Bruno and, much later, Fischer would become governors of the Bank of Israel.

Financial Reforms

From 1974, the government used administrative controls to channel private savings into government bonds. Prior to the July 1985 program, the government monopolized financial markets in order to fund its massive deficits. It dominated the raising of funds, controlled the allocation of credit, and determined the returns that could be paid on financial assets.

It also subsidized the interest rates on loans that it made to favored sectors. Until the failed reform of 1977, it tightly restricted the movement of funds in and out of the economy.

The 1977 foreign exchange reform failed because it was introduced in a highly unstable economy suffering large budget and balance of payments deficits, large internal and external debts, and rapid inflation. After 1985, the emphasis was therefore placed on gradual liberalization taking into account the facts that inflation was still faster in Israel than in its trading partners, and that the public sector debt remained high. The reform, therefore, initially favored the business sector rather than households and institutional investors. Restrictions on capital inflows were eliminated before those on capital outflows. Between 1987 and 1998, the movement of capital in and out of the economy was almost completely liberalized, with the exception of some restrictions on institutional investors.[43]

In 1987, a series of reforms affecting money, capital, and foreign exchange markets were introduced. The main money market reform was the reduction of liquidity ratios imposed on the banks and a unification of their rates. Another reform was the introduction of foreign exchange-linked loans; foreign exchange-linked deposits were already in existence. Numerous other restrictions were abolished and two monetary tools were introduced: monetary loans and deposits, and the issue of Treasury bills. In the capital market, the government reduced the share of pension and savings funds that had to be invested in government bonds from 93 percent in 1976 to 40 percent in 1998. In 1987, the corporate sector was allowed to issue bonds and the government increased the share of its tradable bonds.

Conclusions

The economy experienced rapid if uneven growth in the 1950s and 1960s whereas policy moved toward greater reliance on market forces. The 1967 Six Day War pushed the economy out of recession and it onto a fast-growth path. The dramatic victory in that war was the backdrop to a rise in social tensions that led to a large and partly unfunded increase in social spending. The 1970s brought severe economic difficulties as a result of the Yom Kippur War and a legacy of even internal and external borrowing. Economic mismanagement after 1977 and the expensive agenda of the Likud government

---

[43] Ben Bassat, Avi. 2002. "The Obstacle Course to a Market Economy in Israel," in Avi Ben Bassat, ed. *The Israeli Economy, 1985–1998: From Government Intervention to Market Economy*. Cambridge, MA and London: MIT Press, 9–22.

that came to power in that year led directly to hyperinflation, a deterioration of the balance of payments, and foreign debt, as well as slow economic growth. The very successful stabilization program introduced in July 1985 reduced government intervention largely by cutting subsidies to consumers and producers. These changes brought a range of prices closer to those that the market would dictate and were a major move toward a liberalized economy. The legacy of the 1985 program and the events that led up to it was a very strong bias towards fiscal and monetary conservatism that led to large reductions in allocations to the welfare state.

FOUR

Macro-Economic Developments, Growth, and Policy

The Israeli economy has experienced dramatic changes since 2000. In that year, it moved from a short, sharp boom to the beginning of one of the worst recessions in its history. Then, in 2003, it turned a corner to become one of the fastest-growing economies in the developed world. In the summer of 2008, the economy showed the first signs of deceleration as a result of worsening international conditions. Economic policy aimed to reduce the role of the state and the budget deficit. As a result, the internal debt has fallen as a share of national income. These developments have also helped strengthen the balance of payments in a fundamental way. This chapter examines the factors explaining economic growth, changes in the structure of the economy, and the improvement of balance of payments in recent years. It begins with providing the background by examining developments since 1985.

Macroeconomic Development since 1985

Following the 1985 stabilization program, economic policy aimed to maintain stability rather than restart economic growth. As a result, in the period 1985–1989, GDP grew by an annual average of 3.8 percent. The growth of GDP since 1990 is illustrated in Figure 4.1. It shows that the moderate growth of 1985–1989 was followed by a nearly unbroken upswing in 1990–1996. The turnaround was due to the massive immigration from the former Soviet Union accompanied by large imports of capital. This was followed by three years of much slower growth in 1997–1999, the result of slower immigration and much tighter fiscal and monetary policies. Behind these developments was the growth of the high-technology sector that resulted in major structural changes that are examined in this chapter and in Chapter 5. The upswing in 2000 was the shortest on record

Figure 4.1. GDP annual growth rates, 1990–2009.

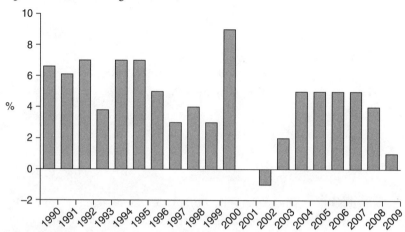

Source: Ministry of Finance. Survey of Macro-Economic Conditions for the 2008. Budget Bank of Israel, Annual Report 2008; CBS Press Release. First Estimate for the Second Half of 2009: GDP Increased At An Annual Rate Of 2.9%.

and was followed by two years of negative growth and one year of slow growth, resulting in three years of falling GDP per capita. This downturn was due to the recession in high-technology markets that came to a head with the National Association of Securities Dealers Automated Quotations (NASDAQ) crash in the autumn of 2000 and the beginning of the Second Intifada at almost the same time. In the period 2004–2009, GDP grew by an average annual rate of 4.2%. The reasons for this recent period of fast growth were quite different from those in earlier fast-growth phases and are explored further in this chapter.

By the end of 1989, it became apparent that huge numbers of immigrants from the Soviet Union were about to make their way to Israel. The economic growth rate had to be accelerated if mass unemployment and unacceptable burdens on the state budget were not to result, taking the economy back to where it had been before July 1985. The government realized that an increase in the labor force resulting from the immigration would have to be matched by a rise in the supply of capital. The lessons of the late 1940s and early 1950s, when there was a large influx of immigrants and little capital to fund their absorption, had been learned. The government therefore applied to the United States for $10 billion worth of loan guarantees. In 1991, President George H. Bush refused the request made by the Likud Prime Minister Yitzhak Shamir on the grounds that they might be used to expand Israeli settlements in the West Bank and Gaza. After the Israeli elections held in June 1992, they were agreed on with the Labor Prime Minister Yitzhak Rabin, who gave assurances that public funds would not be used to expand settlements. The loan guarantees enabled Israel to borrow on more favorable terms than would have otherwise have been possible and thus finance the balance of payments current account deficit with greater ease.

Although the combination of large increases in labor and capital was a major factor behind the rapid acceleration of growth in the early 1990s, political developments also played a role. The peace process with the Palestinians that culminated in the so-called Oslo Agreements of 1993, and the signing of the peace treaty with Jordan in 1994 created a wave of optimism in Israel and abroad. There was hope that the conflict in the Middle East – the longest-running in the world – would end and that this would bring major economic gains. This encouraged both foreign and domestic investment in Israel. It also led to a major improvement in Israel's international status and the establishment or development of diplomatic relations with a number of countries that were to become significant markets, most notably China and India. Economic growth remained fast until 1996, with a temporary slowdown in 1993 as a result of the security situation. The 1996 elections were preceded by an increase in government spending and the installation of a Likud government after the elections resulted in a change in economic policy. This took some time to evolve, but in 1997, the government began to squeeze public spending, and the Bank of Israel raised interest rates.

These measures were designed to reduce the budget deficit and inflation respectively and they succeeded, but the price was a much slower economic growth rate that endured, with the exception of the first nine months of 2000, until 2003. This was not only because of the squeeze on government spending and the deflationary effects of high interest rates, but also because of what might be called a perverse effect of high interest rates. High interest rates made the shekel relatively attractive compared with foreign currencies and encouraged the flow of funds into Israel. As a result, the shekel exchange rate rose. This had negative effects on price-sensitive Israeli exports by making them more expensive in foreign currency terms than they would have been otherwise. It also made imports cheaper. The industries most sensitive to these developments were traditional ones that paid low wages and already had been affected by the liberalization of trade with so-called third-world countries with which Israel did not have trade agreements. Conversely, the hi-tech sector, which paid high wages, was much less price sensitive and was virtually unaffected by these policies. In addition, the number of immigrants arriving in Israel fell in those years, which had deflationary effects.

The year 2000 was exceptional, with GDP growth of 8.9 percent, the fastest rate of growth in more than twenty years. This growth was the culmination of rapid development in the high-technology industries (see Chapter 5). When shares on the NASDAQ collapsed in the autumn of that year, the high-technology sector in Israel went into a sudden and sharp recession.

Between 1995 and 2008, there were major changes in the structure of GDP. Private consumption increased by 68 percent whereas public consumption increased only by 28 percent, reflecting the continued liberalization of the economy. Investment rose by 29 percent, and the globalization of the economy was reflected in the growth rates for exports (135 percent) and imports (86 percent) (see Appendix 4.1). The fall in the share of investment and its relatively slow growth compared with that of GDP and its other components was one of the consequences of the end of mass immigration in the second half of the 1990s. The economy moving further away from government domination toward the freer markets may have resulted in fewer but more effective and efficient investments. On the demand side, exports, especially of high-technology products, increased rapidly. Between 2003 and 2008, GDP rose by almost 27 percent, private consumption by 26 percent, public consumption by only 8 percent, investment grew by 35 percent, exports by 46 percent, and imports by 37 percent. Investment therefore grew much faster than GDP and other domestic components. It seems that rapid growth encouraged an upsurge of investment, although, of course, it was also the explanation of fast growth.

Sources of Growth

The growth of output is conventionally explained by the growth of inputs (labor and capital) and by the growth of total factor productivity (TFP) (a measure of changes in efficiency and technological development). In the period 1971–1990, GDP rose by 137 percent, and TFP contributed one-third of this. When the increase in TFP is decomposed, the contribution of education in those years was measured at 12 percent, domestic research and development (R&D) at 17 percent, and foreign R&D at 8 percent. Israel's achievements in those years were not exceptional when compared with countries at a similar level of development. Some 70 percent of the rise in its GDP was explained by an increase in hours worked and investment in machinery, structures, and equipment – in other words, by increases in the volume of inputs or factors of production. Despite this, investment was largely made possible by the increase in productivity, which in turn was due to improvements in education, investment in R&D,

Table 4.1. *Business sector inputs and total factor productivity, 1990–2008 (average annual rate of change, percent)*

	1990–1999	2000–2008
Gross capital stock	6.7	4.4
Civilian labor force*	4.4	2.4
Total factor productivity	0.0	1.5

* Including Palestinian and other foreign workers
Sources: Calculated from Bank of Israel, Annual Report 2004, Table 3, p. 10, Annual Report 2005, Table 2.5, p. 53, and Annual Report 2007, Table 2.5, p. 46. Annual Report 2008.

and knowledge spillovers from other countries. R&D investment had the highest rate of return.[1]

In the 1970s, TFP grew by an average annual rate of 1.6 percent, in the 1980s, by 2.5 percent, and experienced no growth in the 1990s. The background to these changes in productivity growth was as follows. Between 1970 and 1972, Israel experienced fast growth followed in 1973 by war, massive disruption of the economy, slow growth, and accelerating inflation. The 1980s began with hyperinflation, followed by the 1985 stabilization program and slow growth. In the first half of the 1990s, there was the massive immigration from the former Soviet Union and very fast economic growth. In the second half of that decade, growth slowed sharply.[2] Table 4.1 shows the improvement in TFP between the 1990s and 2000–2008. The capital stock grew rapidly in the period 1993–1999 and more slowly in the period 2000–2008. The supply of labor rose rapidly in the period 1990–1999, then decelerated to 2005, and then accelerated in 2006–2008.

The reasons for the zero rate of growth of TFP in the 1990s included political and security problems, the adverse effects of government policies, and the slowdown in the international economy. Another cause was, ironically, the increase in the labor force, made possible by the large immigration from the former Soviet Union.[3] The entry of many immigrants into

[1] Helpman, Elhanan. 2003. "Israel's Economic Growth: An International Comparison." *Israel Economic Review*. Vol. 1. No. 1. 1–10. http://www.bankisrael.gov.il/publeng/publeslf.php?misg_id=22&publ_num=Vol%201,No.1
[2] Bank of Israel. 2007. *Annual Report 2006*. 41.
[3] Passerman, Daniele. 2007. Do High Skilled Immigrants Raise Productivity? Evidence from Israel, 1990–1999. Samuel Neaman Institute, Technion-Israel Institute of Technology. Science, Technology and the Economy Program series. STE-WP-26-2007. 1–2, 24–28.

the labor market reduced average productivity, because initially what may be called their relevant skills and Hebrew language levels were low. This was despite the fact that their education levels were relatively high. The severity of this effect was considerable considering that many productivity-enhancing developments took place at this time, including the elimination of barriers to international trade, increasing foreign investment, and the continuing effects of the revolutionary developments in information and communications technology. In the period 1987–2005, the quality of labor in the business sector increased by 0.29 percent a year. This accounted for one-third of the rise in TFP. The quality of labor increased because of the rise in the return to education.[4] Over time, the relevant skill levels of new immigrants rose as they learned Hebrew and grew accustomed to the economic environment in Israel.

Between 2004 and 2008, rapid economic growth was closely related to the boom in the global economy and especially in high-technology markets. As a result, the demand for Israeli exports was strong, as was domestic demand. Fiscal and monetary policies supported growth with declining interest rates and, from 2006, an expansion of government spending. On the supply side, the labor market exhibited considerable flexibility largely because of a rise in the labor participation rate. Increased demand for Israeli goods raised their prices relative to imports, resulting in a real appreciation of the shekel. This in turn led to a deterioration of the foreign trade account in 2007–2008 (see section on the balance of payments below and Figure 4.8).

Long-term productivity growth reflected, among other things, greater efficiency of the means of production, technological developments, exploiting relative advantages, an increase in human capital, improved infrastructure, and reforms in public policy. It is largely determined by supply factors: the stock of human capital (the share of the labor force with higher education and the total number of workers, both Israeli and foreign), international technological developments, and new capital equipment as a proportion of the capital stock. Technological developments, which increased the economy's productive potential, also contributed to higher productivity.[5]

[4] Zussman, Noam and Amit Friedman. 2008. "The Quality of the Labor Force in Israel. Bank of Israel Research. Department Discussion Paper." Jerusalem: Bank of Israel; Bank of Israel. *Annual Report 2006*. 41–42.

[5] This is reflected in the Tech-Pulse index (a summary statistic that tracks the health of the technology sector of the economy. It is computed monthly from a number of data series that move with the technology sector as a whole) (Federal Reserve Bank of New York. 2008. Taking the Pulse of the Technology Sector. http://www.newyorkfed.org/survey/TechPulse/tech_pulse_index.html). It is also reflected in the volume of capital

In the short term, productivity was also affected by cyclical factors and temporary shocks. These included factors relating to business turnover, the convergence of productivity toward its long-term equilibrium level, reflecting the reduction of the impact of temporary shocks, and the rate of unemployment in previous periods that reflected the impact of demand pressures. When the economy grew, the demand for workers increased, and new workers – generally less skilled and less-educated – joined the labor market. These factors had a dominant effect on productivity growth: Falling unemployment rates during the period 2004–2006 contributed to a 1.5-percent reduction in the growth of productivity. In recent years, there have been several sharp fluctuations in productivity, including a rapid increase in the early 1990s and a decline at the end of the 1990s, culminating in a significant fall during the 2001–2003 recession followed by an increase when it ended until 2007 (see Table 4.1).

Apart from the negative impact of reducing demand, the deterioration in the security situation also generally results in the allocation of more resources to less productive activity, such as security and protection. Immigration to Israel initially had a negative impact on productivity because the human capital (skills and language) of the new immigrants was incompatible with the needs of the local market. Nevertheless, the massive immigration of the 1990s did result in greater productivity in the long term due to the high percentage of well-educated immigrants and their successful absorption into the economy.

Although the main channel through which taxation affects production is its impact on the factors of production, in the short term, taxation can also affect the utilization of the factors of production. Direct taxation has a negative impact on productivity, whereas indirect taxation has no impact. The sensitivity of productivity to the income tax rate was 12 percent, which meant that a decline in the direct tax rate in 2002–2006 of some 16 percent made a cumulative contribution of 2 percent to productivity, or some 14 percent of its entire increase during this period.[6] For this reason, income tax reductions have been a central theme of government policy in recent years.

The Labor Supply

The main developments in the supply of labor during the last ten years are detailed in Table 4.2. It shows that the population of working age grew at

investment that results in new equipment coming into use, thus making the capital stock more productive.

[6]   Bank of Israel. 2008. *Annual Report 2007*. 47–50.

Table 4.2. *Labor market indicators, 1998–2008 (annual averages, thousands)*

	1998	2000	2003	2008	Growth 1998–2008, percent
Population	5,968.0	6,289.2	6,689.6	7,305.6	22.4
Working age population	4,242.2	4,486.7	4,791.8	5,232.9	23.4
Civilian labor force	2,271.6	2,435.0	2,610.0	2,957.0	30.2
Unemployed	195.0	213.8	279.7	180.4	−7.5
Employees	2,269.7	2.513.4	2,572.5	3,031.0	33.5
–Israelis	2,076.6	2,217.8	2,330.3	2,776.7	33.7
–Palestinians*	53.0	98.0	40.7	61.0	15.1
–Other foreigners*	140.2	197.5	201.5	203.3	45.0
–Total Palestinians and other foreigners*	193.2	295.5	242.2	264.3	36.8

* legally employed workers

Source: Bank of Israel: Annual Report 1998, Annual Report 2003, Annual Report 2008.

a similar rate to that of the population as a whole. The civilian labor force grew somewhat faster as a larger share of the population of working age sought work. The increased participation rate reflected policy and general economic changes. The number of employees rose by almost 30 percent, with the growth in the number of Israelis exceeding that rate, whereas the number of legal foreigners grew even faster. The implications of using Palestinian and other foreign workers are examined in Chapters 5 and 7. The rise in the number of employees reflected economic growth, and the number of Israelis willing to join the labor force rose.

Labor Force Participation

Although the labor supply has increased as a result of immigration and the import of Palestinian and other foreign workers, the Israeli labor force participation rate is low by international standards (see Appendix 4.2). There are two main reasons for this. The first is the existence of a conscript army that removes thousands of young people from the labor market. The permanent army does the same thing, but this exists in comparator countries (see Chapter 6). Second, many men in the Jewish ultra-orthodox community and women in the Arab community do not work (see Chapters 8 and 9). Between 2002 and 2007, largely as a result of changes in economic policy, there was an increase in the labor participation rate of just over 2 percent.

Human Capital

The quality of labor has long been recognized as a key ingredient in the process of economic growth. Although Israel has made major investments in technological and scientific education that have had beneficial effects on its economic development, there are a number of worrying trends.

During the period 1995–2005, large numbers of immigrants who had arrived in the early 1990s were absorbed in the labor force. In 1995, immigrants accounted for 13 percent of the labor force and in 2005, for 19.3 percent. In addition, the share of women in the labor force rose from 34.4 percent to 38.4 percent, part of a long-running trend. These two groups had, on average, lower levels of education, measured by the number of years of schooling, than the average in the labor force. On the other hand, there was an overall increase in the share of highly educated immigrants in the labor force. The lower earnings of immigrants and women were due more to their lower productivity rather than to discrimination. In the period 1987–2005, the labor input of Israelis increased by 68.7 percent and the quality-adjusted labor input rose by 79.8 percent. There was therefore an average annual quality increase of 0.35 percent. During that period, total factor productivity (not adjusted for quality) rose by an annual average rate of 0.59 percent. The increase in labor quality therefore explains 40 percent of the improvement in productivity. Labor quality was influenced by education: The share in labor input of people with 16-plus years of education rose from 15.9 percent in 1987 to 27.5 percent in 2005. The increase in the number of immigrants and women in the labor force lowered the average levels of education of the labor force. The improvement in labor quality in Israel was low by international standards. It was lower than Germany that absorbed millions of workers from the former East Germany, and much lower than in other large Western countries. When the effects of immigration are excluded, the effect of education in Israel remains low.[7]

Investment and the Capital Stock

Between 1995 and 2008, investment rose at less than half the rate at which the economy grew (see Appendix 4.1). As has been suggested earlier in the chapter, this was possible because of the greater efficiency with which resources

---

[7]   Bank of Israel. 2007. *Annual Report 2006*. 45–50; Getz Dafna, Dan Peled, Yair Even- Zohar Zippi Butnik, Sivan Frankel and Marion Tachuko. 2007. *Indices of Science, Technology and Innovation in Israel*. Haifa: The Shmuel Neʾeman Institute, The Technion and Central Bureau of Statistics, 60–61.

were used, reflected in the growth of total factor productivity. There were, however, a number of subperiods, each of which had different characteristics. After fast growth in the period 1990–1996, there was a policy-induced slowdown in 1997, followed by a high-technology-driven recovery in 1999 and 2000. Between 2001 and 2003, the high-technology recession and the Second Intifada resulted in large falls in investment. In 2003, investment was 18.5 percent below its 2000 peak. In 2006, the level of investment was 1.7 percent below the 2000 peak, but GDP was 17.9 percent higher. This suggests that there was an increase in the capital output ratio: The efficiency of investment rose. Between 2003 and 2006, the economy recovered and GDP grew by 16.5 percent and investment by 20.7 percent. In 2007, with the exhaustion of this process, investment in the business sector in particular and the economy more generally increased. In that year, gross domestic capital formation rose by 12 percent in real terms, compared with an average rate of about 7.7 percent in the preceding three years.[8] Table 4.3 shows that between 2000 and 2007, real value of the net capital stock, excluding dwellings, increased by almost 21 percent. That of the manufacturing sector rose by 19.6 percent.

Economic Policy

Since 1985, economic policy has been dominated by two aims: stabilization and liberalization. The main method to achieve both objectives was to reduce the share of government consumption in GDP. This made it possible to reduce the share of taxation in GDP and to cut the budget deficit, which in turn led to a fall in the public sector debt. In 1980–1984, public sector spending averaged 73 percent of GDP; in 1985–1987, it was 66 percent and in 2008, it fell to 43 percent (see Figure 4.2). This constituted a major change in the structure of the economy and in the role of the state (see Appendix 4.1). There was a break in the trend in the early 1990s, when more expansionary fiscal and monetary policies were implemented to accommodate the large immigration. By 1996–1997, this had changed and deflationary policies were introduced. Since then, in most years, the growth of public spending was kept below that of the economy, thus reducing its share.

There have also been significant changes within the budget (see Figure 4.3). In the early 1980s, defense accounted for about 20 percent of GDP and interest payments on central government debt accounted for another 10 percent. These two items have fallen steadily since then. The share of defense declined

---

[8] Calculated from the Central Bureau of Statistics. *Statistical Abstract of Israel 2008*, p. 614. http://www.cbs.gov.il/shnaton59/st14_02x.pdf

Table 4.3. *The net capital stock, 2000-2007 (year-on-year change, percent, beginning-of-year data)*

Year	Agriculture	Water-works	Industry	Construction equipment	Electricity	Transport & communications	Private services	Intangible assets	Business sector	Public services	Total
2000	0.9	1.3	6.5	3.1	4.5	6.3	10.0	4.3	6.3	4.5	5.8
2001	3.2	1.1	5.9	7.6	1.2	7.4	7.8	6.3	6.1	4.3	5.7
2002	-0.2	0.7	2.8	3.6	1.5	7.2	4.9	6.2	4.6	4.1	4.5
2003	1.6	-0.4	1.8	1.5	2.0	3.3	2.6	2.5	2.5	3.5	2.7
2004	-0.1	2.8	0.4	0.7	4.0	2.1	2.0	3.0	1.7	2.5	1.9
2005	1.9	6.8	1.0	-0.4	1.2	2.5	1.5	2.9	1.9	1.5	1.8
2006	2.6	4.3	1.3	1.8	-0.4	2.4	2.3	7.4	2.0	1.6	1.9
2007	4.3	4.8	4.2	6.4	-2.3	3.8	2.3	13.0	3.4	1.5	2.9

Source: Bank of Israel, Annual Report 2008.

Figure 4.2. Central government revenues and expenditure, 1980–2008.

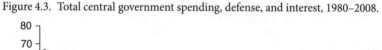

Source: Bank of Israel. Annual Report 2000, 2006, 2008.

Figure 4.3. Total central government spending, defense, and interest, 1980–2008.

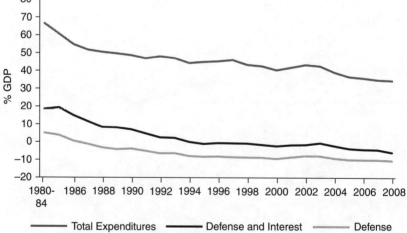

Source: Bank of Israel. Annual Report 2000, 2006, 2008.

because of cuts in spending and periods of slower growth than that of GDP. Interest payments fell because the debt and average rate of interest on it fell. The fall in debt was made possible by the reduction of the deficit, so there was something of a cumulative effect. In the 1990s, there was a large increase in welfare spending, partly because of the needs of new immigrants but also

Figure 4.4. The budget deficit, 1998–2008.

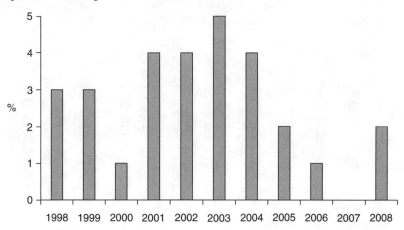

Source: Bank of Israel, Annual Report 2008.

because of political pressures (see Chapter 11). This was largely accommodated by reductions in the share of defense spending. By 2003, with the economy in deep recession and the Second Intifada raging, defense spending increased and welfare spending was cut in order to bring the budget into balance.

The effects of changes in fiscal policy are summarized in Figures 4.2–4.4. These show the fall in the budget deficit in 1997 that was policy-induced and the sharp but temporary fall in 2000 due to a rise in tax revenues associated with the high-technology boom. The increase in the deficit in 2001 and the high levels prevailing until 2004 were due to falling tax revenues as a result of the recession and the reductions in GDP that occurred in 2001 and 2002. The decline since 2004 was due to the growth of the economy and cautious fiscal policies. The aim of government policy was to reduce the deficit so as to cut the public sector debt. This also furthered the aim of reducing taxation.

Since 1985, the underlying aim of fiscal policy has been to maintain economic stability. To achieve this, the government and the Bank of Israel decided that the ratio of internal debt to national income had to be reduced to the level prevailing in comparable economies. Over the last twenty five years, this has been achieved and the main method was to hold the growth of public spending down. In recent years, annual growth was limited to 1.7 percent, similar to that of the population. This constraint caused many problems in the public sector: For example, the number of children has grown by more than 1.7 percent, and so expenditure per head has fallen. In addition, the standard of Israel's infrastructure and its social services are, in many respects, lower than in comparable economies. The Finance Ministry has often said that public

Figure 4.5. Public debt as percentage of GDP, 1998–2008.

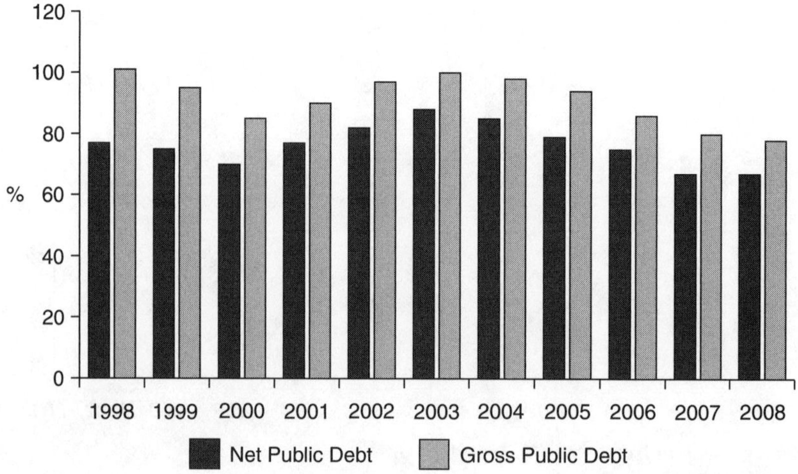

Net Public Debt   Gross Public Debt

Source: Bank of Israel, Annual Report 2008.

services could be improved if there was greater efficiency in the public sector. Although this is true, in the long run, without an increase in funding, even the most efficient systems cannot always meet needs when demand is growing. In January 2010, the Finance Minister announced a change in the formula used to calculate how much public spending may rise. Instead of a fixed 1.7-percent maximum, the rate would be determined by the maximum ratio of debt to GDP allowed in the Maastrict Agreement, divided by the expected rate in Israel. The result of this calculation is then multiplied by the rate of growth of the economy. Hence a debt/GDP ratio of 79 percent and a GDP growth rate of 3.4 percent would allow public spending to raise by 2.6 percent.[9] This would allow a significant relaxation of fiscal policy as long as the economy was growing but would, in theory, allow less flexibility in periods of slow growth when expansionary fiscal policy would be required.

Policy makers were keen to bring the public sector down to the average level of OECD countries. They were aided by privatization receipts and the decline in the value of the dollar in which about a quarter of public debt was denominated.[10] The reduction in the debt is shown in Figure 4.5. It shows that between

[9] Arlozorov, Meirav and Moti Bassok. 2010. "Udi Nisan: Government spending has reached the desired level – it is now possible to expand the budget." *Ha'aretz* and *The Marker*, 23 February, 6.
[10] Ministry of Finance. 2008. Economic Outlook June 2008, pp. 6–7. http://www.mof.gov.il/research_e/EconomicOutlook

Table 4.4. *The 1999 and 2009 budget proposals: Main*
components (percent)

	1999	2009
Civilian expenditures	15.5	17.9
Transfers and supports	29.5	28.8
Defense	17.0	16.2
Investment and credits	6.7	5.6
Debt repayment	31.3	31.5

Source: Ministry of Finance, Budget in Brief 2009–2010, p. 61.
http://www.mof.gov.il/BudgetSite/StateBudget/Documents/ikarey2010.pdf

1998 and 2008, the gross public debt as a percentage of GDP fell by 30 percent. This was made possible by the fall in the share of government consumption along with a much more gradual decline in the share of taxation. The fall would have been more continuous and faster had it not been for the recession of 2000–2002 and the effects of the international financial crisis in 2008.

Table 4.4 compares the 1999 and 2009 budget proposals. Despite the reduction in the debt as a share of the budget, the share of debt servicing rose slightly. In 2009, debt and defense accounted for almost 48 percent of the budget. This was despite the fall in the share of interest payments. These items, together with transfer payments and other forms of support, took 77 percent of the budget. This left only 23 percent for what the Finance Ministry called discretionary spending, on items that it believed were economically beneficial. The allocation for investment and credit fell by more than 1 percent and reflected the continuing failure to increase public spending on the infrastructure.

In comparison, the U.S. federal budget proposal for 2008 included discretionary allocations that accounted for 38 percent of total spending; 22 percent for defense (including funding for U.S. forces in Iraq) and the global war on terror and 62 percent for mandatory spending (that included 9 percent for interest payments).[11]

Government spending is largely financed by tax revenues, and as a consequence of its relatively high defense allocations, the tax burden in Israel is higher than the average in OECD countries. This is illustrated in Figure 4.6. It also shows how, since the late 1980s, the burden has declined as the share

---

[11] Calculated from the U.S. Government Printing Office. Budget of the United States Government: Browse Fiscal Year 2008, Summary tables, p. 168, Table S7. http://www. gpoaccess.gov/usbudget/fy08/pdf/budget/tables.pdf

Figure 4.6. The tax burden in Israel and the OECD, 1970–2007.

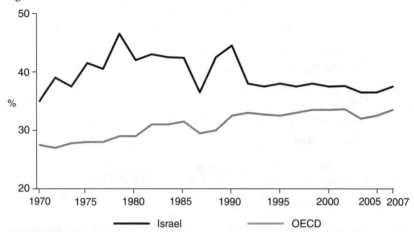

Source: State Revenue Commission 2007 Report. http://www.mof.gov.il/hachnasot/
doch07/docs/perek22.pdf

of government spending in national income has been reduced, but in 2007 it was still higher than in 1970.

There have also been major changes in monetary policy since the stabilization program of 1985, designed to liberalize the way in which banks operated and credit was allocated. These changes did not, however, go as far as they did in the United States or the United Kingdom, and as a result, Israel did not suffer as much as those and other economies when the international financial crisis of 2008–2009 began (see Chapter 5).

Structural Change

Table 4.5 shows how the structure of the business sector changed between 1998 and 2008. The shares of industry transport, communication, and construction all declined slightly whereas that of services rose. This disguised the fact that considerable change did take place within the industrial sector. Although the share of industry in GDP fell, manufacturing production rose sharply. The share of the business sector in GDP increased by more than 8 percent, reflecting cutbacks in the public sector as well the growth of the former. The most significant aspect of structural change has been the growth of manufacturing output, especially high technology.

Between 1998 and 2008, manufacturing output rose by an annual average rate of 3.6 percent, agricultural output rose by 4 percent, transport and communications by 4.5 percent, construction output (about half of which

Table 4.5. *The structure of the business sector, 1998–2008 (percent)*

	1998	2000	2008
Industry	24.0	26.5	21.5
Agriculture	3.0	2.7	2.8
Transport and Communication	12.0	12.1	11.0
Construction	10.0	7.2	7.3
Water and electricity	2.0	2.9	3.1
Services	50.0	53.0	58.8
Implied banking services and errors	−1.0	−2.3	−4.5
Total	100.0	100.0	100.0
Business sector GDP as percent of GDP	71.8	69.2	73.9

CBS Macro-Economic Statistics Quarterly October–December 2008, Table 1.1.
http://www.cbs.gov.il/publications09/macro0109/pdf/t1_1.pdfs
Source: BankofIsrael,AnnualReports,1997–2008andCBS,http://www.cbs.gov.il/www/publications/
macro0308/excel/t1_1.xl

was accounted for by housing construction) fell by 1.7 percent, commerce and service sector output rose by 6.1 percent, electricity and water rose by 3.4 percent, and the business sector as a whole rose by 4.2 percent.[12]

Manufacturing Output

In 2005, the low-technology sector accounted for 22.5 percent of GDP produced in manufacturing industry, the medium-low technology sector accounted for 24.1 percent, the medium-high for 16.3 percent, and the high-technology sector for 37.1 percent.[13]

The development of manufacturing output between 1995 and 2008 is shown in Table 4.6. Total output rose by 56 percent; low-technology output (food products, beverages and tobacco, textiles, wearing apparel and leather, paper, printing and paper products, wood and furniture) declined by 2.9 percent; output in the medium-low technology groups grew by an average of 28.9 percent; medium-low technology production included mining and quarrying, rubber and plastic products, nonmetallic mineral production, nonferrous and precious metals, iron and steel foundries, ships

[12] Bank of Israel, *Annual Report 2008.* p.72.
[13] Central Bureau of Statistics. 2009. Statistical Abstract of Israel 2008, Table 20.12. http://www.cbs.gov.il/shnaton59/st20_12.pdf

Table 4.6. *Manufacturing production by technological intensity, 1995–2007*
(indices, 2004 = 100)

	Low technology	Medium low technology	Medium high technology	High technology	Total manufacturing
1995	107.9	93.1	94.5	55.0	81.8
2000	107.8	98.2	105.3	96.3	100.6
2001	103.5	95.9	100.1	89.2	95.7
2002	101.2	96.9	101.5	85.1	93.9
2003	97.9	96.8	99.8	86.9	93.6
2004	100.0	100.0	100.0	100.0	100.0
2005	101.3	104.9	102.1	105.4	103.7
2006	104.2	111.4	102.2	127.9	113.9
2007	106.3	117.2	111.3	133.5	119.0
1995–2007 growth percent	−2.9	28.9	25.5	183.5	56.2

Source: Central Bureau of Statistics, Statistical Abstract of Israel 2009.

and boats, metal products, jewelry, and silversmithing. Medium-high tech-nology, which grew by 25.5 percent, included chemicals and petroleum refining, machinery and equipment, electrical equipment and electric motors, and transport equipment. High-technology output, which rose by 183.5 percent, included office and computing equipment, electronic com-ponents, aircraft, electronics, and communications equipment, equipment for control and supervision, and pharmaceutical products. These trends were strongly influenced by foreign trade (see Chapter 5).

Competitiveness

Israel has experienced an increasing income gap with the United States, measured in current prices or by purchasing power parity (see Figure 4.7). This occurred despite the success of the high-technology sector. Between 1995 and 2006, GDP per job in the information-communications manufac-turing sector rose by 80 percent, whereas in the business sector as a whole it went up by only 20 percent.[14]

[14] Central Bureau of Statistics. 2008. Information and Communications Technologies (ICT) Sector 1995–2006. Jerusalem: CBS, p. XXV. http://www.cbs.gov.il/publications/ict_06/pdf/e_print.pdf

Figure 4.7. National income per capita in Israel as a percentage of that in the United States, 1995–2005.

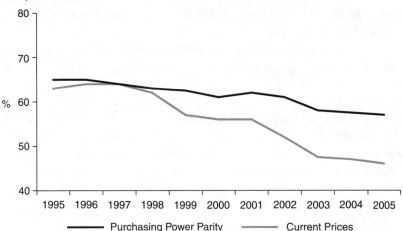

Source: Prime Minister's Office, National Economic Council, Socio-Economic Agenda for Israel, 2008–2010. Jerusalem: Prime Minister's Office, 2007.

The gap between the performance of high-technology sector and much of the rest of the economy (that employed the bulk of the labor force) was greater in Israel than in many Western countries. In 2000, output per worker in the traditional industries sector (textiles, clothing, paper and printing, jewelry, precious stones, and others) in Israel was about $21,000 measured in 2000 prices. In Europe, it was $32,000 and in the United States, it was $44,000. By 2006, output per worker in Israel was $33,000; in Europe, $51,000 and in the United States, $61,000, all in 2000 prices. Israel therefore failed to catch up.[15] As shown in Chapter 5, employment in low-technology, traditional industries fell and as a result, the modest rise in output per worker did not result in an increase in the total output of this group of industries. Given their scale, this was a constraint on the growth rate of the economy as a whole.

Traditional industries and the services sector were the largest employers in the economy but suffered from low levels of labor productivity, lack of technological innovation, and low levels of competitiveness. These factors have resulted in slow growth, limited the demand for labor, and perpetuated low wages.[16]

[15] Prime Minister's Office. 2007. National Economic Council. Socio-Economic Agenda for Israel, 2008–2010, p. 17–26. http://www.pmo.gov.il/PMO/PM+Office/Departments/econ20082010.htm

[16] Prime Minister's Office. 2007. National Economic Council Overview, 6. http://www.pmo.gov.il/NR/rdonlyres/93120D40-2790-4C14-A45E-80457D758FEB/0/NationalEconomicCounciloverview.pdf

The Balance of Payments

Deficits on the current account of the balance of payments were a feature of the Israeli economy from the foundation of the state until the early 2000s. They were the result of the large excess of imports of goods over exports and smaller deficits on the services account. Despite large transfers (gifts from the international Jewish community and United States aid), there were current account deficits in most years and periodically these would lead to crises because they could not be financed by borrowing with ease. The result was always a squeeze on the economy designed to reduce imports and encourage exports, which would bring about slow economic growth, and lower employment and incomes. The medicine usually worked and the economy would emerge from recession to grow again, with the next crisis some years ahead. In 1993–1997, the cumulative current account deficit was $19 billion; in 1998–2002, it was $5.6 billion, and so the emergence of current account surpluses totaling an estimated $28 billion between 2003 and 2009 was of great significance. The change in the current account of the balance of payments and the rate of growth of GDP are shown in Figure 4.8.

Israel has always had a deficit on merchandise trade. The very small deficit on trade recorded in 2004 reflected the recession that affected the economy in the preceding years. Between 2004 and 2007, the trade deficit increased by 90 percent. The balance on services moved from a deficit to a surplus during the period 1995–2007, and a small surplus emerged on the income account (see Appendix 5.1). A more detailed analysis of foreign trade is given in Chapter 5. Between 1995 and 2007, transfers – mainly United States' government aid and donations by the world Jewish Community – were between $5 billion and $7 billion a year. Despite these sizeable inflows, the current account was in deficit until 2004.

There were also significant changes in the capital account. Investment in Israel rose sharply, in the form of, among others, direct foreign investment and portfolio investment. Investments by Israelis abroad rose as a result of the liberalization of capital controls and the accumulation of funds in a growing economy.

The emergence of current account surpluses is significant for three reasons. First, they have been continuous, which had never happened before. Second, they have been large and this has had major effects on the economy, enabling Israel to reduce its foreign liabilities and accumulate foreign assets to such an extent that since 2002 there has been a net surplus of foreign assets (see Appendix 3.1). This meant that income from foreign assets grew and payments on foreign liabilities shrunk, thus strengthening

Figure 4.8. The balance of payments current account and the GDP growth rate, 1980–2009.

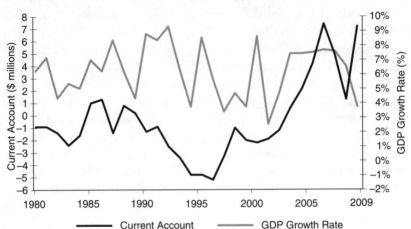

Source: Bank of Israel, Annual Report, 2008; Central Bureau of Statistics, First Estimates of GDP; Central Bureau of Statistics, The Balance of Payments 2009.

the balance of payments further. Third and perhaps the most significant, they have developed at a time of rapid economic growth. All other periods of rapid growth have resulted in deficits that eventually undermined the growth of the economy. The main reason for this was the rapid growth of high-technology exports, examined in Chapter 5. Figure 4.6 suggests that the development path of the economy changed in the late 1990s and early 2000s, from one in which growth was accompanied by current account deficits to one in which exports became the motor of growth. This resulted in growth being accompanied for the first time in a significant and pro-longed way by current account surpluses. In 2009, the current account recorded a surplus of $7.5 billion, compared with a surplus of $1.7 billion in 2008. This was due to a much larger fall in imports than exports.[17]

There was also an important change in the capital or financial account of the balance of payments. The volume of foreign investment in Israel rose sharply: Both direct investment in companies and portfolio investment in stocks and bonds on the Israeli stock market grew. So-called other invest-ments such as loans, deposits, commercial credit, and advance payment

[17] Central Bureau of Statistics. 2010. Press Release. Israel's Balance of Payments 2009. http://www.cbs.gov.il/reader/newhodaot/tables_template_eng.html?hodaa=201009045; 8 March, Table G/1. http://www.cbs.gov.il/hodaot2009n/09_09_116t1.pdf

accounts also increased. This, together with the trends in the current account, encouraged the accumulation of foreign reserves that yielded income and strengthened the balance of payments. In 1995, the Bank of Israel had $8.3 billion of foreign reserves; in 2007, it had $29 billion.[18] In August 2009, the Bank of Israel's foreign exchange reserves reached $60 billion. The increase was the result of the Bank's decision to buy dollars to reduce the appreciation of the shekels' exchange rate.[19]

There were therefore two major changes in the balance of payments: one on the current account and one on the capital account. The elimination of the net foreign debt resulted in an increase in net foreign investment income that increased income inflows on the current account. These developments have been profoundly important for the development of the economy and they represent the successful side of the globalization of the economy.

Capital Inflows and Foreign Debt

During the last ten years, foreign investment in Israel has increased sharply. Direct foreign investment was in Israeli companies, existing or new. Portfolio investment was that in shares on the Tel Aviv Stock Exchange, including privatized companies. This included funds that, elsewhere in the world, have contributed so much to international financial instability because they could be withdrawn quickly.

In the period 1993–1996, an annual average of 63 percent of the current account deficit was covered by foreign investment (direct and portfolio). In 1999, it covered 127 percent, partly because it increased from an annual average of $2.6 billion to $3.3 billion and also because the current account deficit declined. High real interest rates, a strong exchange rate, and the strength of the economy caused the foreign exchange reserves to rise by an annual average of $1.5 billion in 1993–1996 and by an annual average of $4.2 billion in 1997–1999. Despite a current account deficit of $14 billion in the period 1995–1999, Israel's net foreign debt declined by $8.4 billion, from $19.2 billion in 1995 to $10.8 billion in 1999. This transformation of the nation's external finances was in part due to globalization and the consequent increase in foreign investment.

---

[18] Central Bureau of Statistics. 2007. *Statistical Abstract of Israel 2007*. No. 58. Table 15.6. http://www.cbs.gov.il/reader/shnaton/templ_shnaton_e.html?num_tab=st15_06x&CYear=2007

[19] Bank of Israel. "Inflation Report." July-September 2009. no. 28. Table 7. Jerusalem: Bank of Israel. http://www.bankisrael.gov.il/deptdata/general/infrep/eng/inf-09-3e.pdf; Central Bureau of Statistics. Monthly Bulletin of Statistics. No. 10. 2009; Bank of Israel. Israel's External Financial Transactions. http://www.bankisrael.gov.il/deptdata/pik_mth/pikmth_e.htm

Israeli companies, particularly in high technology, have raised considerable amounts in share offerings in New York. In 1999, the total came to $2 billion, of which 75 percent was accounted for by high technology. The ability to raise funds in this way depended not only on the quality of the offerings but also on the state of the capital markets. In 1999, the Bank of Israel has pointed out that there were risks in high-technology investment that discouraged bank lending to the high-tech sector. As a result, funds tended to be raised through the issue of equity, especially in New York. The Bank warned that speculation in share prices might lead to overpricing and then to share price falls with the result that investment would be affected. Israel raised 30 percent of its capital by share issues to non-residents compared with 15 percent of gross capital in emerging markets generally.[20] In the last quarter of 2000, with the collapse of share prices on the NASDAQ, the Bank's warnings were proven correct. In recent years, there has been a large increase in inward direct foreign investment. In 1996–1999, foreign direct investment in Israel totaled $2 billion; in 2000–2003, it came to $3.7 billion and in 2004–2007, to $31.9 billion. Portfolio investment in Israel fell from $3.2 billion in 1996–1999 to $2 billion in 2000–2003 and then rose to $20.6 billion in 2004–2007. Another aspect of globalization was the increase in Israeli investments abroad. Direct and portfolio investments increased from $1 billion in 1996–1999 to $4.5 billion in 2000–2003 and to $56.5 billion in 2004–2007.[21] The development of foreign investment in Israel and Israeli investment abroad is shown in Figures 4.9 and 4.10.

As a result of the liberalization of the capital account of the balance of payments, more Israeli funds have been invested abroad by the corporate sector and by individuals. The aim of the liberalization was to enable Israelis to invest their funds freely so as to maximize their returns with the expectation that this would increase the flow of incomes back into the economy. This was exactly what happened: In 1995–2000, the average annual income from all investments abroad was $1.4 billion; in 2001–2008 it was $4.5 billion.[22]

Although the effects of globalization are examined in Chapter 5, it is worth noting the macroeconomic impact here. Appendix 4.1 shows that between 1995 and 2008, the share of exports and imports in GDP rose from 71 percent to 88 percent. This opening of the economy was the continuation of a very long trend going back to the 1950s. The most important implication for the macroeconomy was that international factors played an increasing role. This

---

[20] Bank of Israel. 2000. *Annual Report 1999*, p. 192. http://www.bankisrael.gov.il/deptdata/ mehkar/doch99/eng/ch6.pdf
[21] Bank of Israel. 2008. *Annual Report 2007*, p. 296 http://www.bankisrael.gov.il/deptdata/ mehkar/doch07/eng/pe_7.pdf
[22] Bank of Israel. Appendix, Table 7, A9.

Figure 4.9. Investment in Israel by non-residents, 1998–2008.

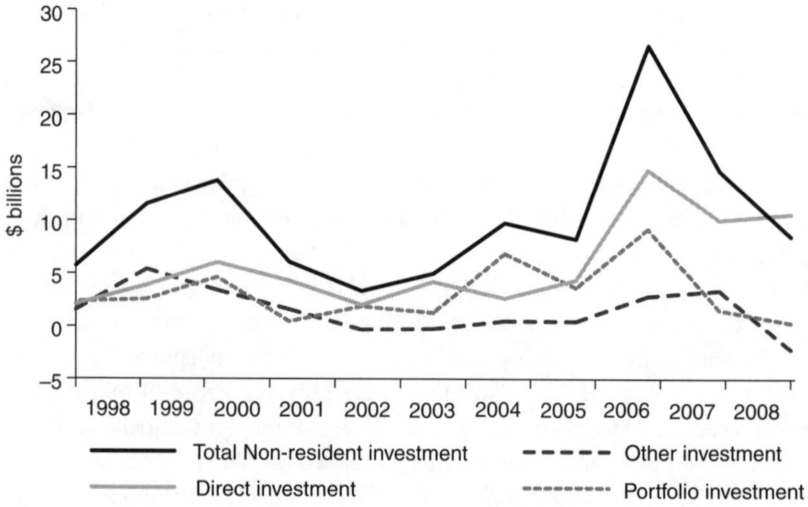

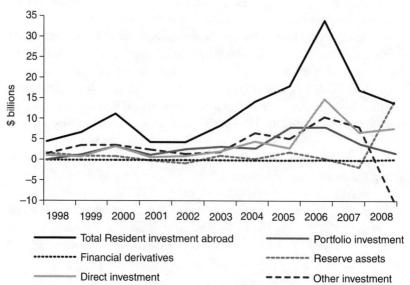

Source: Bank of Israel, Annual Report 2008 Statistical Appendix, Table G12.[23]

Figure 4.10. Investments by Israelis abroad, 1998–2008.

Source: Bank of Israel, Annual Report 2008 Statistical Appendix G12.[24]

[23] See note 2.
[24] See note 1.

meant that when international trade and the world economy grew, the Israeli economy benefited, and when they contracted it suffered. This was amply demonstrated in the changes in the world economy in 2008. Closely connected to this was the inflow of foreign investment that has been examined here, which was both a cause and consequence of the growth of exports and imports.

Conclusions

In recent years, the Israeli economy has experienced very strong growth and structural change. This has been punctuated by sharp recessions largely induced by external factors such as changes in the international economy and the regional security situation. Economic policy has been aimed at reducing the role of the state and its fiscal manifestation, the budget deficit. As a result, the internal debt has fallen as a share of national income, but not as far as policy makers would have liked. The social implications of these policies are examined in Chapter 10.

Economic growth has been made possible by increases in inputs of labor and capital, made possible by immigration, the import of workers, and foreign investment. There has also been a major improvement in the educational level of the workforce (also examined in Chapter 10). The growth of productivity has, however, been somewhat disappointing, although the current decade has brought an improvement compared with the 1990s. The economy was as well placed as any to face the rigors resulting from the international economic crisis that began in the second half of 2008. For the first time in its history, growth has been accompanied by balance of payments current account surpluses, as well as inflows of funds on the capital account. As a result, Israel's foreign debt has been replaced by an accumulation of net assets abroad.

FIVE

Globalization and High Technology

Globalization is a process that involves increased interaction and integration among people, companies, and governments in different countries. It has been driven by international trade and investment and has been reinforced by the development and use of information and communication technology. Globalization has had effects on economic development, political systems, culture, the environment, and human welfare and has played a major role in the development of the Israeli economy in recent years.

The most significant consequence of this has been the development of the high-technology sector. Since the 1960s, the Israeli economy has become increasingly internationalized with the move from import substitution to export promotion. This was achieved by signing free trade agreements with the European Community in the 1960s and 1970s and with the United States in the 1980s. In the 1990s, Israel liberalized its trade with so-called third-world countries, with which it did not have bilateral trade agreements. During that decade, it entered into what has been called the globalized economy, one in which a much wider range of policies were adjusted in order to attain and maintain internationally acceptable standards. Perhaps the most significant of these were limits on public spending, borrowing, and debt. Globalization accelerated the pace of change. An increasing number of people traveled abroad for work on a regular basis in the high-technology sector, especially to the United States. The availability of personal computers, the internet, cable and satellite television, and cheaper telephone communication, as well as increasing travel abroad affected the way people thought and behaved. Through the new media, many Israelis increasingly lived in what Herbert Marcuse called the "world village." Israel has become a consumer-orientated society in which the new media and advertising played an increasing role. This encouraged a shift in values from collectivism to individualism, something favored by conventional economics, but which comes, as will be seen, with a cost.

This chapter analyzes the development of the high-technology sector, changes in foreign trade policy, and the effects of globalization on the labor market. This is followed by an analysis of the development of the construction sector that has relied on cheap, imported labor and has as a result experienced very weak productivity growth. It also looks at the exceptional economics developments of 2000 and 20008–2009. Conclusions are then drawn about the effects on economic growth and equity.

In 2000, Israel was the nineteenth most globalized economy in the world and the most globalized in the Middle East, according to the AT Kearney/ Foreign Policy Globalization Index. Progress toward a more globalized economy has been continuous: In 2006, it was the fifteenth most globalized economy. The index includes indices of trade and investment flows, movements of people across borders, volume of international telephone calls, internet use, and participation in international organizations.[1]

Trade Policy and The Internationalization
of the Economy

In 1950, imports accounted for 39.4 percent of GDP and exports equaled 4.3 percent. In 1970, they accounted for 35.5 percent and 17.8 percent respectively. These shares increased steadily, with an acceleration occurring between 1990 and 2009. The share of imports in GDP rose from 31.1 percent to 37.32 percent and that of exports from 27.8 percent to 39.2 percent (Figure 5.1).[2]

The internationalization of the Israeli economy has been a long process. Israel began its independent history with years of extreme austerity, rationing, and massive state intervention in all areas of the economy, and from the 1950s, industrialization based on import substitution. By the 1960s, the government understood that the growth of Israeli firms (and thus employment and income) was limited by the size of the local market. For the economy to grow, exports would have to increase. Improved access to foreign markets had a price: increased foreign access to Israeli markets. Hence the free trade agreements were signed with the European Community in the 1960s and

[1] Foreign Policy. 2006. The Global Top 20, November-December. 1–8. http://www.atkearney. com/shared_res/pdf/Globalization-Index_FP_Nov-Dec-06_S.pdf
[2] Calculated from Central Bureau of Statistics, *Statistical Abstract of Israel*, various issues and Central Bureau of Statistics, Israel's National Accounts 2009. Press Release 10 March 2010. http://www.cbs.gov.il/reader/newhodaot/tables_template_eng.html?hodaa=201008049

Figure 5.1. The share of exports and imports in GDP, 1950–2009.

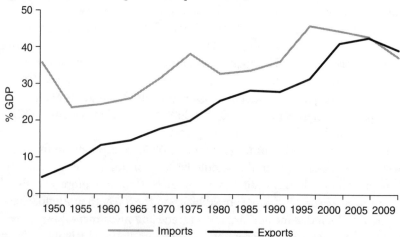

Source: Central Bureau of Statistics. Statistical Abstract of Israel 2009.

1970s and with the United States in 1985 (the first signed by the United States).

In the early 1990s, these measures were followed by the abolition of quotas and the reduction of duties on imports from countries that did not have free trade agreements with Israel. Later, controls on capital movements by companies and individuals were eased. From the 1980s, large numbers of Israelis traveled abroad, something that affected tastes and consumption patterns as well. In addition, Israelis continued to work abroad both on a temporary and permanent basis. In these ways, Israel became part of the global labor market. Some of the connections that the traveling Israelis made, particularly in the United States, led to foreign investment in Israel and the development of Israeli exports, especially in high-technology sectors.

In 1991, a program to remove nontariff barriers (NTBs) on imports from so-called third-world countries – with which Israel did not have free trade agreements – was introduced. NTBs were replaced with tariffs and those were reduced each year according to a predetermined schedule. For most industries – the most important of which were iron and steel, glass products, tires, and refrigerators – the process was completed in 1996. For sensitive industries such as lumber and footwear, 1998 was the final year whereas for textiles the process ended in 2000. By then, tariffs on imports from third countries were 12 percent on finished products and 8 percent on raw materials. In May 1997, a free-trade agreement between Israel and

Turkey came into force. As a result of this process and the improvement in Israel's international political position, its trade with China, India, Russia, and Turkey, among others, increased sharply. Imports from those four countries increased from $1 billion, or 3.5 percent of total imports, in 1997, to $2.2 billion, or 6.3 percent of total imports, in 2000, and to $8.7 billion, or 13.4 percent of total imports, in 2008. Exports to them rose from $911 million, or four percent of total exports, in 1997 to $1.4 billion (4.4 percent) in 2000 and 4 to $6 billion, or 9.8 percent of total exports, in 2008.[3] Most industrial goods have been tariff-free since January 2000. The overall direction of trade is shown in Appendix 5.2.

Israel is a member of the World Trade Organization (WTO) and the Government Procurement Agreement. It has free trade agreements with its main trading partners, the United States and the European Union, as well as with the European Free Trade Association (EFTA) countries, Canada, Mexico, and Turkey. Most favored nation (MFN) agreements have been signed with several countries that are not members of the WTO: China, Uzbekistan, Moldova, Russia, Ukraine, Kazakhstan, and Croatia. Israel also has a preferential trade agreement with Jordan. In May 2007, it became a candidate for membership of the Organisation for Economic Cooperation and Development (OECD).[4]

During the 1990s, a number of other developments increased the globalization of the Israeli economy. Foreign investment began to play a very important role in the economy, and the development of high technology, specifically information and communications technology (ICT) sector, linked Israel to the high-technology sector in the United States and elsewhere, resulting in parts of the labor market becoming significantly internationalized. In addition, there were significant political changes. In the early 1990s, the beginning of the peace process with the Palestinians and the signing of the Oslo Accords led to a major improvement in Israel's international relations. It led to strong expectations of peace among large sections of the Israeli population and among many industrialists. This encouraged domestically financed investments as well as foreign investment. Many countries – in Eastern Europe, the former USSR, and elsewhere in Asia and Africa – established or re-established diplomatic and trade links, something that opened new markets for Israeli exports

---

[3] Central Bureau of Statistics. *Statistical Abstract of Israel 2008*, no. 59, Table 16.10 and 1999, no. 50, Tables 8.6 and 8.9; Foreign Trade Statistics Monthly, January 2009, Table D.1. http://www.cbs.gov.il/www/fr_trade/td1.htm

[4] Organisation for Economic Cooperation and Development. http://www.olis.oecd.org/olis/2007doc.nsf/LinkTo/NT00004872/$FILE/JT03237381.PDF

and provided new sources of imports. Perhaps the most important was China with which diplomatic relations were established in 1992, following years of low-level contacts.

The flood of immigrants, mainly from the former Soviet Union, that began at the end of 1989 was a major factor in generating rapid economic growth that lasted until 1996. Between 1990 and 1995, 700,000 immigrants arrived, and between 1996 and 2000, 350,000 more. The population increased from 4.8 million in 1990 to 6.3 million in 2000, an increase of 31 percent over the decade. The immigrants from the former Soviet Union were mainly motivated by the desire for higher living standards that they felt would be available in Israel, rather than by ideological factors. As is shown Chapter 10, this immigration provided a large increase in the labor force, and many of the immigrants had a level of education or human capital that would make them potentially (after learning Hebrew, sometimes retraining, and acclimatizing to life in a new country) very productive.

The growth of the economy meant that Israel became a much more important market for foreign firms. From the mid-1980s, Arab markets in the Gulf and elsewhere had declined in importance as oil revenues fell. The Middle East peace process also brought the end of the Arab secondary boycott – that of companies that traded with Israel.* As a result, there was an upsurge of interest in Israel by foreign companies both as a market and as a place to invest.

---

*   The Arab boycott of the Yishuv was formally declared by the Arab League Council in December 1945. It called for all Arab institutions, organizations, and individuals to boycott Jewish products and later Israeli goods. In 1948, the boycott has evolved into one against the State of Israel, and consists of three components. The primary boycott prohibited direct trade between Israel and Arab states. The secondary boycott was directed at companies that did business with Israel. The tertiary boycott involved the blacklisting of firms that traded with other companies that did business with Israel. After concluding peace treaties with Israel, Egypt and Jordan abandoned the boycott. Israel has low-level commercial relations with some of the Gulf States and with Morocco. In the 1990s, the secondary and tertiary boycotts were abandoned by the Gulf Cooperation States following the signing of the Oslo Accords.

There are no estimates of the overall costs of the boycott for Israel. The inability to import from neighboring countries raised transport and insurance costs because goods had to come from further away. The inability to sell in those countries had negative effects because the comparative advantage implied by proximity was denied. Perhaps more serious was the secondary boycott. Until the 1990s, many foreign companies, afraid of losing their Arab markets, refused to sell to Israel. This reduced competition on Israeli markets and increased costs, resulting in economic losses.[5] The fact that Israel was forced to sell in more developed markets in Europe and North America meant that there was more pressure to improve quality and develop new products than if it had exported mainly to the Middle East.

5   Fershtman, Chaim and Neil Gandel. 1998. "The Effect of the Arab Boycott on Israel: The Automobile Market." *The Rand Journal of Economics*. Vol. 29. No. 1. 193–214

Globalization

There are several channels through which globalization affected the economy. The first was the high-technology product market that was dominated by trade with United States. The Free Trade Agreement with the United States and the liberalization of capital markets were crucial for this. Capital market liberalization enabled capital to move into Israel and has enabled Israeli companies to invest abroad. A very important aspect of high-technology development has been the creation by Israelis of companies in the United States and subsequent investment in Israel by these companies. The role of Israel's military links with the United States was important, and this is examined in Chapter 6.

The second globalization channel was the traditional product markets. Trade liberalization has meant that Israel opened its economy to imports initially from developed countries and then from so-called third-world countries. This primarily affected the import substitute industries set up in the 1950s and early 1960s. The liberalization of trade with developing countries was a consequence of the free trade agreements with European Union and United States under which Israel effectively gave preference to imports from expensive suppliers. In the early 1990s, the government decided to abolish quotas and reduce tariffs on imports from third-world countries so as to end this distortion. As a result, Israeli consumers gained access to a wide range of cheaper goods, especially from China, that had major consequences for basic industries.

The third channel was the import of foreign workers who replaced Palestinians. From the late 1960s until the 1990s, Israel relied on cheap Palestinian labor. When security considerations made it no longer possible to permit large numbers of Palestinians to work in Israel, other foreign workers were recruited, mainly from Southeast Asia and Africa. They came in tens of thousands, both legally and illegally.

In the period since 1961, changes in world trade and security have explained about two-thirds of the economic growth, whereas macroeconomic developments and tax changes explained the other one-third.[6] In 2003–2004, the transition to fast economic growth was the result of the growth of world trade and the improvement in the security situation in Israel. This conclusion is reinforced by findings of the International Monetary Fund (IMF) that there is a very close relationship between the Israeli economy and that of the

---

[6] Flug, Karnit and Michel Strawczynski. 2007. Persistent Growth Episodes and Macroeconomic Policy Performance in Israel. Bank of Israel Research Department Discussion Paper no. 2007.08, 26.

United States. In 2008, the United States accounted for 33 percent of Israel's exports. It was also the main foreign source for financing the high-technology sector. The IMF found that a 1 percent increase in United States' quarterly growth implied a 0.5 percent increase in Israeli quarterly growth over two quarters. Growth in the United States was also the single most important factor explaining changes in Israeli growth rates after the first quarter. It also found that the Israeli economy was less sensitive to changes in growth in the European Union, to changes in global stock markets (with the exception of NASDAQ), and to changes in international oil prices. Crucial was the Israeli reliance on U.S. sources of finance for high-technology investment well as the volume of trade in high-technology products.[7]

High Technology

The development of high technology has been Israel's success story: It has been the main source of economic growth in the last twenty years, and there is much optimism about its future. Various definitions of high technology are used in Israel. The first is the level of technological intensity, illustrated in Table 5.1. This classifies industries by the amount of capital equipment per worker and the age of the capital stock. Another definition is by sector: The information and communications technology sector (ICT) is considered largely high technology, but it is not identical because computers and other sophisticated equipment are used elsewhere in the economy. The difference between manufacturing and services in ICT is illustrated in Appendix 5.3.

High technology has been the leading sector of the Israeli economy in the last twenty years. It includes office and computing equipment, electronic components, aircraft, electronic communication equipment, equipment for control and supervision, and pharmaceuticals. Medium-high-technology industries are chemicals and petroleum refining, machinery and equipment, electronic equipment and electrical motors, and transport equipment. Medium-low-technology industries are mining and quarrying, rubber and plastics, nonmetallic mineral products, basic metals, ships and boats, jewelry, and silversmiths articles. Low-technology industries are food products, beverages and tobacco, textiles, wearing apparel and leather, paper, printing, and wood products.[8]

[7] International Monetary Fund. 2009. *Israel: 2008 Article IV Consultation-Staff Report. Washington DC: Country Report No. 09/57 2009.* Central Bureau of Statistics, Israel's Foreign Trade by Country. Press Release, 20 January, 46.

[8] Bank of Israel. Presentation by Governor Stanley Fischer. Israel Hi-Tech Conference 2007. http://www.bankisrael.gov.il/deptdata/neumim/neum242e.pps#381,7,Slide 7

Table 5.1. *Manufactured exports by technology intensity, 1990–2008 ($ millions)*

	Low technology	Medium Low technology	Medium High technology	High technology	Total
1990	1,492	1,537	2,390	2,278	7,697
1995	1,823	2,542	3,388	4,549	12,302
2000	1,812	3,171	4,833	11,188	21,005
2005	2,087	4,751	6,962	11,767	25,566
2008	2,278	8,081	13,125	17,150	40,634

Source: Central Bureau of Statistics, Statistical Abstract of Israel 2008. http://www.cbs.gov.il/shnaton59/download/st16_11x.xls; Foreign Trade Statistics Monthly, May 2009. http://www.cbs.gov.il/www/fr_trade/tc4.htm

As the high-technology revolution spread in the 1990s, especially in telecommunications and computers, Israel's output and exports of these and related products expanded rapidly. Although manufacturing industries' share in GDP declined, there was rapid structural change within that sector. In 1970, traditional industries accounted for 67 percent of manufacturing output and so-called advanced industries took 26 percent. In 1995, the traditional industries accounted for 50 percent and advanced for 42 percent. In 1998 – using a broader definition – the high-technology sector accounted for 50 percent of output in manufacturing, 37 percent of labor input, and 73 percent of exports.

Between 1986 and 1995, according to the narrower, ICT definition, which includes manufacturing (office and accounting machinery, computers, electronic components, electronic communications equipment, industrial equipment for control and supervision, and instruments for measuring, testing and navigating) and services (telecommunications, computer and related services, research and development, and start-up companies), output rose 2.8-fold, or by about 10 percent a year, compared to an annual average of 4 percent for the business sector. In 1995, it accounted for 9 percent of business sector GDP and 6 percent of overall GDP; in 2007, it accounted for 17 percent of business sector output and 12 percent of GDP. The capital-intensive nature of ICT is reflected in the fact that in 2006, it accounted for only 8 percent of business sector employment (184,000).[9]

Furthermore, some of the high-technology companies that were sold to large U.S. corporations had relatively few employees and, as was customary,

[9] Central Bureau of Statistics. 2008. Information and Communication Technologies (ICT) Sector 1995–2006. Table 1. Jerusalem: CBS.

Figure 5.2. Manufacturing employment by technological intensity, 1995–2007.

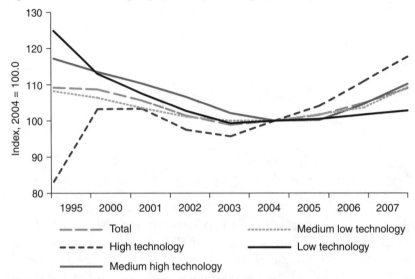

Source: Central Bureau of Statistics, Statistical Abstract of Israel 2008.

payments to employees included options to buy shares. As a result of the sale of these companies, a number of employees, some of whom had been in employment for only a few years or less, received millions of dollars in shares or cash. The owners or founders of these companies did even better. This had had effects on the distribution of wealth and income and thus on consumption patterns.

Employment as well as wages rose much faster in high technology than elsewhere in the economy. This is shown in Figure 5.2. In the high-technology sectors, the increases were fast, with electronic components almost doubling and computers much more than doubling. One of the main reasons for the increase in earnings inequality was the rise in wages paid in high-technology sectors. As the high-technology labor force was more skilled than those in other sector, it was better paid. In periods of fast growth, there were shortages of skilled labor, and high-technology firms bid workers away from each other by increasing wages. This further increased average pay in the sector and pushed it above levels paid elsewhere in the economy.

There are several overlapping explanations of Israel's technological success. The first is that it is a response to adversity. The country has experienced wars and boycotts since its foundation and has had to develop technology in order to survive. The defense relationship with the United States has given Israel access to technology from the most sophisticated economy in the world, and close business links have developed as a result. Israel has a very informal culture – the Zionist socialists rebelled against the formality of life in Europe – and some say that its management culture in both the civilian and military sectors are influenced by this.[10]

This sector, which represents globalization more than any other in the Israeli economy, had its origins in import substitution applied to the defense sector and to government involvement more generally. The high-technology sector was closely connected to developments in Israeli defense policy and in government investments made in academic research and other research. In 1948, Israel Defense Forces established the Science Corps charged with developing weapons and equipment for the IDF. (During the Mandate, the Hagana defense organization began underground weapons production.) In the 1950s, military industry developed to meet the country's needs for armaments and technologies it could not obtain from abroad. Israel had the best institutions of education and scientific research in the Middle East: two technological universities, the Technion, the Israel Institute of Technology in Haifa (founded in 1924), and the post-graduate Weizmann Institute of Science in Rehovot (founded in 1933). In addition, Israel now has five universities and numerous degree-awarding colleges. In the early 1960s, Israel set up two nuclear research plants.

By the 1960s, most research and development (R&D) was carried out in the public sector and thus focused on technological R&D. Since then, the private sector has played an increasing role. Output was concentrated first in ICT hardware and then in ICT software. The aim of R&D was to create new products, and the government saw the private sector as the main agent for carrying out these activities. It increasingly confined itself to providing funds and encouraging the diffusion of know-how from the military and the universities to the private sector.

One of the most important factors in enabling Israel to develop high technology was the willingness to experiment. In a country that has always been at war and has experienced many years of shortages, the need to devise ad hoc solutions has become second nature. This was particularly true in the IDF and the military industries and has permeated all sectors of the economy. The "hands-on" approach is the essence of learning by doing, which ultimately is a significant source of economic growth.[11] Israel imported military and civilian equipment but seldom ordered "turnkey" projects. The aim was always

---

[10] Senor, Dan and Saul Singer. 2009. *Start Up Nation: The Story of Israel's Economic Miracle.* New York: The Hachette Book Group, 67–83.

[11] Arrow, Kenneth J. 1962. "The Implications of Learning by Doing." *The Review of Economic Studies.* Vol. 29. No. 3. 155–173.

to learn how to operate equipment, to train Israeli personnel, and often to improve what was acquired abroad to adapt it to local conditions and needs.

Israel has achieved a comparative advantage in R&D based on the development of defense and academic institutions. The government's focus on the enhancement of technological cutting-edge capabilities enabled firms to develop new products using the latest technologies. This made it possible for Israeli information technology companies to supply the rest of the world. Success came first in hardware and then in software. From the early 1970s, the aim of policy was to create new R&D-based products. The government saw the private sector as the main means of generating R&D; its job was to help with the supply of capital and encourage the diffusion of know-how from the defense sector, the universities, and other public sector bodies. It encouraged public-private sector cooperation and links with foreign firms when appropriate. All this was made possible by investments in education, the encouragement of R&D in the defense sector (see Chapter 6), and policies that gave high priority to science and technology. This was partly facilitated by the informal but close links between key political leaders and the scientific and technological elite. Another important step taken by the government was the creation in 1968 of the Office of the Chief Scientist (OCS) in different government ministries. Those created in the Ministry of Defense and the Ministry of Trade and Industry were of particular economic significance. The latter was given a budget to invest in R&D in the public and private sectors.

Until the late-1960s, support was confined to national R&D laboratories, academic R&D, defense-related R&D, and agricultural research. Between 1969 and 1987, as a result of the new impetus, industrial R&D expenditures grew at 14 percent per year, and high technology exports increased from $422 million in 1969 (in 1987 dollars) to $3.3 billion in 1987. The next major development was the passing in 1985 of the Law for the Encouragement of Industrial Research and Development. This has been the main piece of legislation that has defined government policy toward industrial R&D ever since. The aims of the law were to develop science-based, export-oriented industries, which would promote employment and improve the balance of payments. To do this, the legislation was designed to provide the financial means to expand and exploit the country's technological and scientific infrastructure including its high-skilled human resources.

The 1985 law offered a number of financial incentives. Companies of any size that met the criteria specified in the legislation were entitled to receive matching funds for the development of innovative, export-targeted products. The OCS funded up to 50 percent of R&D expenses in established companies and up to 66 percent for start-ups. The OCS supports and administers a wide range of additional programs, the main ones being *Magnet*, a program to encourage precompetitive generic research conducted by consortia; a program of technological incubators; and various programs involving bilateral and multilateral international R&D collaboration.[12] The volume of grants given under the law fell from a peak of 0.75 percent of GDP in 1997 to 0.45 percent in 2006, whereas the share of tax benefits in total benefits has increased continuously.[13]

In 1976, the Israeli and U.S. governments set up the Bi-national Industrial Research and Development (BIRD), with an endowment of $110 million that reached $205 million in 2007. Its aim was to encourage cooperation between Israeli and U.S. companies to jointly develop and market new products.[14] Over time, it had brought many Israeli and U.S. firms together: by 2007, it had approved 776 projects, provided $255 million in grants, and its investments had yielded $4.5 billion in sales.[15] Since the 1990s, an increasing volume of funds have been raised from venture capitalists in the United States and Israel.* This was made possible by the maturity of the high-technology industry, the stability of the economy, the globalization of international capital markets, as well as government programs directed toward the venture capital sector.[16]

The Development of Exports

The main motor of economic growth in recent years has been exports. They have grown in absolute terms, as a share of national income, and in relation

---

[12] Trajtenberg, Manuel. R&D Policy in Israel: An Overview and Reassessment. National Bureau of Economic Research. Working Paper no. 7930. October 2000.

[13] Bank of Israel. *Annual Report 2006.* 7 4.

[14] Breznitz, Dan. 2007. *Innovation and the State.* New Haven and London: Yale University Press, 42–45.

[15] Israel-U.S. Bi-national Industrial Research and Development (BIRD) 2007 Annual Report. http://www.birdf.com/_Uploads/193BIRD_AR2007.pdf

* Venture capital is a type of private equity capital usually made in early-stage, high-potential growth companies. The aim is to generate a return through the floatation of shares by an initial public offering (IPO) or trade sale of the company. Venture capital investments are generally made as cash in exchange for shares in the invested company. Venture capital investors identify and back companies in high technology industries such as biotechnology and ICT. Venture capital usually comes from institutional investors and rich individuals who are brought together by investment firms. Venture capital firms typically comprise small teams with technology backgrounds (scientists, engineers and researchers) and/or those with business training or relevant experience in the industry concerned.

[16] Avnimelech, Gil and Morris Teubal. 2002. "Israel's Venture Capital (VC) Industry: Emergence, Operation and Impact." January. http://economics.huji.ac.il/facultye/teubal/VCPaper1%20-%20Dilek%20Book.pdf

to imports. This has had beneficial effects on income, employment, and the balance of payments. Export growth has also been one of the reasons why Israel has been able to attract high levels of foreign investment.

Table 5.1 shows how rapid the growth of exports has been in recent years. Between 1990 and 2007, the high-technology sector increased its overseas sales sevenfold compared with a 4.5-fold increase in total manufacturing industry. Those of the medium-technology group rose fourfold, and the low technology sector increased its exports by 50 percent. There was therefore an absolute increase in exports and a dramatic change in their composition. Between 1900 and 1995, total exports rose by 60 percent; between 1995 and 2000, they increased by 70 percent. The high-technology crisis of 2000 resulted in slower growth, and in 2000–2005, total exports rose by less than 22 percent, but in 2005–2007, they rose by almost 34 percent, largely as a result of high-technology growth.

Employment in Manufacturing

Figure 5.2 provides the details of changes in manufacturing employment for the period 1995–2007. It shows that total employment in this sector was virtually stagnant. Employment in the low-technology sector fell by almost 18 percent, in the medium-low-technology sector it grew by 1 percent, and in the medium-high-technology sector it fell by almost 6 percent. In contrast, the high-technology sector experienced growth of more than 40 percent.

The decline in employment in the low-technology sector resulted in growing unemployment among low-skilled workers. These tended to be of Sephardic origin or Arabs. The increase in employment in the high-technology sector was among better educated workers who were native-born Israelis or immigrants from the former Soviet Union or the West. The increased return to education resulted in both an earnings and an unemployment gap.[17] This was something that Israel experienced alongside other countries.[18] Between 2001 and 2008, employment in manufacturing industry increased by 14.4 percent. Employment in manufacturing sectors classified as education-intensive rose by 32 percent, and in computer

[17]　Ribon, Sigal, Karnit Flug and Nitsa Kasir. 2000. "Unemployment and Education in Israel: Business Cycles, Structural Change, and Technological Change, 1986–98." *Economic Quarterly*. Vol. 47. No. 3. 374–416.

[18]　Greenaway, David and Douglas Nelson. 2000. "The Assessment: Globalization: The Labour Market." *Oxford Review of Economic Policy*. Vol. 16. No. [AU: issue number?]. 1–13. Slaughter, Matthew J. 1999. "Globalization and Wages: A Tale of Two Perspectives." *The World Economy*. Vol. 22. No. 5. 609–629.

Figure 5.3. Average monthly wage per employee post, 1990–2007.

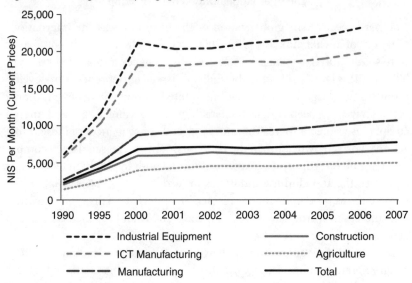

Source: Central Bureau of Statistics: Statistical Abstract of Israel 1991, 2005, 2008; Information and Communication Technologies (ICT) Sector 1995–2006.

services by 48 percent. In manufacturing sectors classified as intensive users of unskilled labor, employment rose by only 2 percent.[19]

Earnings

The growth of inequality in earnings is a worldwide phenomenon and is the result of a number of closely connected factors. The most important is that the demand for educated workers in the high-technology sector has grown and as a result, the return to education has increased. The wages of those with less education and employed in traditional industries have been constrained by the competition those sectors have faced from foreign sources of supply using abundant low-wage labor. This effect became much more potent with the lowering of trade barriers on imports from third-world countries in the early 1990s. As a result, earnings differentials have widened. This is shown in Figure 5.3. In 1990, monthly earnings in the highest-paid sector were 2.6 times the average for the economy and 1.07 times those in manufacturing. By 2006, they were 3.1 times the average for the economy and 1.2 times the manufacturing average.

[19] Bank of Israel. *Annual Report 2008*. Jerusalem, Bank of Israel. Table 5.A.10.

The Internationalization of Ownership

Another aspect of the globalization of the economy was the internationalization of ownership. In 1999–2000, ten Israeli high-tech companies were sold to foreign – mainly U.S. – corporations for a total of almost $12 billion.[20] This largely reflected the ability of Israeli entrepreneurs to develop products that large U.S. corporations wanted to buy. Firms in traditional sectors have also been sold as the Israeli market became larger and foreign companies wanted a share. There were several consequences of these transactions. Foreign ownership in the Israeli economy increased. Israeli companies have invested increasing amounts abroad both in U.S. high technology and in textile and clothing industries in Jordan and Egypt. The latter had consequences for employment in Israel. The internationalization of ownership increased in the late 1990s and early 2000s and reached its peak in 2006.

In May 2006, Warren Buffet, chairman of Berkshire Hathaway, a huge conglomerate holding company, announced that his company would pay $4 billion for an 80-percent stake in Iscar, the privately held Israeli cutting-tools company – its first-ever acquisition outside the United States. Founded in 1952 to manufacture metal-cutting tools, by the 1990s, Iscar had become a major player, with subsidiaries in 60 countries and factories in Europe, Asia, and the Americas. The company specializes in precision tools for the automotive, aerospace, and die-and-mold industries.[21] Israel has the largest number of NASDAQ-listed companies outside North America. Intel and Microsoft both opened their first overseas R&D centers in Israel. Intel has eight locations in Israel. Intel's Israeli base in Haifa has since 1974 been a multidisciplinary development center for software and hardware. The Israel sales office also includes Intel Semiconductors Ltd. The center was established with a total investment of $300,000 and initially employed five workers. The plant employs 1,600 people. Intel has a large plant in Kiryat Gat, which manufactures some of the world's most advanced computer chips. It uses state-of-the-art technology that constitutes the basis of advanced computers. The plant was established with a total investment of $1.8 billion, $600 million of which was invested by the Israeli government, under the Law for the Encouragement of Capital Investments. This was the

[20] Shulman, Sofi. 2000. "Galileo sold to Merval." *Ha'aretz*, 18 October, 3
[21] Sandler, Neal. 2006. "Buffet Takes a Cut Out of Iscar." *Businessweek*, 8 May. http://www. businessweek.com/globalbiz/content/may2006/gb20060508_953503.htm

largest investment ever made in Israel by a private company. In 2008, Intel employed 3,700 people in Israel.[22]

The high-technology sector was highly concentrated geographically: In 2000, 80 percent of high-tech jobs were in the Greater Tel Aviv area.[23] This geographic pattern reinforced the occupational differences between traditional and high-tech industries, making it even harder for workers to move from one to the other.

The Internationalization of the Labor Market

Globalization and technological development resulted in changes in the demand for labor, a process that began in the 1970s. Other, institutional changes affected the labor market. The Histadrut – which was both a trade union organization and an employer through its ownership of industrial companies, banking, insurance, and other assets – contracted and its share in employment fell. The strength of national trade unions declined as personal contracts became more widespread and the use of labor, without the payment of social benefits, supplied through manpower companies became more important. Bargaining over wage and conditions moved away from the national to the local or plant level and to the individual level. Unions remain very powerful in the publicly owned monopolies.

Following the Six Day War of 1967, Israel began to employ Palestinian workers from the West Bank and Gaza. Many were employed in the construction industry, others in agriculture, services, and basic industries. In 1970, Palestinian workers accounted for 2.1 percent of the labor force (about 15,000); by 1987, they took 7.2 percent (over 100,000). In 1993, following a spate of terrorist incidents, the government introduced restrictions on the entry of these workers, and the number crossing the Green Line (between Israel and the occupied territories) fell sharply each day (see Chapter 7). At the same time, the Israeli population was increasing relatively rapidly. Between 1990 and 1995, the population increased by 16 percent as a result of the immigration from the former Soviet Union, and one of the most serious challenges facing the economy was to provide housing. The construction industry could not function without the cheap labor that the Palestinians provided, and pressure was put on the government to permit the entry of foreign workers from Southeast Asia and Eastern Europe.

[22] Ministry of Trade Industry and Employment. Intel Israel – Thirty Years of Successful Growth. http://www.moital.gov.il/NR/exeres/49CA1B09–31FC-4D88-A603-FFD3D78A973C.htm
[23] Schmuel, Avi. 2001. "Hi-tech Prosperity Does Not Reach Periphery." *Ha'aretz*, 6 June, 5.

Since 1990, other foreign workers have been imported. They accounted for 0.2 percent of employees in 1990, 4.3 percent in 1995, and 5.1 percent in 1999 (see Figure 5.4). The number of permits issued to foreign workers rose sharply, from 6,000 in 1993 to 106,000 in 1997. (These figures are for the beginning of each year.) Between 1997 and 1999, the number of foreign workers with permits fell from 90,192 to 70,172. By February 2001, however, it had risen to 94,174.[24] Since 1997, there have been a stream of government decisions to deport illegal entrants, fine those who employ them, and impose fees on those who use foreign workers legally, but substantive action has been limited. Thousands overstayed their visas or worked while visiting as tourists.[25]

Many developed countries have imported workers to carry out low-skilled jobs that the local labor force does not want to carry out. These jobs tended to be concentrated in the nontradeable sector where there was no international competition or in sectors where international trade barriers were strong, such as agriculture. Employers were able to bring in foreign workers who were virtually indentured. They were employed by Israeli or foreign manpower companies that sometimes deducted the cost of flying them to Israel from their earnings.[26] Some were not been paid because foreign manpower companies did not pass on payments made to them. These conditions discriminated against legal foreign workers, legal Palestinians, and Israelis. The presence of illegal foreign workers and indentured legal workers put downward pressure on wages in certain sectors and resulted in job losses and unemployment among Israelis. Although the government exerted nominal control through the issuing of work permits, real control over recruitment, allocation, and terms of employment remained in the hands of the employers, especially the Association of Contractors and Builders (an employers' association).[27]

Palestinian and foreign workers together accounted for 8 percent of business sector employment in 1994 and 12.8 percent in 1999; the latter was a high proportion by international standards. In 1997, the number of illegal workers was variously estimated by official sources at 128,000 and

[24] *Ha'aretz*, 14 March 2001.
[25] Ministry of Finance. 2000. *Economic Outlook*. November. 19–21.
[26] Amir, Shmuel. 2000. Overseas Foreign Workers in Israel: Policy Aims and Labor Market Outcomes, Falk Institute Discussion Paper no. 2000.01, 2. This is not unique to Israel or to the 1990s. Its historical context is discussed by Chiswick, Barry and Timothy Hatton in "International Migration and the Integration of Labor Markets, National Bureau for Economic Research." November 2000. National Bureau of Economic Research. Chapters series no. 9586. http://www.nber.org/chapters/c9586.pdf
[27] Amir, Shmuel. 2002. "Overseas Foreign Workers in Israel: Policy Aims and Labor Market Outcomes." International Migration Review. April. 3.

Figure 5.4. The Israeli labor force, 1970–2007.

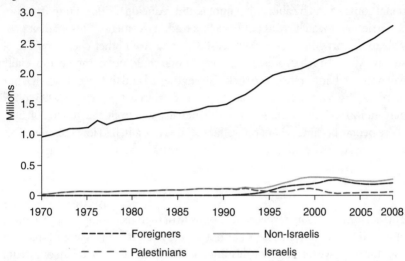

Source: Bank of Israel, Annual Report 1999, Annual Report 2008.

190,000.[28] The presence of large numbers of foreign workers, both legal and illegal, as well as Palestinians, depressed wages and discouraged the technological modernization in certain sectors, especially construction. This has had negative effects on productivity at the sector level and thus on the economy as a whole.

The inflow of foreign workers had a substitution effect: because they competed for jobs held by unskilled or low-skilled Israeli or Palestinian workers. As a result, wages in certain sectors were depressed and jobs were lost. Between 1996 and 2000, 36,000 Israelis left or lost their jobs in the construction sector (see Appendix 5.4). By reducing labor costs, a rise in the supply of foreign workers increased the level of economic activity and thus boosted the demand for other kinds of labor. It also made the distribution of income more unequal.[29]

Since 1990, the gap between earnings in traditional and high-tech sectors has increased. One reason for the rise in costs in basic industries was an increase in the minimum wage: Between 1987 and 1997, it was set at 45 percent of the average wage. In 1997, it was increased to 47 percent of the average wage, and the linkage system was tightened. As the average wage began to be influenced by the rapid rise in wages in high-tech, so the minimum wage

---

[28] Bank of Israel, *Annual Report 1999*. 99, footnote 2.
[29] Amir, Shmuel. "Overseas Foreign Workers in Israel: Policy Aims and Labor Market Outcomes," 15.

increased more rapidly.[30] In the 1990s, Israel opened its markets to international competition by abolishing quotas and reducing tariffs on imports from countries with which it did not have free trade agreements. This made it possible to import goods from Southeast Asia and from other cheap sources of supply. Many Israeli producers of basic goods could not compete, especially when the exchange rate of the shekel strengthened and the cost of Israeli labor increased.[31] As a result, unemployment rose, from 6.3 percent in 1995 to 8.9 percent in 1999. In absolute terms, the increase was from 142,400 to 208,500. More people became reliant on welfare and, as a result, had low incomes. This had effects on the distribution of earnings that are examined in Chapter 10.

The Construction Sector

This sector is in many respects the opposite of high technology because most of its activity is domestic. This has not always been true of its labor force that was, for many years, largely Palestinian and is now partly made up of foreign workers. Appendix 5.4 shows that the share of construction in the output of the business sector declined from 10 percent in 1998 to 7.3 percent in 2008. This was partly because of the decrease in demand due to the end of the large-scale immigration from the former Soviet Union in the late 1990s, but it was also due to supply constraints. These have meant, among other things, that the average amount of time taken to build an apartment rose from 15 months in 1991 to 25.7 months in 2008, having peaked at 26.1 months in 2005![32]

Between 1980 and 2008, output rose by 64 percent compared with 216 percent in the manufacturing sector. Between 1980 and 1990, construction output rose by only 3.5 percent, whereas between 1990 and 2008, it increased by 59 percent. In 1980–1990, the labor force in construction grew by 21 percent whereas between 1990 and 2008, it increased by 53 percent. This indicates a dismal record for labor productivity.

The construction sector has in large part failed to industrialize and relied on cheap and inefficient labor-intensive technology.[33] The industry

---

[30] Clifton, Eric. 1998. The Decline of Traditional Sectors in Israel: The Role of the Exchange Rate. International Monetary Fund (IMF) Working Paper no. WP/98/167, 7.

[31] Ministry of Finance. 2001. Economic Outlook, June; Gabai, Yoram and Rafael Rob. 2002. "Trade Liberalization and the Unification of the Exchange Rates: Implications for the National Economy," in Avi Ben Bassat, ed. *The Israeli Economy, 1985–1998: From Government Intervention to Market Economics*. Cambridge, MA: MIT Press.

[32] Central Bureau of Statistics. Monthly Bulletin of Statistics, August 2008. http://www.cbs.gov.il/reader/yarhon/yarmenu_e_new.html#15

[33] Kun, George. 2003. Low Labor-Input Technology Utilization in the Construction Industry. *Central Bureau of Statistics*. http://www.cbs.gov.il/publications/singapore.pdf

Figure 5.5. Employment in construction, 1980–2008.

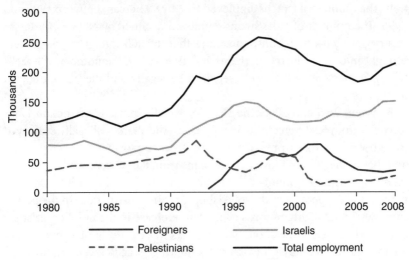

Foreigners   Israelis

Palestinians   Total employment

Source: Bank of Israel, Annual Report 1999, Annual Report 2008.

was largely to blame for this situation because it successfully lobbied for cheap labor. In the mid-1990s, when Israel limited the entry of Palestinians for security reasons and there was pressure to build homes for immigrants from the former Soviet Union, it pushed for access to other foreign workers, hundreds of thousands of whom were brought in (see Figure 5.5).

The construction sector was the largest employer of Palestinian and foreign workers and it was here that cheap, imported labor had the most dramatic effects on productivity. Details of employment, output, and output per head are given in Appendix 5.3. The sector can be divided into two subsectors. The subsector involved in the construction of office and other commercial building, as well as roads, was technologically sophisticated. The second, involved in housing construction, was relatively primitive and relied in large part on unskilled or semi-skilled labor. Output fluctuated mainly because of changes in demand due to immigration, but output per head remained virtually unchanged between 1990 and 1999. Between 1991 and 1995, productivity, measured in terms of net domestic product per hour worked, rose by an annual average rate of 1.6 percent in industry and by only 0.8 percent in construction. In the period 1996–1999, it rose by an average of 1.8 percent in the manufacturing sector but fell by an average of 3.2 percent in construction.[34]

---

[34] Calculated from: Central Bureau of Statistics. 2000. Productivity, Compensation of Employees and Capital Return 1995–1999. Current Statistics, no. 23/2000 (November) and Current Briefings in Statistics, no. 15, 1996.

There were significant changes in the pattern of employment in construction. The number of Israelis employed rose by 98 percent between 1990 and 1996. The number of Palestinians employed declined by 48 percent due to security-related restrictions, and more than 60,000 foreign workers were brought into the industry. In the period 1996–1999, the number of Israelis fell by 20 percent as they were replaced by legally and illegally employed foreigners.

Between 1995 and 2000, the share of Israelis in the construction labor force fell from 63.3 percent to 50.9 percent. The share of illegally employed foreign workers rose from 6.6 percent of total employment to 10.6 percent, and that of illegally employed Palestinians from 8.6 percent to 18.2 percent. As a result, the total number of illegally employed workers rose from 15.2 percent to 28.8 percent of the total labor force in construction. In the period from 2005 to 2007, there was a significant increase in the number of Israeli employed in the construction industry. This was the result of a government attempt to replace foreign workers by offering Israelis incentives to work there.

Economic Developments in 2000

Whereas growth in the early 1990s was consumption-led, by 2000, it had become export-led. Total exports of goods rose by 26.6 percent in nominal dollar terms, with high-tech (communication, medical and scientific equipment, electronic components, and computers) exports leading the way with a 59-percent increase. Other exports went up by 14.8 percent. In the last quarter of 2000, the economic climate changed due to the slowdown in the U.S. economy, the fall of the NASDAQ, and changes in the political conditions in the Middle East. Although the influence of the NASDAQ on the Israeli economy was strong, Israeli high-tech companies were less vulnerable to the crisis because most of them were not Internet-based, "dotcom" companies. Initially, the Palestinian uprising that began in October 2000 affected tourism, construction, and agriculture. Tourism, always very sensitive to geopolitical changes, was the first to be affected, with foreign and domestic revenues decreasing. The construction sector, 30 percent of whose workforce consisted of Palestinians, and the agriculture sector, with 12 percent Palestinian workers, were particularly affected. By 2001, all sectors of the economy were affected.

There were also significant nominal effects. The development of prices in 2000 was affected by the inflow of capital and the rapid increase of exports. These factors resulted in an appreciation of the shekel against both the dollar and the currency basket, and influenced the prices of tradable goods as well as those denominated in foreign currency. The shekel appreciated by 5 percent in the first nine months of 2000. The development of prices during the year was also greatly influenced by exchange rate shifts, and in most months when the shekel appreciated against the dollar, the consumer price index declined, and vice versa. In the first nine months of 2000, monetary policy involved the reduction of nominal interest rates, but as inflation expectations also fell, real short-term interest declined only moderately. The relatively high level of real interest helped moderate the level of price increases during the period reviewed.[35] Fiscal policy also contributed to the deceleration of inflation.

The Crisis of 2008–2009

Most of the problems that led to the financial crisis that began in the autumn of 2008 in the United States and elsewhere did not exist in Israel. In recent years, it has had a balance of payments surplus and a low fiscal deficit. There was no speculative bubble in the housing market: The number of apartments for sale actually fell from an average of 13,000 during the years 2004–2007 to 9,500 in 2008. The liability-to-asset ratio in mortgages did not normally exceed 90 percent and was usually closer to 60–70 percent. The Israeli capital market did not reach the level of complexity of its American counterpart: Trading in structured products in Israel was small compared with the United States. As a result, neither credit default swaps (CDS) nor mortgage-backed securities (MBS) existed in Israeli financial markets. Although Israeli institutions invested in CDS and other derivatives abroad, these investments were limited.

In addition, the availability of credit in the Israeli capital market was much less than in the United States. As a result, the level of leverage was lower than in the United States. Israel was well positioned to face the global crisis after five years of rapid growth because the economy was diversified, with a conservative fiscal policy. Nevertheless, as a small and open economy, Israel was affected by the crisis. There was a sharp decrease in the public's wealth due to the continued losses in the equities markets, and the volume of exports fell as foreign markets went into recession. There were also difficulties in raising credit from banks, and on capital market, companies with high leverage ratios in real estate were hardest hit. Some of the changes expected in worldwide regulation are relevant to Israel as well.

---

[35] Ministry of Finance. 2001. *Economic Outlook*, 13.

The largest Israeli rating agencies are branches of leading agencies from the United States and thus were expected to be affected by regulatory changes in the United States.[36]

Conclusions

Globalization has had profound effects on the Israeli economy. The most important example has been the development of the high-technology sector in which Israel is a world leader. The development of high technology led to an acceleration of growth without a concomitant increase in imports. As a result, the balance of payments was transformed and economic growth became more sustainable than ever before. Globalization also encouraged the development of a dual economy: One sector led and others were far behind. There were a number of mechanisms at work, all made possible by globalization.

The internationalization of the labor market enabled Israel to import cheap labor and subvert mechanisms designed to improve employment conditions, raise minimum wages, and reduce unemployment. It also was an incentive for the construction industry to continue avoiding technological development. There were also implications for Israel's delicate social fiber that already suffered from large income, educational, and other inequalities between Jews and Arabs and between different sections of the Jewish community.

In the high-technology sector, wages were pulled up by international pressure and by competition between Israeli companies due to the shortage of skilled labor. These two factors resulted in increased inequality in the distribution of earnings. The increase in wages in the high-technology sector pushed up the average level of wages and thus the legal minimum wage. This was one of the factors that reduced profitability in traditional industries, causing, inter alia, job losses.

The high-tech sector pulled in large amounts of foreign capital that affected the exchange rate. The high level of the exchange rate was another factor contributing to the difficulties faced by traditional industries. These trends have been described as symptoms of an Israeli variant of the Dutch Disease.[37]

---

[36] Ministry of Finance. 2008. Appendix to the National Budget 2009. Jerusalem: Ministry of Finance, 15–17. http://www.mof.gov.il/research_e/2009/stateBudget2009.pdf

[37] The Dutch Disease was identified in the 1960s, when the Netherlands experienced a large increase in its wealth after discovering natural gas deposits in the North Sea. Unexpectedly,

As Israel became an increasingly individualistic society, the role of consumerism has increased. Spending on advertising and the media available for it (cable and satellite television, commercial radio stations, the internet and mobile telephones) has risen. Foreign companies have invested in order to benefit from the growth of the market, and Israelis, who travel abroad in increasing numbers, demand products and services at standards that prevail abroad. This is a profound implication of globalization.

Globalization has also affected the economy through the multilateral trade agreements that Israel signed. The decision, taken in the early 1990s, to reduce the restrictions on imports from so-called third-world countries had major effects on production and employment in basic industries. The revolution in telecommunications and computer technology that brought the internet, satellite, and cable television to millions of people has had a major influence on tastes, consumption, and production. Rising real income enabled a much larger share of the population to engage in foreign travel. This had effects on tastes and consumer demand. The widespread use of English, including the fact that it is a compulsory school subject, has helped facilitate globalization. As is shown in Chapter 6, the development of technology and technological education, especially in the IDF, was vital.

this ostensibly positive development had negative repercussions on sectors of the country's economy, as the Dutch guilder became stronger, making non-oil exports less competitive. Although this is generally associated with natural resource discoveries, it can occur from any development that results in a large inflow of foreign currency.

SIX

Defense: Service or Burden?

In 1950, Israel spent some $400 million on defense, equal to approximately 8.5 percent of GDP. By 1975, this had increased thirty-five-fold in real terms to reach approximately $14 billion, or 30 percent of GDP. By 2009, it had fallen to an estimated $12 billion, or approximately 8 percent of GDP (these figures are all in 2005 prices). This chapter examines the defense budget as well as other defense-related spending in the state budget. It then details the extra-budgetary costs of defense that are largely associated with the conscription of manpower. This is followed with an analysis of the costs of conflict and the development of military industries. The chapter concludes by analyzing the role of defense in decision making and its effects on economic growth.

Is defense a burden or a service? If a country is threatened and decides to defend itself, then defense is a service that it buys, like education or health. It ensures that life can continue and in this respect, defense is like other publicly provided service. If defense is viewed as an expenditure that results from the pressures of the military-industrial complex, or because of mistaken political policies, then it may be regarded as a burden. The funds spent on defense could go to improving civilian services or reducing taxation. The truth lies in between these definitions: Defense provides a service that many would prefer not to need. The allocation of resources to defense reduces the costs of insecurity. At the same time, it reduces the volume of resources available to the civilian economy. There are static and intertemporal effects and all have to be considered in calculating how much to spend.[1] Most Israelis agree that defense spending is necessary; however, most would also prefer the volume of this defense spending to be lower.

---

[1] Shiffer, Zalman. 2007. "The Debate over the Defense Budget in Israel." *Israel Studies.* Vol. 12. No. 1. 2007. 199.

The Defense Budget

The defense budget covers some of the costs of the manpower used in the Israel Defense Forces (IDF), purchases of weapons, ammunition and other equipment, pensions of military personnel, and other items. In 2008, the budget was funded by the government (38 billion shekels), by profits and income from Ministry of Defense-owned companies (1.3 billion shekels), and by grants from the United States ($2.4 billion) that were mainly used to help buy American equipment. The total budget, including expenditures dependent on income from government-owned military industries, was 51.3 billion shekels, or $10.3 billion. (The implied exchange rate for 2008 used when the budget was drawn up in 2007 was $1=4.97 shekels.)[2] In 2006, just over 40 percent of the defense budget was allocated for manpower costs, 24 percent for purchases of equipment, and the balance of nearly 36 percent went to other current costs.[3] As will be seen, the defense budget does not cover all the costs of defense.

The Development of Defense Expenditure

One of the most important elements of Israel's economy is the very high level of defense expenditure. Israel spends a greater share of its national resources on defense than most Western countries and has done so for more than twenty years. In 2007, defense expenditure equaled 8 percent of GDP in Israel, compared to 4 percent in the United States and 2.6 percent in the United Kingdom.[4] These costs were not always so high: The era of high volumes of defense spending in Israel began in the 1960s.

The Six-Day War of 1967 pushed up defense costs, as did the War of Attrition along the Suez Canal that followed it. Each war brought a rise in absolute levels of defense spending, and after the Yom Kippur War, spending did not return to previous levels. The growing cost of military equipment and the need to increase the size of the armed forces to match those of the Arab countries led to an increase in defense spending. The peak in budgeted defense expenditures was reached between 1973 and

---

2   Ministry of Finance. The Budget in Brief 2008. 1 and 65. http://www.mof.gov.il/budget2007/docs2008/301.pdf

3   Ministry of Defense. 2007. Report issued in accordance with the Law for the Freedom of Information. 115. http://www.mod.gov.il/pages/about_office/pdfs/2007.pdf

4   Stockholm International Peace Research Institute. 2008. *SIPRI Yearbook 2008.* Oxford: Oxford University Press, 228, 230, 232.

1975, when defense consumption equaled a crippling 32 percent of GNP.[5] In 1990, defense expenditure funded by domestic sources (excluding U.S. military aid) was 58 percent higher in real terms than in 1970. During this period, national income had increased by only about 52 percent. Between 1970, a year of fighting along the Suez Canal, and 1990, a year in which the country experienced quiet along its borders, the burden had therefore increased.

From 1967 onward, an important trend in the defense budget was the increased share spent on arms and military supplies purchased in the United States. These purchases were largely financed by U.S. loans and grants. From the mid-1980s, purchases of equipment from Israeli companies were also partly funded by the United States, mainly for the development of the Lavi fighter by Israel Aircraft Industries. Funds received by the Israeli government were exchanged for local currency, which was then used to pay domestic companies for work on the Lavi. The dollars were sold by the government to other sectors in the economy, thus reducing its need to raise revenues by other means.

Another large share of the budget covers salaries in the IDF and the Ministry of Defense that employs several thousand civilians. Permanent members of the armed forces are also paid salaries according to civil service wage scales. Pensions and other benefits of these officers are higher than those paid in the civil service and have become a major share of the budget.

The real level of defense spending has risen in recent years (see Figure 6.1), although the rise has not been constant. The Intifada that began in 2000 pushed up defense spending and as it was one of the factors behind the fall in GDP in 2001 and 2002, so the share of defense in GDP rose significantly. By 2005, it was possible to reduce the volume of spending but in 2006, as a result of the war in the Lebanon that summer, it rose again. Further increases occurred in 2008 and 2009 as a result of the multiple threats facing the country, including that from Iran, and the need to improve military equipment and training after the 2006 war. Figure 6.2 shows that in every year since 1996, the revised budget was higher than the original budget. In 2000–2004, years of the Second Intifada, and in 2006 when the Second Lebanon War took place, these overruns were considerable. It also shows that between 2005 and 2009, the budget rose by about 20 percent in real terms.

---

[5] Bank of Israel. 1985. Annual Report 1984. 45.

Figure 6.1. The defense budget, 1996–2009.

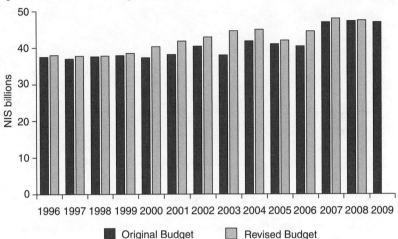

Source: Ministry of Finance. Budget in Brief 2009.

Figure 6.2. Defense consumption expenditure, 1960–2006.

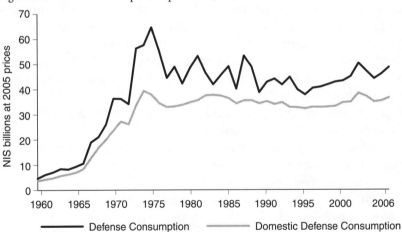

Source: Central Bureau of Statistics. 2007. Defence Expenditure in Israel 1950–2006. Publication No. 2007/10.

Figures 6.1–6.3 provide long-term perspectives on the growth of defense spending. Figure 6.3 shows that the volume of defense spending, measured in 2005 prices, increased sharply between 1960 and 1975. This was due to the Six Day War of 1967, the War of Attrition that followed it on the Suez

Figure 6.3. Defense consumption expenditure as a percentage of GDP, 1950–2006.

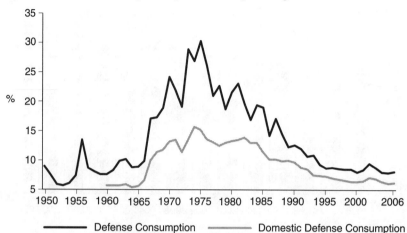

Source: Central Bureau of Statistics. 2007. Defence Expenditure in Israel 1950–2006. Current Statistics. Publication No. 10/2007.

Canal until 1970, and the Yom Kippur War of 1973. It then fell gradually until the mid-1990s and has risen since then. These trends were more pronounced for total defense spending that includes United States aid than for domestic spending that is almost entirely funded by the Israeli government. Figure 6.2 also shows that in 2006, total spending was about ten times higher in real terms than in 1960, and domestic spending was about seven times higher.

Up to 1966, government expenditures were financed by tax revenues, and domestic public debt was limited. After the Six Day War of 1967, the rise in defense spending was not matched by a decline in civilian spending, and tax revenues did not increase by enough to cover them both. As a result, the budget deficit increased and thus pushed up the domestic debt that caused the burden of interest payments made by the government to grow.

High and rising levels of defense spending were one of the main causes of economic slowdown and crisis in the late 1970s and early 1980s. In 1973, as a result of the Yom Kippur War, defense spending rose by almost 64 percent, and in 1974–75, it grew by almost 15 percent a year. In 1976–77, it began to fall but by 1987, it was still nearly 40 percent higher than in 1972. In 1986, there was a 14-percent reduction in defense spending. In 1987–1991, it grew by an annual average of 1.8 percent, slower than the growth of the economy, and in 1992–1995, it fell by an average of 3.4 percent annually. In the period 1985–1995, there was a tradeoff between domestic defense spending and civilian consumption. In the late 1990s, defense spending was restrained while transfer payments rose without increasing the budget deficit.[6]

From the mid-1980s and especially in the 1990s, the economy grew more quickly, enabling Israel to maintain defense spending in real terms and at the same time reduce it as a share of GDP. The reduced levels of defense spending and total public spending contributed to the improvement in the condition of the economy and the rate of growth. This is shown in Figure 6.3. Since 2005, it has increased in real terms.

Military Manpower

The IDF is composed of three elements. The conscript force is made up of eighteen- to twenty-one-year-old men and eighteen- to twenty-year-old women who are paid a token salary. In 2006, some 72 percent of Jewish males (about 35,000) and 65 percent of females (30,000) reaching eighteen years of age were conscripted. As men are conscripted for three years and women for two years, assuming no change in the number reaching the age eighteen or the rate of conscription, the total size of the conscript force in 2006 was 165,000 (35,000 x 3 = 105,000 men + 30,000 x 2 women = 60,000).[7] Most ultra-orthodox men and all ultra-orthodox women do not serve in the army, which means that the length of service for those who do is longer than it would otherwise be. The fact that this group does not serve and that some others manage to avoid serving in the IDF is a source of considerable resentment. Arabs also do not serve, although Druze and some Bedouin men do.

The permanent force consists mainly of officers who volunteer to serve in professional and fighting units. They are paid a market-related wage and receive full pensions upon reaching retirement, usually in their forties or fifties. There is also a budget for pensions and compensation to retired and wounded soldiers and their families, which rose fourfold in real terms between 1988 and 2008.[8] The third group is the reservists who usually serve for up to a month each year and are compensated for their service

---

[6] Lifshitz, Yaacov. 2003. *The Economics of Producing Defense Illustrated by the Israeli Case.* Boston, Dordrecht, New York, London: Kluwer Academic Publishers, 89, 99.

[7] Grinber, Mijal. 2007. "IDF: Nearly 28% of Israeli (Jewish) Males Avoided Conscription in 2007." *Ha'aretz*, 6 December; *CIA Factbook* https://www.cia.gov/library/publications/the-world-factbook/geos/is.html#Military (accessed 21 September 2008). The CIA says that the number of eighteen-year-olds was 44,000, but this includes Arabs who account for an estimated 20 percent.

[8] Calculated from Ministry of Finance. "Budget in Brief 2008." 68. http://mof.gov.il/budget2007/docs2008/301.pdf

through the National Insurance Institute. In 2008, the reserve force was estimated at 445,000.[9]

Extra-Budgetary Costs

Extra-budgetary costs are defense-related costs not covered by the defense budget. A true estimate of total defense costs includes these extra-budgetary items. The most important element of extra-budgetary costs has already been mentioned: The IDF does not pay the full cost of its use of conscripts and reservists. Conscripts, who are paid a nominal wage, bear the opportunity cost of their military service (their loss of income from alternative, civilian employment) almost completely; they do not receive a significant material reward for the service they provide to the country. Reservists do not receive their regular salaries while in uniform; rather they receive payments equal to their regular salary from national insurance funds to which they and their employers contribute.

The amount that each extra full-time soldier would produce if he or she left the army for civilian employment has been calculated in the following way. Labor's contribution to output is equal to 56 percent of the net product less taxes and subsidies.[10] Calculating this amount on a national basis and then dividing it by the number of workers in the labor force gives an estimate of output per person. In 2007, GDP was 662.5 billion shekels; labor's share equal to 56 percent, equal to 371 billion shekels. The number of workers who produced this was 2.68 million.[11] Output per capita was therefore 138,433 shekels or $33,698 (at an exchange rate of $1=4.108). This calculation assumes constant returns to scale: The addition of each worker (or indeed a whole demobilized army) added to the labor force would not change economic conditions so as to alter the estimate of output per person. In reality, any addition to the labor force changes economic conditions, and a substantial demobilization would have significant effects that cannot be estimated here. The annual cost of conscription on these assumptions equaled about $5.6 billion, or 3.5 percent of GDP, in 2007. The assumption of constant returns is unrealistic in that the addition of

[9] Institute for National Security Studies. 2008. Middle East Military Balance." http://www. inss.org.il/upload/(FILE)1206270841.pdf

[10] Central Bureau of Statistic. 1999. *Statistical Abstract of Israel 1998; Statistical Abstract of Israel 2008*; National Accounts 1995–1998, Current Statistics, no. 27; Labor Force Survey 1998, Current Statistics, no. 7, 1999, and author's calculations.

[11] Bank of Israel. *Annual Report 2007*. Table 5.A.3. http://www.bankisrael.gov.il/deptdata/mehkar/doch07/eng/e_3_e.xls

165,000 new workers (or about 6 percent of the workforce) would certainly lower the average level of productivity. It is more realistic to assume that they would have half the level of productivity, at least in the short and medium term, and so the loss would have come to about 1.75 percent of GDP. The 2009 budget estimates the cost at 1.7 percent of GDP, or about $2.8 billion.[12] Assuming that reservists served an average of one month per year, the annual cost of reserve duty came to 445,000/12 = 37,083 man/years. With labor's share of output valued at $33,698, the total loss of output in the economy was 37,083 x $33,698= $1.25 billion, or 0.8 percent of GDP. The total extra-budgetary manpower cost consisted of the cost of conscription (1.7 percent of GDP) and the reserves (0.8 percent), totaling 2.5 percent, or about $4.1 billion.

Although the cost of conscription to the economy is considerable, reducing the size of the army would, at least in the short term, present serious problems. The Israeli economy, with a total labor force of about 2.9 million, would find it difficult to absorb an increase in the labor supply represented by the demobilization of 165,000 conscripts at once. This would be true even in an environment of lower defense spending that might make more resources available for the generation of alternative employment. The question is therefore one of the time scale: Over time, the adjustment would be easier; the economy could adjust to a series of incremental changes more easily than to a single large adjustment. The longer the period over which demobilization occurs, the lower the adjustment cost. The Central Bureau of Statistics has also estimated these extra-budgetary costs (see Appendix 6.1). The additional cost of labor due to conscription and reserve service, including a risk premium due to the danger of military service, was estimated at 1.7 percent of GDP in 2000 and 1.5 percent in 2005.[13]

Another extra-budgetary cost is that of pensions: Government employees do not make contributions during their working lives to official pension funds; this situation applies to both civilian employees of the Ministry of Defense and career soldiers. These costs have been estimated at between 1 and 2 percent of GDP. Further, the stockpiling of fuel and other essential commodities for military purposes is estimated to cost the equivalent of 0.5 percent of GDP. Facilities for stockpiling must be built, maintained, and guarded. The funds used to buy fuel and other stockpiled items could

---

[12] Ministry of Finance. Budget in Brief 2009. 83. http://www.mof.gov.il/budget2007/docs2009/c01.pdf

[13] Central Bureau of Statistics. Defence Expenditure in Israel 1950–2006. Current Statistics, Publication No. 10/2007. http://www.cbs.gov.il/webpub/pub/text_page_eng.html?publ=7&CYear=2006&CMonth=1. 32

otherwise earn foreign currency. Civil defense in terms of building shelters alone may cost another 0.5 percent of GDP.[14] Total extra-budgetary costs calculated here therefore come to about 6 percent of GDP.

Other costs are incurred by central and local governments under different budget headings. The defense establishment owns land in the center of the country for which it does not pay rent; the rent these parcels of land could yield from other uses is also lost, which is another implicit economic cost. The public and private sectors employ guards and equipment to maintain security in schools, shops, places of entertainment, transport facilities, factories, hotels, and other institutions. The costs for the public sector are included in Appendix 6.1, insofar as they can be calculated. These include allocations for security in public institutions such as airports and railway stations. The security costs of the private sector are not known, although superficial observation of life in Israel – where most restaurants have a guard – suggests that they are significant. It would be reasonable to assume that they are at least as large as those of civilian ministries. The data in Appendix 6.1 shows them to have been about $200 million in 2005.

Another incalculable cost is that of disruption of the labor force; although this is most obvious during periods of war, it also occurs in peacetime. The mobilization of reservists each year means that workers are unable to report for work. The loss of output is not only what they would have produced had they remained at work, but also includes the cost of disruption caused by their absence. One person's absence affects the output of other workers; managers have to double or triple their responsibilities when their colleagues go on reserve duty, with negative consequences for efficiency and production. Reservists are usually notified when and for how long they must serve, but mobilization exercises are also conducted to test the efficiency of the system, and these tests can cause unplanned disruptions. These costs have to be met in normal conditions; when war breaks out, there are additional one.

United States' Aid

As an indicator of the defense burden, the calculation of defense costs as a share of national income is somewhat misleading because Israel has access to resources in addition to its national income. These include U.S. loans and grants, details of which are given in Figure 6.4. An accurate definition of

[14] Berglas, Eitan. 1983. *Defense and the Economy: The Israeli Experience*. Jerusalem: Falk Institute for Economic Research in Israel, 21–23.

Figure 6.4. United States military and civilian aid to Israel, 1997–2007.

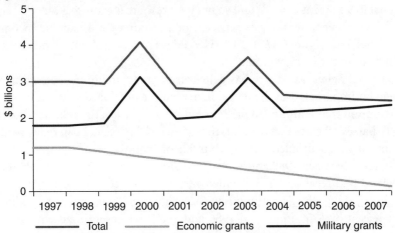

Total ——— Economic grants ——— Military grants

Source: Ministry of Finance. Non-classified items in the Defense Budget 2009.

available resources would also include a deduction for debt repayment. A serious complication is the need to calculate what sum to consider as a result of the military threat to Israel. Economic assistance from the United States and Jewish communities outside Israel is closely related to Israel's strategic position: At times of threat, United States' assistance has increased.

In 1980, loans from the U.S. government equaled 7.1 percent of GNP; grants came to 7.4 percent. Other loans and transfers equaled 9.4 percent; the total inflow of resources from abroad was equivalent to 23.9 percent of GNP. The United States provided large-scale military loans to Israel from 1971 until 1984. In 1974, following the Yom Kippur War and the tremendous burden that it placed on the Israeli economy, the United States began providing grants. The gap between total and domestic defense spending in Figures 6.2 and 6.3 reflects the role of U.S. military assistance. This peaked in the mid-1970s as a result of large increases in aid associated with the Yom Kippur War and the implementation of the peace treaty between Egypt and Israel signed in 1979. By 1985, grants had replaced loans as the primary form of defense aid, and as a result, the volume of funds allocated for debt repayment declined. Between 1951 and 1962, U.S. grants were provided for economic purposes and were renewed in 1972; however, they are now being phased out, and Israel has been partly compensated with a small increase in military aid.

In 1980, total resources, defined as GNP plus inflows from abroad, came to 123.9 percent of GNP. Net total resources are defined as GNP plus the inflow of aid and loans minus debt repayments. Debt repayments were equal to 9 percent of GNP, and so net total resources came to 114.9 percent of GNP. Over time, the gap between total resources and national income declined (see Figure 6.4). In 2008, U.S. aid was equal to about 1.5 percent of GDP, all in the form of grants.

United States' assistance has helped Israel meet the immediate costs of defense imports but in the past it increased the debt burden. A number of significant trends are apparent. Between 1980 and 1989, the volume of loans fell sharply whereas that of grants increased by 78 percent. Loan repayments more than quadrupled and the burden of interest payments more than doubled. Between 1980 and 1989, gross aid declined by 5 percent whereas net aid (aid received less repayment) fell by 60 percent. In real terms, the value of aid declined continuously. These figures include civilian aid, which increased by $750 million in 1986 and 1987 as a result of an emergency assistance package granted in connection with the July 1985 economic stabilization program. In 1990, to help overcome costs resulting from the Gulf War, the United States provided Israel with an additional $750 million of military assistance.

What is the total cost of defense? In 2005 (the most recent year for which there is a comprehensive official breakdown), according to the figures in Appendix 6.1, total direct defense costs came to $10.3 billion and additional extra-budgetary costs were $2.2 billion. The cost of security in the private sector was not included in the table and has been estimated at $225 million, similar to the additional costs in civilian ministries. The total came to $12.7 billion, equal to almost 9.8 percent of GDP. United States' aid equaled $2.2 billion and so the total cost to the Israeli economy was $10.5 billion, or 8.1 percent of GDP. Figure 6.1 shows that in 2009, the defense budget was about seven billion shekels, or about $1.7 billion higher than in 2005 (in 2009 prices).

The Cost of Conflict

Israel allocates large resources to defense on a regular basis but when there is conflict, allocations and costs rise. Since the Yom Kippur War, Israel has fought two Palestinian uprisings, the First Intifada (1987–1993), the Second Intifada (2000–2005), and two wars in Lebanon, the 1982–2000 war and the 2006 war. In addition, there has been conflict in and near Gaza since 2006, culminating in the Gaza war of December 2008–January 2009.

One of the most serious repercussions of high and fluctuating military expenditure is the rapid rate of change and uncertainty it produces in the economy. The largest fluctuations were in the construction sector, associated with the withdrawal of the IDF from Sinai following the peace treaty with Egypt. For example, in 1980, domestic purchases from the construction sector rose by 52 percent. This situation necessitated importing workers from abroad to avoid causing shortages in the local industry and thus causing inflationary pressures. Fluctuations in purchases of goods and services from the defense budget in areas other than construction are much more significant because of the size of these items in the budget. The implications for the economy are examined below.

The Iraqi invasion of Kuwait in August 1990 and the Gulf War in January–March 1991 resulted in losses of approximately $3 billion in the Israeli economy. Tourist revenues fell by $500 million, and imports of oil cost $400 million more than in the corresponding period of 1989–1990. There was a loss of output worth $1.1 billion when the missile attacks on Israel brought the economy to a temporary standstill. Direct damage from the missile attacks is estimated at $60 million, and budgetary costs (mainly due to increased military activity) came to $750 million. Balance of payments costs, loss of export earnings, and higher interest charges equaled about $250 million. The 2003 war in Iraq also caused damage to the Israeli economy, and the United States decided to make further loan guarantees available.

The cost of Israel's military involvement in Lebanon between 1982 and 1985 has been estimated at $5 billion.[15] This estimate includes additions to the national debt caused by the war and the cost of Israel's military buildup to keep pace with the Syrian army, which followed the period of most severe fighting in 1982. Net interest payments abroad rose from $600 million in 1979 to $1 billion in 1982 and $1.7 billion in 1984.[16] Not all of the increase was caused by the war; changes in economic policy during 1981 that increased private consumption also contributed to the rise in the foreign debt. Other costs of war include increased reserve duty, losses of military equipment and fuel, losses of industrial and other output, reduced tourism, and, of course, increased casualties. An immeasurable cost of the war in Lebanon was the considerable damage to military and national morale, which may have resulted, inter alia, in more emigration and less immigration. It is not known over how long a period the $5 billion cost will be incurred: Some costs, such as purchases of equipment, are immediate,

---

[15] Barkai, Haim. 1986. "Reflections on the Economic Cost of the Lebanon War." *The Jerusalem Quarterly.* No. 37. 95–107.
[16] Bank of Israel. 1985. *Annual Report 1984.* 114.

whereas others, including the effect of higher taxation on work incentives, investment, and civilian output, will be carried into the future. In 1982, the Bank of Israel noted that spreading the cost of replenishing military supplies and equipment over several years would lighten the economic burden in 1982 but would prolong it thereafter, thus impeding economic growth and making budget cuts more difficult.[17]

Reserve duty increased when the first Intifada broke out in 1987. Between 1988 and 1991, about $500 million was allocated, mainly within the defense budget, to cover the military costs of the uprising.[18] This situation has also increased the extra-budgetary burden of defense.

The costs of the Second Intifada, which began in the autumn of 2000, were large. Unlike most of the conflicts that Israel has been involved in, this affected the civilian population. Initially the Palestinian uprising affected foreign tourism and Israeli exports to the Palestinian territories. It also reduced, still further, the number of Palestinians working in Israel. The latter had effects on the sectors where most of them worked: agriculture and construction. By the end of 2001, these sectors incurred losses equal to 2 percent of GDP. As the conflict spread and got worse, it began to affect private consumption and investment. Public consumption rose as security needs increased. In 2003, the loss of GDP due to the Intifada came to between 0.7 percent and 1.8 percent of GDP.[19] The economy experienced a recovery in 2003, and in 2004, fast economic growth began. This was in part made possible by the construction of a wall, or fence, in large sections of the West Bank and in Jerusalem, separating Israelis and Palestinians and preventing the entry of terrorists into Israel. The construction of this wall, which was the direct result of the Intifada, involved large costs; between 2003 and 2008, about $2.3 billion was allocated (at the 2008 exchange rate). This was funded through the defense budget that received additional allocations.[20]

The war in Lebanon during the summer of 2006 also affected the economy but on a much smaller scale than the Second Intifada did. The costs of the war have been estimated as follows. Damage to property was estimated at $170 million; the cost of financing the war was $1.8 billion, excluding the

[17] Bank of Israel. 1983. *Annual Report 1982*. 6.
[18] Ministry of Finance. 1990. Main Points of the Budget 1991. Jerusalem: Ministry of Finance.
[19] Bank of Israel. Annual Report 2003. 22–25.
[20] Ministry of Finance. Non-classified items in the Defense Budget 2009. 14. http://www.mof.gov.il/BudgetSite/StateBudget/Budget2009/MinisteriesBudget/Safety/Lists/List/Attachments/2/safety2.pdf

costs of reserve duty. The loss of output was valued at $780 million. Adding these costs and the loss of output gives a total cost of about $2.75 billion, or 1.8 percent of GDP.[21]

In 2006, Israel moved its civilians and military out of the Gaza Strip and closed all its settlements and installations there. The move cost millions of shekels but more significant was the cost of resettling Israelis who had lived there. This is examined in Chapter 7. Since the Israeli withdrawal, areas adjacent to the Gaza Strip came under constant attack from Palestinian missiles until a cease-fire in March 2008. This broke down in December of that year when a one-month war broke out. The conflict resulted in losses of life, injuries, damage to public and private property, loss of production, and costs resulting from the construction of shelters.

Military Industries

The development of military industries has had major effects on the Israeli economy. Despite this, there is no clear definition of what constitutes the defense sector because few companies manufacture solely for the IDF and foreign military markets; most companies produce a mix of military and civilian goods. In 1985, it was estimated that between 58,000 and 120,000 people worked in military industries, depending on the definition used.[22] The lower estimate is equal to 20 percent of the industrial workforce and to between 4 percent and 5 percent of the total labor force, including up to 50 percent of Israel's scientists and engineers.[23] The 1987–1988 Israel Defense Sales Directory advertised 180 companies; in 2008, 216 companies were listed.[24]

Although the origins of military industries predate the state, a major impetus for the development of more sophisticated production came in the late 1960s. In 1967, France – then Israel's major arms supplier – declared an embargo on arms supplies to Israel. To overcome the large gap caused by the embargo, Israel decided to increase local production and purchase equipment from the United States. As a result, the Ministry of Defense has had a strong industrial policy. Its role in the development of industry dates back to the earliest days of the state. In 1948, it set up the Science Corps, renamed the Research and Design Directorate in 1952. In 1958, the Advanced

---

[21] Bank of Israel. Annual Report 2006. 65.
[22] Klieman, Aaron. 1985. *Israel's Global Reach*. London: Pergamon Brassey's, 57.
[23] Klieman, 57.
[24] Ministry of Defense. Sibat. Companies. http://www.sibat.mod.gov.il/sibatmain/catalog/pages/companies-z.html

Weapons Development Authority, known by its Hebrew acronym, Rafael, became a civilian authority producing and advising on weapons systems for the IDF. In 2002, it was incorporated and by 2007, it had almost $1.3 billion in sales, 65 percent of which were abroad. It employed about 5,000 people.[25] Another organization, Israel Military Industries (IMI) produced ammunition and other equipment; it operated as part of the Ministry of Defense and was incorporated in 1990. In 2007, IMI's sales were $517 million and it had 3,200 employees.[26]

Research, development, and production of a wide range of military products increased after the 1967 war, with spin-offs in civilian product areas. The IDF provided a large market for these products and was able to impose high standards and test products. Its use of these items in war became an important sales feature in export markets. An example of this was the decision by a foreign customer to purchase whichever of the two Israeli-produced drones (unmanned mini-aircraft) that the IDF decided to purchase.[27]

In 1961, the ministry pushed for the merger of two companies, Tadir and Ran, to form Tadiran, jointly owned by the government and Koor, the industrial conglomerate belonging to the Histadrut national labor federation. Tadir was a producer of communications equipment, and Ran produced military and civilian batteries. The government sold 50 percent of Tadiran's equity to General Telephone and Electric (GTE) of the United States to acquire U.S. technology, management, and marketing expertise. In 1983, GTE sold its share to Koor. In 1980, Tadiran's sales were $280 million; by 1990, they were $800 million, making it Israel's second-largest manufacturing company. It has since been broken up, and its different sections operate as separate companies.

Israel Aircraft Industries (IAI), Israel's largest industrial company, is also its major defense producer. Its 1990 sales were $1.4 billion, of which $1.1 billion was exported. In 2006, sales reached $2.8 billion, and it employed 15,000.[28] IAI was founded as a maintenance base for the Israel Air Force and El Al Israel Airlines. In the 1970s, it began to design, develop, and later

[25] Rafael Advanced Defense Systems Ltd. Welcome to Rafael. http://www.rafael.co.il/marketing/cor0porate.aspx?FolderID=197

[26] Israel Military Industries. http://www.imi-israel.com/Company/Profile.aspx?FolderID=25

[27] The State Controller. 1984. Report of the State Comptroller no. 35. Jerusalem: State Comptroller's Office.

[28] Israel Aircraft Industries. Company Information. http://www.iai.co.il/Templates/Homepage/Homepage.aspx?lang=EN

produce prototypes of its own fighter aircraft, the Lavi. From its inception, the project was the subject of controversy. Production costs were estimated at over $2 billion, and Israel temporarily joined the very small group of countries individually developing and producing fighter aircraft.[29] In concentrating resources on the Lavi, Israel followed a pattern observed in the United States: a tendency to concentrate on a small number of large projects with rapidly escalating costs.[30] This practice further reinforced the trend toward inflexibility in production. The United States, having been funding part of the program, eventually exerted strong pressure for its cancellation. In 1987, the Lavi was scrapped after a long and heated debate; $500 million was allocated for severance pay and other costs and $350 million for alternative projects.[31] The cancellation of the Lavi resulted in many former employees of IAI and other companies that had been subcontractors setting up new enterprises. These became one of the main bases for the development of Israel's civilian high-technology sector. This was a similar process to that which occurred in California at the end of the Vietnam War. From 1975, U.S. defense spending started to decline, and the aircraft industry went into recession. Engineers and others who lost their jobs as a result turned to the civilian sector and were among the founders of the high-technology revolution that centered in the Silicon Valley.

There are also a large number of private companies involved in military production that have grown in close cooperation with the Ministry of Defense. Perhaps the most important example of private sector activity in this field was the Discount Investment Company (DIC), Israel's largest private holding company. It was founded in 1961 by the Discount Banking Group, with a former commander of the Israel Air force, Dan Tolkovsky, as its managing director and vice-chairman. In the 1960s, Tolkovsky identified the need for Israel to develop a high-technology industrial base for military as well as economic reasons. DIC was instrumental in setting up Biron Electronic Industries, Ltd., an industrial holding group with subsidiaries and affiliates involved in the development, manufacture, and marketing of a range of industrial goods.

The military sector has certain inherent advantages that have benefitted the economy. Companies concentrating on military production tend to

[29] Peri, Yoram and Amnon Neubach. 1985. *The Military Industrial Complex in Israel: A Pilot Study.* Tel Aviv: International Center for Peace in the Middle East. 60–62.

[30] Gansler, Jacques. 1980. *The Defense Industry.* Cambridge, MA: MIT Press, 16.

[31] Tzimuki, Tova and Aries Arad. 1987. "Answer on the Lavi at the End of the Month." *Davar,* 8 March. 1–2.

have relatively good industrial relations, partly because they employ skilled and therefore well-paid workers. Employees are conscious of their centrality to the national defense effort, a motivational factor of considerable importance. These firms are also capital intensive and are technologically very sophisticated. They usually have a high degree of product concentration with only limited competition, but this is not always the case: Intense competition at home and abroad between Israel Aircraft Industries and Tadiran for sales of drones, for example, eventually resulted in the formation of a joint company.

Military products produced in Israel are not guaranteed a market in the IDF. The defense establishment policy has generally been to supply the IDF with the best equipment, not necessarily that made at home. The best example of this was the fact that in the 1980s, the Israel Air Force preferred United States' equipment to the Lavi. Domestic production therefore has to compete with imports. The IDF has an incentive to buy abroad when imports are cheaper (given that quality considerations do not outweigh cost), but decisions are also influenced by the desire to provide orders to local producers so as to maintain domestic production capabilities.[32] Reductions in the domestically funded defense budget have led to pressures in the military establishment to buy more basic goods, such as uniforms and sometimes even food, abroad. The budget funded by United States' aid has been large enough to cover the cost of more sophisticated purchases and basic items.

Many countries prefer to manufacture their own arms where possible rather than rely on imports; they are, therefore, of limited value as markets. As there are a significant number of countries that do not maintain diplomatic relations with Israel or are subject to pressure from Arab countries, the weapons market is limited. The dangers of reliance on arms exports are considerable. Most of the funds provided by the United States are tied to purchases of goods made there. The definition of "Made in America" is that at least 51 percent of the product should be made in the United States. In order to meet the U.S. requirement, a number of Israeli companies set up production facilities in the United States so that the U.S. facilities can produce at least 51 percent of the orders financed by U.S. aid.[33] The links with United States have helped Israeli industry and the IDF develop technologically and in other ways.

---

[32] Peri, Yoram and Amnon Neubach. 1985. *The Military Industrial Complex in Israel.* Tel Aviv: International Center for Peace in the Middle East, 84–87.

[33] *Ma'ariv.* Tel Aviv, 2 August 1985.

Structure of the Defense Industry

The significance of the structure of an industry as a determinant of its behavior and growth has been emphasized by a number of economists.[34] The less competitive the industry and its market is, the slower its growth. If the industry is large and uncompetitive, its effect on the economy will be to reduce the rate of growth of GDP. The conditions in an optimal, free-market situation have been contrasted with those that prevail in the United States defense market. A brief examination of United States' defense markets reveals significant Israeli parallels. Among the main characteristics of free markets is the existence of many small producers and consumers, none of whom can have a significant effect on the market. Commodities traded are small and divisible, and prices are determined by competition in the market and respond to changes in supply and demand. There is mobility of factors of production, perfect information (everyone in the market has all the information needed to make decisions), and free movement in and out of markets.

The United States defense market is characterized by monopsony (a monopolistic purchaser), oligopoly, and the indivisibility of products. Prices are determined in relation to total costs and military need (on a cost-plus basis): Weapons systems take years to develop; capital and labor are not mobile, and the government intervenes as regulator, specifier, banker, and judge of claims. Finally, competition is for all or none of a market rather than for shares of it. Barriers to entry include the fact that sales are made to the government through close contact with its purchasing officers. Winning government contracts is a specialized, complex task. Although capital investment needed for defense production may be high, the market is limited to what the defense budget allows plus any possible exports. Lowering prices may not affect sales if military needs have been met, something even more true of Israel than the United States. There are close links between the defense establishment and supplying companies that involve the interchange of personnel.

In defense markets, price is less important than performance: Firms cannot reduce unit costs by duplicating existing products at lower prices, because markets are limited. The pressure is usually to improve performance. Research and development are the keys to product improvement and new systems, but they are expensive activities. The costs involved may

---

[34] Porter, Michael. 1980. *Competitive Strategy: Techniques for Analyzing Industries and Competitors.* New York: Free Press; Gansler, *The Defense Industry.*

not be feasible. Defense ministries may lend equipment to firms in the industry as part of joint projects but may be less willing to do so with new entrants whom they know less well. Given the tendency toward large projects, the size of the investments required may be prohibitive. The defense establishment may demand particular reporting, accounting, management, and other technical systems that are unique to the defense sector and require knowledge before they can be adopted.[35]

There are also factors that prevent or discourage companies from leaving the industry. Defense contracts may encourage financially weak companies to stay in the market rather than seek capital from other sources. Government funding provides an incentive to remain in the hope of making a civilian commercial application as well as military ones. Equipment required for defense production often cannot be converted for use in manufacturing civilian goods. The ability of specially trained personnel to move into civilian production may be limited. For example, defense industry marketing skills are different from civilian ones, and the cost pressures prevailing in civilian markets may be difficult for firms used to operating in a cost-plus environment. Given the increasingly long-term nature of military product development, diversification may take years to plan. Local companies may not want to abandon the market to foreign suppliers, nor may governments want them to.[36]

Israel's defense industry has many of these characteristics. The defense sector is only partly subject to competitive pressures; its importance in the economy means that this lack of competitiveness exerts a significant influence on the system as a whole. Its civilian markets are too small for economies of scale to be achieved in domestic production as often as economies of scale are achieved in larger economies. Monopoly and oligopoly are widespread, and prices are often either controlled by the government or strongly influenced by it. Capital is immobile because the state dominates the capital market, and labor mobility is limited by trade union and other agreements.

The availability of United States aid meant that the IDF could buy equipment without using the shekel budget financed by Israeli taxpayers, leaving it with more funds for other things. In 1979, the IDF was given control over its budget including that for weapons' development and acquisition. It has always preferred to buy equipment off-the-shelf rather than wait for local products to be developed. These factors weighed against the domestic

---

[35] Gansler, *The Defense Industry*, 217–221.
[36] Gansler, 246–247.

defense industry that increasingly had to rely on exports to maintain its production runs.[37]

In the 1980s and 1990s, the defense industry experienced a decline in the demand for its products both at home and abroad. As a result, major restructuring were made by closing plants and reducing the labor force. Between 1992 and 2008, nearly 21 billion shekels were invested in this effort, but the industry's problems have not been solved. This is because of inflexible labor agreements resulting in, among other things, high labor costs and excess capacity. Restructuring has been achieved by privatization and the concentration of production in Israel Aircraft Industries and Rafael. The gradual reduction in the number of companies in the sector (especially in the publicly owned part of it) conformed to a worldwide trend. In recent years, the market for defense products abroad has grown. At home, the demand grew as a result of decisions to reequip the IDF after the 2006 Lebanon War.[38]

Defense and Its Prominence in Decision Making

Israel is unique in having been founded in war and having remained so ever since. Few countries have been subject to so much active and passive hostility by so many and for so long. Defense has almost always come first in terms of the overall allocation of resources. Great efforts have been made by the political leadership to obtain financial and technological resources for the IDF and military industries.

The centrality of the defense effort in Israeli life has been described in the following terms: "The control of the execution of centralized policies and decisions is performed through the Israeli social structure, where managers are much better acquainted with each other than they are in countries with populations similar to that of Israel. This is true mainly because of Israel's geo-political position, its relatively isolated and self-centered economy and its business managers being associated with each other in different social systems, primarily in their service in the IDF's reserves."[39]

The IDF is a significant socializing agent in Israeli society; it also provides many with a common motivation. Although the consensus on political and

---

[37] Sadeh, Sharon. 2001. "Israel's Beleaguered Defense Industry." *Middle East Review of International Affairs.* Vol. 5. No. 1. 64–77. http://meria.idc.ac.il/journal/2001/issue1/sadeh.pdf

[38] Ministry of Finance. Main Points of the Budget 2009. 91–92. http://www.mof.gov.il/budget2007/docs2009/c01.pdf

[39] Weinshall, Theodore D. 1972. "The Industrialization of a Rapidly Developing Country – Israel," in Robert Dubin, ed. *Handbook of Work, Organisation and Society.* Chicago: RandMcNally College Publishing Co., 949–987.

economic issues has declined in recent years, the army still plays a unifying social role.[40] The size of the IDF and of the industrial complex with which it is associated has been one reason why the government has played an important role in the economy. Defense industries have either been run by the government directly or by former army officers or reservists whose outlook, ideology, and motivation were affected by their army service. The size and preponderance of the military sector also mean that many of the decisions in the economy are made as a result of military rather than economic considerations or, at most, with economic factors being only one of the deciding criteria. Many important decisions affecting the economy are made within the confines of the defense establishment, with minimal external influence.

In the 1980s, defense had a reduced priority. The domestic consensus about the nation's political-military aims weakened. This change resulted from controversy about the settlement program in the West Bank and Gaza as well as from intense dissatisfaction with the conduct of the war in Lebanon. The peace treaty signed with Egypt and the Iran-Iraq war of 1980–1988 made many, including the General Staff, feel that Israel was in a relatively strong position in the region. During 1988, this belief began to change with the end of the Iran-Iraq war and the continuation of the Palestinian uprising in the West Bank and Gaza. This change in belief was reinforced by Iraqi missile attacks on Israel during the Gulf War of 1991.

The deteriorating performance of the economy made the allocation of resources for defense more difficult. Social services were cut to a point where the opportunity cost of defense spending became clearer to the public and the government. This action was one of the factors behind the cancellation of the Lavi. Since 2000, the Second Intifada, the Second Lebanon War of 2006, and the Gaza war in early 2009, as well as the roles of Iran, Hamas, and Hizbollah, have changed the strategic balance. Israel feels more threatened: Plans to reduce the period of conscription were delayed in 2006 and defense spending has increased.

Defense and High Technology

The IDF and military industries have played a crucial role in the development of the high technology sector and continue to do so. Technological know-how and experience is frequently transferred from the military to the civilian

---

[40] Radom, M. 1968. "Military Officers and Business Leaders: An Israeli Study in Contrasts." *Columbia Journal of World Business.* Vol. 3. No. 2. 27–34.

sector, and the IDF does not seek property rights or patents on technologies development under its sponsorship. The IDF also forms a source of personal status, cultural codes, and a network of contacts that serves people in the civilian sector. They knew each other in the army, or knew of each other, or are able to assess each other on the basis of their service in specific units. The IDF has created and maintains highly innovative and potentially internationally competitive technologies that set standards for those working with them or helping develop them. Many of those involved in these activities are doing their compulsory military service and are therefore young, which means they are at the beginning of their career. These systems of work, training, and experiences and the networks surrounding them lower the transaction costs of doing business in software and other high-technology sectors. It is significant that a very conservative type of organization – an army – has developed systems that have produced something very dynamic: technological development. This is because the emphasis has been on problem solving in an ad hoc and low-cost environment, and because young people are used, encouraged, and promoted.[41] The IDF jump-starts young technologists with special training programs and gives them managerial responsibilities at a young age. Many of them later join high-technology companies, and some of them have created very successful ones.[42]

Outsourcing and Privatization

Over the last twenty-five years, the IDF has privatized some of the services it used to provide. This began in the catering industry and in the early 1990s was extended. The Israel Air Force issued a tender for the maintenance of training aircraft of its Central Flying School and allowed external firms to participate. This involved allowing civilian contractors to perform ongoing work inside military facilities, on the aircraft lines. More recently, a civilian firm was contracted to provide flights by unmanned airborne vehicles for intelligence gathering.[43] There are plans to extend these processes further

[41] Honig, Benson, Miri Lerner and Yoel Rabin. 2006. "Social Capital and the Linkages of High-Tech Companies to the Military Defense System: Is There a Signaling Mechanism?" *Small Business Economics*. Vol. 27. 421; Peled Dan. 2001. Defense R&D and Economic Growth in Israel: A Research Agenda. Samuel Neaman Institute, The Technion. 18–19. http://econ.haifa.ac.il/~dpeled/papers/ste-wp4.pdf

[42] Senor, Dan and Saul Singer. 2009. *Start-Up Nation: The Story of Israel's Economic Miracle*. New York: The Hachette Books Group, 69–83.

[43] Ivry, David. 2003. Privatization of Military Services and Its Implications. The Fisher Brothers Institute for Air and Space Strategic Studies. 1–4. http://www.fisherinstitute.org. il/Eng/_Articles/Article.asp?ArticleID=37&CategoryID=25

in order to cut costs and thus make resources available for other military needs. The IDF has also recently privatized part of its medical services

Conclusions

Military necessity has forced the government to play a major role in the economy. A key question is whether Israel's economy would have developed in a different way without government intervention through the defense effort. The ideas put forward by Gerschenkron suggest that countries trying to develop in the mid-twentieth century cannot succeed without government intervention.[44] Germany in the latter part of the nineteenth century had to involve the banks in the development of industry in a way that had not been necessary half a century before in the United Kingdom. Germany also had to compete with the already industrialized United Kingdom and so needed a different development mechanism. Russia, before the revolution, experienced massive state investment in basic industries, which had not happened in the United Kingdom or Germany. Postwar Japan developed on the basis of very close links between the government and industrial conglomerates. Against this background, the development of military industries can be seen as a means by which the Israeli government was able to push economic development forward. However, since 1973, Israel's large-scale military spending has been accompanied by periods of stagnation, and some commentators have suggested that the government has gone too far, from an economic point of view, in developing military production.[45]

The most superficial statistical investigation bears this assertion out. As the defense burden has grown, the rate of economic growth has fallen. In the 1980s, the defense burden stabilized and then fell slightly, but it remained at a very high absolute level. After allowing for the fact that inputs of labor and capital grew more slowly in recent years, this correlation between high levels of defense expenditure and slow economic growth suggests that there is a threshold beyond which defense spending does have a negative effect. The nature and existence of such a threshold is a matter for further research. In the early 1990s, the stability or even reduction in defense spending was accompanied by faster economic growth. Showing a correlation between high defense/national income ratios and slow national income growth does not mean that the former is the cause

[44] Gerschenkron, Alexander. 1962. *Economic Backwardness in Historical Perspective.* Cambridge, MA: Harvard University Press.
[45] Peri and Neubach, *The Military Industrial Complex in Israel.*

of the latter. There is, however, a priori evidence for such a conclusion: The output of the defense sector does not yield conventional economic benefits apart from security; it is not meant to.

Foreign aid has accounted for an increasing share of the defense budget, and this situation has caused the ratio of defense expenditure to GNP to be biased upward. It has been shown, however, that after allowing for debt repayment for military borrowing, the true ratio was not lower. Extra-budgetary costs need to be added to the calculation.

If it is assumed that the whole of the metals, electronics, and electrical sectors was the result of military-inspired government intervention, then their contribution to the economy can be set off against the costs of defense. What cannot easily be calculated is what the level of exports would have been in a low defense spending situation and precisely what the level of indirect defense imports was. Finally, for a complete picture, it would be necessary to calculate the level of civilian imports required by the reduced level of domestic production.

Had the government decided not to set up military industries and stimulate arms production, it could still have pushed economic development in other ways. The alternatives were not "defense" and "no growth." The government could have found ways to stimulate civilian output through either the public sector or the private sector, or both. Arms imports might have been higher but exports might have more than compensated for them. The trade-off between economic growth and defense spending is complex. If growth is assumed to be synonymous with increased exports, then in any one year, there is a trade-off between allocations for exports and those for defense. The government can spend money on one or the other. In addition, allocations for domestic expenditure stimulate local demand, thus increasing imports and at the same time reducing the room for, and incentive to, export. Promotion of exports may therefore be at the expense of defense consumption, which yields noneconomic benefits in the short term, or defense investment, which yields noneconomic benefits in the future. However, allocations for defense at the expense of export development reduce the size of future national income and thus the economy's ability to fund future defense spending.[46] Civilian investment can be substituted for export allocations in this argument.

As a result of Israel's political and military situation, the country developed a very close relationship with the United States, which resulted in

---

[46] Halperin, Ariel. 1986. Military Build-up and Economic Growth in Israel. Jerusalem: Maurice Falk Institute Conference Paper. June. 18–22.

flows of aid and military hardware, accompanied by significant effects on the economy, especially in terms of technological development.

There is no consensus in economic literature on the effects of defense expenditure on economic growth and development, but Israel's current experience leads to certain conclusions. The defense buildup led to major industrial development, but the costs of military spending increased the size of the state budget and the budget deficit. These were important factors behind the acceleration of inflation and the slowdown of economic growth in the mid-1970s and early 1980s. Israel's move into high-technology military production resulted in slower growth of civilian output than otherwise would have occurred. Traditional industries were upgraded at a slower rate, and as a result they were left behind technologically and denied skilled manpower. According to an estimate made in the mid-1980s, shifting 1,000 technologically trained personnel from military to civilian research and development could have increased GNP growth by 1 percent.[47] Even if these estimates of the costs are overstated, the effect is considerable. This effect, combined with the burdens described above, amounts to a considerable economic loss. Against this, the training of thousands of soldiers in the use of technology should be considered.

The IDF, the military industries, and the Ministry of Defense have been subject to much greater criticism since the Yom Kippur War of 1973 and the huge losses that it entailed. Since then, there have been many events that have resulted in public criticism but, insofar as the armed forces and the defense sector are subject to government control and parliamentary oversight – albeit nominal one – the majority of the public continues to believe in the IDF and serves in it willingly.

---

[47] Halperin, Military Build-up and Economic Growth in Israel, 19.

SEVEN

Israel and the Palestinians

This chapter examines the costs of building, maintaining, and guarding Israeli settlements in the West Bank and other territories that Israel occupied in 1967. It then looks at how Israel's relations with the Palestinians have affected the economy.

Settlements

In the June 1967 Six Day War, Israel occupied the Golan Heights, the West Bank, the Gaza Strip, and the Sinai Peninsula. Soon after, it began to build the first settlements for Jews in those areas. At the end of 1967, the head of the Ministerial Committee for Settlements, Yigal Allon, began to plan the state's settlement map that envisaged the establishment of Jewish settlements in the eastern part of the West Bank. The aim was to create a security border along the Jordan River valley on the eastern slopes of the West Bank hill ridge, over which Israel would retain rule. The hills of the West Bank with its cities would be returned to Jordan in the framework of a peace treaty whereas 40 percent of the West Bank would remain under Israeli sovereignty.[1] An Israeli civilian presence in the Jordan Valley was in accordance with the security ideology that was in the Allon Plan. A number of settlements were also constructed in the Gaza Strip.

In 1977, the Likud government led by Menachem Begin changed and accelerated the settlement policy. Dozens of settlements were established at the end of the 1970s and the beginning of the 1980s. In contrast to the policies of its Labor predecessor, the aim was to build settlements near Palestinian towns in the heartland of what was considered the biblical Land of Israel in such a way that the West Bank could not be separated from

---

[1]   Efrat, Elisha. 2006. *The West Bank and the Gaza Strip*. Abingdon, Oxon: Routledge, 25.

Israel. In addition, the government built suburban settlements close to the eastern side of the 1967 border. These would provide housing for commuters into Israel's cities. The government offered numerous incentives to Israelis to buy homes in the West Bank, thus making the area attractive not only to the ideologically motivated settlers, who were often but not always religious, but also to those who simply wanted cheaper accommodation and the amenities that living in the West Bank, rather than in crowded Israeli cities, offered.[2] Between 1967 and 1977, under the Labor governments of Levi Eshkol, Golda Meir, and Yitzhak Rabin, the population of the settlements reached 5,000. In 1978, after one year of Likud government, the number of settlers had reached 7,800. By 1980, it was 12,500 and by 1985, it had reached 46,100.[3]

In addition, Israel began to expand the Jewish suburbs of Jerusalem over the cease-fire line (known as the Green Line) that had prevailed between 1949, when the War of Independence ended, and 1967. In Jerusalem, this also included building beyond the city's municipal boundary. Most of this development became the subject of a barrage of Palestinian, Arab, and international opposition and was the subject of much controversy inside Israel. It is significant that such a large public enterprise was undertaken without a national consensus.

The West Bank and Gaza

In September 1967, the first Israeli settlement in the territories occupied in the Six Day War was established. It was called Kefr Etzion, near Hebron, and was built on the site of a Jewish settlement that had been abandoned in the 1948 war.[4] Since then, numerous other settlements, some the size of towns, have been built, and their total population today is in the hundreds of thousands. They have been one of the most contentious elements in Israeli-Palestinian relations. For a number of reasons that are explored here, they have been a major burden on the Israeli economy.

These settlements were initially built in four main areas. The first group of settlements was in the West Bank. The second was close to Jerusalem or part of it, within and outside its municipal area, on the non-Israeli side of the Green Line, or 1967 border. The third group of settlements was in the

---

[2]   Efrat, *The West Bank and The Gaza Strip*, 27–33; Gorenberg, Gershom. 2006. *The Accidental Empire*. New York: Times Books, Henry Holt and Company, 368.

[3]   Peace Now. http://www.peace.now

[4]   Gorenberg, Gershom. 2008. "The Etzion Illusion." *Ha'aretz*, 29 September.

Gaza Strip, all of which were closed when Israeli settlers and the Israeli army left in 2006. The fourth group was built in the Golan Heights, formerly a part of Syria. A small number of settlements were also built in the Sinai and these were closed when Israel returned that area to Egypt after the 1979 peace treaty between the two countries was signed. In addition, smaller settlements were built elsewhere in the West Bank with varying amounts of official approval and funding. In 2003, according to an official report, there were at least 105 of these "unauthorized outposts." Their construction began in the mid-1990s, after the construction of settlements in the West Bank and Gaza was frozen by the Rabin government. Although the government ceased to be involved in the establishment of new settlements from the mid-1990s, public authorities and government bodies played a major role in establishing the unauthorized outposts.[5] Construction of apartments peaked in 1991, when there were 7,750 building starts in the West Bank, 9.3 percent of the total in Israel. The share peaked in 2000 when 4,960 starts were recorded, equal to 10.8 percent of all building starts in Israel.[6] At the end of 2007, there were 119 official Jewish localities in the West Bank.[7]

In a country with a relatively fast population growth rate and improving living standards, the government was faced with choices of how to develop the economy geographically. Traditionally there was a bias toward the periphery – the Negev and the Galilee – where Israel's pioneering spirit would continue. Both before and after the creation of the state, the cities were considered bourgeois and not where a society with a socialist orientation should put its resources. As a result, the agricultural sector in the north and south of the country, especially the kibbutzim, was favored until the 1950s. Then the emphasis shifted toward industry, but development towns for new immigrants were also constructed in the periphery. Many of the towns in the Galilee and Negev struggled economically and were in need of more investment. The settlement effort in the West Bank came at the expense of that investment and has been one of the factors behind the continued lagging behind of the periphery.

It is against this background of pioneering ideology that the creation of settlements in the West Bank and Gaza should be seen. An additional factor

[5] Summary of Opinion Concerning Unauthorized Outposts – Talya Sason http://www.mfa.gov.il/MFA/Government/Law/Legal+Issues+and+Rulings/Summary+of+Opinion+Concerning+Unauthorized+Outposts+-+Talya+Sason+Adv.htm

[6] Central Bureau of Statistics. Construction in Israel 2007. http://cbs.gov.il/publications/build2007/pdf/t09.pdf

[7] Central Bureau of Statistics. *Statistical Abstract of Israel, 2008.* http://www.cbs.gov.il/reader/shnaton/templ_shnaton_e.html?num_tab=st02_07x&CYear=2008

that played a key role was the development of a kind of religious messian-ism that took hold of parts of Israeli society after the dramatic victory in the Six Day War. This fervor even affected some of the secular, socialist rulers of the country. The religious groups keen to create or recreate settlements in the West Bank (and, to a lesser extent, in other areas) were seen by some in the Labor movement as a new generation of *chalutzim*, or pioneers. From the late-1960s, they were willing to do what socialists had done from the beginning of the twentieth century: to live in remote areas, not necessarily for financial gain, and redeem the land of Israel. They were to prove very different from the socialists in terms of their political behavior, and their willingness and sometimes even desire to confront the Palestinians next to whom they were living deepened the already painful conflict still further, which has had enormous political and therefore economic consequences ever since.

Israeli Settlements in the Golan

Israel has built a number of kibbutzim, moshavim, and a small town in the Golan Heights. As most of the small, Syrian population fled in 1967, there was little territorial conflict between Israelis and Syrians there. As a result, there has been much less controversy within Israel about these settlements. It is, however, clear to most Israelis that a political settlement with Syria will require either their abandonment or transfer to Syria if some kind of leasing arrangement cannot be negotiated. At the end of 2000, there were thirty-seven Jewish settlements in the Golan, the largest of which was the town of Katzrin with a population of 6,500.[8]

The Population of West Bank Settlements

Figure 7.1 shows that between 1972 (the first date for which there are offi-cial statistics) and September 2009, the population of the settlements in the West Bank and Gaza grew 201-fold, compared to a national increase of 129 percent. In recent years, the annual growth rate has exceeded 5 percent, compared with a total population growth rate of about 1.8 percent. In 1972, 0.5 percent of the Jewish population of Israel lived in the territories; in 2007, it was nearly 5 percent. This growth was even more remarkable given that

---

[8]   Central Bureau of Statistics. *Statistical Abstract of Israel, 2008.* http://www.cbs.gov.il/ reader/shnaton/templ_shnaton_e.html?num_tab=st02_07x&CYear=2008; Central Bureau of Statistics. Population of localities numbering above 1,000 residents and other rural population on 30. 09. 2008. http://www.cbs.gov.il/population/new_2008/table3.pdf

Figure 7.1. Population of Jewish settlements in the West Bank and Gaza, 1972–2008.

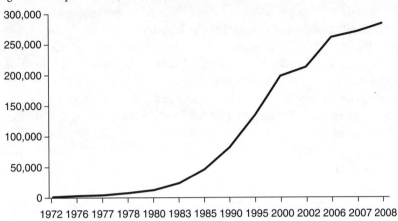

Source: Central Bureau of Statistics, *Statistical Abstract of Israel*, 2003, 2007, 2008, 2009.

about 8,000 Jews left Gaza in the summer of 2006. It should be noted that these figures exclude thousands of Jews living in the West Bank illegally. Expansion of the Jewish population in the West Bank, Gaza, and the Golan was made possible by large-scale public spending. In this sense, the population and its growth is endogenous, a factor to be explained, rather than an exogenous factor to be used for calculating total costs.

Figure 7.1 excludes the population of suburbs and settlements built contiguously with Jerusalem. Although the Palestinians consider these areas to be the same as the settlements, many Israelis do not. The population of Jerusalem has grown faster than the national average, partly because the birth rates of the large Arab and Haredi populations there are high and because the Israeli government and Jerusalem municipality invested massively in expanding the city to the north, east and south after 1967. In 2006, the population of areas of Jerusalem built over the Green Line was 176,000, or about 24 percent of the total population of the city.[9]

The Jewish population of the West Bank has become increasingly dominated by the ultra-Orthodox. Between the end of 2003 and the end of 2007, the population of the exclusively ultra-Orthodox town of Beitar Ilit rose by 40 percent, from almost 23,000 to more than 32,000. The population of Modi'in Ilit, the other ultra-Orthodox town, rose by 55 percent, from

---

[9] Arieli, Shaul. 2008. Jewish Population over the Green Line. September. http://www. shaularieli.com; Central Bureau of Statistics. *Statistical Abstract of Israel 2008*. Table 2.5.

almost 24,300 to 38,000, during the same period.[10] Much of the increase in the ultra-Orthodox population is due to natural growth because they have the highest birth rate of any part of the Jewish population of Israel (or the West Bank settlers). In the early 2000s, about 70 percent of children born to West Bank settlers were ultra-Orthodox families. In addition, there was substantial growth due to migration to ultra-Orthodox settlements from Israel given the housing shortage for this group in Israeli cities. The other main settlements were the towns of Ariel, with a 2007 population of nearly 17,000, and Elad with 30,300.[11] In 2008, there were some 80,000 ultra-Orthodox Jews living in the West Bank, accounting for nearly 30 percent of all Israeli settlers.

The Cost of West Bank Settlements

The Israeli economy has been severely burdened by costs of construction, maintenance, and guarding of these settlements. What were the costs? If the settlements that now accommodate hundreds of thousands of people had not been built, then alternatives inside the Green Line would have had to be constructed. They could either have been new settlements or they could have been expansions to existing ones. In either case, they could have reinforced the development of existing peripheral areas such as the Galilee or even more, the Negev that is underpopulated and underdeveloped, helping to achieve economies of scale. These are the first costs of the West Bank settlements that should be calculated, but they have never been done as they involve asking very complex, hypothetical questions. The Ministry of Finance has noted that the economy of the Negev will benefit from the current construction of a group of new military bases and a town for military personnel and their families. This could have been replicated many times over if resources allocated to settlement building had gone there or to the Galilee instead.[12]

The second set of costs is that related to security. The location of the settlements in Palestinian areas, sometimes near or even in populated areas, gave rise to high security costs that would not have arisen if they had been

[10] Central Bureau of Statistics. *Statistical Abstract of Israel 2008.* http://www.cbs.gov.il/shnaton59/download/st02_15.xls and http://www.cbs.gov.il/population/new_2005/table1_2005.pdf

[11] Peace Now. http://peacenow.org/policy.asp?rid=&cid=1644; Central Bureau of Statistics. Population of localities numbering above 1,000 residents and other rural population on 30. 09. 2008. http://www.cbs.gov.il/population/new_2008/table3.pdf

[12] Ministry of Finance. Main Points of the Budget 2009. 85. http://www.mof.gov.il/budget2007/docs2009/c01.pdf

built inside the green line. This is not to deny that the latter would require some security.

The third cost is that of dismantling settlements. Israel abandoned the settlements it built in the Sinai when the area was returned to Egypt in the early 1980s, including the small town of Yamit that had been built on the North Sinai coast. In 2006, Israel left the Gaza Strip and closed four settlements in the northern part of the West Bank. Thousands of settlers were re-housed and compensated. The total cost of the evacuation of Israeli settlements in Gaza has been estimated at 10–11 billion shekels (about $2.5 billion), or more than 2 percent of GDP, spread over a two- to three-year period.[13] This figure is a transfer cost imposed by the government on taxpayers and is not necessarily equal to the loss to the economy. The economic loss is measured by the effect of higher taxation (or deficit financing) that the government imposes. If it creates disincentives to work then it will result in a loss of output; if it does not, it may lead to a loss of welfare for taxpayers but not necessarily to a commensurate loss for the economy. Although the government budget has been nearly balanced in recent years, this has not been a costless process: Many painful cuts have been made in public spending, and the internal debt remains high. Offsetting the costs of relocation by increasing taxation helps maintain the budget in balance, but indirect, negative effects on growth mean that national income is smaller than it otherwise would be and so the budget deficit/GDP ratio will also be higher. No estimates have been made of these effects in Israel. A peace treaty with the Palestinians will require abandoning large numbers, if not all, of the settlements, with thousands of homes and other facilities in which billions of shekels have been invested.

Table 7.1 shows that between 1967 and 2003, Israel spent 50.5 billion shekels, equal to $14 billion on the settlements, or $450 million a year, excluding security costs (in 2008 prices). Security costs have been calculated at between 1.5 and 2.5 billion shekels a year, depending on the level of violence. If an average of 2 billion shekels ($450 million) a year is used, then the annual cost, including security, averaged $900 million, or nearly 0.5 percent of GDP in 2008. A rough calculation based on these figures suggests that between 1967 and 2008, Israel spent about $28 billion on West Bank settlements and security.

The first item in Table 7.1 is transfers to local authorities made by central government. This item consists of grants of various kinds designed to

[13] Tov, Imri. 2005. The Disengagement Price Tag. *Strategic Assessment*. Vol. 8. No. 3. http://www.inss.org.il/publications.php?cat=21&incat=&read=194

Table 7.1. *Spending on settlements in the territories,1967–2003 (billions of shekels, 2008 prices)*

Transfers to local authorities	11.8
Income tax benefits	1.7
Grants	0.5
Housing	12.2
Roads	11.1
Jewish Agency	3.0
Industrial Development	0.7
Water	1.3
Electricity	1.2
Police	1.6
Lottery Funding	1.6
Health benefits	1.9
Education benefits	1.9
Total	50.5

Source: Author's calculations from: The Cost of Settlements Supplement. 2003. *Haaretz* 26 September, p. 44.
http://www.haaretz.com/hasen/pages/ShArt.jhtml?item No=344399&contrassID=2&subContrassID=14&sbSubContrassID=0&listSrc=Y

enable local authorities to provide services. They are provided to many local authorities in Israel according to welfare criteria: Those authorities that do not have enough income to provide a nationally specified standard of services receive government help. In addition, those authorities that were selected for development programs of national importance receive assistance for their capital budgets. Until 2006, settlements in the West Bank and Gaza received significantly more assistance for current and capital purposes than other authorities in Israel. The differential between the amount granted to local authorities in the West Bank and that granted to local authorities reflects the government's preference for settlements on the West Bank rather than the criterion used inside the Green Line: compensation for their economic situation.

In 2006, local authorities in the West Bank and the Golan received 1,105 shekels per capita in government grants for their current budgets (in 2007 prices). The average grant in Israel was 370 shekels (prosperous local authorities received nothing). Development towns in Israel received

773 shekels, and Israeli Arab local authorities 940 shekels. The population of the West Bank settlements was estimated at 261,500 (see Table 7.1), and there were about 17,000 Israelis living in the Golan.[14] This suggests that the current grant was 3.1 billion shekels, or nearly 2.1 billion shekels higher than it would be if the per capita amount was the national average in Israel.

In addition, the government provides services directly to local authorities, and these were also differentiated. In 2006, Jewish West Bank and Golan local authorities received services worth 2,132 shekels per capita, compared with an average of 1,351 shekels in Israel, 1,557 shekels in development towns, and 1,548 shekels in Arab local authorities. The total value of the government services provided in the West Bank and the Golan was therefore 5.9 billion shekels. The extra value of services in the West bank and the Golan compared to the average level in Israel was 2.2 billion shekels, or 781 shekels per capita.

In 2006, investment per capita made by local authorities in the West Bank and Golan averaged 1,316 shekels, compared with 1,040 shekels in Israel as a whole, 1,067 in development towns, and 682 shekels in Arab local authorities. The difference between the West Bank and Golan and the Israeli average was 276 shekels per capita and the total value of this difference was 770 million shekels. The difference between the three items – current budget grants, government services provided, and capital grants – totaled 5.02 billion shekels ($1.23 billion at 2007 exchange rates).[15]

One of the costliest aspects of settlements has been the construction of roads. This is because they have to be linked to the center of the country and because in the West Bank, they require an almost separate network from the Palestinians for security reasons. In 2000–2006, the length of roads started per resident of the West Bank and Gaza was 2.5 times that for Israel (including the West Bank and Gaza).[16] In November 2008, it was estimated that 250 million shekels had been wasted on unused roads connecting settlements as a result of the construction of the separation wall and continuous adjustments in its route.[17]

[14] Central Bureau of Statistics. *Statistical Abstract of Israel 2007*. Table 2.10. http://www.cbs. gov.il/reader/shnaton/shnatone_new.htm?CYear=2007&Vol=58&CSubject=2

[15] Swirsky, Shlomo, Etty Konor-Attias and Ehud Dahan. 2008. Government Preferences in Financing Local Authorities 2000–2006. *Adva Center*. 15–64. http://www.adva.org/UserFiles/File/settlements%202000–2006%20final.pdf

[16] Swirski, Shlomo. 2008. The Cost of Occupation: The Burden of the Israeli-Palestinian Conflict, 2008 Report. *Adva Center*. http://www.adva.org/view.asp?lang=en&articleID=509

[17] Harel, Amos. 2008. "Israel Wastes 250 million Shekels on Settlement Roads to Nowhere." *Ha'aretz*, 21 November. http://www.haaretz.com/hasen/spages/1039508.html

There have been other negative effects of Israeli settlement building. It is beyond the scope of this book to evaluate their contribution to the Arab-Israeli conflict, but they have had direct effects on Israel's foreign economic relations. The most obvious example was the unwillingness of President George H. W. Bush to extend loan guarantees to Israel in 1991 because of settlement building. With the election of a Labor-led government under Yitzhak Rabin in June 1992 and the announcement of a change in priorities away from spending on settlements, the United States agreed to provide loan guarantees. As the Israeli government continued to spend money on settlements, a total of $1.36 billion was deducted from the volume of loan guarantees that were made available.[18]

How far did Israel's settlement activity contribute to the conflict and how much did that cost? These are very controversial issues, and one Israeli organization has tried to provide answers. It suggested that most of Israel's woes can be accounted for by the occupation of the West Bank (and Gaza) together with the construction of settlements.[19] The implication that an Israeli withdrawal from the territories occupied in 1967 would bring peace is questionable, but this does not invalidate the view that occupation and settlements have exacted high costs.

The *additional* cost of the settlements – above what they would have cost if they had been built in Israel – has been estimated at $8 billion for the period 1979–2008, or about 0.3 percent of annual national income.[20] This does not allow for the fact that had the settlements been built in Israel (either as separate villages and towns or as extensions of existing ones), then economic development inside the Green Line, Israel's 1967 border, would have been enhanced.

Economic Relations with the Palestinians

The Israeli economy has been affected by the occupation of the West Bank and Gaza in two main ways. The first is that these regions provided a source of cheap labor from 1967 until the 1990s. In 1992, the Palestinian workforce employed in Israel peaked at almost 115,600, or 7 percent of total

---

[18] Swirsky, Konor-Attias and Dahan, 64.

[19] Swirski, The Cost of Occupation.

[20] Kleiman, Ephraim. 2009. "'Not All the Result of the Occupation' – The Influence of 40 Years of Israeli Rule of the Palestinian Territories on the State of Israel," in Ephraim Lavie, ed. *40 Years of Occupation: The Effects on Israeli Society*. Tel Aviv: The Tami Steinitz Center for Peace, Tel Aviv University,191.

employees there. The second is that they formed markets that were almost exclusively supplied by Israel (see further in this chapter).

The Main Features of Israeli Policies
in the Territories

After Israel conquered the West Bank and other territories in 1967, a dispute broke out between the defense minister, Moshe Dayan, and Pinhas Sapir, the finance minister, about economic policy vis à vis the Palestinians. Dayan wanted an open border for goods and labor so as to tie the territories to Israel as tightly as possible. Sapir did not, fearing the growth of Palestinian nationalism and world opinion.[21] Initially the anxieties expressed by Sapir dominated government policy, but gradually Dayan's policies were implemented. This is reflected in the rise in the import of Palestinian labor from 1970 (see Figure 7.2).

Israeli policies had several aims. The first was to minimize the burden on the Israeli budget of administering the territories. The second was to prevent the entry of Palestinian agricultural or industrial goods into Israel where they had a price advantage over Israeli products. The final aspect of Israeli policy was to prevent the entrance of Palestinian workers into Israel where they too had the advantage of lower wages.[22] The restrictions on the movement of Palestinian labor broke down within a couple of years. Limits on Palestinian imports were maintained until the Oslo Agreements were signed. The development of Israeli settlements took land and water from the Palestinians. After 2002, the construction of the wall built by Israel to prevent the entry of terrorists had further consequences for Palestinian movement and access to land.

After 1967, the Israeli authorities took responsibility for maintaining basic welfare and ensuring employment in the territories, but limited both taxation and government spending. They did not, however, set themselves the task of developing the Palestinian economy. In 1968, the population of the West Bank was 579,100 and that of Gaza was 360,800.[23] The Palestinian private sector was weak, both because it was undeveloped and because the political and economic environment did not encourage risk taking. The

---

[21] Arnon, Arie, Israel Luski, Avia Spivak and Jimmy Weinblatt. 1997. *The Palestinian Economy*. Leiden: Brill, 4.16.

[22] Gazit, Shlomo. 2003. *Trapped Fools: Thirty Years of Israeli Policy in the Territories*. London and Portland: Frank Cass 16–17.

[23] Bregman, Arie. Economic Growth in the Administered Areas 1968–1973. Bank of Israel Research Department 1974. 29.

Figure 7.2. Employment of Palestinian West Bank and Gaza residents in Israel, 1968–2005.

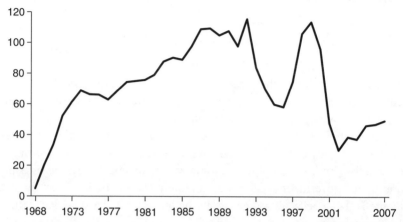

Sources: Israel, Central Bureau of Statistics, Publication no. 1012, (1996) National Accounts of Judea, Samaria and Gaza Area, 1968–1993; Bank of Israel Annual Report 2007.
* Includes employment in Israeli settlements in the West Bank and Gaza.

financial system was primitive and so savings could not easily be loaned to the private sector. Savings were largely channeled into housing: Investment in construction (mainly housing) rose from 2.3 percent in the West Bank and 4.6 percent in Gaza in 1968 to approximately 15 percent in both areas in 1986–1987. Under Israeli rule, public investment in the West Bank peaked at 6.5 percent of GDP in 1969 and in Gaza at 10 percent in 1975.[24] In 1987, housing accounted for 78 percent of private sector investment and 68 percent of total investment. Public sector investment was very low: In 1987, it equaled only 17 percent of total investment. Between 1987 and 1991, government investment fell by 32 percent. One of the most significant consequences of the pattern of investment was that firms remained very small.

In Gaza, the investment pattern, like much else, was more extreme. Although in 1991, total investment accounted for about 25 percent of GDP, 80 percent of it was in housing. The very large share of housing in total investment in Gaza was a permanent feature of the economy after 1967. By 1991, housing accounted for 66 percent of total investment in the West Bank. The combined effect of a weak private sector, political and economic uncertainty, and little government initiative meant that overall investment levels were low. This meant that infrastructure development was limited and that economic growth was severely restricted.

[24] Calculated from Arnon et al. 24, 122 and 125.

The Palestinian Economy

In the war that followed Israel's declaration of independence, the West Bank of the Jordan was conquered by forces of the Hashemite Kingdom of Jordan, whereas the Gaza region was conquered by Egypt. In 1950, Jordan annexed the West Bank. In that year, the West Bank had a population of 400,000 and Gaza had 200,000, both having absorbed hundreds of thousands of refugees from areas that became Israel. These refugees were supported by the United Nations through its United Nations Relief and Works Agency (UNRWA) that operates in refugee camps in those areas up to today.

In the period up to 1948, the East Bank of the Jordan had been reliant on the dynamism of the Jewish and Arab Palestinian economy. After 1948, the West Bank was left dependent on the much weaker East Bank. With limited resources available, the Hashemite kingdom concentrated investment on the East Bank, where the number of Palestinian Arabs was relatively small compared to the West Bank. The economy of the latter was dominated by agriculture that provided 50 percent of employment. Services were also important partly because of tourism in Jerusalem, which the government in Amman promoted. The amount of data on the West Bank economy for the period 1948–1967 is very small given that it was governed as part of Jordan from 1950. The Jordanian economy as a whole grew in those years, and the West Bank participated in that growth, something that enabled it to maintain a population that grew to 900,000 in 1967 after significant emigration.

The economy of Gaza was also dominated by agriculture and, to a lesser extent, trade. The presence of Egyptian army units, the Palestine Liberation Army, and UNRWA all provided additional sources of income and employment.[25]

Between 1968 and 1986, the gross national product of the West Bank and Gaza rose almost fivefold in real terms. As a result, GNP per capita increased by a factor of 3.38. Between 1986 and 1991, GNP rose by 40 percent in real terms; GNP per capita rose by 13 percent. The gap between GNP and GDP grew rapidly from 1968 because income earned in Israel played an increasingly important role in the economy. This rose from 3.3 percent of GDP in 1968 to 34 percent in 1986.

A macroeconomic overview suggests a major success story. Between 1968 and 1986, national disposable income rose 3.8-fold, in real terms, in the West Bank and 4.2-fold in Gaza, resulting in large increases in living

---

[25] Van Arkadie, Brian. 1977. *Benefits and Burdens: A Report on the West Bank and Gaza Strip Economies Since 1967*. New York and Washington, DC: Carnegie Endowment for Peace, 23–27.

standards. In fact, the economic development of the West Bank and Gaza was much more problematic because there was a great deal of instability, especially from the mid-1980s. In addition, from the 1980s, reliance on income and transfers from abroad played a much bigger role in the economy than in the late 1960s and 1970s but were much more unstable sources than domestic production.[26]

The creation of the Palestinian Authority in 1994 resulted in the large majority of the population of the West Bank coming under its control. This was also a period in which the fundamentalist Hamas organization started to attack Israeli civilians inside the Green Line. This led to the closure of the Israeli labor market and consequently a sharp fall in Palestinian income. Despite this, economic activity increased, as Israeli trade restrictions were eased and foreign aid flowed in. In 1994, although GNP, which included income earned by Palestinians abroad (largely in Israel), fell by 2.3 percent. GDP, which only includes income generated within the Palestinian territories, increased by 5.4 percent. In 1995, GNP fell by 9.4 percent and GDP fell by 5.5 percent, but in 1996, GNP fell by 6.9 percent whereas GDP increased by 8.1 percent.[27]

The outbreak of the Second Intifada in the autumn of 2000 resulted in widespread destruction and in that year, GDP fell by 5.4 percent. In 2001, it fell by 15 percent and in 2002 by 14.5 percent. In 2003, there was a modest recovery, but by the end of that year, GDP was more than 30 percent below its 1999 level.[28] The recovery continued in 2004–2005, when GDP grew by 6 percent a year. Then in 2006, following the victory of the fundamentalist Hamas in the Palestinian general elections and its takeover of Gaza, the economy crashed, recording negative growth in 2006 and 2007.[29]

The Import of Labor

The rapid growth of the Palestinian population in the West Bank and Gaza meant that the population of working age rose sharply and as a result the labor force increased. The working-age population rose from 521,000 in 1970 to 1.9 million in 2005. The share that worked outside the home or

---

[26] Rivlin, Paul. 2009. *Arab Economies in the Twenty First Century*. Cambridge and New York: Cambridge University Press, 192–217.

[27] Palestinian Monetary Authority, Department of Research and Monetary Policies. 1997. Monthly Statistical Bulletin July 1997. Ramallah, Palestinian Monetary Authority. 11.

[28] Economist Intelligence Unit. The Occupied Territories Country Profile 2005. London: Economist Intelligence Unit. 29.

[29] Economist Intelligence Unit. The Occupied Territories Country Profile 2008. 17.

looked for work there rose. The labor force rose from 147,000 in 1968 to 826,000 in 2005, a 5.6-fold rise compared to a 3.6-fold increase in the working-age population. As in other Arab countries, the population of working age has grown faster than that of the total population. Due to emigration, this was not reflected in the population statistics that measure the number of residents.

Since 1970, the reliance on employment in Israel meant that when – for security reasons – this was restricted, the economy suffered. Employment in Israel peaked in 1987, when 109,000 Palestinians were legally employed in Israel, equal to 39 percent of total Palestinian employment.[30] The trends since 1968 can be seen in Table 7.2. This shows the rapid increase from 1970, when the Israeli labor market was opened to Palestinian workers. They were attracted by the fact that there were jobs available and that those jobs paid more than those at home. Since the late 1960s, there have also been thousands of Palestinians who worked in Israel illegally. Reliance on the Israeli labor market meant dependence on Israel, something that benefited Israel in the short term. In the 1990s, Israel stopped importing Palestinian workers and replaced them with other foreign workers. This prevented serious damage to the Israeli economy, inflicted major damage on the Palestinian economy, and the political stalemate continued.

The start of the First Intifada in December 1987 resulted in a fall in Palestinian employment in Israel. The First Intifada ended in 1992, but terrorist attacks in Israel following the signing of the Oslo accords led to restrictions on the movement of Palestinians into Israel and their replacement by foreign workers, mainly from the Far East. In the second half of 1993, the Palestinian labor force numbered approximately 315,000 (16 percent of the population) and 260,000 were in employment. Each Palestinian at work had to support an average of seven people. Half of the West Bank and Gaza population was less than 15 years of age; the population became younger in the 1980s due to increasing fertility and declining child mortality. By 1995, some 66,000 Palestinians were employed in Israel and Israeli settlements in the West Bank and Gaza. In 1999, this rose to a peak of 135,000 but that represented only 12 percent of total employment. By 2002, the number had fallen to 49,000, or 9.6 percent of employment.[31] The jobs lost in Israel have not been made up elsewhere in the economy. Between 2000 and 2005, total employment increased by 37,000; that in the West Bank and Gaza grew

---

[30]   Arnon, Luski, Spivak and Weinblatt, *The Palestinian Economy*, 75.
[31]   World Bank. 2005. The Palestinian Economy and the Prospects for Its Recovery. Economic Monitoring Report to the Ad Hoc Liaison Committee, no. 1, 9.

Table 7.2. *Israeli net exports to and imports of goods from the West Bank
and Gaza, 1967–2008 ($ millions)*

	Exports to the West Bank and Gaza	Exports to West Bank and Gaza as percent of total Israeli exports	Imports from the West Bank and Gaza	Imports from West Bank and Gaza as percent of total Israeli imports
1970	55	7.5	16	1.1
1980	351	6.6	111	1.4
1990	714	6.2	181	1.2
1995	1,521	8.6	242	0.8
2000	1,535	5.4	280	0.8
2005	2,097	5.7	312	0.7
2007	2,604	5.7	531	0.9
2008	3,256	6.3	566	0.9

Source: Central Bureau of Statistics Statistical Abstract of Israel, 1996, 2008, 2009.
Arnon, Arie, Israel Luski, Avia Spivak and Jimmy Weinblatt. 1997. *The Palestinian Economy*.
Leiden: Brill.

by 88,000 while that of Palestinians in Israel fell by 52,000. The labor force
rose by 131,000 and as a result unemployment increased by 94,000. (The
figures do not add up because of rounding) By 2005, the population of the
West Bank and Gaza had reached 3.5 million and the labor force was about
790,000 (23 percent of the population), of whom 590,000 were in employment (75 percent of the labor force and 17 percent of the population).[32]

Although there have been fluctuations as a result of the Second Intifada,
the labor force grew even faster than the working-age population because of
an increase until 2000 in labor force participation. Between 2001 and 2005,
the labor force participation rate fell from 40.9 percent to 38.6 percent,
although the labor force increased from 675,000 to 826,000, or 22 percent.
Employment in Israel fell from 116,000 in 2000 to 64,000 in 2005, and that
in the West Bank and Gaza fell from 435,000 to 241,000.[33] Female labor
force participation was much lower than in other Arab countries: In 2000,
it was only 13 percent, compared to 22 percent in Egypt and 40 percent in
Morocco. The figure for Gaza was 10 percent.[34]

[32] World Bank. 2006. West Bank and Gaza Country Economic Memorandum, Vol. 1 Report
no. 36320 WBG. Washington DC: World Bank, 2.
[33] World Bank. 2005. World Bank Monitoring Report. December, 9.
[34] World Bank. 2002. Long Term Policy Options for the Palestinian Economy. 34.

Trade between Israel and the Territories

In 1992 and 1993, Israeli and Palestinian negotiators held secret talks in Norway that led to the Oslo Agreement, signed on September 13, 1993, in the White House in Washington, DC. The agreement was a declaration of principles, including mutual recognition: Israel recognized the Palestine Liberation Organization (PLO) as the legitimate representative of the Palestinian people, and the PLO recognized Israel's right to exist. The declaration stated that negotiations would begin to establish a Palestinian Authority that would have would have limited powers for an interim period of five years. During that period, negotiators planned to reach a permanent settlement.*

---

* In 1993, The Oslo Accords, officially called the Declaration of Principles on Interim Self-Government Arrangements or Declaration of Principles (DOP), were signed. It was the first directly negotiated agreement between the government of Israel and political representatives of the Palestinian people. It was intended to be the framework for future negotiations and relations between Israel and the Palestinians, within which all outstanding "final status issues" between the two sides would be dealt with.

Negotiations concerning the agreements were completed in Oslo, Norway, on 20 August 1993, and the Accords was officially signed subsequently at a public ceremony in Washington, DC, on 13 September 1993 in the presence of Palestinian Liberation Organisation (PLO) chairman Yasser Arafat, Israeli Prime Minister Yitzhak Rabin, and U.S. President Bill Clinton. The Accords provided for the creation of a Palestinian National Authority that would have responsibility for the administration of the territory under its control. The Accords also called for the withdrawal of the IDF from parts of the Gaza Strip and West Bank.

It was anticipated that this arrangement would last for a five-year interim period, during which a permanent agreement would be negotiated (beginning no later than May 1996). Permanent issues such as Jerusalem, Palestinian refugees, Israeli settlements, security, and borders were deliberately left to be decided at a later stage. Interim self-government was to be granted by Israel in phases.

Along with the principles, the two parties signed *Letters of Mutual Recognition* – the Israeli government recognized the PLO as the legitimate representative of the Palestinian people, whereas the PLO recognized the right of the state of Israel to exist and renounced terrorism and other violence, as well as its desire for the destruction of the Israeli state. The aim of Israeli-Palestinian negotiations was to establish a Palestinian Interim Self-Government Authority, an elected Council, for the Palestinian people in the West Bank and the Gaza Strip for a transitional period not exceeding five years, leading to a permanent settlement based on UN Security Council Resolutions 242 and 338, both integral parts of the peace process. To ensure the Palestinians govern themselves according to democratic principles, free and general political elections would be held for the Council. Jurisdiction of the Palestinian Council would cover the West Bank and Gaza Strip, except for issues that would be finalized in the permanent status negotiations. The two sides viewed the West Bank and Gaza as a single territorial unit.

The five-year transitional period would commence with Israeli withdrawal from the Gaza Strip and Jericho area. Permanent status negotiations would begin as soon as possible between Israel and the Palestinians. The negotiations would cover remaining issues

The 1994 Paris Accord

In April 1994, an economic agreement between Israel and the PLO was signed in Paris that has been largely determined by the political framework. As no border between Palestine and Israel was defined (an issue that was supposed to be determined later), the economic options were limited. A free trade agreement (FTA), under which each party maintained its own external tariff, would have required a border between the two parties to prevent imports into the party with the lower external tariff leaking into the one with the higher external tariff, given that no internal tariffs are permitted in an FTA. With no border fixed in the Oslo Agreement, this option was rejected. Another option would have been complete separation (as has largely happened since 2000). This would also have required a border and would also have prevented Palestinians working in Israel, something that the Palestinian negotiators in Paris were anxious to avoid. As a result, a

including: Jerusalem, Palestinian refugees, Israeli settlements, security arrangements, borders, relations and cooperation with other neighbors, and other issues of common interest. There would be a transfer of authority from the IDF to the authorized Palestinians concerning education and culture, health, social welfare, direct taxation, and tourism. The Council would establish a police force, whereas Israel would continue to be responsible for external defense. An Israeli-Palestinian Economic Cooperation Committee would be established to develop and implement in a cooperative manner the programs identified in the protocols.

The Gaza-Jericho Agreement was signed in Cairo in May 1994 under the patronage of the United States, Russia, and Egypt, and dealt with the implementation of the Declaration of Principles. This agreement marked the beginning of the Interim Period and determined the arrangements for the Israeli withdrawal from Gaza and Jericho and the establishment of a Palestinian Self-Governing Authority (the Palestinian Authority) bearing legislative and executive powers and authorities.

The "Interim Agreement" of September 1995, officially entitled "The Israeli-Palestinian Interim Agreement for the West Bank and Gaza Strip," was the Second Interim Agreement signed between Israel and the Palestinians. The objective of this Agreement was to regulate the relations between Israel and the Palestinians during the interim period toward negotiations for a Permanent Status Agreement. The Interim Agreement was a part of the Oslo Process, which began with the Declaration of Principles. The principles of the declaration were intended to lead Israel and the Palestinians toward a Permanent Status Agreement on the basis of The Framework of Future Negotiations with the Palestinians, signed between Israel and Egypt as a part of the 1978 Camp David Accords. According to the Declaration of Principles, Israel is required to gradually transfer powers and authorities to a Self-Governing Palestinian Authority over a five-year interim Period, during which time, negotiations for a Permanent Status Agreement would commence. According to this framework, the Gaza-Jericho Agreement was signed between Israel and the Palestinians, which established a Self-Governing Palestinian Authority in Gaza and Jericho (the Palestinian Authority [PA]). The signing of the Gaza-Jericho Agreement marked the beginning of the Interim Period. The objective of the Interim Agreement was to regulate the relations between the parties within the aforementioned period. In fact, the Interim Agreement

customs union (in which the countries or parties in the union maintain a common external tariff and remove restrictions on trade between them) or something close to it was the only option. Under the Paris agreement, Israel and the Palestinian Authority were to have similar import policies. The Palestinian Authority was allowed to import mutually agreed goods at customs rates differing from those prevailing in Israel and to import goods from Arab countries in limited quantities.

The agreement provided for the free movement of goods manufactured in the autonomous areas into Israel and vice versa. Agricultural produce from the autonomous areas could enter Israel freely for the first time, with limited and temporary exceptions for which there would be quotas. Tourists would be allowed to move freely between Israel and the autonomous areas. The Palestinian Authority was permitted to establish a monetary authority whose main functions would be the regulation and supervision of banks, but there would not be a Palestinian currency. The

replaced the Gaza-Jericho Agreement as well as two additional detailed agreements dealing with the transfer of powers and authorities to the Palestinians (see note 26). The Interim Agreement deals with security arrangements, the elections to the Palestinian Legislative Council, transfer of authorities, justice, economics, and other joint issues. Israel's military administration will withdraw from the central cities of the West Bank. The West Bank and Gaza Strip will be divided into three areas: area A – jurisdiction over security and administrative responsibilities will be transferred to the Palestinians; area B – control over security will remain in Israel's hands, however, administrative duties will be transferred to the Palestinians; area C – Israel would retain security and administrative jurisdiction.

Israel would no longer retain administrative responsibilities in areas A and B. Administrative duties in those areas would be assigned to the Palestinians. The West Bank and Gaza Strip would be recognized as a Single Territorial Unit, with the exception of issues that will be negotiated in Permanent Status negotiations. Elections for the Palestinian Legislative Council and for the head of the executive authority of the Council would take place. They would be elected for a time period not exceeding five years from the signing of the "Gaza-Jericho Agreement." The elected Palestinian Council would have legislative authority, executive authority, and the power to oversee and enforce police matters in the territories under its control; however, it would not have the authority to manage an independent foreign policy. Except for issues that would be addressed in Permanent Status negotiations, jurisdiction over the territory of the West Bank and Gaza Strip would be transferred to the Palestinian Council. The transfer would take place gradually and would be completed within eighteen months from the time of establishment of the Council. A Palestinian police force would be established to maintain order and internal security, whereas Israel would retain responsibility over external security. Palestinian police officers in uniform would be authorized to carry weapons. A joint committee including Israel, Jordan, Egypt, and the Palestinians would decide the admission criteria for persons who were displaced from the West Bank and Gaza Strip in 1967. Permanent Status negotiations would cover the historical issues between the two parties and would commence no later than May 4, 1996. Within two months of the establishment of the Council, the Palestinian National Council would convene and formally ratify the obligation of the PLO to change all relevant clauses of the Palestinian National Charter which refer to the destruction of the State of Israel.[36]

Palestinian Tax Administration would conduct its own direct tax policies. Israel would transfer to the Palestinian Authority 75 percent of the
revenues from income tax collected from Palestinians employed in Israel.
Israel would continue to collect import duties on goods destined for the PA
but would transfer those funds to the Authority. A value added tax (VAT)
would be operated by the Palestinian Authority with rates up to 3 percent
higher or lower than in Israel. Finally, Israel agreed to keep its labor market
open for Palestinian workers while reserving the right to place restrictions
on the inflow for security reasons.[37]

There have been a range of critiques of the Paris protocols by Palestinians,
Israelis, and others. One Palestinian critique was that the protocols served
tactical political interests: They were designed to support the political
agreements that gave the Palestinians autonomy in limited areas of the West
Bank and Gaza. It was not clear whether peace would bring about improvements in the Palestinian standard of living or vice versa. In the end, neither
has occurred. The mechanics of the protocol also enabled Israel to avoid
transferring funds fairly to the Palestinians, and as a result, the stronger side
was able to bankrupt the weaker one. Although a full political agreement
was not necessarily a precondition for economic success, the economic
agreement needed to be fairer if it was to support political moves toward
a final settlement.[38] Another critique, made by some Israelis, was that the
agreement was drawn up against a background of political and economic
inequality between the parties and in effect froze them in that position. The
economic agreement did not take into account Palestinian political aspira-
tions. It set custom duties at rates that suited Israel rather than Palestine
(or at rates weighted by their relative needs). It enabled Israel to close its
labor market to Palestinians when security concerns prevailed, leaving the
Palestinians without control over either their trade or employment. It was

[36] Ministry of Foreign Affairs. 1993. Declaration of Principles on Interim Self-
Government Arrangements. 13 September. http://www.mfa.gov.il/MFA/Peace+Process/
Guide+to+the+Peace+Process/Declaration+of+Principles.htm; Ministry of Foreign
Affairs. 1994. Agreement on the Gaza Strip and Jericho Area. 4 May. http://www.mfa.
gov.il/MFA/Peace+Process/Guide+to+the+Peace+Process/Agreement+on+Gaza+
Strip+and+Jericho+Area.htm; Ministry of Foreign Affairs. 1995. Israeli-Palestinian
Interim Agreement on the West Bank and the Gaza Strip. 28 September. http://www.
mfa.gov.il/MFA/Peace+Process/Guide+to+the+Peace+Process/THE+ISRAELI-
PALESTINIAN+INTERIM+AGREEMENT.htm.

[37] Israel, Ministry of Foreign Affairs Website, http://www.mfa.gov.il (accessed 14 September
2005).

[38] Kanafani, Nu'man. 2004. "Economic Foundations for Peace," in Hassan Hakimian and
Jeffrey B. Nugent, eds. *Trade Policy and Economic Integration in the Middle East and North
Africa*. London: Routledge Curzon, 271–289.

what has been called an "incomplete contract," because it failed to specify what was to happen in all contingencies. This was not because the political agreements were transitory and designed to be followed by negotiations on final status agreements, but because they did not specify what was to happen in all eventualities. As a result, when political and military conditions deteriorated, the Paris Protocol was doomed. Although a full political agreement did not have to *precede* economic agreements, the latter had to contain major political changes for it to succeed.[39]

In this context it is interesting to note that the United Nations outlined conditions for economic cooperation between an Arab and a Jewish state in its 1947 resolution dividing Palestine.*

Between 1967 and 1994, the trading pattern between Israel and the West Bank and Gaza partly resembled that between those Arab states in the Mediterranean with European Union (EU) partnership agreements and the EU. The main Arab/Palestinian export (agricultural products) was restricted or even banned whereas the main EU/Israeli export (industrial goods) was permitted. In the case of the EU, this was implemented immediately; in the case of Israel, it was implemented from 1967. Palestinian industry was fully exposed to Israeli competition whereas its agricultural production was barred from Israeli markets until 1994. Although the Paris accord opened Israeli markets to Palestinian produce, the extremely weak state of Palestinian industry

---

[39] Arnon, A. and J. Weinblatt. 2001. "Sovereignty and Economic Development: The Case of Palestine." *Economic Journal.* F291–F308.

* In November 1947, the United Nations General Assembly adopted Resolution 181 calling for an end of the Mandate as soon as possible and the creation of independent Jewish and Arab states in Palestine. It also called for an economic union to be created between the two new states. This is significant in view of attempts in the 1990s to developed economic relations between Israel and the Palestinian authority.

According to the United Nation's resolution, the objectives of the Economic Union of Palestine would include a customs union; a joint currency system providing for a single foreign exchange rate; the operation in the common interest on a non-discriminatory basis of railways; inter-state highways; postal, telephone, and telegraphic services, and port and airports involved in international trade and commerce; joint economic development, especially in respect of irrigation, land reclamation, and soil conservation, and access for both states and for the City of Jerusalem on a non-discriminatory basis to water and power facilities.

A Joint Economic Board would be established, consisting of three representatives of each of the two States and three foreign members appointed by the Economic and Social Council of the United Nations. The foreign members shall be appointed in the first instance for a term of three years; they shall serve as individuals and not as representatives of States. The Board's purpose would be to implement measures necessary to realize the objectives of the Economic Union. The two states were to commit themselves to put into effect the decisions of the Joint Economic Board that would be taken by a majority vote.

The functions of the Board would be to plan, investigate, and encourage joint development projects, but it would not undertake such projects except with the assent of both

meant that it had little to export. Furthermore, in the early 1990s, Israel liberalized its foreign trade and that meant Chinese and other cheap sources entered its markets, making it harder for the Palestinians to compete.

In 1968, Israel accounted for 66 percent of the exports of the West Bank and Gaza and 65 percent of imports. By 1973, it accounted for 90 percent of imports into the Territories (the West Bank and Gaza) and 66 percent of their exports.[40] The Territories were much less important to Israel's foreign trade (see Table 7.2).

Although Israeli exports of goods and services to the West Bank and Gaza rose in nominal terms, their share in total Israeli exports fell. In 1988, they were $808 million, or 7.1 percent; in 2008, they came to $3 billion, or 4 percent. Palestinian exports of goods and services to Israel also rose from $161 million to $753 million over the same period, but their share of total Israeli imports fell from 1.2 percent to 0.9 percent.

Conclusions

Israel has spent billions of dollars building villages and towns in the territories occupied in 1967. These settlements have added to costs because Israelis have settled in hostile areas and may have to be moved out as they were from Gaza in 2005–2006 and from the Sinai following the peace treaty with Egypt. They have stretched resources that could have been used to develop peripheral settlements in Israel, limiting the gains from economies

States and the City of Jerusalem, in the event that Jerusalem is directly involved in the development project.

Under the joint currency system, the currencies circulating in the two States and the City of Jerusalem would be issued under the authority of the Joint Economic Board, which would be the sole issuing authority and which shall determine the reserves to be held against such currencies. A common customs tariff would be created with complete freedom of trade between the States, and between the States and the City of Jerusalem. The tariff schedules would be drawn up by a Tariff Commission, consisting of representatives of each of the States in equal numbers, and would be submitted to the Joint Economic Board for approval by a majority vote. In case of disagreement in the Tariff Commission, the Joint Economic Board would arbitrate the points of difference. In the event that the Tariff Commission fails to draw up any schedule by a date to be fixed, the Joint Economic Board shall determine the tariff schedule (United Nations. 1947. General Assembly Resolution 181 (II) The Future Government of Palestine. 29 November. http://unispal.un.org/unispal.nsf/0/7F0AF2BD897689B785256C33 0061D253). The resolution to create Arab and Jewish states was accepted by the governing body of the Jewish community in Palestine and rejected by the Arabs. The passing of the resolution led to a major increase in violence between the two communities in Palestine that were nominally under British rule.

[40] Calculated from Arie Bregman. 1975. *Economic Growth in the Administered Territories, 1968–1973*. Second edition. Jerusalem: Bank of Israel, 84.

of scale and concentration. As a result, development inside the country has been slowed.

By locating Israelis in the West Bank and in East Jerusalem (and previously in Gaza), conflict with the Palestinians has increased. Building access roads, sometimes exclusively for these settlements, has consumed even more land that the Palestinians, much of the international community, and many Israelis consider belonging to the Palestinians. Guarding the settlements and the roads leading to them has added to defense costs each year. Their removal will have to be paid for by the government through taxation and/or borrowing at home. All these have welfare implications and effects on economic growth, although if done in the right political context, they may yield political and economic gains in terms of peace.

Israeli policies have severely restricted Palestinian development, which created dependence on Israeli labor markets. The latter had negative effects on the construction industry and other sectors of the Israeli economy. The failure to allow or encourage Palestinian industrialization had major negative effects on the Palestinian economy, social structure, and politics, discouraging the development of the middle class and contributing to the rise of the Hamas. This has deepened and lengthened the conflict, with major implications for the Israeli economy. None of this lessens the responsibility of the Palestinians. The conduct, at least until recently, of the Palestinian authority regarding corruption and monopolies and the destruction of their own infrastructure by the Palestinians in the Second Intifada all seriously damaged their economy.[41]

---

[41] Rivlin, *Arab Economies in the Twenty-First Century*, chapter 9.

EIGHT

The Economics of Religion

Religion plays an unusual and large role in the Israeli economy. This is mainly because of the ultra-orthodox Jewish community (known in Hebrew as Haredi, or fearful of God) that numbers about 600,000, or about 8 percent of the population.[1] There are a range of estimates of the size of the ultra-orthodox community depending on the measures used.[2] Its population is heavily concentrated in Jerusalem and Bnei Brak, near Tel Aviv, and is spreading to other towns, especially in the West Bank. As a result of its religious beliefs and the political power it has accumulated, the ultra-orthodox community has been able to limit its interaction with the rest of society while obtaining large economic benefits from it. As a result, it has been able to maintain a way of life that limits participation in the labor force, reduce the amount of secular learning (mathematics, science, humanities, civics, and English) in its schools, and avoid army service. It also has a high birth rate resulting in large families and rapid growth of its population, largely made possible by government assistance. These factors impose heavy costs on the economy that are almost unique to Israel. To understand the economics of religion in Israel, it is essential to understand the politics of religion. This is examined here and in Chapter 11. This chapter concludes with an analysis of the allocation of public funds for religious services that are, in theory, available to the whole community. It will show how these have been largely captured by a section of the population that monopolizes their use.

---

[1] Bank of Israel. *Annual Report 2007.* Chapter 8. http://www.bankisrael.gov.il/deptdata/mehkar/doch07/eng/pe_8.pdf and CBS, Statistical Abstract of Israel 2008. Table 2.1.

[2] Gottlieb, Daniel. 2007. *Poverty and Labor Market Behaviour in the Ultra-Othodox Population in Israel.* Jerusalem: The Van Leer Jerusalem Institute; Berman, Eli. 2000. "Sect, Subsidy and Sacrifice: An Economist's View of Ultra-Orthodox Jews." *Quarterly Journal of Economics.* Vol. 115. No. 3. 43.

The Ultra-orthodox

Ultra-orthodox, or Haredi, is the most theologically conservative form of Judaism. Haredi is derived from the Hebrew word meaning fear or anxiety, and is interpreted in the biblical context as "one who trembles in awe of God." Ultra-orthodox Judaism is highly ritualistic and attempts to preserve the lifestyle – including the clothing – of the Eastern European village of hundreds of years ago.

Ultra-orthodox Jews consider their belief system and religious practices to date back to the giving of the Torah to Moses on Mount Sinai as described in the Bible. As a result, they regard non-ultra-orthodox streams of Judaism to be unacceptable deviations from authentic Judaism. The phenomenon of ultra-orthodox Judaism dates back to a period in which Jews in Eastern and Central Europe were beginning to become secular, and it was a form of reaction to what they considered the abandonment of Judaism.[3] The majority of ultra-orthodox Jews were Ashkenazi or of Eastern European origin, but in the last twenty years, the Sephardic ultra-orthodox movement has overshadowed it, at least politically. The ultra-orthodox community has adopted a policy of strict separation from the rest of society, but at the same time it is politically active, considering itself the protector of Judaism and seeking to preserve its position in a largely secular society.

The issues that divide the ultra-orthodox and the rest of the Jewish community in Israel date back to the late nineteenth century and the rise of the Zionist movement. Zionists and other Jews were profoundly influenced by the secular trends that became powerful in late-nineteenth-century Europe. The ultra-orthodox rejected this in general, as well as Zionism in particular. The objection to Zionism was its claim that Jewish political independence could be obtained without divine intervention and the coming of the Messiah. Any attempt to force history was seen by the ultra-orthodox as a rejection of Judaism. This was reinforced by the rejection by many Zionists of religion in general and ultra-orthodoxy in particular. Many Zionists considered the ultra-orthodox outdated or even primitive and often parasitic. The ultra-orthodox often considered the Zionists as tyrannizing heretics. This *Kulturkampf* still exists in Israeli society.

The modus vivendi that exists today, with all its tensions, dates back to compromises reached between the Labor leadership of the Yishuv and the ultra-orthodox leadership during the British Mandate. A division of labor

[3] Berman, 9.

was established in which the Zionist leadership had political authority but delegated control over marriage, divorce, conversions to Judaism, burials, and other religious matters to the ultra-orthodox and orthodox communities. The Orthodox (sometimes referred to as "modern Orthodox") have similar beliefs to the ultra-orthodox but carry out their religious obligations with a modern style of life (including dress) and are part of the Zionist mainstream. After the creation of the state, an agreement was reached between the government and the religious parties, including the ultra-orthodox, that the government would exempt 400 religious scholars from military service so that they could pursue their studies. This number now exceeds 40,000 who do not serve in the conscript army and over 60,000 who do not serve in the military reserves.

Until the 1980s, despite these arrangements, many ultra-orthodox groups maintained an apolitical stance. The Ashkenazi ultra-orthodox was split into two political movements: Agudat Israel that cooperated with the government and the others that fiercely opposed it. Agudat Israel was invited to participate in governing coalitions. It agreed but did not appoint any ministers since doing so would have implied full acceptance of the legitimacy of non-religious actions taken by the government. It has therefore appointed deputy ministers and chairmen of the powerful Knesset finance committee. These politicians are appointed by the rabbis who control much of the life of the ultra-orthodox community. Furthermore, the ultra-orthodox population has grown rapidly, giving it a larger power base. In the 1977 Knesset elections, ultra-orthodox parties won four seats and gradually increased the number to eight in 1984, ten in 1992, fourteen in 1996, and twenty-two in 1999. In 2003, they won sixteen seats; in 2006, they won eighteen seats, and in 2009 they won sixteen seats. For much of the last thirty years, they have controlled the balance of power between the country's two major parties, but in the 2003 general election, they lost seats and were not included in the government. Major policy changes were made that undermined one of their most important achievements. This centered on the issue of child allowances, discussed further in this chapter.

Until the early 1980s, ultra-orthodox political activity had been confined to the Ashkenazi community. In 1984, a Sephardic ultra-orthodox party, Shas, was founded. The party was formed under the spiritual leadership of Rabbi Ovadia Yosef, who remains its leader today. In founding the party, Yosef received help and guidance from one of the leaders of the Ashkenazi ultra-orthodox. To restore Sephardic pride and religious observance, Shas has created cadres of newly religious and semi-religious men and women who often had an animosity toward the country's secular European leadership. Its supporters have been loyal and obedient to the teachings of its spiritual leader. By the mid-1990s, Shas was mired in a scandal after the indictment and subsequent conviction and imprisonment of its former party leader, Aryeh Deri, on corruption charges. Even though Rabbi Ovadia Yosef distanced the party from Deri, many Shas voters saw him as the victim of a discriminatory political witch hunt against the Sephardic community and continue to support him. Following Deri's conviction, in the 1999 elections, Shas gained seventeen seats, its strongest showing ever. In the 2003 election, Shas was reduced to eleven seats and was not included in the governing coalition. In the elections of 2006, it gained twelve seats and joined the government, and in the 2009 elections, it won eleven seats and joined the government. A disproportionate number of Shas politicians have been convicted and imprisoned for corruption and other crimes.

There are four main interrelated characteristics of the ultra-orthodox community that need to be examined. The first is that the majority of ultra-orthodox men and women do not work. The second is that they do not serve in the army. The third is that they have large families, and the fourth is that many of them are poor.

These factors are vividly illustrated in an official report on the town of Beitar Ilit. Construction of the town, located southwest of Jerusalem and in the West Bank, began in 1990. It was designed for the ultra-orthodox population that could no longer find affordable housing in such traditional centers as Jerusalem or Bnei Brak. At the end of 2003, it had a population of 23,000, 94 percent of whom were ultra-orthodox. At that time, the average number of people living in each home was 4.9, and over 20 percent of homes had six or more people living in them. Nearly 10 percent of women and 7 percent of men had an academic education. Thirty-five percent of women and 58 percent of men had other education beyond high school. In the case of men, this usually meant religious education. Among those of working age, 52.5 percent did not work; 64.3 percent of men and 45.8 percent of women. The main reasons given by women for not working were work at home (63.4 percent) and unemployment (26.7 percent). Among men, religious study was the explanation given by 79.7 percent whereas unemployment was the explanation given by 5.4 percent.[4] In 2006, the population of Beitar Ilit was 29,100 and in 2007, it was estimated at 35,000 – an increase of 20 percent in one year![5] Beitar Ilit is a town in which

---

[4] Degani, Avi and Rina Degani. 2004. Characteristics of the Housing Market in Beitar Ilit and Recommendations for Marketing Land in the Settlement. Geocatography Knowledge Group, for the Ministry of Housing, 47–57. http://www.moch.gov.il/NR/rdonlyres/B5711295-153D-4A66-89FC-28D492D5BF89/1572/sekerYeshuvBeytarIlit.pdf

[5] Ministry of Interior. Local Authorities in Israel 2006. Publication No. 1315. http://www.moin.gov.il/Apps/PubWebSite/publications.nsf/All/7EDFB6D72D07F81FC22574B30031

over half of the population of working age does not work. Only 17.4 percent of those who did not work said this was because they were unemployed, with the implication that they wanted to work. These patterns are similar in other new ultra-orthodox settlements in the West Bank, such as Modi'in Ilit and Emanuel. It may become true in the ultra-orthodox town of Harish planned to be built in Wadi Ara in Northern Israel.[6]

Allocations to the Ultra-orthodox
and Their Implications

Most of what is spent on religion goes to the ultra-orthodox community. This is partly because it receives large welfare benefits. The justification for this is that most ultra-orthodox families are poor. Most of their entitlements are not exclusive: Others who have similar needs also receive almost the same benefits. Some benefits, however, such as those for housing in specifically ultra-orthodox or income supplements for ultra-orthodox students, are exclusively for them. What is specific to the ultra-orthodox is the way in which the state has created the situation in which a whole community has largely come to rely on welfare.

Government allocations to the ultra-orthodox community have significant economic effects. The state-funded, but not state-controlled, ultra-orthodox education prepares boys for a life of religious study. Thousands complete school and then continue in institutions for religious education at the higher level, known as yeshivot or kollelim (seminaries). Their studies at these institutions are free, unlike students who go to university or colleges of higher education. In addition, they and their families are eligible for a range of benefits including implicit housing subsidies, local tax reductions, reduced national insurance payments, rent subsidies, and allowances for their children's nursery education. For those aged 18–22, a condition for receiving army service deferments is that they study and do not work. This whole procedure has resulted in an increase in the burden of military service on the rest of the population, and is a deeply divisive issue.

The main effect of state allocations to ultra-orthodox students has been a massive rise in their number. Traditionally, in Eastern Europe, in the nineteenth and early twentieth century, a life of religious study was reserved for the most able students and was funded by their families or by private

F767/$FILE/Publications.pdf; Shragai, Nadav. 2008. "Open Element and Ultra-Orthodox Jews Deliver a Population Boom to the West Bank." *Ha'aretz*, 14 August.

[6] Ministry of Construction and Housing. Press Notice 5 August 2008. http://www.moch. gov.il/NR/exeres/6CAED619–3D14–4914-B9A9-C2E9EDFAD1D0.htm

charity. In Israel, a much larger priesthood has been created, including many students who do not pass any objective tests to measure their suitability for these studies. This community has come to rely on state handouts, something that is very significant given the large size of most ultra-orthodox families. The most important of these are child benefits that were, until 2002, strongly biased toward large families, payments to students in religious study programs, other welfare benefits, and charitable donations.

The most significant way in which this developed was the right given to ultra-orthodox men to indefinitely defer army service (both the compulsory conscription of men for three years and then reserve duty) if they study in a religious seminary. In 1977, restrictions on the number receiving such deferments were lifted. In 1997, 3,000 deferments were granted, equal to about 7.5 percent of the males eligible for call-up.[7] In 1999, 9.2 percent were granted deferments, equal to about 3,800, and the number has continued to rise since then.[8] The condition of maintaining deferment and eventually changing it into an exemption is that the deferment holder does not work. The effects of this were not only on the budget, in terms of allocations of spending, but also in terms of losses of output.

Figure 8.1 shows how the number of male students in religious seminaries has increased since the early 1970s. Nearly all of these students get exemptions from military service. Initially this applies to the 18–21-year-olds (*greater yeshivot*) who are at the age of compulsory military service. If they continue to further study in *kollelim* then their exemption continues and they do not serve in the reserves.

Output Losses

The fact that a significant number of men were able to devote themselves to religious study meant that they did not participate in the labor force. Those that did enter the labor force after studying in a religious seminary were likely to earn less and/or suffer more from unemployment than those that did not. The economy lost production and the state lost tax revenues on the earnings forgone. Table 8.1 presents an estimate of the value of output lost to the economy using the method outlined in Chapter 6. It shows how much more output was lost during the period 1998–2007. There is an overlap with the figure for

7   Berman, Eli and Ruth Klinov. 1995. Human Capital Investment and Nonparticipation: Evidence from a Sample with Infinite Horizons. Jerusalem: The Maurice Falk Institute for Economic Research in Israel, Discussion Paper Series, no. 97. 24–27.
8   Berman and Klinov, 3–5. Ilan, Shahar. 2009. "The Knesset Is Evading the Draft." *Ha'aretz*, 17 September.

Figure 8.1. Number of religious seminary students, 1971–2007.

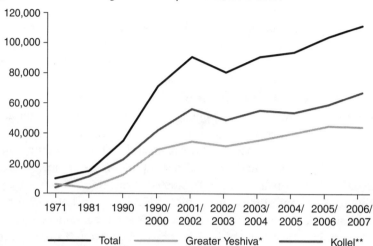

These figures include some non-Israelis.
* unmarried men 18 years and over
** married men
Sources: Eli Berman and Ruth Klinov, Human Capital Investment and Nonparticipation: Evidence from a Sample with Infinite Horizons; Ministry of Religion, Budget 2000; Central Bureau of Statistics, Statistical Abstract of Israel 2008.

output losses in Chapter 6 because both include the loss due to ultra-orthodox men aged eighteen to twenty-one years not being in the labor force.

Between 2002 and 2007, the share of ultra-orthodox men participating in the labor force rose from 42 percent to 53.5 percent whereas that of ultra-orthodox women fell from 53.3 percent to 51 percent, having peaked at 58.6 percent in 2004.[9] The participation rate of ultra-orthodox women was lower than that of Orthodox women and much lower than that of secular women.[10]

Fertility and Child Allowances

The most outstanding feature of ultra-orthodox life in Israel is the large average size of their families. This is illustrated in Table 8.2 that shows the fertility rate in six Israeli towns that have an almost entirely Jewish population. The first three towns have a largely secular population and the second

[9] Central Bureau of Statistics. Press Announcement. http://www.cbs.gov.il/reader/newhodaot/ hodaa_template.html?hodaa=200819206
[10] The Knesset. 2008. Encouraging Employment of Haredi Women. *Research and Information Center.* http://www.knesset.gov.il/mmm/data/pdf/m02006.pdf

Table 8.1. *Output losses due to ultra-orthodox non-participation in the labor market, 1998–2007 (current prices)*

	1998	2006/7*
1. Net Domestic Product (NDP), millions of shekels	283,895	622,746
2. Share of labor in national income	0.75	0.58
3. Labor's share of NDP (1 x 2), millions of shekels	212,921	316,193
4. Number employed, million	2.077	2.969
5. Labor's of share of NDP /head (3/4), shekels	102,514	121,657
6. Number of male students in religious seminaries	34,230	112,000
7. Loss of output (5 x 6), millions of shekels	3,509	13,625
8. Exchange rate ($=shekels)	3.8	4.11
9. Loss of output in millions of dollars (7/8)	923	3,317
10. Loss of output as share of GDP	0.8	2.0

* Based on estimated data

Source: Ministry of Religious Affairs 1990–1998 budgets (Jerusalem, 1989–1997); CBS, Statistical Abstracts of Israel, 1998 and 2008; National Accounts 1995–1998, Current Statistics, no. 27, 1999; Labor Force Survey 1998, Current Statistics, no. 7, 1999; and author's calculations.

Table 8.2. *Fertility rates in selected communities with populations of 10,000 or more, 2007*

Community	Fertility Rate
Kochav Yair	1.5
Nazareth Ilit	1.8
Kiryat Motzkin	1.8
Modi'in Ilit	8.2
Beitar Ilit	7.5
Elad	6.5

Also compare Jerusalem with other cities.

Source: CBS Press Notice, 16 November 2008, no. 231/2008.

three have an almost totally ultra-orthodox population. In 2006, the ultra-orthodox family had an average of 4.1 children, compared with 2.1 children for the rest of the Jewish population.[11]

Research covering the period 1999–2005 has found that child subsidies, in the form of National Insurance allowances paid to mothers, have a direct effect on fertility. The effect is most pronounced among the poor and the more religious sections of the Jewish and Arab populations because the prohibitions on family planning are strongest there. During this period, there were two main changes to the child allowance system. In 2001, there was an increase in the allowance for the fifth and successive child of between 33 and 47 percent, as a result of a bill introduced by an ultra-orthodox Knesset member. In 2003, there was a large cut in child allowances introduced by the government that was implemented over the following six years.

In 2009, Prime Minister-designate Benjamin Netanyahu agreed with the ultra-orthodox parties to an increase of about $375 million in child allowances over a three-year period. In the first stage, monthly allowances would rise by 40, 66, and 105 shekels for the second, third, and fourth child in a family, respectively. This stage would cost $125 million. In 2011, this allowance would be increased again, at a cost of $250 million.[12]

Table 8.3 shows how the strong bias of the child allowance system toward large families. In 2000, the allowance for a sixth child was 3.75 times that for the first child, although the costs of a first child are the highest. (The bias against secular or small families was so great that no allowance was paid for the first child until it was introduced by the Rabin government in the early 1990s). This was despite the fact that there are economies of scale in raising children, and the cost of the first child is always the highest. This principle is recognized elsewhere in the Israeli welfare system: National Insurance pensions for elderly couples are less than twice those for single people. In 2001, child allowance differential rose to a factor of five, and the lower amount for the seventh and subsequent child was abolished. From 2002, a series of cuts were made, closing the gap between the amount paid for the first and second child and subsequent children. Between 2001 and 2005, the amount paid for the seventh child fell by 53 percent and the amount for the first child fell by almost 30 percent. These changes had major effects on the income of large families who were poor because child allowances formed a substantial part of their income. The reductions in

[11] Bank of Israel. *Annual Report 2007*. 348. http://www.bankisrael.gov.il/deptdata/mehkar/doch07/eng/pe_8.pdf

[12] Zrahiya, Zvi. 2009. "Netanyahu Agrees to Raise Child Allowances." *Ha'aretz*, 23 March.

Table 8.3. *Child allowances, 2000–2009 (shekels per month per child)*

Number of children	2000	2001	2002	2003	2004	2005	2006	2007	2008	2009
1	171	171	157	144	120	120	144	144	144	144
2	171	171	157	144	120	120	144	144	144	144
3	342	343	312	195	168	156	173	159	152	144
4	693	694	633	454	417	360	320	248	197	144
5	582	856	782	522	479	401	320	248	197	144
6	642	856	782	522	479	401	320	248	197	144
7+	599	856	782	522	479	401	320	248	197	144

Sources: Cohen, Alma, Rajeev Dehejia and Dimitri Romanov. 2007. "Do Financial Incentives Affect Fertility," 19; NBER Working Paper. http://www.nber.org/papers/w13700; Ophir, Michael and Tami Eliav. 2005. "Child Allowances in Israel: A Historical View and an International Perspective." Jerusalem: National Insurance Institute, Research Paper no. 91. http://www.btl.gov.il/מחקר%20ופיתוח/Pages/קצבאות%20ילדים%20בישראל%20היבט%20היסטורי.aspx.aspx

Figure 8.2. Total cost of child allowances, 1970–2007.

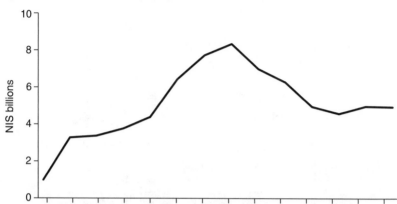

Source: Calculated from National Insurance Institute, *Statistical Quarterly*, July-September 2008 Statistical Quarterly, July-September 2005.
* Between 1970 and 1994, an additional child allowance was paid to families of those who completed army service. This was phased out by 1997. The amounts paid are included here.

child allowances also had large and negative effects on fertility. The 2003 reform cut the benefit for newborn children relative to the fourth and fourth-plus child. This affected ultra-orthodox and Arab Muslim families the most because they had large families. A woman with four children would have received an extra 782 shekels a month for the fifth child in 2002, but only received 144 shekels in 2003 and after.[13] Between 2001 and 2006, the average number of children up to two years of age in ultra-orthodox homes in Beitar Ilit and Modi'in Ilit fell by 18 percent because the birth rate fell by 10 percent.[14]

The reductions in child allowances led to a decline in their total cost, as shown in Figure 8.2. The total saving between 2002 and 2008 was estimated at 19 billion shekels, or about $1 billion a year.[15]

In its first fifty years, the state therefore successfully encouraged fertility among two groups of the population that are outside the Zionist mainstream in Israeli society: the Arabs (mainly Muslims) and ultra-orthodox

[13] Cohen Alma, Rajeev Dehejia and Dimitri Romanov. 2007. Do Financial Incentives Affect Fertility. NBER Working Paper, 19. http://www.nber.org/papers/w13700
[14] Bank of Israel. *Annual Report 2008*. 345. http://www.bankisrael.gov.il/deptdata/mehkar/doch07/eng/pe_8.pdf
[15] Ilan, Shahar. 2008. "State Saves NIS 19 Billion Due to Cut in Child Allowances since 2002." *Ha'aretz*, 11 August.

Jews. In so doing, it has also generated poverty and increased the burden of welfare on the rest of society.

Poverty

Low family income due to a lack of paid employment and large average family size meant that many in the ultra-orthodox community lived in poverty. The share of the ultra-orthodox that lived in poverty before taxes and transfers was the highest of any identifiable group in Israeli society. Between 1997–2000 and 2001, the increase was 10 percent as a result of the rapid growth of the ultra-orthodox community and its low earnings. Between 2001 and 2007, the increase of 5 percent was largely the result of the reduction in child allowances. The rapid growth of the ultra-orthodox population – by an estimated 6 percent a year – meant that between 2001 and 2006, the number of ultra-orthodox poor rose from an estimated 223,000 (16 percent of the poor in Israel) to 327,000 (18 percent). In those five years, the number of ultra-orthodox poor rose by nearly 47 percent.[16]

Ultra-orthodox Education

There are three school systems in Israel. The first is the state system divided into the mainstream secular stream and the smaller state religious one that caters to children from Orthodox homes. This system is state-funded and teaches the core curriculum fully. The second is the so-called "recognized unofficial" school system that is 75 percent state-funded and is supposed to adopt 75 percent of the core curriculum. The third is the so-called "exempt" system that is supposed to include 55 percent of the core curriculum. According to a Knesset report issued in 2003, the number of hours actually devoted to core subjects in the recognized unofficial and exempt schools was much lower.[17]

In the school year 1998–1989, there were 124,636 children in ultra-orthodox and Arab Christian schools, or 10.1 percent of the total school population. (The Ministry of Education classifies them together.) In 2007–2008, there were 194,682, equal to 13.5 percent of the total. Between those years, the total school population rose by 18 percent, whereas the number of pupils in these schools rose by 56 percent. This was a reflection of

---

[16] Bank of Israel. *Annual Report 2008*. 332 and 348. http://www.bankisrael.gov.il/deptdata/mehkar/doch07/eng/pe_8.pdf

[17] The Knesset Research and Information Center. 2003. The Core Curriculum. 12–13. http://www.knesset.gov.il/mmm/data/pdf/m00557.pdf

demographic trends: The ultra-orthodox population grew much faster than the population as a whole.[18] The number of pupils in Arab Christian schools was between 20,000 and 25,000 in this period. Their syllabi include secular studies and their educational achievements are high (see Chapter 9). The number of children in ultra-orthodox schools has grown rapidly and is a cause for great anxiety because children in this system do not get a basic general education. They learn little, if any, mathematics, science, English, digital skills, humanities, or citizenship. Despite this, their studies are largely funded by the state.[19] Furthermore, the state has abandoned its role as inspector by allowing the ultra-orthodox systems to monitor themselves.[20] For ideological reasons, most children in these schools do not take the official high school leaving exams that are a requirement for college or university entrance. To do so would imply recognition of the state.

In July 2008, the Knesset passed a law exempting ultra-orthodox schools from teaching the core curriculum. The law enabled the Education Ministry to continue funding ultra-orthodox high schools at a rate of 60 percent of what ordinary high schools receive. Thus after almost sixty years in which the state funded these schools in violation of the law, as of September 2008, this funding became legal. The core curriculum consists of the basic subjects the Education Ministry requires every school to teach, such as mathematics, English, and civics. Until the passing of the new law, the State Education Law forbade state financing of schools that did not teach this curriculum. The fact that a great many ultra-orthodox schools received government funding in contravention of this law has been known for years, but nothing was done about it. Ultra-orthodox elementary schools teach a few non-religious subjects, but the ultra-orthodox high schools teach none at all. The new law defines a new type of so-called culturally unique schools. These educational institutions, which are ultra-orthodox high schools, will receive 60 percent of the funding per student given to regular high schools, even though they will not teach the core curriculum. They will not be able to receive funding beyond this from the Education Ministry, but will receive additional funding from local authorities.[21] In 2006, 46 percent of all children in the twelfth

---

[18] Ministry of Finance. 1999. Ministry of Education Budget 2000. Jerusalem, Ministry of Finance. 49 and 196. http://www.mof.gov.il/budget2007/fbudget.htm; Ministry of Education Budget 2009. Jerusalem, Ministry of Finance 2008. 34 and 173. http://www.mof.gov.il/budget2007/docs2009/hinuch.pdf

[19] Arlosoroff, Meirav. 2008. "Hard Look: Handing the Haredim a Noose." *Ha'aretz*, 10 April.

[20] Shiffer, Varda. 1999. The Haredi Educational in Israel: Allocation, Regulation and Control. Jerusalem: The Floersheimer Institute for Policy Studies. http//www.floershiemer.org.il

[21] Ilan, Shahar and Zvi Zrahiya. 2008. "Knesset Makes It Legal: Yeshivas Don't Need to Teach Math and English." *Ha'aretz*, 25 July.

grade met university entrance requirements (i.e., earned high enough grades in their school leaving exams). Among ultra-orthodox pupils, the share was only 4.1 percent. The share of ultra-orthodox pupils sitting the exams and passing them at any level was also much lower than the national average.[22]

The nature of the ultra-orthodox education system means that its graduates, especially men, earn significantly less than other groups. This results in poverty and higher welfare spending. The major incentive not to work is that this is a condition for deferring military service. Deferment of military service is possible for ultra-orthodox men on condition that they are studying at a yeshiva. As a result, government regulations provide an incentive not to work, or to work illegally and thus not pay taxes. Note the double effect: lower earnings because of the nature of the education system and disincentives to work.

The Costs of Ultra-orthodox Education

The total budget for education rose by 31 percent in nominal terms between the budget proposals for 2000 and 2009, from almost 21 billion shekels to 27.6 billion shekels. The sections of the budget identified as exclusively for ultra-orthodox education rose by 69 percent, from 1.7 billion shekels to 2.9 billion shekels. In 2000, 8.1 percent of the budget was for the ultra-orthodox systems and in 2009, the share was 10.5 percent. These are only part of the expenditures on this type of education: There were others that cannot be identified. These include the fact that the ultra-orthodox school system is very fragmented – it is made up of a number of different systems. This results in small schools and classes and thus higher costs than in the main state system.[23]

In the academic year 2008–2009, 63,000 young men were expected to begin studying in kollels, yeshivas, or Talmudic academies for married men. The cost of funding these studies in 2008–2009 was estimated at 5 billion shekels – just over 18 percent of the budget and significantly more than the share of ultra-orthodox students in the education system. These students received an allowance of 8,460 shekels ($2,260) a year from the Education Ministry. In the regular ultra-orthodox yeshivas, in which most students are at the age that most Jewish Israelis are serving in the military, some 30,000 students were enrolled in 2008, a figure that is also expected to increase.

[22] Central Bureau of Statistics. *Statistical Yearbook of Israel 2008.* http://www.cbs.gov.il/ reader/shnaton/templ_shnaton_e.html?num_tab=st08_25&CYear=2008
[23] Shiffer, Varda. 1999. The Haredi Educational in Israel. 8 and 12.

They received 4,800 shekels ($1,280) a year from the Education Ministry. The number of students enrolled in yeshivas and kollels in 2008–2009 was expected to reach a record 95,000, compared with 88,000 in 2007–2008. The budget for supporting these students in 2008–2009 was 685 million shekels, but it may have to be increased by 60 million shekels to meet growing demand. The 95,000 students in kollelim and yeshivot represent 3.5 percent of the population of working-age men.[24] Students who complete their army service receive a grant toward further education or other approved expenses. The amount depended on their type and length of service and usually covered one or two years of college fees. In 2009, a total of 1.5 billion shekels was allocated for this grant, which is included in the defense budget. This compares with a total of 5.7 billion shekels allocated for ultra-orthodox students, as itemized earlier in the chapter.[25] In 2008–2009, the total allocation for ultra-orthodox school education plus that for higher education for ultra-orthodox single and married men therefore came to 8.6 billion shekels, or about $2 billion. This was funded by taxpayers and insofar as the ultra-orthodox community has a low labor force participation rate, its share in income tax paid is also low. As a result, much of this very large sum was a transfer to the ultra-orthodox from the rest of the community to pay for forms of education that are economically a dead-end.

The Allocation of Public Funds
for Religious Services

This section examines the allocation of public funds for religious services. These mainly consist of education, places of worship, burial, marriage, the provision of kosher food, and monitoring observation of the Sabbath and religious courts. The government recognizes Orthodox Judaism as the only form that can provide these services for the Jewish community. Hence conservative, reform, or secular Jews cannot officiate in marriage ceremonies, organize burials, or carry out other activities with state recognition. In most western countries with which Israel compares itself, religion is a private matter separate from the state. In Israel, not only is the state involved, but it has chosen the form of religion for the Jewish majority.

There are a number of definitional problems that make the use of the term "cost of religion" problematic. Is spending on religion consumption

[24] Ilan, Shahar. 2008. "Record Yeshiva Enrollment Predicted to Cost Economy NIS 5 Billion." *Ha'aretz*, 28 August.
[25] Ministry of Finance. Ministry of Defense 2009 Budget. 87–88. http://mof.gov.il/BudgetSite/StateBudget/Budget2009/MinisteriesBudget/Safety/Lists/List/Attachments/1/safety1.pdf

(like that on culture or entertainment) an investment (the ultimate: that in the afterlife) or is it, from a strictly economic point of view, a waste? Putting spending on religion into one of these categories is appropriate for an individual deciding, over time, how to allocate resources. When we look at the economy as a whole, the analysis is complicated by the fact that in Israel, there is large-scale public spending on religious services.[26]

The classical rationale for public spending is that there are some goods and services that will not be provided privately (e.g., national defense) or will not be well provided (education). It is therefore in the public interest that these be publicly provided. Is religion one of them? There are also a number of closely related issues including the effect of religious activities on labor force participation and thus on the level of output in the economy; effects on family size which in turn affect poverty levels and therefore welfare budgets. In addition, there are efficiency losses from the high levels of taxation imposed in Israel due to the large volume of government spending, including that on religion.

The focus here is on public spending. The share of the budget or GDP devoted to religion is an indication of priorities, but not in a straightforward way. Because the Israeli electorate has traditionally been divided between left and right on territorial issues, religious parties have often held the balance of power between the secular left and the secular right. They have therefore been able to extract concessions from both of the larger groups, many of which have had financial implications. The size of these budgets therefore reflects the cost of coalition making rather than public preferences. The most important element that the economist wants to identify is the subsidy provided by the secular to the religious through allocations of public funds, because this reflects the loss of welfare to that group. Insofar as the religious population pays tax, its contribution to these expenditures has to be calculated. The costs of religion consist of budgetary allocations by government at the central and local levels and by individuals for services that are, in principle, available to the public as a whole. There are also subsidies to institutions for religious education and others for those that study in them and for their families. The main source of information on budgetary allocations is the state budget and that for local authorities. Budgetary information is not straightforward – spending on religious services takes place in a number of ministries, and the identification of the relevant clauses in each budget is complicated by changes in the definitions of budget clauses each year.

---

[26] I am obliged to Ruth Klinov for this point.

Local authority budgets are not readily available in any one place and only those of the larger cities receive any publicity. Apart from allocating funds for religious purposes, central government and local government authorities also give funds to charitable foundations, many of which have been set up for religious purposes; identification of these funds is even harder. Another complication is that the budget for education covers the expenses of those in religious schools or colleges. In many cases they receive more per student from the state than those in the majority, secular system.

The Ministry of Religious Affairs has been responsible for the provision of religious services to the public. It was abolished in 2003 and its budgets that came to about $350 million were transferred to the prime minister's office. The services that it funds include synagogues, religious courts (that handle marriage, divorce, and other issues), ritual baths (mikvot), the chief rabbinate, local rabbinical authorities, and burial services. They are all administered by Orthodox rabbis and officials. Some of these activities are funded through local government. During the period of the Likud government of 1996–1999, the religious affairs budget rose nominally by 39 percent whereas the total budget rose by 24 percent. In 1998, 65 percent of the Ministry's budget was devoted to support for seminary students and on other items that exclusively benefited ultra-orthodox groups. In 2008, it was restarted, although its budget of about $73 million was included in that of the prime minister's office.[27] It should be noted that seminary students also received support by the Ministry of Education and the Ministry of Labor and Social Welfare.

By far the largest allocations for religious spending are made by the Ministry of Education. This is because the ministry funds not only the majority (secular) education system, but also the state-religious system and so-called non-state systems for the ultra-orthodox. The latter are private systems that, although they are funded and recognized by the ministry, are not subject to government inspection. What and how children are taught in those schools is a controversial matter, partly because many feel that they do not provide children with useful skills and thus prevent them from joining the workforce, or at least limit their participation. This applies more to boys, who are prepared to become students of religion, than girls who are more likely to acquire economically useful skills.

The funding per child in the school system is higher in the state-religious system than in the secular system and is highest in the ultra-orthodox

---

[27] Ministry of Finance. Office of the Prime Minister 2009 Budget. http://www.mof.gov.il/budget2007/fbudget.htm

systems. There are two reasons for this. The first is that class sizes are smaller in the ultra-orthodox and state-religious systems than in the state-secular system, which also provides for most of the Israeli Arab population. The second reason is that teachers employed by the state-secular and the state-religious systems cost less than those in the ultra-orthodox systems.

Another adjustment that should be made is to allow for the fact that the average size of schools in the secular system is larger than that in the state-religious system, whereas the average size in the ultra-orthodox systems is even smaller than in the state-religious system. This means that the overheads are lowest in the secular system and highest in the ultra-orthodox ones. It has not been possible to include the effect of school size into our calculations of costs.

There are several reasons for the differences in school size. The first is that the religious population (both religious and ultra-orthodox) is much smaller than the secular one. In any town, there are less likely to be as many religious children to fill a large school than there are secular children. The exception to this has been Jerusalem, which had a large and growing religious and ultra-orthodox population, and Bnei Brak, which had an almost exclusively ultra-orthodox population. In the last two years, ultra-orthodox Jews have been moving to dominantly secular communities in sufficient numbers for schools to be built for them. In addition, there are special funds solely for the use of the ultra-orthodox.

Given that all children between the ages of six and sixteen years must attend school by law, the cost of religion in the education system can be estimated as the difference between the cost for a secular child and that for a religious child and an ultra-orthodox child, multiplied by the number of children in the latter two systems.

In addition to services provided to the public a whole, the Ministry of Labor and Welfare provides direct subsidies to ultra-orthodox students and training courses for religious professions.

The Ministry of Housing and Construction provides funds for the construction of religious institutions and sells apartments to religious families at subsidized prices. The latter cannot be calculated with much accuracy because the subsidies are implicit: For example, government-owned land is provided more cheaply than in other cases. Once again, some items can be obtained from the state budget and others have to be estimated. Furthermore, government-owned companies provide benefits to different sections of the population, which are not included in the state budget. The ultra-orthodox community is growing rapidly. No figures are available for the breakdown of the budget by community (secular, religious, ultra-orthodox). The Ministry of Interior provides funds for the development of religious activities at the local authority level.

Much finance is provided through the National Insurance Institute. The effects of religion on budgets for welfare are very significant, but calculating them is, in some respects, so sensitive a matter that it has hardly ever been done. The ultra-orthodox community has a much larger average family size than the rest of the population. It includes many of Israel's poorest citizens, and so a considerable share of the welfare budget is accounted for by the ultra-orthodox community.

Welfare benefits other than child allowances have been estimated on the basis of the share of the ultra-orthodox in the total population of Jerusalem and Bnei Brak and a small number of other places. It is likely that the number receiving welfare among the ultra-orthodox in Jerusalem exceeds its share in the city's population. As a result, the estimate of welfare costs is biased downward. Some local authorities provide city tax reductions to those studying in seminaries, as well as other forms of aid. In some areas, any building containing a synagogue is not subject to local taxes: A synagogue can be one room devoted to prayer. As a result, towns with large ultra-orthodox populations, including Jerusalem and Bnei Brak, have low city-tax bases and are among the poorest in Israel. The concentration of poverty in Jerusalem and Bnei Brak is closely linked with employment patterns and family size, which can, in turn, be largely explained by ultra-orthodox religious practice.

The Politics of Religion

In July 2008, the Knesset, passed the second and third readings of a law exempting Haredi (ultra-orthodox) schools from teaching the core curriculum. The law enables the Education Ministry to continue funding Haredi yeshiva high schools up to 60 percent of what state high schools receive. Thus after almost sixty years in which the state funded these yeshivas in violation of the law, as of September 2008, this funding became legal. The core curriculum consists of the basic subjects the Education Ministry requires every educational institute to teach, such as math, English, and civics. Until July 2008, the State Education Law forbade state financing of schools that did not teach this curriculum. Haredi elementary schools teach few non-Torah subjects, but Haredi yeshiva high schools teach none at all. Thus various parties and the high school teachers' union petitioned the High Court of Justice against the illegal funding of these schools. Under the High Court's ruling, if the law had not been passed, state funding of ultra-orthodox high schools would have been discontinued as of the coming school year. For this reason, getting the law passed became the Shas party's top priority. The law defines a new type of school – "culturally unique" schools. These educational institutions, meaning the ultra-orthodox yeshiva high schools, will receive 60 percent of the funding per student given to regular high schools, even though they will not be teaching the core curriculum. They will receive additional funding from local authorities.

Shas invested huge efforts to get this law passed promptly. The law was approved mainly thanks to the votes of ultra-orthodox and Arab members of the Knesset. Members of the Kadima and Labor factions absented themselves from the vote. The law was opposed by the Meretz party and one Labor Knesset member. The vote was also made possible by Shas's decision to refrain from voting against the appointment of a Labor member as chairman of the Knesset Finance Committee. In exchange, the government coalition assisted Shas with the core curriculum law. The then-Prime Minister Ehud Olmert's representatives offered Shas an increase of 250 million shekels ($62.5 million) in the budget for child allowances in exchange. That offer was made on the eve of the Finance Committee's vote on the appointment because the coalition was afraid it did not have a majority. The parliamentary leader of Shas refused, demanding a 1–1.5 billion shekel ($250–375 million) increase in child allowances.[28] This kind of deal, which negated advice given, among others, by the Prime Minister's economic advisor, was the direct result of weak multiparty government.[29] The price was paid not so much in terms of overspending the budget but by misallocating resources with the budget and by passing laws with such severe negative *social* as well as economic effects.

Conclusions

In 2006–2007, the low labor force participation rate of the ultra-orthodox resulted in a loss of output at estimated $3.3 billion, equal to about two percent of GDP. The cost of ultra-orthodox education at all levels was estimated at about $2 billion, which is a form of transfer payment largely paid for by the non-ultra-orthodox population. In addition, there were welfare

---

[28] Ilan and Zrahiya. "Knesset Makes It Legal: Yeshivas Don't Need to Teach Math and English."

[29] The National Economic Council, The Prime Minister's Office. Socio-Economic Agenda for Israel 2008–2010. Jerusalem: Prime Minister's Office, 2007. 67–75. http://www.pmo. gov.il/PMO/PM+Office/Departments/econ20082010.htm

transfers due to the high level of poverty in the ultra-orthodox community, something that is, at least in part, self-imposed.

Much of the expenditure on religion carried out privately in Western countries is done in Israel by the state. This has implications for equity and for efficiency. High levels of taxation that prevail in Israel have long been recognized as a disincentive to work, and one of the ways in which taxes can be reduced is to cut public spending. Spending on religion is largely current spending and, insofar as it is concentrated in the public sector, it contributes to the current bias in the state budget against investment, which has had a negative effect on economic growth.

Given that a large share of Israel's population is secular, reducing the subsidies to the religious minority would have important welfare implications. This assumes that the secular population was in favor of such a move.

In the education budget, there is a large element of discrimination in favor of the religious population, especially the ultra-orthodox. Yet the economic benefits of ultra-orthodox education, especially for boys, are highly questionable. The extra amounts spent on ultra-orthodox education are at the expense of the majority systems that are under financial pressure despite the fact that they produce the main economic gains in terms of skills needed in the labor force. The discrimination against the majority of children is also an equity issue that demands attention. The failure of the ultra-orthodox education system to include the core curriculum means that future generations will lack the skills that would enable them to support themselves and their families. This will guarantee the continuance of significant levels of poverty.

The effect of benefits for ultra-orthodox students and their families, including the structure of child benefits, is to encourage a section of the population not to join the labor force and to live off state benefits. Exemption from army service is conditional on them not working. Furthermore, the benefit system encourages large families. This tends to lower income per head to a point where many ultra-orthodox families need income support, which is provided by the state. The extreme concentration of the ultra-orthodox population in a small number of cities and towns also placed large burdens on those local authorities and on central government that provides some financial assistance to local government.

NINE

The Arab Minority

Introduction

The Arab community comprises a fifth of the population of Israel and faces serious economic, social, and political problems. This chapter begins with a review of the economic theory of minorities and that of discrimination, the aim being to see what light theoretical work can throw on the status of the Arabs in Israel. The second section examines demographic, economic, educational, and employment development since the British Mandate. Conclusions are then drawn about the relative strength of what might be called endogenous and exogenous factors in explaining the economic development of the Arabs in Israel. Endogenous factors include religion and culture. Exogenous factors are the environment in which the community lives: Is it encouraging or discouraging and discriminatory? Is the state active or passive or even negative in helping the minority develop? Endogenous factors such as motivation, education, and even culture and beliefs are affected by exogenous factor over time. This differentiation, although tenuous, is analytically useful.

The Economic Theory of Minorities

Most of the theoretical work on minorities has been about economically successful ones. It has analyzed which traditions, cultures, and beliefs minorities have that have enabled them to succeed. Most of the work on minorities has been on groups, such as Jews, Huguenots, and the overseas Chinese, that succeeded in the face of discrimination.

Various explanations have been made for the success of minorities. Weber emphasized that religious values affect economic behavior. He stated that Calvinist Protestantism was based on asceticism that in turn favored saving and investment rather than consumption.[1] Landes has suggested that religious values per se are of secondary importance: More important was the rationality associated with Protestantism, which developed alongside religious values.[2] The idea that the higher ethic of Calvinist businessmen was the reason for their success has been disputed by those who claim that it was in fact their ability to be at least as ruthless in business as others, or more so, that led to their success. Mathias and Grief have pointed out that minorities provide a social network for getting business done. This works in different directions depending on circumstances.[3] Mathias's examples are positive, but Grief's work on Maghribi traders suggests that reliance on kinship may be a sign of weakness, due to the lack of development of the market, although the difference in the periods considered is important.[4]

An initial conclusion is that some minorities have done well because they have the endogenous factors, such as religious beliefs or patterns of behavior influenced by religious beliefs, that enable them to play a significant role in the economy, even though they may be discriminated against politically, socially, and economically. Endogenous factors have not traditionally been the province of economists largely because they are hard to quantify. Furthermore, they are highly controversial, and the desire for political correctness has limited discussion especially among non-economists. There have been some changes in recent years, one example being the work of Deepak Lal. Lal has supplied a framework for analysis of endogenous factors, especially the role of religion in economic development. He distinguishes between three sets of equilibria that define economic development. First there is the market process of supply and demand. Second are factors generating material beliefs that determine the pattern of economic organization, and third are cultural factors that determine cosmological beliefs. He contends that Christian beliefs are much more favorable to economic growth than Muslim ones.[5] Kuran has shown how Islamic law regarding interest and inheritance has hindered capital accumulation and economic development. This is also an endogenous explanation.[6]

[1] Weber, Max. 1930. *The Protestant Ethic and the Spirit of Capitalism*. London: George Allen and Unwin, 156–157, 171–183.
[2] Landes, David. 1998. *The Wealth and Poverty of Nations*. New York and London: W.W. Norton, 174–181.
[3] Mathias, Peter. 1999. "How Do Minorities Become Elites," in Elise S. Brezis and Peter Temin, eds. *Elites, Minorities, and Economic Growth*. Amsterdam: Elsevier, 115–128.
[4] Grief, Avner. 1993. "Contract Enforceability and Economic Institutions in Early Trade: The Magrhribi Trader's Coalition." *American Economic Review*. Vol. 83. No. 3. 525–540.
[5] Lal, Deepak. 1998. *Unintended Consequences*. Cambridge, MA: MIT Press, 11–12.
[6] Kuran, Timur. 2004. *Islam and Mammon: The Economic Predicaments of Islamism*. Princeton: Princeton University Press, chapter 6.

Exogenous factors can be summarized in one word: discrimination. Neoclassical theory suggests that discrimination is irrational: Paying one group less implies paying another group more and therefore there is no net gain to the employer. The only ones to gain are the better-paid workers. Marxists and adherents to traditional institutionalism, using different methodologies, suggest that the net effect is to lower the total wage bill, thus benefiting employers. Lewin-Epstein and Semyonov conclude that the results predicted in neoclassical theory best fit their observations on Israel. Discrimination took two forms: denying Arabs access to jobs/ firms/industries/sectors and limiting their promotion prospects within any employment framework that they were offered.[7] These kinds of analysis are static and do not allow for dynamic factors that affect minorities.

The official inquiry into the riots and deaths in October 2000 made the following points about the minority status of the Arabs of Israel that have often been forgotten. The first was that sixty years ago, this minority was a majority. The alteration in status this change brought about was hard to absorb, especially over a relatively short time. The second was the fact that Israel's Arabs are part of the majority population in the Middle East (something that is especially true for the Muslims) made their minority status in Israel even harder to accept.[8]

Demography

The Arab community is divided into three groups: the majority is Muslim, and there are two minority groups: the Christians and the Druze. At the end of 2008, there were 1.24 million Muslim Arabs, 153,100 Christian Arabs (as well as a small number of non-Arab Christians) and 121,900 Druze. These groups accounted for 24.5 percent of the population.[9] In 2008, the Arab birth rate was 26.9 per 1,000 of the population and the death rate was 2.7 per 1,000. Among Muslims, the birth rate was 26.1 per 1,000 and the death rate was 2.2 per 1,000. The national birth rate was 20.1 per 1,000 and the national death rate was 6 per 1,000. The higher Arab and Muslim

---

[7]   Lewin-Epstein, Noah and Moshe Semyonov. 1993. *The Arab Minority in Israel's Economy.* Boulder, CO: Westview Press, 30–35, 77–82.
[8]   Report of the Commission of Enquiry into the Clash between Security Forces and Israeli Citizens, October 2000. Jerusalem: The High Court of Justice, 2003. Section A, paragraph 6. http://elyon1.court.gov.il/heb/veadot/or/inside_index.htm
[9]   Central Bureau of Statistics. *Statistical Yearbook of Israel, 2009.* Table 2.2. http://www.cbs. gov.il/reader/shnaton/templ_shnaton_e.html?num_tab=st02_02&CYear=2009

Table 9.1. *Demographic trends, 1919–1949 (thousands)*

Year		Arab population*	Jewish population	Total
1919	March	583	65	648
1922	October	668	84	752
1931	November	859	174	1,033
1939	December	1,056	450	1,506
1947	December	1,269	630	1,899
1948	November	156	759	915
1949	December	160	1,014	1,174

* Muslims, Christians, and Druze

Source: Nadav Halevi and Ruth Klinov-Malul. The Economic Development of Israel. 15; CBS, Statistical Yearbook, 2003.

birth rates were due to higher fertility rates and the age structure of those populations.[10]

The Arab population of Palestine grew rapidly during the Mandate, almost doubling in the twenty years following World War I. This was largely due to natural growth – high birth rates and falling death rates – but was also fed by some immigration, as a result of growth in the Jewish economy.[11] Demographic growth after the creation of the state was entirely due to natural causes. The Arab minority in Israel was once the majority population in Mandatory Palestine, an area that included the West Bank and Gaza. Its class structure and educational background changed with the exodus of Arabs from what became Israel in 1947–1949. Table 9.1 shows how the balance between Jews and Arabs changed between the end of World War I and the end of the War of Independence.

During the Israeli War of Independence, the West Bank and Gaza were occupied by Jordan and Egypt, respectively, and thousands of refugees fled to these areas. Others fled to Lebanon and Syria. Those that remained constituted 13.6 percent of the population of Israel in December 1949. By the end of 1990, they numbered 873,000 and constituted 18.1 percent of the population. At the end of 2000, they numbered almost 1.2 million, or 18.7

[10] Central Bureau of Statistics. *Statistical Yearbook of Israel, 2009*. Table 3.12. http://www.cbs.gov.il/reader/shnaton/templ_shnaton_e.html?num_tab=st02_02&CYear=2009 and http://www.cbs.gov.il/reader/shnaton/templ_shnaton.html?num_tab=st03_11x&CYear=2008

[11] Gottheil, Fred. 2003. "The Smoking Gun: Arab Immigration into Palestine, 1922–1931." *Middle East Quarterly*. Winter. http://www.meforum.org/article/522

percent of the population, and at the end of 2008, almost 1.5 million, equal to 20 percent of the population (see Table 10.3).

In the early years of the state, two factors dominated the situation of the Arabs in Israel. The first was the mass exodus of Arabs from Palestine when Israel was created. The second was the relatively underdeveloped state of the Arab economy prior to the creation of the state. This meant that the Arabs were much weaker than the Jews in economic and other terms: In 1947–49, they lost the majority of their population, including much of the urban middle class and intelligentsia. According to Schnell, Sofer and Drori, "[t]he social, economic and cultural elite abandoned the country en masse, leaving behind traditional farming villages located in several peripheral regions of the country. Nearly all of the Arab population remaining in the country lived in settlements that lacked even a minimal modern infrastructure, with the exception of Nazareth and Shefar'am. Almost the entire population lacked basic formal education. Such conditions alone would have made it difficult for the Arab economy to develop, but at least until the late 1960s, the Israel government, placed even more obstacles in its way."[12]

In demographic terms, the Arabs of Israel have been a growing minority both in absolute and relative terms. This phenomenon begs many socioeconomic questions. Did this dramatic development occur because of endogenous and/or exogenous factors? In other words, was it caused by decisions made by the Arabs on the individual, social, or political level, or was it the result of decisions made (or not made) by Israeli governments, or both? How far is demographic growth on this scale typical of underprivileged minorities? Does demographic growth reinforce the underprivileged status of the Arabs or was it a consequence, or both?

Figure 9.1 shows that during the last fifty years, differences in fertility rates within the Arab community were greater than those within the Jewish majority (also see Table 10.5). It also shows that the growth rates of all the communities have been converging toward the Jewish rate. It should be noted that the latter rose slightly between 1990 and 2002, partly because of the effects of subsidies to the ultra-Orthodox community, including child allowances. The higher fertility rates among the Muslims Arabs and Druze is an indication of the power of endogenous factors in the early years of the state. Christian Arabs experienced the same discriminatory environment (an exogenous factor) but had much lower fertility rates.

---

[12] Schnell, Izhak, Michael Sofer and Israel Drori. 1995. *Arab Industrialization in Israel: Ethnic Entrepreneurship in the Periphery.* Westport, CT: Westview, 24.

Figure 9.1. Total fertility rates, 1960–2008.

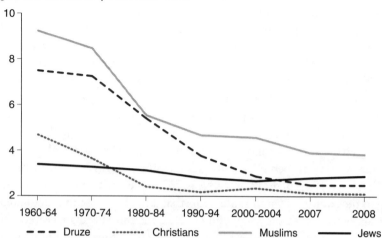

Source: Central Bureau of Statistics, Statistical Abstract of Israel 2009.

The large differences in fertility rates have resulted in variations in the age structures of the communities. The Arab population is much younger than the Jewish population. In 2007, 50 percent of the Arab population was aged 0–19 years, compared with 33 percent in the Jewish population. In this respect, the Israeli Arab population resembles the Palestinian populations of Gaza and the West Bank and those of neighboring Arab states and presents major budgetary challenges in terms of provision of education and employment.

The Arab Economy

The Arab economy in Mandatory Palestine was much less developed than the Jewish one. According to Metzer and Kaplan, it was a "low income, primarily rural and relatively backward" economy.[13] Agriculture was traditional and extensive, although by the 1930s, there was a decline in the role of agricultural employment. Much agricultural output was marketed using the transport and trade sectors that formed a significant share of the Arab economy. Industry was dominated by home production. Between 1922 and 1935, per capita income increased by an average of 5 percent a year – an impressive rate given a population growth of 2.5 percent.

[13] Metzer, Jacob and Oded Kaplan. 1985. Jointly but Severally: Arab-Jewish Dualism and Economic Growth in Mandatory Palestine. The Maurice Falk Institute for Economic Research in Israel. Research Paper no. 180, 328.

In the mid-1930s, only 25 percent of the Arab population lived in towns.[14] The urban-rural breakdown of the population is a key indicator for changes in development. The village has been associated with traditional life: Women worked at home with large numbers of children, men were employed in agriculture and exposure to the modernity emanating from towns and cities was limited. Changes came with urbanization and the relative expansion of the urban population versus the rural one. In 1944, almost 70 percent of the Muslim population lived in villages and less than 12 percent in towns of 45,000-plus inhabitants. Among Christians, this breakdown was 20 percent and almost 53 percent, respectively, and among Jews, almost 35 percent and 64 percent.[15] In the 1940s, agriculture remained paramount in Arab employment. It was, however, less important than the service sector in output terms. The Jewish economy was far more industrialized and had a smaller agricultural sector both in employment and output terms.[16]

In 1948, there were only two cities in the Arab sector, Nazareth and Shefar'am, that had been incorporated by the British mandate. The population lacked basic infrastructure and had a very low education level. It was concentrated in three areas: the Galilee, the Triangle (in the Northern part of the Sharon Plain), and, to a much lesser extent, in the Northern Negev. In the 1950s, the Arab economy was dominated by the village: It provided its own needs and despite the fact that much of its land was lost, agriculture remained dominant.[17]

As soon as fighting ended in 1948, Israeli Arabs were placed under martial law that lasted until 1966. Until 1954, they lived in total closure and were even prevented from visiting other villages.[18] In the early days of the state, the development of the Arab economy was restricted by regulations, administrative policies, and a lack of positive measures. A feeling that the Arab minority was a potential fifth column underlay the state's relations with them. Since the 1960s, legal restrictions on the Arab population have

[14] Lewin-Epstein, Noah. 1990. The Arab Economy in Israel: Growing Population Mismatch. Tel Aviv University Pinchas Sapir Center for Development. Discussion Paper No. 14–90, 3.

[15] Government Printer, Palestine. 1946. A Survey of Palestine, Prepared in December 1945 and January 1946 for the information of the Anglo-American Committee of Inquiry Vol. I, April. 153.

[16] Meltzer, Jacob. 1998. *The Divided Economy of Mandatory Palestine*. Cambridge: Cambridge University Press, 142

[17] Lewin-Epstein, Noah and Moshe Semyonov. 1993. *The Arab Minority in Israel's Economy*. Boulder, CO: Westview Press, 45–46.

[18] Schnell, Sofer and Drori, *Arab Industrialization in Israel Ethnic Entrepreneurship in the Periphery*, 24.

been lifted, but there are two areas in which they still suffer what might be called legalized discrimination. The first is that they were not allowed to buy or build homes on land owned by the Jewish National Fund. This has been successfully challenged in the courts, and some changes in the land ownership system were planned in early 2009 to overcome these problems. The second is that Arabs do not serve in the IDF (Druze and some Bedouins do). They face discrimination because of this, although the reason why they were not required to serve is not only fears about their loyalty but also an unwillingness put them in a position where they might be obliged to fight other Arabs who could be members of their own family.

By 1959, the Arab population had increased to 230,000 (Muslims, Christians, and Druze). The supply of land for this mainly rural population had declined as a result of land expropriations. Demand for labor in the Jewish economy had increased and immigration had declined. There were therefore pressures to bring Arabs into the labor force. The 1959 Employment Service Law made this possible by ending discrimination in the state employment service. Arab citizens joined the Histadrut and more Arabs traveled to work outside their villages in Jewish areas.[19] They moved into low-status jobs whereas those who remained in the Arab sector had jobs at the higher- and lower-status levels. As a result, ironically, economic integration resulted in relative occupational disadvantages: The Arabs were unable to convert their improving educational levels into higher-status jobs.

The Arab population has become much more urbanized but, compared with the total population, it remains relatively rural and resident in small towns. In 1972, there were 30,600 Arab workers in agriculture; in 1983, there were only 11,800. The fastest growth sector was of professionals and technical workers, mainly employed by the public sector.[20] Another significant change was the decline in self-employment and entrepreneurship. In 1972, a total of 53.1 percent of the nonagricultural labor force was either self-employed or an employer; by 1983, this had declined to 31.2 percent.[21] In recent years, a number of initiatives have been taken to reverse this.

Between the 1970s and the 1980s, the mismatch between educational achievements and occupational levels for Arab workers increased. In 1972, there was no "market discrimination" against Arabs in that their occupational status corresponded to their age and educational characteristics. By 1983, they had, on average, lower occupational status than their age and

---

[19] Meltzer, *The Divided Economy of Mandatory Palestine*, 205–206.
[20] Lewin-Epstein and Semyonov, Table 3.3, 53.
[21] Lewin-Epstein and Semyonov, Table 3.2, 52.

educational characteristics would suggest.[22] After 1967, Israeli Arabs were sometimes replaced by Palestinian workers who were cheaper to employ. In the 1990s, they also faced competition from other foreign workers. When Israel closed its borders to Palestinian workers, this had a positive effect on the wages paid to Israeli Arabs.[23]

An estimate of the size of the Arab economy in Israel has been made and it throws light on the factors that have militated against the community at the macroeconomic level. In 2005, 11.5 percent of those in employment were Arabs. The labor participation rate of the Arab community was 68.7 percent of the national rate. The Arab share of income from work was therefore 11.5 percent multiplied by 68.7 percent, or 7.9 percent. In 2004, the GDP was $118 billion, and the Arab share was $9.3 billion.[24] Assuming the same proportions, the 2008 figure was estimated at 7.9 percent of GDP, or $15.2 billion. GDP per capita in 2008 was therefore $10,413 in the Arab community and $31,725 in the Jewish community. There were two main reasons for the large gap. The first was the much lower participation rate in the labor force in the Arab community, especially of women. The second reason was the lack of access of the Arab community to well-paid industrial jobs – an explanation that subsumes other causes such as education and discrimination.[25]

Arab labor force participation rates are low because of the low participation rates of women and because of the early retirement rates among men. These rates cannot be fully explained by the factors that usually determine labor force participation rates. The decline in male participation rates reflects the fall in demand for unskilled labor, a result of technological change encouraged by globalization. It also reflected the substitution of Israeli Arab workers first by Palestinians and later by other foreign workers. In the early 2000s, reductions in welfare benefits, as well as tighter criteria for eligibility, seemed to have reversed the downward trend. The extent of religiosity did not affect labor participation rates, but religious affiliation did. Christian Arab men had higher participation rates than Muslims or Druze.[26] This may have been because they had higher skill

---

[22] Lewin-Epstein and Semyonov, 57.
[23] Asali, Muhammad. 2006. Why Do Arabs Earn Less than Jews in Israel. The Maurice Falk Institute for Economic Research in Israel, 31–35. http://pluto.huji.ac.il/~msfalkin/pdfs/paper%2006-3.pdf
[24] Sadan, Ezra. 2006. The Share of the Arab Sector in the Economy. The Abraham Fund Initiatives, 4. http://www.abrahamfund.org
[25] Sadan, 5–6.
[26] Bank of Israel. Annual Report 2008. 204–209.

levels and thus did less physically exhausting work. These are cultural, or endogenous, factors.

The main reason why so few Arab women worked outside the home was that they had a relatively large number of children to tend. As fertility rates fall, this is changing. Another, closely related reason was that in traditional societies, women remain at home, but this is changing too, and there is increasing evidence that discrimination and a lack of employment are the main factors limiting the number of Arab women entering the labor market. This is also true in the ultra-Orthodox Jewish community, although it is changing in both the Arab and Jewish communities as a result of economic pressures. One of the factors that determines access to well-paid industrial (and service sector) jobs is the suitability of the candidate. The most important aspect is the level of education.

Education

The Arab community suffers from lower educational levels than the Jewish majority. This is due to a relative lack of investment in the Arab educational system by the state, higher dropout levels, and less supportive home environments. An indication of differential investment levels is given by the average number of pupils per class. In 1999–2000, the figures were 29.8 in the Arab sector and 25.9 in the Jewish one. Nine years later, the figures had changed to 29.6 and 25.6, respectively.[27]

Despite this, there has been a major improvement in the average level of education of the Arab minority. There are also striking differences between Christians and Muslims. It is not clear whether this is because of religious reasons or because religious differences reflect socioeconomic factors such as urbanization. In 1997 and 2007, the Arabs had a lower median level of education than that of the Jews. In 1997, the median Arab number of years of schooling was 10.6 years and the Jewish median was 12.4 years. By 2007, the figures had reached 11.3 and 12.6 respectively; as a result, the educational gap between the communities had fallen by 50 percent. There was also an increase in the share of Arab pupils gaining high school certificates and university entrance (see Chapter 10). One of the challenges that the Arab education system had to face was the much faster increase in population than in the Jewish sector. In addition, Israeli Arabs have to ask the question: Would

---

[27] Ministry of Finance. Ministry of Education Budget 2009. 38. http://www.mof.gov.il/BudgetSite/StateBudget/Budget2009/MinisteriesBudget/socialBudget/Lists/List/Attachments/2/education%202.pdf

more education be a worthwhile investment if discrimination means that access to good jobs was limited even to those suitably qualified?

Employment and Earnings

A key parameter determining the supply of labor is the participation rate: the share of the working age population that wants to work outside the home. In 2007, the participation rate of Arab men was 62 percent, similar to that of Jewish men (aged fifteen years and older). The participation rate of Arab women was much lower than men, at 20.5 percent. The total Arab participation rate, for men and women, was 39 percent, compared with 57 percent for Jews. Furthermore, the participation rate for Arab men fell between the late 1980s and 2007 from 68 percent to 62 percent, whereas for Jewish men, it fell from 62 percent to 60 percent.[28] The participation of Arab women rose slightly, from 17 percent in 2003 to 20.5 percent in 2007. The overall Arab participation rate was therefore about 40 percent, compared with about 60 percent in the Jewish community. These low participation rates were one of the main causes of low family incomes and high poverty rates. In 2007, the national unemployment rate was 7.3 percent; among the Arabs it was 10.9 percent.

The demand for labor is determined by macroeconomic factors, but at the sectoral or industrial level, it is determined by the willingness of employers to take on particular individuals, regardless of their suitability in terms of education, training, and experience. The negative expression of this is discrimination, often manifest in jobs that are barred to Arabs for security reasons or because of prejudice. The local public sector in Arab towns is virtually reserved for them, but as public sector budgets have been cut, this source of employment has been constrained.

A survey of employment patterns in 1986 and 1996 compared the situation of Arabs between those years. It showed that in 1986, they were substantially underrepresented in the sample of forty-eight factories surveyed, both in number and in rank. The survey was repeated in 1996 and concluded that the position was even worse. Between those years, although industrial employment had increased, the employment of Arabs had worsened as a result of employers' preferences for newly arrived Jews from the Soviet Union and a result of the First Intifada (1987–1992).[29]

---

[28] CBS. The Arab Population in Israel 2003 and CBS Labor Force Survey 2007. http://www.cbs.gov.il/www/saka_y/08_01.pdf

[29] Levanon, Gad and Yaron Raviv. 2007. "Decomposing Wage Gaps between Ethnic Groups: The Case of Israel." *Southern Economic Journal.* Vol. 73. No. 4. 1066–1087.

In 1995, there were 109,700 employees in the high-tech industry of whom only 2,800 (2.6 percent) were non-Jews. In 1999, there were 145,700 and 4,700 (3.2 percent), respectively. Most of the non-Jews were Arabs, but a precise figure is not available. In 1995, the average wage per employee post in the high-tech sector was 77 percent higher than in the economy as a whole; in 1999, it was 109.5 percent higher. Arabs were underrepresented in this well-paid sector both because they had, on average, lower educational achievements and because of discrimination.[30] In 2007, it was estimated that only 2 percent of high-technology workers were Arabs, despite that fact that 10 percent of the country's engineering graduates were Arab.[31]

Apart from discrimination – the result of prejudice or security consider-ations (sometimes an excuse for prejudice) – the Arab community suffers other handicaps in the labor market. It is concentrated in areas of the coun-try that have relatively little industry. Due to low-income levels, some Arab families lack means of private transportation that would enable them to overcome geographic hurdles. Hebrew is their second language and English their third – a significant disadvantage in more sophisticated sectors of the economy. Lack of experience in and exposure to the labor market is a hin-drance, and there can be consequent psychological barriers that affect those looking for work.[32]

The pattern of employment in the Arab community and the whole economy is outlined in Table 9.2. It shows that agriculture and construc-tion played a bigger role in the Arab economy than the whole economy, and manufacturing played a smaller role. Business services, which include much high technology, were also much smaller in the Arab economy, as were banking, insurance, and other financial services. The table also shows the underrepresentation of Arabs in the public sector. This is very worrying given that it is the government that should be pushing for change.

In 2004, 74 percent of Arabs employed in the industrial sector were in traditional sectors, 16.5 percent in textiles and clothing and 9.5 percent in technological sectors. Among Arab women, the shares were 60 percent, 36.6 percent, and 3.4 percent, respectively. Between 1995 and 2004, the volume

[30] Pepperman, Beni. Increasing Employment for Israeli Arabs. Ministry of Industry, Trade and Employment, Research and Economics Authority. 12, 17–18. http://www.moital.gov.il/NR/rdonlyres/FF6BBCA2-B2F9–4452–9EB6-CEC4DECC957A/0/taasukaarvim.pdf
[31] Goldstein, Tani. 2007. "Arabs out of Israeli Hi–tech." *YNet News.com*, 9 August. http://www.ynet.co.il/english/articles/0,7340,L-3447252,00.html
[32] Pepperman, Beni. 2006. Increasing Employment for Israeli Arabs. Ministry of Industry, Trade and Employment, Research and Economics Authority. 4. http://www.moital.gov.il/NR/rdonlyres/FF6BBCA2-B2F9–4452–9EB6-CEC4DECC957A/0/taasukaarvim.pdf

Table 9.2. *Employment by sector, 2007 (%)*

	Arabs	Israeli economy
Agriculture	3.0	1.6
Manufacturing (mining and industry)	12.7	15.7
Construction	20.6	5.6
Wholesale and retail trade, and repairs	16.2	13.4
Accommodation services and restaurants	5.8	4.6
Transport, storage and communications	6.4	6.4
Banking, insurance and other financial services	0.7	3.5
Business activities	6.1	14.0
Public administration	2.5	4.5
Education	13.9	12.8
Health, welfare, and social work services	7.1	10.0
Community, social, personal, and other services	3.2	4.6
Services for households by domestic personnel	0.4	1.8
Other, unidentified	1.4	0.9
Total	100.0	100.0

Source: CBS, Labor Force Survey 2007, http://www.cbs.gov.il/www/saka_y/08_03.pdf and http://www.cbs.gov.il/www/saka_y/02_20.pdf

of industrial employment in the Arab sector fell by 25 percent, whereas the volume of industrial employment of Arab women fell by 52 percent. This was due to the nationwide decline in basic industries as a result of globalization (see Chapter 5). Unlike the rest of the economy, there was very little growth in alternative industrial employment. Technological employment rose from 2,100 in 1995 to 2,900 in 2004.[33] In 2007, only 5.2 percent of civil servants (including administration and education) were Arabs, despite government announcements that the share would rise to 10 percent by 2012.[34]

The net effect of these employment trends was large and growing income inequality between Arabs and Jews. One measure of this is monthly gross income per household. This is an indication of the amount earned by members of a household and depends on the number of people going out to work

[33] Pepperman, Increasing Employment for Israeli Arabs, 12.
[34] Haider, Ali, ed. 2008. The Sikkuy Report 2007. Haifa and Jerusalem: Sikkuy: The Association for the Advancement of Civic Equality in Israel. Table 4.7.3. http://www.sikkuy.org.il/english/en2007/sikkuy2007pdf

Figure 9.2. Arab and Jewish household monthly income, 1997–2006.

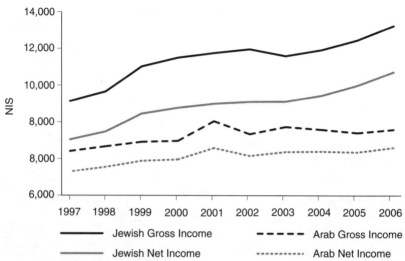

Jewish Gross Income · · · · · Arab Gross Income

Jewish Net Income ·········· Arab Net Income

Source: Central Bureau of Statistics: Arab Households Expenditure and Income 2006. Based on a survey of 1,353 (1997) to 2,138 (2006) Arab households and 11,593 (1997) to 12,195 (2006) Jewish households.

as well as what they earn. Data on household earnings is given in Figure 9.2. Where they worked in the same sectors, with the same education and experience levels, Arab earnings were often lower than Jewish ones.[35]

In 2006, there were 267,900 Arab households and 1,676,200 Jewish households; the Arab population was 1.4 million and the Jewish population was 5.35 million. This meant that the average Arab household consisted of 5.2 people and the average Jewish household consisted of 3.2 people. In 2006, gross income per capita in the Arab community was 1,406 shekels a month ($330) and net income was 1,272 shekels ($288). In the Jewish community, the figures were 4,139 shekels ($929) and 3,352 shekels ($752).

In 1997, Arab gross household earnings were 70 percent of Jewish earnings; by 2000, they had fallen to 61 percent, and in 2006, they equaled 59 percent. In 1997, Arab net household earnings were 75 percent of Jewish earnings; by 2000, they had fallen to 68 percent, and in 2006, they equaled 62 percent (see Figure 9.2). The gap in net earnings widened faster than that in gross earnings because the tax and benefit system became less effective in redistributing income (see Chapter 10). Within the Arab community, there were also inequalities by religion and by locality. The Bedouin were

[35] Levanon, Gad and Yaron Raviv. Decomposing Wage Gaps between Ethnic Groups: The Case of Israel.

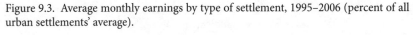

Figure 9.3. Average monthly earnings by type of settlement, 1995–2006 (percent of all urban settlements' average).

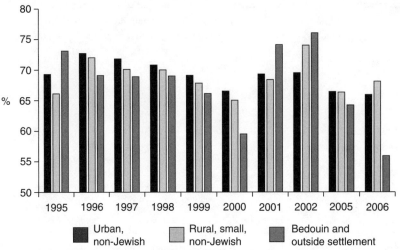

Source: Calculated from Jacques Bendelac. Average Salaries and Earnings by Settlement and by Other Economic Variables, 1994–1995. National Insurance Institute, Periodic Report no. 154, 1998; Jacques Bendelac. Average Wages and Incomes and Their Distribution by Various Economic Variables, 2000–2001. National Insurance Institute, Periodic Report no. 189, 2003; Jacques Bendelac. Average Wages and Incomes and Their Distribution by Various Economic Variables, 2004–2005. National Insurance Institute, Periodic Report no. 210, 2007; Jacques Bendelac. Average Wage and Income by Locality and by Various Economic Variables, 2006. National Insurance Institute, Periodic Report, no. 219, 2008.

the most underprivileged in terms of income, employment, and education. The total population included in Figure 9.3 in 2002 was 2.57 million. In the non-Jewish urban settlements, the population was 207,355. In small, rural non-Jewish settlements, the population was 7,546, and in the Bedouin and so-called outside settlement sector, there were 6,000. Non-Jews earned 30 percent less than the average for the all-urban group, and in the period 1994 to 2002, the one of considerable economic development, this gap changed little.

Table 9.3 gives an indication of the depth of earnings inequality and how it has changed. The first point to note is that the share of earners earning up to the minimum wage rose in all urban settlements from 38.4 percent in 1995 to 45 percent in 2006. In 1995, in the urban non-Jewish sector, the base was higher at 44.1 percent and it rose much more, to 54.6 percent in 2006. In the small, rural non-Jewish sector, the increase was more moderate, but in the Bedouin sector, it was nearly as strong, although there was a

Table 9.3. *Share of wage and salary earners earning up to the minimum wage, by type of settlement, 1995–2006 (%)*

	All urban settlements	Urban, non-Jewish settlements	Rural, small, non-Jewish settlements	Bedouin and other population outside settlements
1995	38.4	44.1	43.3	44.0
1996	37.5	43.6	41.6	46.4
1997	33.7	41.0	39.0	41.9
1998	39.4	50.3	46.0	49.7
1999	40.0	53.8	49.7	54.4
2000	40.3	55.9	52.1	59.5
2001	39.6	53.9	49.2	54.8
2002	40.9	53.2	48.2	51.5
2006	45.0	54.6	50.2	58.7

Source: Calculated from Jack Bendlak. Average Salaries and Earnings by Settlement and by Other Economic Variables, 1994–1995. Periodic Report no. 154; to 2001–2003. Periodic Report no.189; to 2004–2005 (2007) 2006 (2008). Jerusalem: National Insurance Institute.

significant decline between 2000 and 2002 and then a sharp increase in the period 2002–2006.

The Israeli labor market is characterized by large numbers of low and very low earners. The number and share of this group has risen in recent years, and this was true more for non-Jews than for the total population. A mismatch between educational attainments and employment has been found using 1972 and 1983 census data. Education levels increased rapidly since then, but despite improvements, the Arab economy sector lagged behind. As a result, there were few opportunities for the higher-skilled Arab workers, something that remained true in 2007.[36]

Poverty

In 2007, 58 percent of the Arab population was classified as poor before taxes and transfer payments and 51.4 percent were poor after taxes and transfer payments.[37] The extent of poverty in the Arab community is one of

[36] Lewin-Epstein, Noah. 1990. The Arab Economy in Israel: Growing Population Mismatch. Pinchas Sapir Center for Development, TAU, Discussion Paper 014–90, 131.
[37] National Insurance Institute. 2008. Poverty and Social Gaps in 2007 Annual Report. Jerusalem: National Insurance Institute Research and Planning Administration, 16.

Figure 9.4. The rate of poverty among Arabs, 1997–2008.

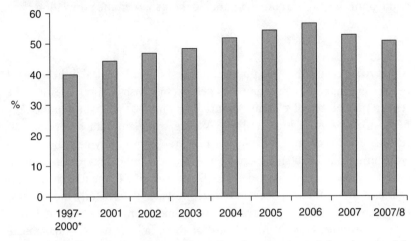

Source: Bank of Israel, Annual Report 2008. Based on survey carried out between July 2007 and June 2008. 1997–2000: annual average.

the most serious failings in Israeli society, not only from a socioeconomic point of view, but also from a political perspective. In the period 1997–2006, the relative probability of Arabs being poor, exclusive of the effect of demographic variables, increased. The extent or depth of poverty also increased in the Arab community. The main reason for the increase in the last decade was the reduction in child allowances that cut the income of large and poor families. In 2007–2008, there was a decrease in the rate of poverty due to improvements in the economy that resulted in an increase in employment. These trends are shown in Figure 9.4 and are compared with the poverty rate for Jewish population, excluding the ultra-Orthodox.

The reduction in welfare payments in 2002–2003 and the deterioration in the economic situation of the Arab population during recent years also resulted in a small increase the labor force participation rate of Arab women. Ironically, this led to a rise in unemployment among them rather than to a growth in employment.[38] In 2000, there were 85,900 Arab families classified as poor after taxes and transfers. By 2007, that number had increased by 66 percent, to 143,000. The corresponding increase in the Jewish community was 23 percent. In 2000, Arab families accounted for 28 percent of total

http://www.btl.gov.il/English%20Homepage/Publications/Poverty_Report/Documents/oni2007-E.pdf

[38] Bank of Israel. Annual Report 2006. 341 and 343. http://www.bankisrael.gov.il/deptdata/mehkar/doch07/eng/pe_8.pdf

number of families in poverty; in 2006–2007, they accounted for 41 percent of the poor in Israel – more than double their share in the population.[39]

Local Authorities

About 70 percent of the Arab population lives in 116 Arab local authorities, 24 percent live in mixed communities, 1 percent in Jewish communities, and the remaining 4 percent live in unrecognized, mainly Bedouin communities.[40]

Most of the Arab local authorities were small and had few resources, reflecting the economic situation of the Arab community and the lack of government aid. In 2004, 45 percent of Arab local authorities were in the two lowest socioeconomic categories and 97 percent were in the four lowest categories.[41] Many did not collect local taxes or water charges fully, did not pass tax payments to central government, and some did not pay their employees fully or on time. One of the reasons for these failings was the inadequate infrastructure, including a lack of public transport within Arab towns as well as between them and other urban centers. The industrial employment base is weak in part because there are proportionally fewer industrial estates in Arab municipal areas than in Jewish ones. The government has a policy of compensating weaker local authorities whose local tax base is too low to fund basic services: It provides an equalization grant to weaker local authorities. In 2002, it provided 2.3 billion shekels to Jewish local authorities and 952 million to Arab and Druze ones. In 2008, the allocation to Jewish local authorities had fallen by 28 percent, to 1.65 billion shekels, and that to Arab and Druze local authorities fell by 1 percent, to 943 million shekels.[42] It should be added that Arab municipalities suffer serious problems of maladministration: Contracts are awarded on the basis of family connections, as are jobs in city administration, and accountability is weak.

---

[39] National Insurance Institute. 2008. Poverty and Social Gaps in 2007 Annual Report, Jerusalem: National Insurance Institute, Research and Planning Administration, 45; National Insurance Institute. 2002. Poverty and Income Inequality 2001, 21. http://www.btl.gov.il/Publications/oni_report/Documents/oni2001.pdf

[40] Agency for the Development of the Arab Sector in Israel. Prime Minister's Office. 2008. The Arab Population and the State of Israel: Economic Integration Strategy. http://www.pmo.gov.il/NR/rdonlyres/76DFC487-D52D-4A4F-919D-166BDF0476FC/0/ecopaper.pdf

[41] Rivlin-Tsur, Goni and Emad Zoabi. 2005. The State of Infant Education in the Arab Sector in Israel: Characteristics, Data and Conclusions. The Abraham Fund Initiatives and The Citizens Accord Forum between Jews and Arabs in Israel, Newe Ilan. http://www.abrahamfund.org/main/siteNew/index.php?page=4#

[42] The Prime Minister's Office. 2008. The Prime Minister's Conference on Arab Local Authorities. Slide 18. http://www.pmo.gov.il/NR/rdonlyres/F071E419–6643–4A2C-8F32–337CD628EAB9/0/int.ppt#316,18

Comparisons with Neighboring States

A comparison of the socioeconomic position of the Arabs in Israel with those in some of the Arab countries neighboring Israel throws light on the situation of the former. Table 9.4 shows that in 2006, the average gross national income per capita in the four neighboring countries, weighted by their population, was $1,562. This was equal to 7.5 per cent of Israel's gross national income per capita. (No comparable figures are available for the Palestinian Territories.) Average annual gross earnings per capita in Israel in 2006 were estimated at almost $10,000, or approximately 48 percent of gross national income per capita. Israeli Arab earnings averaged 38 percent of average earnings, or $3,800. Assuming that the relationship between gross earnings and gross national income[43] is the same in the neighboring countries produces the figures shown in the second row of Table 9.3. (This assumption is necessary because of the lack of data about earnings in these Arab countries.) The data in the Table 9.3 shows that average gross earnings in the neighboring Arab states, weighted by their population, were $744 and the Israeli Arab level was just over five times higher.

Conclusions

In the early years of the state, the Arab minority was rural, isolated, poorly educated, and lacked services of all kinds. It was therefore in a weak position both "endogenously" and "exogenously" and was also a new and suddenly created minority. None of the minorities that have been examined in the literature have been "created" so quickly. In this and other respects, the Arabs of Israel are very different from other minorities. This became less true over time as being a minority became the norm for them. Government restrictions on movement and employment reinforced the separation of the Arab and Jewish economy until the 1950s.[44]

In the highly centralized state that Israel became, the Arab community was underfunded. Many Arabs lived in municipalities that did not get a fair share of government allocations. As a result, basic services, including education, remained substandard. One of the consequences was that economic development has been restricted and Arabs have had to work outside their communities. This did not help their integration into the wider, Jewish

---

[43] Gross national income is equal to GDP less net taxes on production and imports, less compensation of employees and property income payable to the rest of the world, plus the corresponding items receivable from the rest of the world.

[44] Meltzer, *The Divided Economy of Mandatory Palestine*, 206.

Table 9.4. *Gross national income per capita in the Middle East, 2006 ($)*

	Israel	Israeli Arabs	Egypt	Jordan	Lebanon	Syria
Gross national income per capita	20,920		1,260	2,650	5,630	1,560
Estimated average gross earnings per capita	9,998	3,800	602	1,266	2,670	745

Source: World Bank Country Data Profiles. http://ddp-ext.worldbank.org/ext/ddpreports/View SharedReport?REPORT_ID=9147&REQUEST_TYPE=VIEWADVANCED

economy.[45] There has been a greater recognition of these issues, and more funding has been made available to Arab local authorities by the Ministry of the Interior. In addition, initiatives were taken in the prime minister's office to raise capital for Arab businesses, encourage Arab women to go to work, and improve the physical infrastructure of the Arab school system. On the other hand, the political environment has worked against integration with the rise of more extreme voices in Arab and Jewish political circles.

The most outstanding development in the Arab community was demographic. Between 1948 and 2008, the Arab population increased by a factor of 9.6, compared with a total population rise of a factor of just over nine. As a result, its share in the total rose from 18 percent in November 1948 to 20 percent at the end of 2008, despite huge waves of Jewish immigration. Demographic trends are converging in that the Arab Muslim fertility rate is falling, thereby slowing the overall rate of growth of the Arab minority.

Education levels have risen since 1948, and there is a clear difference between the various religious groups that make up the Arab minority. The large differences in the educational achievements of Muslims and Christians are due in part to attitudes toward education and traditions in the two communities, in turn related to their class structure. The Christian community is more urban and more middle class. Whereas the Muslim community is more rural and working class. This is in part a heritage of the events of 1947–1949. In 1944, almost 53 percent of the Christian population lived in towns of 45,000 or more residents, whereas the share among the Muslims was less than 12 percent. This was endogenous but could be

[45] Lewin-Epstein and Semyonov, 149.

changed by the external environment. Differences in educational achievements have not led to a corresponding difference in earnings. Here the external environment – discrimination – plays a role. In recent years, the increase in Arab entrepreneurship may be due to the decline of the public sector in Arab towns due to cuts in public sector budgets throughout the economy.

Catching up has been a powerful explanation of the transmission of growth between countries. It also has potential within them. The educational improvements of recent years in terms of higher attendance rates and high school achievement levels are optimistic signs in an otherwise gloomy picture of discrimination and political disaffection. Whether this potential can be translated into more employment, higher earnings, and greater equality depends on the economic and political trends that prevail in the coming years.

The frustration of the Arab community combined with the onset of the Second Intifada led to serious riots and deaths in October 2000. According to the official commission's report on the riots, they were the result of "deep-seated factors that created an explosive situation in the Israeli Arab population." The state failed to provides comprehensive solutions to the serious problems faced by the Arab community. Over many years, the government's handling of the Arab sector was neglectful, discriminatory, and insensitive. The state did not do enough to create equality or enforce the law in the Arab sector, and so illegal and other undesirable phenomena had taken root there. As a result, serious distress prevailed in the Arab sector including poverty, unemployment, a shortage of land, serious problems in the education system, and a very defective infrastructure.[46]

On the theoretical level, this chapter suggests that the terms "endogenous" and "exogenous" need to be used with care. What might be considered endogenous in one period may well be the result of exogenous factors operating over a longer period. The high fertility rates that prevailed for many years were related to the traditions of village life. As the community became urbanized and better educated, fertility rates declined. As in other countries, the education of women was crucial in changing decisions about the number of children in a family. In this way, what initially was taken as an endogenous factor became influenced by socioeconomic conditions and was thus influenced by exogenous factors.

---

[46] The Official Summary of the Or Commission. 2008. *Ha'aretz*. http://www.haaretz.com/hasen/pages/ShArt.jhtml?itemNo=335594

TEN

Demographic Developments and Socioeconomic Divisions

Introduction

Immigration has played a major role in the growth of the Israeli population and has affected the ethnic composition of the Jewish majority. The change in ethnicity has, along with other factors, had significant political effects that, in turn, have influenced economic policies and the structure of the economy. The first section of this chapter examines the demographic trends that have prevailed in Israel.

Israel has also experienced significant changes in the distribution of income and poverty rates in recent years. The second section of this chapter relates these changes to stabilization, liberalization, and globalization, the three main developments that have dominated the economy in recent years. Social developments were not only the by-product of economic policies; they had economic effects manifested in unemployment and other phenomena.

Demography

Between 1948 and 2008, the population of Israel increased ninefold, or by over 6 million, and the number of immigrants and returning Israelis was just over 3 million (see Table 10.1). Natural growth of the population played a major role despite the fact that the birth rate fell much faster than the death rate (see Appendix 10.1). The rate of demographic growth was characteristic of developing countries, as Israel was classified in 1948. Rapid growth continued even when the economy reached a level of maturity, with relatively high income levels; the reason for this was immigration.

Israel is a country of immigration. The ingathering of the exiled Jewish population from the Diaspora was the central tenet of Zionism and has

Table 10.1. *The sources of population growth, 1948–2008 (thousands)*

	Population at beginning of period	Natural increase	Total net migration balance	Total growth	Population at end of period	Annual growth (percent)	Migration balance/ total growth (percent)
1948–2007	805.6	3,951.6	2,448.0	6,399.4	7,243.6	3.8	38.3
1948–1960	805.6	475.4	869.4	1,344.8	2,150.4	8.2	64.6
1961–1971	2,150.4	562.0	339.8	901.8	3,120.7	3.2	37.7
1972–1982	3,115.6	752.7	183.5	936.2	4,063.6	2.4	19.6
1983–1989	4,033.7	494.8	31.1	525.9	4,559.6	1.8	5.9
1990–1995	4,559.6	465.9	593.5	1,059.4	5,619.0	3.5	56.0
1996–2000	5,612.3	460.8	296.2	757.0	6,369.3	2.6	39.1
2001–2006	6,369.3	628.4	119.1	747.4	7,116.7	1.9	15.9
2000	6,209.1	98.7	61.4	160.1	6,369.3	2.6	38.3
2005	6,869.5	104.9	16.3	121.2	6,990.7	1.8	13.5
2006	6,990.7	109.3	16.6	126.0	7,116.7	1.8	13.2
2007	7,116.7	111.6	15.4	127.0	7,243.6	1.8	12.1
2008	7,243.6	128.3	12.8	130.0	7,371.9	1.8	9.8

Sources: Central Bureau of Statistics. Statistical Abstract of Israel 2009, no. 60. http://www.cbs.gov.il/reader/shnaton/templ_shnaton_e.html?num_tab=st02_038&CYear=2009

been one of the most important phenomena affecting its development ever since. In the last decade, the share of immigration in total population growth declined sharply. This also contributed to the slower growth of the population. There was also significant emigration; by the end of 2007, an estimated 650,000 Israelis lived abroad, equal to 9 percent of the population.[1]

In the first twenty-five years, immigrants formed a majority of Israel's population. By 2008, the Israeli population included 3.9 million Jews born in Israel and 1.6 million born abroad. Immigrants therefore constituted 29 percent of the Jewish population and 22 percent of the total population. There were also several hundred thousand immigrants from the former Soviet Union who were not classified as Jews.[2]

Although overall birth and fertility rates have fallen, they varied significantly by ethnic origin. As was shown in Chapter 9, the natural growth rate of the Arab population of Israel was always much higher than that of the Jews. Within the Arab community, there were significant differences between Muslims and Christians. Within the Jewish community, there were also significant differences depending on the level of religiosity. As was shown in Chapter 8, the fertility rates among ultra-Orthodox women were much higher than among other Jewish women, and as a result, the rate of growth of the ultra-Orthodox population was much higher than that of the Jewish population as a whole. The decline in the crude birth rate was mainly due to the declining number of births per woman, from an average of 4.16 in 1950–1955 to an estimated 2.75 in 2005–2010.[3] Since 1950, the birth rate has fallen by almost 40 percent and the death rate by almost 26 percent.

Between 1990 and 2007, the dependency ratio – which measures the relationship between the population below and above working age and that of working age – fell from 95 percent to 68 percent. The share of children (aged 0 to 19 years) in the population declined from 52 percent to 45 percent, and the share of individuals aged 65 or older rose from 4.9 percent to 9.8 percent. During the same period, the dependency ratio for more developed areas fell from 49 percent to 48 percent, whereas that in West Asia (which includes Israel) fell from 76 percent to 61 percent. Israel's relatively high dependency ratio is due to the relatively large proportion of young people

---

[1] Central Bureau of Statistics. *Statistical Abstract of Israel 2008*. Tables 2.1 and 2.25.

[2] UN: Population Division of the Department of Economic and Social Affairs of the United Nations Secretariat. World Population Prospects: The 2006 Revision and World Urbanization Prospects: The 2005 Revision, Medium variant. http://esa.un.org/unpp/p2k0data.asp

[3] UN: World Population Prospects. The 2006 Revision. http://esa.un.org/unpp/index.asp?panel=2

Table 10.2. *The age structure of the population, 1960–2008*

	Working age	Total non-working age	of which 0–19 years	of which 65+ years	Ratio of working age to non-working age population
1960	51.3	48.7	43.8	4.9	1.05
1970	50.0	50.0	43.3	6.7	1.00
1980	49.5	50.5	41.8	8.7	0.98
1990	50.5	49.5	40.4	9.1	1.02
2000	53.0	47.0	37.3	9.7	1.13
2008	53.9	46.1	36.4	9.7	1.17

Source: Statistical Abstract of Israel 2008, no. 59. http://www.cbs.gov.il/shnaton59/download/st02_21x.xls; Statistical Abstract of Israel 2009, no. 60. http://www.cbs.gov.il/reader/shnatonenew_site.htm

in the population, something that it has in common with other West Asian countries.[4] These trends are illustrated in Table 10.2.

Ethnic Balance

Israel was created as a Jewish democracy, and the Law of Return gives all Jews the right to immigrate and become citizens. From the day of its foundation, it had a significant Arab (Muslim, Christian, and Druze) minority that was accorded equal rights in law. Although the Arab minority suffered serious discrimination, its population increased more than ninefold between 1948 and 2007 (end of years), almost entirely due to natural growth. This compares to a near eightfold increase in the Jewish population. As shown in Chapter 8, high population growth in the Arab community was associated with low living standards.

The composition of the Jewish population is significant in political terms, because there is an ethnic component in voting patterns as well as in educational achievement levels and recruitment to managerial and political posts. The main division is between Jews who came from the West, which includes the former Soviet Union (Ashkenazim), and those who came from

---

[4] Central Bureau of Statistics. The Emigration of Israelis-2005. Jerusalem: Central Bureau of Statistics, 2008. http://www.cbs.gov.il/reader/newhodaot/hodaa_template.html?hodaa=200701153; Associated Press, "Absorption Ministry Seeks to Bring Israelis Living Abroad." Reprinted in *Ha'aretz*, 10 December.

Table 10.3. *The ethnic origin of the population,*
1948–2008 (thousands)

	Total	Jews	Arabs	Other*
1948	827.7	716.7	156.0	
1950	1,370.1	1,203.0	167.1	
1960	2,150.4	1,911.3	239.1	
1970	3,022.1	2,582.0	440.1	
1980	3,921.7	3,282.7	638.9	
1990	4,821.7	3,946.7	875.0	
2000	6,369.3	4,955.4	1,188.7	225.2
2008	7,374.0	5,569.2	1,487.6	317.1

* Non-Jewish immigrants were classified separately from 2000.
Sources: Central Bureau of Statistics: Statistical Abstract
of Israel 2008, no. 59. http://www.cbs.gov.il/shnaton58/
download/st02_01.xls; Monthly Bulletin of Statistics, June
2009, no. 6. http://www.cbs.gov.il/www/yarhon/b1_e.htm.
NB end of year except 8 November 1948.

the Middle East and North Africa (Sephardim). The Sephardim account
for many of the lower occupational, income, and educational groups in
Jewish-Israeli society. This is gradually changing because improvements in
education, housing, and other services are having their effect and because
of intermarriage between members of the two communities, but the differences are still significant. The other, wider division is between Jews and
Arabs. The Arab community is also heterogeneous: The majority is Muslim
and the minority is Christian, but there is also a significant Druze community. In addition, there are very small Circassian, Bahai, and other communities, each with different income levels and educational achievements (see
Table 10.3).

Appendix 10.2 shows how the pattern of immigration has changed. Most
of the immigrants who came before 1948 were from Europe and were affected
by the social and political changes that developed there in the latter part of
the nineteenth century (see Chapter 2). After 1948, an increasing share of
immigrants came from the Arab countries of the Middle East as well as Iran
and Turkey. Although there were many differences between the immigrants
from the different Middle East states, most of them had not been exposed to
secularization, at least not for as long or as deeply as Jews from Europe. For
most, though not all, the socialism of the Labor movement, and especially

Table 10.4. *The Jewish population by origin,*
1948–2008 (percent)

	Born in Israel	Born abroad	Asia	Africa	Europe-America
1948	35.4	64.4	8.2	2.7	54.8
1961	37.8	62.2	25.5	22.9	34.8
1972	37.3	52.7	11.8	13.0	29.9
1983	57.5	42.5	8.9	9.7	23.9
1995	60.7	39.3	5.5	7.1	26.7
2008	67.7	32.3	3.4	5.4	23.5

Source: CBS, Statistical Abstract of Israel 2009, Table 2.25. Years 1995 and 2008 include non-Arab Christians and others not classified by religion.

the Kibbutz, was anathema. The attempt to maintain an extended family in which the grandfather was the head came into conflict with the mores of the new society that Labor Zionism was creating. Although the early generations of immigrants were grateful to David Ben Gurion, the first Prime Minister and leader of the Labor movement, for enabling them to reach the Promised Land, they and their children and grandchildren paid a price in terms of discrimination that was to have long-term political significance. Appendix 10.2 is based on data for immigration, and it should be noted that emigration has been a significant phenomenon.

The arrival of the immigrants changed the ethnic structure of the Jewish population. In May 1948, when the state was created, almost 36 percent of the population had been born in Palestine. This hardly changed in the following quarter-century as wave after wave of immigrants arrived. The share of the population born in Israel or Europe and America fell sharply from just over 90 percent in 1948 to just over 68 percent in 1972. Then the share of native-born Israelis rose sharply and the volume of immigration subsided. In the 1990s, with the arrival of nearly one million immigrants from the former Soviet Union, the share from Europe rose but that of native-born Israelis in the total population also continued to rise. The immigration from the former Soviet Union, which included large numbers of non-Jewish family members, changed the ethnic balance and the political landscape yet again (Table 10.4).

The influx of large numbers of immigrants has not only changed the ethnic makeup of the Israeli population but also its politics. One of the most important implications was a change in public attitudes toward welfare and other social values. The arrival of a million immigrants from the former Soviet Union in the 1990s increased the number of people on welfare. In addition, the number of ultra-Orthodox who benefited from welfare increased continuously (see Chapter 8). As welfare budgets rose, Israel became increasingly divided between Jews and Arabs, secular and religious, immigrants and veterans. As the political process promoted sectoral interests so the consensus about universalistic values such as welfare declined. After 1985, this also coincided with the need to restrain public spending to avoid macroeconomic instability.[5]

Fertility Rates

Table 10.5 shows how the rate of fertility (the number of children born to a woman) has fallen over the last fifty years from 3.85 to 2.96. These rates were significantly higher than in other developed countries. As in many other countries, the fall in fertility was due to changes in income, education, urbanization, and the increased tendency of women to work outside the home. The national figure disguises very large variations between the different sections of the Israeli population. In 1960–1964, the fertility rate among Muslim women was almost 2.4 times the national average. By 2007, it was 34 percent above the average. Within the Arab community, in 1960–1964, the Muslim fertility rate was much higher than that of Christians. However, the difference has declined since then. The national fertility rate declined until 2005 as a result of the convergence of rates among the different communities.[6]

Since 2000, there has been an increase in the Jewish fertility rate. As Jews accounted for about 80 percent of the population, this pushed up the national rate. The rise in the fertility rate in the Jewish community reflected the growing share of the ultra-Orthodox population that has a much higher fertility rate than the rest of the Jewish and non-Jewish population. The high fertility rate also explains the growth in the share of this community in the total and Jewish populations. The reasons for the high rate of fertility

[5]   Doron, Avraham. 2007. "Multiculturalism and the Erosion of Support for the Universalistic Welfare State: The Israeli Experience." *Israel Studies*. Vol. 12. No. 3. 92–108; Ben-Rafael. Eliezer. 2007. "Mizrachi and Russian Challenges to Israel's Dominant Culture: Divergencies and Convergencies." *Israel Studies*. Vol. 12. No. 3. 68–91.

[6]   Della Pergola, Sergio. 2007. Actual, Intended, and Appropriate Family Size in Israel: Trends, Attitudes and Policy Implications: A Preliminary Report. New York: Population Association of America, March 29–31.

Table 10.5. *Fertility rates (number of births per woman), 1960–2008*

	1960-64	1965-69	1970-74	1975-79	1980-84	1985-89	1990-94	1995-99	2000-2004	2005	2006	2007	2008
Total population	3.85	3.83	3.80	3.47	3.13	3.07	2.93	2.93	2.92	2.84	2.88	2.90	2.96
Jews	3.39	3.36	3.28	3.00	2.80	2.79	2.62	2.62	2.67	2.69	2.75	2.80	2.88
Muslims	9.23	9.22	8.47	7.25	5.54	4.70	4.67	4.67	4.57	4.03	3.97	3.90	3.84
Christians	4.68	4.26	3.65	3.12	2.41	2.49	2.18	2.56	2.35	2.15	2.14	2.13	2.11
Druze	7.49	7.30	7.25	6.93	5.40	4.19	3.77	3.24	2.87	2.59	2.64	2.49	2.49
Population not classified by religion								1.76	1.55	1.49	1.55	1.49	1.57

Source: CBS, Statistical Abstract of Israel 2009, Table 3.13.

in the ultra-Orthodox community and some of its consequences are examined in Chapter 9.

Overall birth and death rates have fallen, although there have been significant differences between sections of the population. Although there is evidence that these differences are declining. The ethnic composition of the population has changed mainly within the Jewish majority. The share of Jews born in the Middle East and North Africa in the population rose sharply in the 1950s. In the 1990s, the large immigration from the Soviet Union and former Soviet Union changed the balance once again. Throughout its history, the share of the population born in Israel has risen, but the share of the Arab community in the total population has remained broadly constant. Demographic developments, dominated by immigration, have had major effects on the way that Israel has developed. They have strengthened the economy by providing an increase in the supply of labor but have made the society much less homogenous. Israel's politics have been affected by the development of sectoral interest groups often based on ethnic divisions. This has played a role in the breakdown of the welfare state and other changes that are examined in Chapters 8 to 11.

Income Distribution

The distribution of income in Israel has become more unequal in recent years. Figure 10.1 shows that between 1980 and 2007, the Gini coefficient of income distribution before taxes and transfers rose by 18 percent. Between 1997 and 2007, it rose by 1.8 percent. The Gini coefficient is defined as a ratio with a range from 0 and 1 (or 0 percent to 100 percent). A low Gini coefficient indicates more equal income or wealth distribution, with zero corresponding to perfect equality (everyone having exactly the same level of income), whereas higher Gini coefficients indicate more unequal distribution, with one corresponding to perfect inequality (a situation with more than one individual, where one person has all the income). To be validly calculated, no person can have negative net income or wealth. These figures suggest that the factors causing inequality have weakened in recent years. Between 1980 and 2007, the index for income after taxes and transfers increased by 18 percent and between 1997 and 2007, it rose by 15 percent, indicating that government measures, in the form of taxes and benefits, to redistribute income had weakened. The separation between pre-tax and benefit incomes and post-tax and benefit incomes captures only part of the effect of government policy. As will be shown, the way the labor market functions and determines earnings

Figure 10.1. The Gini coefficient of income distribution of the whole population, 1980–2007.

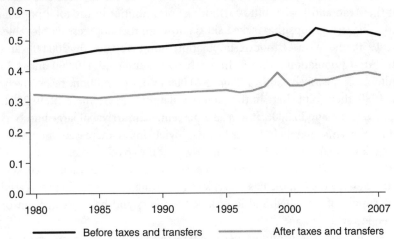

Before taxes and transfers ————— After taxes and transfers

Source: National Insurance Institute. Annual Survey, 2007; Report on Measures of Poverty and Social Gaps, 2007. Annual Survey 1997–1998.

and their distribution is also related to economic policy. Government therefore influences pre-tax and benefit income as well as post-tax and benefit income. The Gini index is an overall index: It does not specify how inequality developed. In Israel, as in many other countries, the growth of inequality in the distribution of income before taxes and benefits has largely been due to the rise in income of the highest earning group. This suggests that as the economy generated less inequality, the tax and benefit system has redistributed less.

Between 1994 and 2003, there was a dramatic rise in the inequality of earnings. The share of all deciles of earners fell except those of the highest two groups while the shares of the lowest earners did worst. The deterioration in the position of middle-level earners was also significant. In real terms, the income of the lowest-paid decile actually fell by 1.3 percent whereas that of the top decile rose by 37 percent. The average rise for the whole population was 17.4 percent. During this period, GDP grew by 32.5 percent in real terms. There were a number of reasons for the growth of earnings inequality. The first was the rise in unemployment that affected the low-earning population the most. In 1994, the unemployment rate was 7.8 percent, meaning that 157,800 people were without work. In 2003, the rate was 10.7 percent, with 279,800 unemployed. The absolute number of unemployed therefore rose by 77 percent. By 2008, the unemployment rate

declined to 6.1 percent or 180,400 people.[7] The second factor that influenced the distribution of income was the increase in the size and share
of the Arab and Jewish ultra-Orthodox communities in the total population, the two groups that lacked skills and were therefore less employable.
In 1980, the ultra-Orthodox population numbered nearly 200,000 and
the Arab population 640,000. In 2001, they numbered 410,000 and 1.25
million, respectively, and in 2006, 570,000 and 1.44 million, respectively.
In 1980, their joint share in the total population was 21.3 percent, in 2001,
25.6 percent, and in 2006, it was 28.2 percent.[8] The arrival of large numbers
of immigrants, mainly from the former Soviet Union, increased unemployment and weakened the bargaining power of low-paid workers by increasing their supply. From the early 1990s, Israel also began to import workers
from outside the Middle East to replace Palestinians. This further increased
the supply of unskilled and low-skilled workers and helped constrain or
even lower their wages.[9]

From 2003, the economy began to recover and efforts were made to
reduce the number of legal and illegal foreign workers in Israel. These
changes had effects on the labor market. In 2007, the unemployment rate
fell to 7.3 percent, or 211,800, some 67,000, or 24 percent, fewer than in
the peak year of 2003.[10] The share of Palestinians and other foreign workers legally employed in the business sector labor force fell from a peak of
16.5 percent in 1999 to 13.9 percent in 2003 and 11 percent in 2007.[11] As
shown in Table 10.1, the increase in the inequality of pre-tax and benefit
earnings distribution stabilized in 2003 and then declined slightly between
2004 and 2007.

Table 10.6 shows that between 1995 and 2000, the inequality of income
before tax and benefits increased as a result of the deterioration of the
position of low earners (in fact, the position of the bottom 60 percent

[7] Bank of Israel. *Annual Report* 2004. Table A.2.7. http://www.bankisrael.gov.il/deptdata/
     mehkar/doch04/eng/d2004ta2.htm; Central Bureau of Statistics. 2009. Monthly Bulletin
     of Statistics no. 11, Table K1. http://www.cbs.gov.il/www/yarhon/k1_e.htm
[8] Calculated from Annual Report 2007. http://www.bankisrael.gov.il/deptdata/mehkar/
     doch07/eng/pe_8.pdf and CBS. Statistical Abstract of Israel. 2008 no. 59 http://www.cbs.
     gov.il/shnaton59/download/st02_02.xls
[9] Saporta, Ishak, Salem Abo Zaid and Dotan Leshem. 2006. Inequality in the Distribution of
     Income among Household and Wage Earners in Israel, 1967–2003. The Van Leer Institute,
     Economics and Society Program Policy Research Paper no. 2. Jerusalem, 11–15.
[10] Bank of Israel. *Annual Report 2007*. 223. http://www.bankisrael.gov.il/deptdata/mehkar/
     doch07/eng/pe_5.pdf
[11] Bank of Israel. *Annual Report 2007*. 217. http://www.bankisrael.gov.il/deptdata/mehkar/
     doch07/eng/pe_5.pdf

Table 10.6. *The distribution of income before and after taxes and benefits: The share of each decile in total income per standard person, 1995–2007*

	1995		2000		2005		2007	
	Before benefits and taxes	After benefits and taxes	Before benefits and taxes	After benefits and taxes after	Before benefits and taxes	After benefits and taxes	Before benefits and taxes	After benefits and taxes
1	1.59	3.27	0.0	2.7	0.0	2.0	0.8	2.0
2	3.03	4.66	1.3	4.1	0.9	3.5	1.6	3.6
3	4.30	5.17	3.2	5.1	2.9	4.6	2.9	4.8
4	5.56	6.88	4.6	6.3	4.4	5.9	4.3	6.0
5	7.01	8.01	6.3	7.6	6.2	7.4	6.3	7.5
6	8.49	9.26	8.2	9.1	8.2	9.0	8.1	9.0
7	10.43	10.73	10.5	10.7	10.5	10.8	10.3	10.7
8	12.99	12.65	13.5	12.8	13.6	13.1	13.3	12.9
9	17.22	15.60	18.3	15.9	18.4	16.5	17.9	16.2
10	29.38	23.17	34.3	25.6	35.0	27.4	34.5	27.3
Ratio of 1+2 to 9+10	10.09	4.89	40.5	6.1	59.3	8.3	12.4	7.8

Sources: National Insurance Institute, Jerusalem. Indices of Poverty and Social Inequality 2007 (2008), 2006 (2007), Annual Survey 1995–1995; 2001. http://www.btl.gov.il

deteriorated) and the improvement of that of high earners. The same pattern can be observed for the period 2000–2005, with the six lower deciles experiencing a fall in their share and the top four experiencing an increase. (The zero figure for income before taxes and benefits for 2000 and 2005 should be interpreted with care. It probably reflects measuring difficulties and should be interpreted as a very low figure close to zero). Between 2005 and 2007, there was an improvement in the position of the lowest two deciles and a deterioration of that of the top four.

In 1995–2000, the share of income after tax and benefits of the bottom six deciles declined whereas the top three deciles experienced an increase. In 2000–2005, the bottom six deciles experienced deterioration in their share and the top three experienced an increase. This was the result of reductions in state benefits designed to reduce the budget deficit and encourage more people to find work. In 2002, total transfer payments per head fell by 5.2 percent in real terms, and in 2003, they were cut by a further 5 percent. The sharpest reduction was in payments to the unemployed by the National Insurance Institute: In 2002, they were reduced by 31.7 percent, and in 2003, by a further 12.4 percent. In 2001–2003, the reduction in unemployment benefits came to 43 percent. Between 2001 and 2004, spending on child allowances fell by 41 percent (see Chapter 9).[12] In 2005–2007, there was no change in the share of the bottom decile, but the second to the sixth deciles all saw improvements whereas the top four experienced deterioration in their share.

The development of high-technology industries that placed great emphasis on human capital meant that well-paid jobs were created for those with high levels of education. The increase in the number of these jobs contributed to the growth of inequality in earnings. This was illustrated in Figure 5.3. As in other countries, earnings inequalities within companies increased. This was also true of the public sector where, between 1993 and 2004, earnings of the top 1 percent rose by 64.8 percent, compared with an average rise of 22.5 percent. The earnings of managers of public companies trading on the stock exchange rose by 92.2 percent.[13] In the permanent (non-conscript) army, differentials widened. In order to retain senior personnel, the army also increased salaries at differential rates. Between 1994 and 2008, the real average salary of full generals rose by 94 percent whereas that of the most junior officer rank rose by 16 percent, and average military salaries went up by nearly 27 percent.[14]

Figure 10.2 shows how unemployment rose between 1988 and 2008; the overall figure is broken down by years of education. There were clear cyclical episodes, with major rises in unemployment in 1988–1992 and in 1996–2003. In addition, the rate of unemployment was much higher than average among those with low levels of schooling and much lower among those with high levels. It should also be noted that the growth of the labor force meant that a constant rate of unemployment resulted in higher absolute numbers of unemployed. Between 1999 and 2005, the labor force grew by almost 17 percent and the unemployment rate rose from 8.9 percent to

[12] Bank of Israel. *Annual Report* 2004. 220. http://www.bankisrael.gov.il/deptdata/mehkar/doch04/heb/p1_5.pdf

[13] Yotav-Solberg, Idit. ed. 2008. The Appointment and Reward of Senior Managers in Public Companies and Authorities. Bank of Israel Survey, January, 19. http://www.bankisrael.gov.il/deptdata/mehkar/seker81/surv81_1.pdf

[14] Ministry of Finance. The Non-Classified Defense Budget 2009. 38. http://www.mof.gov.il/budget2007/docs2009/bitachonLoMesuvag.pdf

Figure 10.2. Unemployment rates by years of education, 1998–2008.

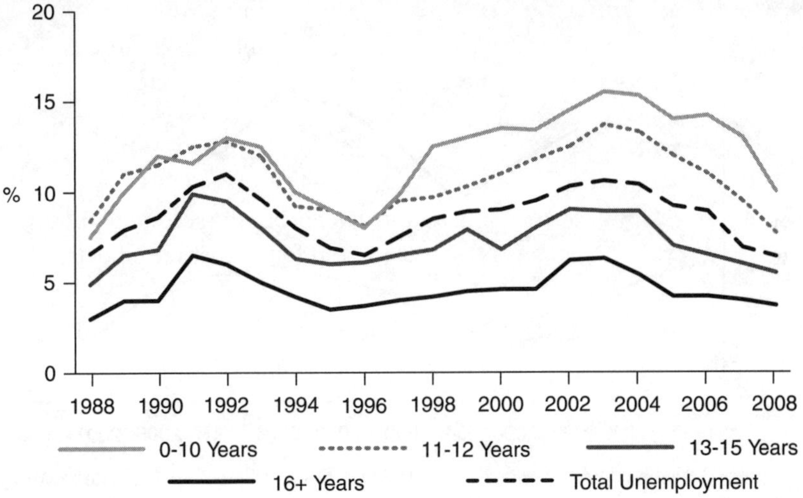

Source: Bank of Israel Annual Report 2008.

9 percent. Despite the very small rise in the rate, because of the increase in the size of the labor force, the number of unemployed increased by 38,000, or 18.2 percent. The only group not to experience an increase in unemployment was that with 16-plus years of education. This was also true of the cyclical increase of 1988–1993 but not in 2000–2003, which was partly due to the international crisis in the high-technology sector.

Poverty

In Israel, the poor are officially defined, using a relative poverty measure, as those having an income below 50 percent of the median income. In the OECD, the rate is 60 percent, although figures for 50 percent and 70 percent are also reported. The standard of living of a household depends not only on its income but also on its needs determined by its size. The additional income needed by each additional person in a family declines as family size increases due to the economies of scale. To measure poverty, an equivalence scale is constructed to calculate what each member of a family needs. The economies of scale assumed abroad are much greater than those in Israel, which is one reason that more people are recorded as poor in the latter.

In 2007–2008, 1.48 million people, or 22.3 percent of the population, lived in poverty. (This excludes the Arab population of Jerusalem, many of whom have Israeli resident status and are thus registered with the National

Figure 10.3. Incidence of poverty among individuals according to different measures, 1997–2007.

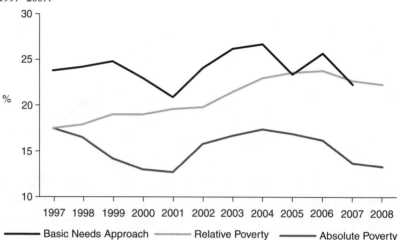

%

Basic Needs Approach ———— Relative Poverty ———— Absolute Poverty

Source: Bank of Israel Annual Report 2008.

Insurance Institute.)[15] Depending on which measures are used, the rate of poverty had remained stable or declined slightly in the period 2005–2008. The relative poverty indexes show stability whereas the absolute poverty index shows a fall and the one based on basic needs shows an increase (see Figure 10.3). The rate of poverty is one of the highest in Western countries.

Using the international (Luxemburg) standard reduces the number of poor in 1987 from nearly 18 percent of the population to 14 percent, and in 2005, from 24 percent to slightly less than 21 percent. It does not, however, change the upward direction of poverty, which increased by 50 percent according to the international measure and by 30 percent according to the Israeli measure.[16]

There are several reasons for the high rates of poverty. The first is low earnings: Many Israelis in full-time employment earn less than the official minimum wage, and there are even public sector employees who are entitled to income supplements from the National Insurance Institute because they earn less than the official minimum. The low-skilled labor force grew with the import of Palestinian and then other foreign workers. This helped moderate wage rises for the lower-paid workers. Furthermore, the availability of low-paid jobs in the manufacturing sector has been reduced by

15 Bank of Israel. *Annual Report 2008*. 328.
16 Bank of Israel. 2006. Recent Economic Developments. November. http://www.bankisrael. gov.il/develeng/develeng115/develeng.pdf; National Insurance Institute. 2008. Measures of Poverty and Social Gaps 2007. November.

the effects of globalization. The resulting unemployment of Israelis (unemployed Palestinians and other foreigners leave the Israeli labor market when demand for labor falls) also puts downward pressure on wages. The second is a set of factors special to Israel and associated with two minority groups: the Arabs and the ultra-Orthodox communities. In recent years, rates of poverty have been affected by two contradictory factors: reduced government spending on welfare programs and faster economic growth.

Although the government provided substantial welfare payments to the poor – which were cut in 2003 – it did little to develop alternative vocational training or employment programs for them. In fact, its policies have undermined the position of the poor in the labor market by allowing or even encouraging the entry of large numbers of Palestinians and later other foreign workers into the economy.

How do welfare payments affect poverty? On the one hand, they alleviated it by providing the poor with alternative sources of income that reduced the number in poverty by the amounts shown in Appendix 10.3. On the other hand, they encouraged a culture of reliance on handouts rather than on work.[17] Large families mean lower savings rates for families, which in turn reduces income from capital.

The numbers in poverty increased between 2002 and 2008 (see Appendix 10.3). The absolute number of people in poverty before tax and benefits rose by 9.8 percent, the number of families by 7.4 percent, and of children by 12.5 percent. After tax and benefits, the number of people living in poverty rose by 25 percent, the number of families by 26.9 percent, and the number of children also by 26.9 percent. Between 2006 and 2008, there was a small decline in the share and absolute number of people, families, and children living in poverty. There was also a rise in the share of the poor who were lifted out of poverty by the tax and benefit system. There was, however, a deepening of poverty in that the poor became relatively poorer. The improvement in the economy and the labor market in recent years meant more employment and higher incomes for the employed. It also raised the poverty level so more would fall below it. In general, the larger the share of the population employed, the lower the level of poverty, although this is partly negated by low earnings.

The poor can be classified in various ways. The first is by family size; the second is by the state of employment of the head of the household. The third is the level of education of the head of the household. Other groups for which there are measures in Israel are pensioners, Jews, Arabs, and immigrants.

The incidence of poverty varies considerably by family size. In 2007, the poverty level after taxes and benefits among all families with children was 24.8 percent. Among families with one to three children, the poverty rate was 18.4 percent. Among families with four or more children, it was 56.5 percent, and among families with five children or more, it was 66.7 percent. It also varied significantly by the employment status of the head of the family and the number of breadwinners. Poverty after taxes and benefits among families whose head of family worked was just over 12 percent. Among those who were of working age but did not work, the share was 69.8 percent. Among families with only one breadwinner, the rate of poverty was 23.5 percent, and among those with two breadwinners, it was 2.8 percent. There was also a correlation between the number of years of education of the head of the household and poverty. Among those families whose head of the household had up to eight years of education, the poverty level after taxes and benefits was 44.3 percent. Before taxes and benefits, it was 69.4 percent. This reflects the very low levels of earnings paid to many of the relatively unskilled in Israel. Between 2006 and 2007, both the pre- and post-tax and benefit figures deteriorated slightly. Among families whose head of household had between nine and twelve years of education, the pre-tax and benefit rate was 32.6 percent and the post tax and benefit rate of poverty was 20.9 percent. Among those families whose head of household had thirteen years or more of education, the poverty rate before taxes and benefits was 13.4 percent and remained unchanged after taxes and benefits. Among the elderly, the rate of poverty before taxes and benefits was 40.2 percent whereas after taxes and benefits (measured by the official retirement age), it was 18.8 percent. Among immigrants, it was 55.9 percent before taxes and benefits and 22.6 percent after them. The most dramatic difference was between Jews and Arabs. The poverty rate among Arabs before taxes was 58.9 percent and after taxes and benefits was 51.4 percent. Among Jews, the corresponding figures were 28.3 percent and 15 percent. These figures are significant not only because of the large difference between the poverty rates among the two communities, but also because the tax and welfare system was much less effective in relieving poverty among Arabs than among Jews. The reason was that the welfare system was much more effective in reducing poverty among small families, single people, and pensioners than among large families, regardless of their ethnic origin. The share of large families was much larger among Arabs than Jews, with the exception of the ultra-Orthodox.

In 2007–2008, the ultra-Orthodox accounted for about 8 percent of the population and 17 percent of the total number of individuals living in

Figure 10.4. Poverty by population group, 1997–2008.

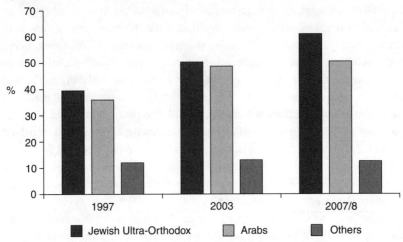

Source: Bank of Israel Annual Report 2008.

poverty. The poverty rate among the ultra-Orthodox was 60 percent before taxes and transfers (see Figure 10.4). The Arab community (including the Arabs of Jerusalem) accounted for 20 percent of the population and 45 percent of the poor. The poverty rate among the Arabs was 54 percent. The non-ultra-Orthodox and non-Arab sections of the population accounted for 38 percent of poverty and had a poverty rate of 12 percent. What is the rate of poverty of the population excluding the ultra-Orthodox? Appendix 10.3 indicates that in 2007, there were 1.63 million in poverty after taxes and benefits. Using the 2007–2008 figure for the share of the ultra-Orthodox in the total number of the poor of 17 percent suggests that there were 1.35 million non-ultra-Orthodox poor in Israel, or slightly less than 20 percent of the population. The rate of poverty among Jews (and other non-Arabs) was 13 percent. The national poverty rate was 23.3 percent and among non-ultra-Orthodox Jews and other non-Arabs, it was 10 percent (see Figure 10.4).

In 2007, those in work accounted for 74.7 percent of the population; of them, 42.1 percent were poor measured before tax and benefits and 45.7 percent after taxes and benefits. Those of working age not in employment accounted for 9.3 percent of the population; of them, 26.3 percent were poor before tax and benefit and 32.6 percent after tax and benefit.[18]

---

[18] Bank of Israel. *Annual Report 2006*. 341. http://www.bankisrael.gov.il/deptdata/mehkar/doch07/eng/pe_8.pdf

The growth of poverty among children is one of the most worrying aspects of the socioeconomic picture. Insofar as poverty is inherited or has lasting negative effects on individuals, then the most urgent task is to reduce poverty among children. As poverty is measured relatively, being poor today means being better off than in the past. For children perhaps more than for adults, relative poverty hurts badly. It not only affects them at home but also at school where they may well lack books and the means to participate fully in school activities. In 1980, the share of children living in poverty before taxes and transfers was 15.4 percent; after tax and transfers, it was 8.2.[19] In 2007, for the first time in recent years, there was a fall in the number and share of children living in poverty before tax and benefits. The number of children living in poverty after tax and benefits rose, although the share declined (see Appendix 10.1).

According to the Organisation for Economic Cooperation and Development (OECD), Israel has the largest share of people living in poverty in the developed world. In 2005, 19.9 percent of Israel's residents lived below the poverty line, a larger share than in Mexico (18.4 percent), Turkey (17.5 percent), or the United States (17.1 percent). The rate in Israel is nearly twice as high as the average OECD poverty rate of 10.6 percent among its thirty member nations (see Figure 10.5).

Among the reasons for Israel's poor showing it had many large families. About a third of Israeli families have at least three children, compared to about 20 percent in most developed countries. Another reason is that the level of government support for the unemployed and the poor in Israel is one of the lowest in the Western world.[20]

Relative poverty measures mean that the standard by which an individual or family is judged to be poor changes as incomes do. In an economy that has experienced rising real income per capita, the poor today are better off than those of the past, assuming that the depth of poverty has not changed. Another objection is that saying that someone is poor because they have 50 percent or less than average income is arbitrary. There have therefore been calls for a more objective measure, and some suggest that the absolute measure of poverty may be appropriate.

---

[19] The Israel National Council for the Child. 2009. Data and information (accessed 26 February). http://www.children.org.il/information.asp?id=30; The Israel National Council for the Child. 2008. Selection of Statistics from the Yearbook: Children in Israel 2008, 19. http://www.children.org.il/Files/File/leket2009.doc

[20] Sinai, Ruth. 2008. "Poverty Report: The Many faces of Destitution." *Ha'aretz*, 24 November.

Figure 10.5. Poverty rates in Israel and selected countries, 1998–2006.

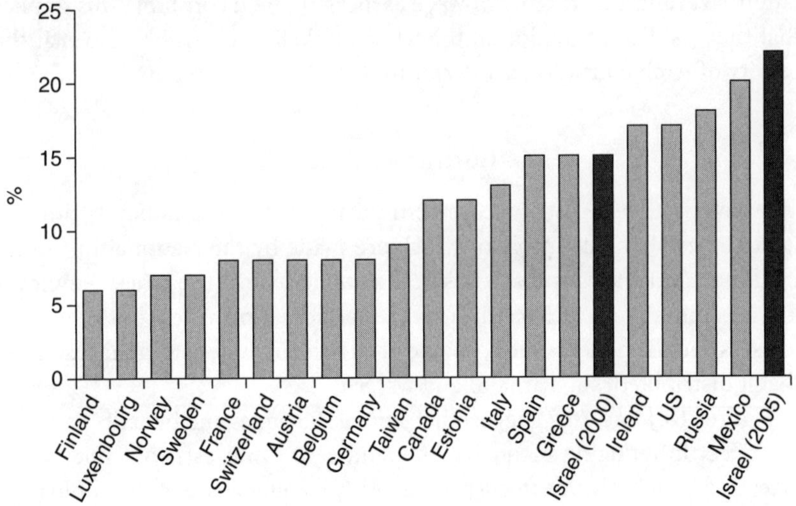

Source: Bank of Israel, Recent Economic Developments, November 2006. Selected countries: poverty rates between 1998 and 2005.

The main determinant of poverty is nonemployment, either due to non-participation in the labor force or unemployment. The existence of more than one wage earner in a household is a near guarantee that a family will not fall below the poverty line. Those communities with high poverty rates are usually characterized as having no or few wage earners. The receipt of transfers reduces the incidence of poverty. Old-age pensions substantially reduce poverty among the elderly, and the income supplement cuts poverty among single-parent families. The extent to which these groups manage to emerge from poverty is closely connected with the size of transfers. Child allowances substantially diminish poverty in large families, but as family size is also endogenously determined, it is not clear whether child allowances reduce poverty in the long run. The probability of being either unemployed or not participating in the labor force is far greater among individuals whose families receive large transfers. In the short run, the key to dealing with the problem of poverty therefore rests with the correct mix of transfers and incentives to work – for those capable of working. Education increases both wages and the employment rate and therefore plays an important role in reducing poverty. The strong negative correlation found between education and the probability of being below the poverty line indicates that the education system is the long-term solution to poverty. There is a relatively high incidence of poverty among the Arab population in Israel, when education, family size, and the number of wage earners are held constant. This implies that there is discrimination in the labor market and possibly also that the quality of Arab education is inferior to that of the Jewish population.[21]

Government Policy

The government redistributes income using direct tax policy (primarily income tax), benefits (most of which are made by the National Insurance Institute), and wages and salaries in the public sector (the largest employer in the economy), as well as through the services it provides (both the costs to users and the benefits they provide need to be included) and the resources that it distributed, such as land and water.[22]

Figures 10.1 and 10.2 suggest that since 1995, taxes and benefits have had less effect in reducing inequality. Appendix 10.3 suggests that since 2002, taxes and benefits have lifted a progressively smaller share of the population out of poverty. In that year, they lifted 11.2 percent of the population out of poverty, and by 2008, they lifted 9 percent out of poverty.

This suggests that government policy has changed. The government has been trying for many years to reduce spending in order to improve the budget balance and reduce internal debt. It has also tried to reduce taxation so as to increase incentives in the economy. All this was part of the liberal market policy followed by all the parties that led governments in recent years. One of the major problems that the Finance Ministry faced was the very sharp rise in social spending in the 1980s and early 1990s (see Figure 10.6). Many felt that this had not led to an improvement of services; the effectiveness of Israel's school system, for example, has long been a source of anxiety. Social spending therefore became a target for spending cuts when these became imperative during the deep recession of 2001–2003. Between 1995 and 2000, real spending on transfer payments per capita rose by about 30 percent. Since then, they have declined gradually. Between 1995 and 2007, general government consumption per capita remained broadly constant (see Figure 10.6).

In 2008, the government adopted two objectives for medium-term socio-economic policy. The first was to increase the employment rate in the 25–64 age group from 69.1 percent to 71.7 percent by 2010. The second objective

---

[21] Flug, Karnit and Nitsa Kasir (Kaliner). 2003. "Poverty and Employment, and the Gulf between Them." *Israel Economic Review.* Vol. 1. 55–80.

[22] Ishak, Saporta, Salem Abo Zaid and Dotan Leshem. 2006. Inequality in the Distribution of Income among Household and Wage Earners in Israel, 1967–2003. Jerusalem: The Van Leer Institute Economics and Society Program Policy Research Paper no. 2.

Figure 10.6. Transfer payments and general government services per capita, 1995–2008.

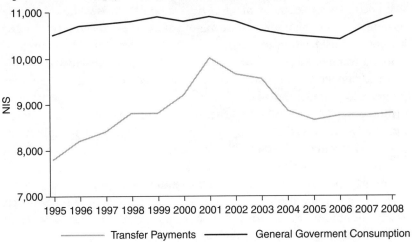

Source: Bank of Israel, Annual Report 2008.

was to reduce poverty by raising the income of the lowest quintile (20 percent) of earners by 10 percent more than the per capita GDP growth rate in the years 2008–2010, whereas the proportion of income from labor in its income was to increase from 43 percent to 45 percent. In the 2009 budget issued in October 2008, the government analyzed the problems in the following terms. Poverty in Israel is distributed unevenly among the population. The ultra-Orthodox and Arab communities account for a quarter of the entire population but account for over half of poor families. The low labor force participation rate among ultra-Orthodox men and Arab women is the main reason for this, and requires a response. This resulted in a decision to encourage vocational training for occupations for which there is a demand in the labor market. This decision was reflected in the 2008 budget, in which 15 million shekels (about $4 million) were allocated for training male engineers and technicians in the ultra-Orthodox sector. In addition, an authority was established to promote economic development in the Arab and ultra-Orthodox communities, with a budget of 50 million shekels ($12 million). The objective was to exploit the economic potential of the minorities' population by encouraging business activity.

The government also recognized the need to improve the skills of the unemployed. Measures to encourage work among the unemployed and groups that have remained outside the labor market for an extended period of time would include an improvement in the program designed to integrate income maintenance recipients in the labor market. In addition, assistance provided through daycare centers has been extended, a measure that encourages the employment of women and increases the disposable income of the populations that use these centers. The 2009 budget included increased subsidization of day/half-day care centers for the children of working women. Measures for promoting employment also include a program for integrating disabled persons in the labor market and another program to examine tools for promoting employment among special population groups. Some 55 million shekels ($13 million) was allocated in the 2009 budget for vocational training in order to replace foreign workers.

Earned income tax credit (EITC or negative income tax) is an additional means for reducing poverty among working families and raising the labor force participation rate by increasing the remuneration for labor of income earners. The program provides a solution for the problem that has arisen as a result of the various forms of support granted to the unemployed and the needy concurrent with the low wages offered to them, which have made entry into the cycle of employment an unattractive proposition. A program to apply EITC in Israel began to operate in September 2008. It provided up to 400 shekels ($100) a month to low-income workers. The largest benefits accrue to families with three children or more and those with two breadwinners whose total monthly gross income does not exceed 10,000 shekels. The program is due to be implemented countrywide in 2010, and a quarter of a million households will be eligible for the benefit once the program is fully applied.[23]

Wealth and Non-work Income

The distribution of wealth has also become much more unequal, partly because of the increased inequality of income but also because of other factors. There is, however, virtually no official data available on this. Inequality in the distribution of income and wealth and income reinforce each other: Income yields wealth that in turn yields income.

Income from sources other than work has become more important over the last decade. In 1998, it equaled 19.9 percent of national income (including incomes from abroad) and in 2007, it came to 25.2 percent.[24] The distribution of wealth is much more unequal than that of income: In 1997, 81

---

[23] Ministry of Finance. 2008. Appendix to the National Budget 2009. Jerusalem: Ministry of Finance. http://www.mof.gov.il/research_e/2009/stateBudget2009.pdf

[24] Central Bureau of Statistics. 2009. Productivity, Compensation of Employed Persons and Capital Return 2004–2007. Publication no. 1350, Table 7. http://www.cbs.gov.il/publications09/prod_07/pdf/t04.pdf

percent of income generated from interest and dividends belonged to 10 percent of households. In addition, 50 percent of rental income belongs to the top 10 percent of earners.[25] A total of 96 percent of non-work income accrued to the top 30 percent of the population. By means of comparison, in the OECD in 1994, the top 10 percent had almost 38 percent of interest income, the top 30 percent had 60 percent, and the bottom 70 percent had 40 percent.[26]

The concentration of business ownership in Israel is one of the highest in the developed world. In 1995–2006, twenty major business groups controlled 160 companies listed on the Tel Aviv stock exchange, accounting for nearly 50 percent of market capitalization. The ten largest groups own 30 percent of market capitalization. These were family-controlled and very diversified by sector, with a concentration in finance. Given that total market capitalization was estimated at $122.6 billion, equal to 74 percent of GDP, the top twenty groups had a total value of almost $61 billion and the top ten had $37 billion, or an average of $3.7 billion each. With ownership concentration (the share of equity owned by the largest shareholder) at 59 percent, one of the highest among the countries surveyed, the richest ten people had an average wealth of $2.2 billion.[27]

Education

The importance of education has increased in recent years with the development of high-technology industries. Employment and unemployment levels vary by education level: The better educated have experienced less unemployment than the less well educated (see Figure 10.2). Part of this was due to emigration: Those who had a degree and could not find suitable employment or lost their jobs were more willing and able to find work abroad. The ability of a small, albeit sometimes fast-growing, economy to supply jobs to all those with higher education is limited, but this does not mean that the incentives for education are lacking for all.

Israel has major and persistent education gaps related to the ethnic origins of the population, something that is true of many countries where there

[25] The Knesset Research and Information Center. 2002. Report and Survey of the Development of the Social Gaps in Israel in the Last Twenty Years. 26. http://www.knesset.gov.il/mmm/eng/doc_eng.asp?doc=me00416&type=pdf P17

[26] Avi Ben Bassat and Momi Dahan. 2004. "Social Rights in the Constitution and in Economic Policy." The Israel Democracy Institute Working Paper no. 41. 71.

[27] Kosenko, Konstantin. 2007. "Concentration of Business Ownership." *Israel Economic Review*. Vol. 5 no. 2. 55–93; Bank of Israel. http://www.bankisrael.gov.il/deptdata/mehkar/iser/10/iser_3.pdf

Table 10.7. *Population aged 15-plus by*
years of schooling, 1997–2007

	1997		2007	
	Jews	Arabs	Jews	Arabs
0	2.8	7.7	1.8	6.2
1–4	1.5	4.8	0.8	3.2
5–8	9.3	22.3	5.9	18.1
9–10	11.2	18.8	8.9	17.9
11–12	36.9	28.4	35.3	35.9
13–15	21.6	11.9	24.6	10.2
16+	16.6	6.1	22.7	9.1
Median	12.4	10.6	12.8	11.3

Source: Central Bureau of Statistics, Statistical Abstract
of Israel 1998, Table 22.1 and 2008, Table 8.3.

is an ethnically heterogeneous population. These gaps are among the causes
of inequality and poverty and are often responsible for the perpetuation of
these phenomena. Table 10.7 gives the educational profile of the population
by ethnic group in 1997 and 2007. It also shows that the level of education,
measured by years of schooling, is higher among Jews than Arabs. It shows
that there was an increase in overall educational levels in both communities
(summarized in the figure for the median number of years of schooling),
and that the gap closed very slightly. In 1997, the median figure for years of
Arab schooling was equal to 85.5 percent of the Jewish figure and by 2007,
it had reached 88.3 percent.

Other measures of the gaps in education and how they have changed
in the last decade are given in Appendix 10.4. Another measure of educational achievement is the share of children in each community who go
to school. In 1991, 41 percent of Arab children of high school age went
to high school; by 2006, the share had more than doubled, reaching 83.5
percent. In the Jewish community, the shares were 81.6 percent and 93 percent, respectively.[28] The large increase in the share of Arab children going
to high school was a precondition for an improvement in educational
achievements. There were other significant gaps beside those between
Jews and Arabs, as well as within the Jewish and Arab communities.

[28] Council for Higher Education, Planning and Budget Committee Annual Report 2005/6.
no. 33. www.che.org.il p. 117

Among the latter, the most significant one was between Christians and Muslims and Druze.

Appendix 10.4 shows that between 2000 and 2006, the share of matriculation candidates who received a school leaving certificate and the share who earned a certificate good enough to meet university entrance requirements rose among all sectors of the population. It is not a full measure of educational inequality because the table does not show the dropout rate before reaching the twelfth grade. This was higher in the weaker sections of society. In terms of obtaining a school leaving certificate, the Christian Arab community did best, whereas in terms of university entrance, Jews of European-American origin did best. Girls did better than boys in both the Jewish and Arab communities both in terms of certificates and university entrance standard certificates. Over time, there was a closing of the gap between Jews and Arabs measured by the share of pupils obtaining a certificate and those obtaining a university entrance level certificate. There was also a closing of the gap within the Jewish community. In 2000, the share of Arab pupils obtaining school leaving certificates at university entrance level was slightly less than 58 percent of the national average. In 2006, it was slightly more than 71 percent. For the Muslim community, the ratio rose from 50 percent to 65 percent. For the weakest Jewish community, that which has its origins in Asia-Africa, the ratio rose from slightly more than 80 percent to slightly more than 85 percent. There was also a closing of the gap in terms of school leaving certificates. In 2000, the Arab community's rate was 82.6 percent of the national rate; by 2006, it had risen to 86.7 percent. The ratio for the Muslim community rose from 77.5 percent of the national average to 81.8 percent during the same period. The Jewish community with Asia-Africa origins also increased its ratio from 92.5 percent to 95.3 percent.

The share of Arab youngsters within two years of finishing high school that went on to higher academic studies in universities, academic colleges, teacher training colleges, and the Open University rose from 10.7 percent in 1991 to 18.2 percent in 2003. Between 1996–1997 and 2006, the share of Arab students in universities, academic colleges, and teacher training colleges rose from 7.6 percent to 11 percent. The total number of students rose by 25 percent and the number of Arab students rose by 37 percent. In the 1990s, 3.6 percent of students studying for a second degree were Arab; by 2006, the share had reached 5.8 percent.[29]

[29] Council for Higher Education. *Annual Report 2005/6.* 117–119.

One of the most important ways to measure the effectiveness of an education system is to examine the extent to which pupils from weaker socioeconomic background succeed. If success is limited to, or concentrated among, those who come from middle class or richer homes, then the education system does little other than translate the success of parents into that of their children. Students in the Jewish education systems were, on average, from stronger socioeconomic backgrounds. Following them in descending order were the Arab-Christian, ultra-Orthodox, and Druze education systems and then the Arab-Muslim and Bedouin students who had the lowest average socioeconomic level. A report on socioeconomic factors and matriculation achievements between 1992–1993 and 2004–2005 summarized the situation in the following terms. The gap between students of different socioeconomic backgrounds in Israel is among the largest in the developed world, and the proportion of poorly performing students is high. The inequality of Israeli students' achievement has far-reaching consequences on socioeconomic polarization that is far more acute than in Western countries.

During the last twenty years, there were five main factors behind this, some of them closely interrelated. First, the share of children from ultra-Orthodox and Arab homes increased. There was also an increase in the share of Muslim and Bedouin children in the Arab school system. These developments not only reflected the higher fertility rates in those communities, but also the lower dropout rates in the school system in general and in the Arab school system in particular. This also reflected the increase in the share of Arab girls going to school. There was a decline in the share of Jewish children going to vocational schools and an increase in the share of Arab children going to them. Second, there was a large influx of immigrants from the former Soviet Union and also from Ethiopia. Third, there was an increase in the number of one-parent families, largely but not only the result of the immigration from the former Soviet Union. Fourth, there was an increase in the number of poor, especially the number of poor children. Fifth, there was a decline in educational spending per child and an apparent decline in the quality of teachers, despite an improvement in their average educational level.[30]

Key variables helping determine a child's performance included parents' educational and income levels. Between 1992 and 2005, the average years of

[30] Zussman, Noam and Shay Tsur. 2008. The Effect of Students' Socioeconomic Background on Their Achievements in Matriculation Examinations Bank of Israel. Research Department Discussion Paper no. 2008.11. 2. http://www.bankisrael.gov.il/deptdata/mehkar/papers/dp0811e.pdf

schooling of mothers rose by one year in the Jewish secular education system and two years in the Arab education system. Nevertheless, the gap in the number of years of schooling between mothers in the Jewish and Arab systems remained high, at the magnitude of 3.7 in 2005. There were similar though somewhat less extreme developments with respect to the father's years of schooling.

In 1992–1993, average family income from salaries and child allowances per capita in the Jewish state education system was double that in the Arab education one. It was much lower among the ultra-Orthodox and among the Bedouin. About 19 percent of students in the Jewish education stream were in the lower 20 percent group of per capita income, whereas in the Arab education system, about 28 percent of students were in the lowest 20 percent and about 44 percent were in the second-to-lowest. This situation remained unchanged in 2004–2005. Between the school years 1992–1993 and 2004–2005, the rate of eligibility for a matriculation certificate among pupils in the twelfth grade rose by nine percentage points whereas the proportion of matriculated individuals who met the criteria for admission into university – one of the measures of the quality of a matriculation certificate – increased by about four percentage points. However, the gaps between the various education streams remained high and in some cases even widened. Whereas in the Jewish secular and state religious systems, the rate of eligibility increased by about thirteen percentage points, to 62 percent in 2004–2005, the rate in the ultra-Orthodox stream remained very low. This was mainly due to the lack of emphasis placed on the core subjects and the low participation rates in tracks leading to a matriculation certificate in this system.

Between 1993–1993 and 2004–2005, the rate of eligibility for a matriculation certificate in the Arab education system increased by eleven percentage points, to 48 percent. The achievements of Arab-Christian students were the best in Arab education system and are close to those of students in the Jewish secular and state religious systems. Following them – in descending order – were the Druze, Muslim, and Bedouin students. Between 1992–1993 and 2004–2005, the rate of eligibility for matriculation certificates among Bedouin students increased by twenty-three percentage points, to 42 percent. The higher achievements of students in the Jewish secular and state religious systems compared to those of students in the Arab system, as well as the ranking of streams within the Arab education system, correlate with the pupils' socioeconomic status.

Students in the Arab education stream were also behind when measured in terms of indicators of excellence, such as the proportion of matriculated students meeting university entrance criteria and the proportion of students achieving high marks in school in core subjects, such as English and mathematics. There was, however, a significant rise in the proportion of those in the Arab education system meeting university entrance criteria and in the proportion of students doing matriculation examinations with four or five study units in English and mathematics that was an indicator of the improvement in the quality of matriculation certificates. The proportion of students in the Arab education stream writing the English matriculation examination in 2004–2005 was much lower than in the Jewish education stream.

The limited success in English among students in the Arab stream was partly the result of it being a third language for them (after Arabic and Hebrew). Furthermore, their exposure to the "global village" (for example, through the Internet) was less than that of Jewish students (excluding the ultra-Orthodox) because of economic factors, which reduced their opportunities for learning English. Achievement on the matriculation examinations, according to the system, was in the following descending order: Jewish State and State Religious, Arab-Christian, Druze, Arab-Muslim, Bedouin, and finally the ultra-Orthodox. During the period between the 1992–1993 and 2004–2005 school years, there was overall improvement in matriculation examination scores (ignoring changes in level of difficulty). There were also significant differences in achievement according to socioeconomic background. Although the gaps in basic achievement narrowed significantly, those in indicators of excellence widened in most cases.[31]

The Share of Labor in National Income

The stabilization of the economy in 1985 has been followed by an almost continuous fall in the share of labor in national income (see Figure 10.7). One of the main factors that have lowered the share of labor in GDP was the weakening of labor unions. In addition, rapid technological progress has resulted in high labor turnover and an acceleration of the rate of depreciation on capital due to the large investment in computers and software. This increased the share of capital. The net return on capital remained fixed because of the increase in the proportion of the capital-intensive communication industry, and also characterized by a degree of monopolistic power in the goods market.

---

[31] Zussman and Tsur, 2–3, 7, 11–12, 16.

Figure 10.7. The share of labor in GDP, 1970–2007.

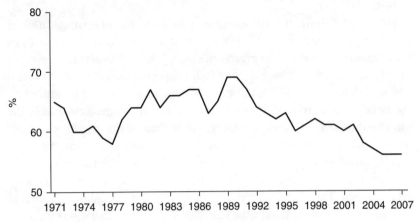

Source: Bank of Israel, Annual Report 2007; Central Bureau of Statistics, Statistical Abstract of Israel 2009.

Globalization creates pressure for a uniform price of labor. The increased exposure of the economy to imports from labor-intensive sectors abroad has reduced the share of labor in capital-intensive economies such as Israel. The increase in imports from developing countries and the increase in the number of foreign workers have worked to lower the share of labor in Israel and in other developed economies. In the short run, the labor share fell during periods of high growth in GDP or total productivity, such as at the beginning of the 1970s and in 2004–2008. This may have been the result of elasticities in the labor market or the increase in capital productivity in the growth process.[32]

Conclusions

Israel faces very serious problems of poverty and income inequality. The level of inequality is greater than the OECD average, as is the level of poverty. This remains true even if alternative measures of poverty are used. The growth of inequality has been a worldwide phenomenon, but is especially worrying in a country with the internal and external political tensions Israel faces. Furthermore, it represents a huge waste of human and other resources. Insofar as poverty is transmitted from parents to children,

[32] Bank of Israel. *Annual Report 2007*. 52. http://www.bankisrael.gov.il/deptdata/mehkar/ doch07/eng/pe_

a new generation is born into poverty and thus may not be able to take its rightful place in society.

This chapter shows that the increase in the inequality of earnings in Israel has been prolonged and deep. There were factors working at both ends of the distribution, making for greater inequality. As well as earnings growing at the higher level, there were many factors keeping the earnings of the less well paid down. In the 1990s, there was mass immigration and the entry into the Israel labor market of hundreds of thousands of foreign workers. The ultra-Orthodox community's rejection of secular schooling and its avoidance of the labor market lowered incomes and earning capacity among a rapidly growing section of the community. It also suffered the effects of large average family size that reduced income per head and therefore lowered savings. The Arab community suffered from a weaker educational system (with the exception of the Christians) and pervasive discrimination in the labor market. The Muslim majority within the Arab community, the Bedouin and, to a lesser extent, the Druze also suffered the effects of large average family size. The government contributed by maintaining pronatal policies until 2003 (when child allowances were reduced), by failing to provide effective retraining programs for workers in the traditional sectors of the economy that were contracting, and by failing to introduce educational reforms.

There was a slight reduction in poverty in 2007–2008. This was the result of the strength of the economy and the increase in employment and incomes it generated. The government began to understand the need for active labor market policies with an emphasis on increasing labor force participation, especially among sections of society with large shares of poverty: the Arabs and the ultra-Orthodox. The first signs that fertility has fallen in the ultra-Orthodox community are an indication of hope for a longer-term decline of poverty in that community. The decline in fertility in the Arab community and improvements in educational achievements will only translate into a reduction in poverty if discrimination in the labor market declines and other steps are taken.

Poverty is not only a social issue: It is also an economic one, with dynamic consequences. The National Economic Council at the Prime Minister's office concluded that deep and widespread poverty is not only a disgrace but threatens the national prosperity of the economy. This is because the increasing budgetary burden resulting from supporting the poor is mainly in the form of relief but does not solve the problem. More importantly, widespread poverty means that about one-third of young workers joining the labor market in five to ten years will do so with major disadvantages in education, health, and other skills needed to utilize their productive potential. In addition, the widening of gaps threatens social unity, with implications for such parameters as crime and the willingness to participate in shouldering the security burden. The widening gap in output per capita between Israel and the United States also threatens to draw away the highest level of young talent – the so-called brain drain. The economy and society are closely intertwined and cannot be dealt with separately.[33]

[33] Prime Minister's Office. 2007. National Economic Council Overview. Jerusalem Prime Minister's Office. 3. http://www.pmo.gov.il/NR/rdonlyres/93120D40-2790-4C14-A45E-80457D758FEB/0/NationalEconomicCounciloverview.pdf

ELEVEN

Conclusions

The Zionist movement set out to create a homeland for the Jews and largely as a result of its policies, the Jewish population of Palestine rose from about 25,000 in 1885 to 600,000 in early 1948. The demographic development of the Yishuv was matched by its economic growth: In the period 1922–1948, national income per capita rose nearly threefold, in real terms (see Appendix 2.1). This extraordinary achievement was made possible by inputs of capital as well as labor and by the very high level of human capital of the immigrants. In 1948, the Jewish population of Israel had one of the highest educational levels in the world, something that made the efficient absorption of capital possible.[1] The successful economic development of the Yishuv was also due to the appropriateness of its economic policies. These emphasized agriculture and the result was to create the foundations needed for industrialization. British economic policies were broadly helpful or at least did not prevent the development of the Yishuv's economy. The increase in demand from the British military in the Middle East during World War II gave industry in the Yishuv a significant boost.

The early years of the state were extremely harsh. In addition to the destruction resulting from the long war of independence, war casualties that amounted to 1 percent of the population and the arrival of huge numbers of immigrants – the raison d'être of Zionism – posed huge challenges. The country lacked the resources to integrate them: Most crucially, there were shortages of housing and employment. In macroeconomic terms, there were large budget deficits, financed by inflationary means, partly suppressed by rationing and other controls. In addition, there were large balance of payments deficits. As a result of these pressures, the government adopted very

---

[1] Easterlin, Richard A. 1961. "Israel's Development: Past Accomplishments and Future Problems." *The Quarterly Journal of Economics.* Vol. 75. No. 1. 63–86.

pragmatic policies that sometimes gave rise to political conflict at home. In the early 1950s, a reparations agreement was negotiated with the Federal Republic of Germany that gave Israel vitally needed foreign exchange, but it was bitterly opposed by opposition parties. The reparations agreements eased the balance of payments constraint and permitted the economy to grow. A second pragmatic policy was the decision – also in the early 1950s – to seek out entrepreneurs from abroad who were encouraged to invest in Israel. Within a framework of import substitution, industrialization was pushed forward. The government offered land, labor, and capital, as well as markets protected from foreign competition. By restricting the number of investments within any sector, the government also limited competition in the home market. This package was enough to encourage a number of vital investments in basic industries such as clothing and textiles. The aim was to increase employment and output and thus supply the local market with the basic products that it needed. By the early 1960s, the development of the economy using import substitution was beginning to weaken. Local markets were becoming saturated with noncompetitively produced goods, and consequently firms were experiencing declines in demand for their products. They needed new markets if they were to continue growing and if the economy was to generate enough new jobs to employ labor market entrants, including immigrants. Once again, pragmatism prevailed and a trade agreement was negotiated with the European Economic Community. This enabled Israel to export industrial products to the EEC with few restrictions, but the price was that Israeli markets would have to be opened to imports. In the 1970s, this agreement was significantly widened; in the 1980s, a free trade agreement was signed with the United States, and in the 1990s, Israel unilaterally reduced restrictions on imports from third-world countries with which it did not have specific trade agreements.

The economy grew rapidly in the 1950s and 1960s, although the growth rate fluctuated as a result of balance of payments constraints, and as a result, living standards rose sharply. Inequality in the distribution of income became a social and political issue, especially after the Six Day War in 1967. The Yom Kippur War of 1973 brought growth to a near standstill, and it took the economy years to recover. This was not only the result of massive damage inflicted by war, but also because of disastrous economic policies adopted in the late 1970s and early 1980s. Underlying these factors was a growing social and political polarization that had resulted in, among other things, the loss of power by the Labor Party in 1977.

Economic stabilization was achieved in 1985, but it took four more years for the economy to start growing rapidly, and this was the result of the massive immigration from the Soviet Union. This immigration was absorbed with much less state intervention than that of the 1950s, but the government undertook to obtain United States' loan guarantees. This meant that there was an adequate supply of capital to match the increase in the supply of labor, and so deficits on the current account of the balance of payments could be financed with relative ease. The absorption of one million immigrants in the 1990s was not an easy task – it presented huge challenges for Israeli society as well as the economy – but over time it was achieved.

The twenty-first century brought the Second Intifada, with numerous terrorist attacks on civilians in Israel, which had major effects on the economy. Its onset in 2001 coincided with the collapse of high-technology shares on the NASDAQ, and these two factors pushed the economy into a sharp recession. The government introduced another stabilization package that largely consisted of cuts in welfare spending, and by 2003–2004, economic recovery began.

The Israeli economy has developed despite enormous challenges. Some of these have been imposed from outside and others have their origins at home. The last ten years have brought economic growth, financial improvements, and growing social gaps. Between 1998 and 2008, the population rose by 22 percent, GDP by 47 percent in real terms, and GDP per capita by 22.5 percent. In 1998, Israel had a balance of payments current account deficit of nearly $1 billion; in 2008, there was a surplus of $2 billion, after five years of surpluses averaging almost $4.5 billion a year. The budget deficit in 1998 equaled 4.1 percent of GDP; in 2008, it was at 2 percent. In 1998, the gross public debt equaled 103.3 percent of GDP; in 2008, it was down to 80 percent. The net foreign debt in 1998 was nearly $11 billion; at the end of 2009, it was negative $55 billion – in other words, net assets had been accumulated. The foreign exchange reserves rose from $22 billion in 1998 to $42 billion at the end of 2008 and $61 billion at the end of 2009.

On the other hand, many socioeconomic indicators have deteriorated. In 1998, there were 1,781,200 people living in poverty before taxes and benefits (32.9 percent of the total population) and 1,088,100 after taxes and benefits (18 percent). By 2008, there were 2,283,300 people living in poverty before taxes and benefits (32.7 percent) and 1,651,300 after taxes and benefits (23.7 percent). The gross figure rose by 22 percent and the net figure by 62 percent. The much faster increase in the net figure reflected the weakening of the redistributive system. In 1998, it lifted almost 15 percent of the population out of poverty, but by 2008, it did the same for only 9 percent. The 1998 figure excludes residents of East Jerusalem, which biases the growth rates upward but does not account for the overall rise in poverty.[2]

The main external challenge has been the conflict with the Palestinians and with parts of the Arab world and in recent years increasingly with Iran. Israel has always been in a state of war, which has resulted in large defense expenditures, periodic wars, terrorism, and much tension. These all have had high costs, but the defense effort has been used to generate formidable technological development. There is no other country in the world that has been at war for all of its history, and to have reached an income per capita level approaching $30,000 is therefore a considerable achievement.

Israel faces a number of economic challenges. The first challenge is presented by the ultra-Orthodox. This community is in large part opposed to Zionism and rejects the state of Israel. Most ultra-Orthodox men and all ultra-Orthodox women do not participate in military service, thereby increasing the burden on those who do. This community is not, however, averse to accepting financial aid from the state that has been willing to provide it. Most ultra-Orthodox men do not work: They study in state-subsidized religious institutions and live off welfare and charity. Ultra-Orthodox families are usually much larger than others (with the exception of the Muslim community) and are therefore major recipients of child allowances that their representatives in the Knesset have fought hard for. The burden on the economy that they represent is compounded by the growth of their population that is now increasingly taking place in ultra-Orthodox towns the West Bank. Changing this situation is a major political challenge that offers the prospect of large economic benefits. It is sometimes suggested that Jews have high levels of literacy due partly to their religious traditions. As this has proven an advantage economically, some suggest that literacy has been even more strongly emphasized in Jewish homes. This is one of the factors explaining the success of Jewish minorities in the Diaspora. In Israel, one group that places great emphasis on literacy – the ultra-Orthodox – has used it almost exclusively for religious study, at the expense of secular learning. As a result, it has created a generation that lacks the skills needed in a modern economy and has thus imprisoned a significant section of the population in poverty.

In 1989–1990, there were 35,000 children in ultra-Orthodox primary schools, accounting for 5.6 percent of the total number of primary school pupils and 7.6 percent of the Jewish ones. In 2008–2009, there were almost 170,000 of them, accounting for 19.7 percent of the total number of primary

[2] Appendix 10.3.

school pupils and 7.6 percent of the Jewish ones.[3] It should be noted that in recent years, the growth in the number of ultra-Orthodox children in primary education has slowed. Most of these children do not get a primary education that provides them with basic skills and will not provide those when they get to secondary school. Government policies are therefore deepening socio-economic divisions. If this problem is not dealt with, Israel ultimately may be overwhelmed by the growth of an uneducated labor force.

Closely related to this is the second challenge, one involving cultural issues. As in other countries, public funding of culture – including theatre, cinema, music, and arts education – have been under continuous threat from budget cuts initiated in the name of conservative economics. In Israel, this issue also relates to the *Kulturkampf* between the ultra-Orthodox minority and the non-ultra-Orthodox majority, because the weakening of secular culture is a victory for the ultra-Orthodox. The threat to humanities and arts in Israel's universities and elsewhere is grave: Departments are being closed and whole bodies of knowledge and tools of analysis are being denied to future generations. Who benefits? Obviously the economy is stronger when the budget deficit is low, but the issue runs much deeper. The purpose of budget cuts is not only to balance the budget but also to facilitate tax cuts, and these benefit those who pay most tax. Although the tax and welfare system reduces inequality and poverty, they have grown considerably. It is not only the rich who benefit more than the poor from this globalized economic model. The ultra-Orthodox may be the unintended beneficiaries of the weakening of mainstream, largely secular society that draws on cultural resources for its spiritual well-being.

The need to integrate the Arab community is the third challenge. This community's identification with the Palestinians in the West Bank and Gaza cannot be "solved" by Israel with money, but its identification with the state would have been stronger had there not been so much long-term neglect of its social and economic needs, especially employment. The unused potential of one-fifth of the population is also an economic loss that Israel has had to bear and that has been officially estimated at 6 percent of GDP.[4] The Arab minority faces major economic and political obstacles. Its position is complicated by the fact that it has familial and political ties with those in neighboring countries who have been or are enemies of Israel.

The cost and future of Jewish settlement of the West Bank is the fourth challenge. The construction of these settlements, together with those in

---

[3] Central Bureau of Statistics. *Statistical Abstract of Israel 2009*. Tables 8.7 and 8.9.

[4] Y-Net News. 2008. "Experts: Failure to Integrate Arabs Costing Israel Billions." 26 November. http://www.ynetnews.com/articles/0,7340,L-3628836,00.html

Gaza until their evacuation in 2006, was primarily an ideological decision, sometimes dressed up as one of security. They have been a major source of conflict with the Palestinians, and the inevitable conclusion is that Israel has damaged its own interests by building them. The settlements on the Golan have resulted in much less friction with the local population because it is small. A peace treaty with Syria will involve the abandonment of these settlements like those in the West Bank. Compensating the Israelis who leave the Golan will be hugely expensive. This book has concentrated on the direct economic consequences of construction and maintenance of settlements in the West Bank. Insofar as they contributed to the Israeli-Palestinian conflict, they have added to Israel's defense costs indirectly as well as directly. The direct costs were estimated in Chapter 7; the indirect costs cannot be estimated in that there were other causes of conflict. The fact that these settlements will have to be abandoned is not only a political consideration but will also involve huge expenditures. In 2006, moving 8,000 settlers out of Gaza and resettling them in Israel cost about 2 percent of GDP, and so the cost of moving much larger numbers out of the West Bank will be much higher, even if the compensation per capita is much lower. This is a political challenge with major economic implications.

The fifth challenge is the cost of defense. For most of Israel's history, the costs of defense did not threaten macroeconomic stability, but the budget and debt positions would have been stronger had expenditures been lower. It is highly unlikely that Israel will be able to reduce its military expenditures significantly in the coming years. A reduction in the length of conscription that will increase the supply of labor and reduce extra-budgetary costs may be possible. Greater oversight of the defense budget by the Treasury, the Knesset, and the state controller might reveal waste that exists in all relatively unaccountable organizations. Given the size of the defense budget, the reduction of waste would have macroeconomic significance. It is also possible that the conflict in the Middle East will worsen, thus raising costs. This could happen regardless of Israel's settlement policies given the threat that Iran poses to Israel's existence and the activities of its proxies, the Hezbollah in Lebanon and the Hamas in Gaza.

The task of solving these challenges is exacerbated by Israel's political system. There are two aspects that affect the economy and economic policy making. The first is Israel's highly fragmented parliamentary system. The second is the set of issues that dominate Israeli politics: security, the future of the territories occupied in 1967, ethnic tensions, and socioeconomic divisions.

Israel's parliament, the Knesset, is elected every four years on a proportional representation system. Any party that receives over 2 percent of the vote gains representation in the Knesset. The political system has become increasingly fragmented, with the two main political parties that led the country for most of its history becoming minority parties, each winning just over a quarter of the seats in the Knesset in the 2006 general elections. The largest party after the elections, Kadima, made up of politicians who had left Likud and Labor, gained only 29 of the 120 seats in the Knesset, having received only 22 percent of the vote. It formed a coalition government with Labor and two other parties, one of which split in two after the formation of the government. Thirteen parties were represented in the Knesset after the 2006 elections. In September 2008, the prime minister resigned due to the pressure of public opinion resulting from numerous police investigations into charges of corruption. Israel's performance in the 2006 Lebanon War was also a contributing factor. Elections were held in February 2009, a year before they were due, and resulted in no party gaining more than 25 percent of the votes. Fragmentation increased: The leading party in the new government, the Likud, won only twenty-eight seats. The government had thirty ministers, equal to a quarter of the Knesset! The Labor Party had only thirteen seats, and the largest party, Kadima, which went into opposition, gained only twenty-nine seats.

Labor and Likud, traditionally the main political parties, differed over foreign policy and defense issues, with Labor following a more pragmatic line based on compromise with the Arabs and the Likud demanding permanent Israeli control over the West Bank. Economic and social issues were never in serious dispute between the two parties, and so Israel lacked a classic left-right set of choices on social and economic issues. This was increasingly true of other Western countries where social-democratic or Labor parties moved to the center or even to the right. Bill Clinton's New Democrats was also an attempt to distinguish his leadership from that of its big-spending Democratic predecessors, as was Tony Blair's New Labor in Britain.

Another important aspect of the Israeli political scene for many years has been the importance of ethnically based voting. From the 1950s, Labor began to be seen as the party of the agricultural aristocracy, the kibbutzim, the intelligentsia, and the many who worked in the public sector that it controlled. The immigrants who had arrived from Yemen, North Africa, and other parts of the Middle East gave their votes to Labor in the early years of the state because it was the Prime Minister, David Ben Gurion, who led the Labor government that brought the state into being and made it possible for them to immigrate. Over time, frustration over their socioeconomic position was reflected in voting patterns, although this often took a generation to manifest itself. In 1977, the votes of many Jews who had their origins in the Middle East and North Africa went to the Likud, a party that had for many years lacked a social program and dwelled on the need to settle the West Bank and Gaza. This, together with a loss of Labor votes to a centrist party, resulted in the Likud, under Menachem Begin, forming a government for the first time. Since the 1980s, there has been an increase in the representation of ultra-Orthodox parties, especially Shas that represents Sephardic Jews. These parties have often held the balance of power and have usually been in government, directly or through political influence. Israel's political economy has a structural bias toward high spending. This is due to the short length of life of recent governments, the fact that they are coalitions, the weakness of the leading party, and, as a consequence, the large number of spending ministries.[5]

The economy has shown many signs of going on auto-pilot. It has grown despite continuous crises in government, as if the latter does not matter. In fact, in a globalized system, if the "financial guidelines" are right, then little else matters at the macroeconomic level, at least in the short term. At the microeconomic level, the socioeconomic level, and in the medium and long term, the costs of badly functioning government are huge.

In a report covering the period to 2006, the International Monetary Fund (IMF) showed how political instability weakened control over the budget. Although fiscal control improved dramatically, adherence to the budget deficit law was limited, and so the public sector debt remained much higher than was considered desirable. From the perspective of 2009, this conclusion seems somewhat unkind. Fiscal control in terms of limiting increases in public spending and limiting the size of the budget deficit has been exemplary, as the IMF stated. In fact, the IMF suggested that fiscal policy needs to be made more flexible in order to cope with recession, and this meant setting a medium-term target for reducing public sector debt. The latter needs to be reduced from about 80 percent of GDP at the end of 2008 to less than 60 percent in the medium term because Israel's geostrategic position is much more exposed than that of the countries that decided to set up the Euro and fixed the 60-percent limit as a condition for membership of the Euro in the Maastrict Treaty of 1992.[6] The problem is not so much the absolute volume of public spending as its composition. Proposing increased

[5] IMF. Israel Selected Issues, 2007, Country Report 07/2. 4–5. http://www.imf.org/external/pubs/ft/scr/2007/cr0725.pdf

[6] IMF. Israel: 2008 Article IV Consultation – Staff Report; Public Information Notice on the Executive Board Discussion; Statement by the Executive Director for Israel. Country Report no. 09/57, 2009 http://www.imf.org/external/pubs/ft/scr/2009/cr0957.pdf

public spending does not win votes: In the 2009 election, the Labor Party advocated increasing public spending by more than the official limit of 1.7 percent a year to push the economy out of recession by Keynesian means. It received a mere 11 percent of the votes after a campaign dominated by security issues following the war in Gaza.

There are two issues involved. The first is the guns-versus-butter argument: Should funds go to defense or education and other civilian services? The second is how funds should be spent within each ministry. All of these issues are profoundly political. According to Mancur Olsen, successful countries give rise to interest groups that accumulate more and more influence over time. Eventually, they become powerful enough to win government favors in the form of new laws or friendly regulators. These favors allow the groups to benefit at the expense of everyone else; not only do they end up with a larger piece of the economic pie, but they do so in a way that keeps the pie from growing as much as it otherwise would. Trade barriers and tariffs are the classic example. They help the domestic manufacturer of a product at the expense of millions of consumers who must pay high prices and choose from a limited selection of goods.[7] Reform is therefore not only a matter of getting government out of the economy, but also a matter of preventing others capturing it. The threat is not only from sectoral groups explicitly represented in the Knesset, but also from the small number of billionaires who control even more of the economy than they own. In December 2009, sixteen families owned 73 percent of the assets in the Tel Aviv Stock Exchange Index of twenty-five leading companies, worth approximately $93 billion.[8] Another obstacle to reform is the existence of powerful labor unions that have secured effective control of key sections of the public sector.

Israel has often adopted systems copied from abroad, particularly the United States, years after they have been introduced there and sometimes have been already abandoned. Over the last thirty years, the idea that big government is the root of all economic problems became dominant.[9] Israel had a much bigger government than the United States and there were more

[7] Olson, Mancur. 1982. *The Rise and Decline of Nations*. New Haven, CT and London: Yale University Press, 75–117.

[8] Morck, Randall, Daniel Wolfenzon and Bernard Yeung. 2005. "Corporate Governance, Economic Entrenchment, and Growth." Journal of Economic Literature Vol. 43. 657–722; Dun and Bradstreet Israel. 2009. Press Announcement: Annual Conclusions about Large Corporate Groups in the Economy. 15 December. http://dundb.co.il/NewsShowHeb1.asp?idnum=475

[9] Madrick, Jeff. 2008. *The Case for Big Government*. Princeton: Princeton University Press; Galbraith. James. 2008. *The Predator State*. New York: The Free Press.

grounds for reducing it than in the United States, but the point has been reached where a change of emphasis is needed. The government now takes a similar share of GDP to the OECD average. Emphasis needs to be placed on improving the quality of what the state does rather than just on the size of government. Israel's economic and social infrastructure is inadequate and needs more investment and better management. The international financial crisis that struck in 2008 suggests the need for more active government in terms of investment, regulation, and administration in support of the market and where markets fail. Israel is failing in this area because of the corruption of its political system that reaches down to the administrative level.

The problems that have been analyzed in this book are also opportunities. The most obvious is Israel's relations with Palestinians. If these improve as a result of a peace treaty, the gains to both parties will be great. Although this may be unimaginable at present, some of the other problems present more realistic opportunities. The most obvious is the gradual integration of more ultra-Orthodox men and Arab women into the labor force. This will simultaneously increase production and reduce poverty. It will also have positive effects on the budget in terms of higher tax revenues and lower welfare spending. The integration of these minorities and improvements in their education would yield other gains including an expansion of domestic markets and a further improvement in the quality of the labor supply. These changes would also improve productivity and stimulate economic growth. The government understands this, but to expand these programs requires political will that it lacks.

The influx of immigrants, combined with a proportional electoral system, has led to an intensification of sectoral politics, which has been very damaging to Israeli society and, in some respects, to its economy. This may change as the huge immigration from the former Soviet Union is gradually absorbed. Intermarriage between Ashkenazi and Sephardic Jews has rendered this differentiation meaningless for an increasing number of families. Over time, this effect will widen, which may reduce the appeal of at least one aspect of sectoral politics – a precondition for the adoption of durable and more universalistic socioeconomic values.

The solution will be to find a path that combines growth and efficiency with equity and integration. These are universal issues that have preoccupied people for thousands of years, as the quotations at the beginning of this book suggest. The benefits of growth and efficiency need to be shared by the whole population and not just accumulated by the richest. Given the inequality in the distribution of income and wealth and the scale of poverty, much needs to be done. This is a challenge that Israel faces with other countries, but because of the security pressures, the urgency of finding a solution is greater, although the means to do so are fewer. One of Israel's constant worries is emigration; in recent years, only the well educated could obtain work permits that would allow them to emigrate to other developed economies. The solution centers on improvements in the education system that inevitably involve the public sector. Although increasing spending on education is not necessarily the answer, shifting resources within the budget and changing attitudes and habits will prove to be a major political challenge. Of course the better educated must have suitable employment opportunities if educational improvements are not to lead to their underemployment or emigration. The nature of the problem is understood; whether there is the political will and national unity to implement change remains an open question. The precedents of the past suggest that change will come but maybe only at the eleventh hour.

Appendices

Appendix 2.1. *The Yishuv: Population, national income, and national income per capita, 1922–1948*

	Average Population (thousands)	Net National Product* (Palestine pounds, thousands, 1936 prices)	Net National Product per capita (Palestine pounds 1936 prices)
1922	83.8	1,625	19.4
1925	121.7	3,202	26.3
1930	164.8	5,666	34.4
1935	322.0	16,388	50.9
1940	460.1	16,684	36.3
1945	549.0	29,945	54.5
1948	671.9	37,394	55.7

In 1936, Palestine pound was worth $4.97 (based on the sterling rate of exchange)

* Net national product = GDP-depreciation

Source: Robert Szereszewski, *Essays on the Structure of the Jewish Economy in Palestine and Israel*. Jerusalem: The Maurice Falk Institute for Economic Research in Israel, 1968, Table 9, p. 56.

Appendix 2.2. *Agricultural, manufacturing, and construction output during the mandate, 1922–1939 (Palestine pounds, 1936 prices)*

	Agriculture		Manufacturing		Construction		Total	Total
	Arab	Jewish	Arab	Jewish	Arab	Jewish	Arab	Jewish
1921	3,188	335	1,254	660	317	488	4,759	1,483
1931	4,493	1,875	2,578	3,454	688	1,231	7,759	6,560
1939	7,765	5,255	3,400	9,453	405	1,621	11,570	16,329

Source: Meltzer, Jacob. *The Divided Economy of Mandatory Palestine*. Cambridge: Cambridge University Press, 1998, pp. 228–231.

Appendix 3.1. *Basic data on the Israeli economy, 2000–2008 (annual averages)*

	2000	2001	2002	2003	2004	2005	2006	2007	2008
Mean population (000s)	6,289	6,439	6,570	6,690	6,809	6,930	7,054	7,180	7,306
Population growth rate (percent)	2.7	2.4	2.0	1.8	1.8	1.8	1.8	1.8	1.7
Israelis employed	2,216	2,265	2,284	2,330	2,401	2,494	2,574	2,682	2,777
GDP (NIS billions, 2008 prices)	557	555	552	562	590	620	652	687	714
GDP ($, 2008 prices and exchange rate)	158	157	156	159	167	176	185	195	202
GDP growth rate	8.9	−0.4	−0.7	1.8	5.0	5.1	5.2	5.2	4.0
GDP per capita ($,000, current prices)	19.7	18.9	17.0	17.6	18.5	19.2	20.4	22.8	27.3
Unemployment rate (percent)	8.8	9.3	10.3	10.7	10.4	9.0	8.4	7.3	6.1
Rate of employment of 25–64 year-olds (percent)	n.a.	66.4	66.0	66.2	66.7	67.5	68.5	70.1	71.0
Public expenditure (percent of GDP)	47.3	49.7	51.1	50.3	47.4	45.2	44.7	44.0	43.3
Tax revenue (percent of GDP)	37.0	36.9	36.2	35.4	35.5	35.6	36.1	36.5	33.9
Budget deficit (percent of GDP)	0.6	4.1	3.5	5.3	3.6	1.8	0.9	0.0	2.1
Gross public debt (percent of GDP, year-end)	85.1	89.9	97.6	99.9	98.2	94.2	85.7	79.4	78.0
Exports of goods and services ($ billion)	39.5	34.9	32.5	35.7	43.1	47.1	53.3	60.7	70.8
Imports of goods and services ($ billions)	40.3	38.4	36.1	37.2	43.6	48.4	53.4	64.1	75.4
Current account (percent of GDP)	−1.8	−1.6	−1.1	0.5	1.7	3.1	5.0	2.6	0.8
Net external debt (percent of GDP)	6.3	3.4	−0.6	−4.3	−8.5	−16.3	−21.8	−24.9	−25.1

Source: Bank of Israel. *Annual Report 2008.* Table 1.1 and author's calculations.

Appendix 4.1. *GDP, 1995–2009 (millions of shekels, 2005 prices)*

	Gross domestic product	Imports of goods and services (f.o.b.)	Exports of goods and services	Gross domestic capital formation	General government consumption expenditure	Private consumption Expenditure*
1995	423,447	164,128	129,395	105,449	126,562	228,469
1996	445,628	176,056	137,081	113,919	132,861	240,146
1997	458,424	183,293	149,339	112,711	135,767	246,501
1998	477,918	186,486	159,163	109,504	139,332	259,536
1999	493,334	215,611	181,581	116,293	143,077	269,405
2000	537,442	241,056	222,755	118,509	145,446	292,743
2001	535,451	228,704	198,010	114,411	150,364	301,848
2002	531,876	226,232	194,011	101,989	157,994	303,926
2003	541,372	223,347	209,540	96,852	153,745	304,804
2004	568,585	249,658	246,113	99,837	151,040	321,124
2005	597,771	258,474	256,640	112,535	153,536	333,534
2006	628,751	267,727	272,228	119,801	157,679	346,770
2007	667,755	297,910	297,545	126,867	165,675	372,276
2008	695,588	305,779	313,732	132,545	168,224	385,644
2009	696,208	259,376	273,100	124,160	169,511	390,864

* Includes consumption of nonprofit organizations

2009 = estimated

Sources: 1995–2006: CBS National Accounts 1995–2007, http://www.cbs.gov.il/publications09/national_accounts95_07/pdf/t01.pdf

Central Bureau of Statistics. 2010. Israel's National Accounts 2009. Press Release 10 March 2010, http://www.cbs.gov.il/reader/newhodaot/tables_template_eng.html?hodaa=201008049

Appendix 4.2. *Share of working-age population in the labor force, 1996–2007*

	1996	1997	1998	1999	2000	2001	2002	2003	2004	2005	2006	2007
Israel	53.7	53.5	53.4	53.8	54.3	54.3	54.1	54.5	54.9	55.2	55.6	56.3
Australia	64.6	64.3	64.3	64.0	64.4	64.4	64.3	64.6	64.6	65.3	65.6	66.0
Italy	47.3	47.3	47.7	47.9	48.1	48.3	48.5	49.1	49.1	48.7	48.9	48.6
United States	66.8	67.1	67.1	67.1	67.1	66.8	66.6	66.2	66.0	66.0	66.2	66.0
Germany	57.1	57.3	57.7	56.9	56.7	56.7	56.4	56.0	56.4	57.6	58.2	
Netherlands	60.2	61.1	61.8	62.5	63.4	64.0	64.7	64.6	64.8	64.7	65.1	65.9
United Kingdom	62.4	62.5	62.5	62.8	62.9	62.7	62.9	63.0	63.0	63.1	63.5	63.4
Japan	63.0	63.2	62.8	62.4	62.0	61.6	60.8	60.3	60.0	60.0	60.0	60.0
France	55.7	55.6	56.0	56.3	56.6	56.7	56.8	56.8	56.6	56.5	56.6	56.7
Canada	64.8	65.1	65.4	65.9	66.0	66.1	67.1	67.7	67.7	67.4	67.4	67.7
Sweden	63.9	63.2	62.8	62.7	63.7	63.6	63.9	63.8	63.6	64.8	65.0	65.3

Source: Central Bureau of Statistics, Labour Force Survey. 2008.

Appendix 4.3. *The net capital stock, 2000–2007 (excluding dwellings, millions of shekels, 2005 prices)*

	2000	2001	2002	2003	2004	2005	2006	2007
Total*	570,954	601,893	627,488	642,279	651,931	661,580	672,336	690,791
Public services*	187,796	196,483	205,984	214,736	221,689	225,030	228,133	232,296
Business sector-total*	383,158	405,410	421,505	427,542	430,243	436,550	444,203	458,496
Manufacturing	124,342	131,887	135,864	138,536	139,294	140,808	142,758	148,674
Agriculture	13,799	12,121	14,036	14,103	14,094	14,313	14,622	15,156
Transport**	64,125	68,541	73,431	73,380	72,517	74,797	77,575	82,926
Communications	29,239	32,080	34,014	34,023	33,022	32,339	31,756	30,606
Other	151,653	158,775	164,160	167,500	171,316	173,293	177,492	181,134

* including capital stock of software

** excluding capital stock of roads that is included in public services

Source: Central Bureau of Statistics. *Net Capital Stock excluding Dwellings.* http://www.cbs.gov.il/publications09/prod_07/pdf/07.pdf

Appendix 4.4. *Israel and the OECD: Gross domestic product and gross domestic product per capita, 2007*

	Gross domestic product per capita		Gross domestic product	
	Based on Purchasing Power Parities (PPP's)	Based on exchange rates	Based on Purchasing Power Parities (PPP's)	Based on exchange rates
	$		$ billions	
Israel	**26,444**	**23,257**	**189.9**	**167.0**
MEMBERS OF OECD				
Austria	37,176	44,647	308.6	370.6
Australia	37,565	44,786	794.6	947.4
Italy	30,538	35,612	1,813.2	2,114.5
Iceland	36,311	65,245	11.3	20.3
Ireland	45,027	59,874	196.2	260.9
United States	45,489	45,489	13,741.6	13,741.6
Belgium	35,382	43,155	375.8	458.4
Germany	34,391	40,312	2,829.1	3,316.1
Denmark	35,961	56,788	196.3	310.1
Netherlands	39,222	47,388	642.4	776.1
Hungary	18,799	13,799	189.0	138.8
United Kingdom	35,656	46,104	2,167.3	2,802.3
Turkey	12,993	8,894	960.3	657.3
Greece	28,423	27,902	318.1	312.3
Japan	33,603	34,283	4,293.5	4,380.4
Luxembourg	80,087	103,822	38.4	49.8
Mexico	14,004	9,646	1,479.9	1,019.4
Norway	53,477	82,549	251.7	388.5
New Zealand	26,911	30,588	114.7	130.4
Slovakia	20,079	13,903	108.4	75.0
Spain	31,586	32,044	1,417.4	1,437.9
Poland	16,091	11,140	613.3	424.6
Portugal	22,824	21,053	242.1	223.3
Finland	34,700	46,494	183.5	245.9
Czech Republic	24,027	16,852	248.0	174.0
France	32,633	40,672	2,080.6	2,593.1
Korea	26,833	21,653	1,300.2	1,049.2
Canada	38,500	43,356	1,269.6	1,429.7
Sweden	36,632	49,554	335.1	453.3
Switzerland	41,215	56,978	314.0	434.1

Source: CBS, *Statistical Abstract of Israel 2009*, no. 60.

Appendix 4.5. *Israel and the OECD: Indices of gross domestic product in purchasing power parities, 2005–2008 (at international prices)*

	At 2005 prices		Volume indices per capita, at current prices			
	2008	2007	2008	2007	2006	2005
ISRAEL	**82**	**80**	**82**	**80**	**80**	**78**
MEMBERS OF OECD	**100**	**100**	**100**	**100**	**100**	**100**
Austria	116	114	113	113	113	113
Australia	111	110	111	110	110	111
Italy	91	93	92	93	94	95
Iceland	116	119	109	111	113	119
Ireland	126	134	125	138	134	131
United States	139	139	139	139	141	141
Belgium	109	108	105	108	108	109
Germany	109	108	106	105	105	106
Denmark	110	112	109	110	112	112
Netherlands	123	121	124	120	119	119
Hungary	58	58	58	57	58	57
United Kingdom	111	111	108	109	109	111
Turkey	38	38	40	40	39	37
Greece	89	87	87	87	86	84
Japan	102	103	102	103	102	103
Luxembourg	233	240	232	245	243	231
Mexico	43	43	43	43	43	42
Norway	160	159	174	163	167	160
New Zealand	80	81	79	81	81	82
Slovakia	66	63	66	61	58	55
Spain	92	92	95	97	95	93
Poland	53	51	53	49	48	47
Portugal	68	69	69	70	69	70
Finland	108	108	106	106	104	104
Czech Republic	75	74	74	73	70	69
France	99	99	98	100	100	99
Korea	82	81	83	82	79	77
Canada	117	118	117	118	118	118
Sweden	109	110	111	112	110	109
Switzerland	121	121	127	124	122	120

Source: CBS, *Statistical Abstract of Israel 2009*, no. 60.

Appendix 4.6. *Israel and the OECD: Average annual growth rates, 1998–2008*

	Israel	USA	Eurozone	OECD
GDP growth rate	3.8	2.7	2.5	3.1
Per capita growth	1/7	1.7	2.0	2.5
Per capita GDP ($000)	19.8	38.5	32.4	28.7
Population growth rate	2.1	1.0	0.5	0.5
Civilian labor force participation rate	54.8	66.0	70.5	73.7
Unemployment rate	8.9	5.0	7.6	6.8
Exports as percent of GDP	32.1	10.7	45.2	40.9
Gross investment as percent of GDP	19.4	19.2	22.1	22.7
National savings as percent GDP	20.3	15.3	21.6	21.9
Current account as percent of GDP	0.6	−4.6	−0.7	−0.8
Public expenditure as percent of GDP	47.5	36.1	46.0	43.5
Tax revenue as percent of GDP	35.9	27.9	38.5	35.9
Gross public debt as percent GDP	91.3	61.5	73.6	62.0

Source: Bank of Israel, *Annual Report 2008*, *Table 1.2* and United States Bureau of Labor, *Employment Status of the Civilian Noninstitutional Population, 1940 to Date*. http://www.bls.gov/cps/cpsaat1.pdf

Appendix 4.7. *Israel and the OECD: Civilian research and development (R&D), 2007*

	Civilian R & D Index of final expenditure per capita (USA = 100)	Expenditure per capita (Dollars)(1)	As percentage of total civilian and defence R&D	As percentage of GDP	Civilian and defence R&D per capita (Dollars)(1)
Israel	**116.1**	**1,259**		**4.8**	
Members of OECD					
Austria	87.8	952	100.0	2.6	952
Australia	62.5	677	94.5	1.9	716
Italy	30.8	334	100.0	1.1	334
Iceland	90.4	980	100.0	2.8	980
Ireland	54.5	591	100.0	1.3	591
United States	100.0	1,084	88.8	2.4	1,221
Belgium	61.0	662	100.0	1.9	662
Germany	80.6	874	100.0	2.5	874
Denmark	84.6	917	100.0	2.6	917
Netherlands	61.7	669	100.0	1.7	669
United Kingdom	52.8	572	89.4	1.6	640
Greece	13.2	143	87.7	0.5	163
Japan	105.5	1,143	98.8	3.4	1,157
Norway	76.7	831	94.7	1.6	878
New Zealand	24.7	268	82.6	1.0	325
Spain	35.2	382	95.2	1.2	401
Portugal	24.8	269	100.0	1.2	269
Finland	109.6	1,188	98.6	3.4	1,206
Czech Republic	33.0	358	96.8	1.5	370
France	56.8	615	90.5	1.9	680
Korea	79.5	861	100.0	3.5	861
Sweden	118.6	1,285	97.4	3.5	1,320
Switzerland	92.5	1,003	100.0	2.9	1,003

(1) Current prices, GDP in purchasing power parity.

Source: CBS, *Statistical Abstract of Israel 2009*, no. 60.

Appendix 5.1. *The balance of payments, 1995–2009 ($ millions)*

		Current account								
		Current transfers (net)		Income(1)		Services		Goods	Imports	
	Balance	Thereof government	Total	Exports	Imports	Exports	Imports	Exports	Thereof: Defense imports	Total
1995	-4,790	3,437	5,673	1,641	4,296	7,956	8,326	19,526	1,293	26,965
1996	-5,175	3,989	6,136	1,702	5,095	8,349	8,902	21,290	1,671	28,654
1997	-3,275	4,040	6,080	1,914	5,882	9,200	9,004	22,574	1,755	28,157
1998	-988	4,077	6,076	2,540	6,605	10,098	9,258	22,779	1,872	26,619
1999	-1,961	4,162	6,273	2,771	7,947	12,315	10,263	25,458	2,070	30,567
2000	-2,210	4,342	6,470	3,631	11,955	15,406	11,905	30,891	1,936	34,748
2001	-1,928	4,283	6,658	2,733	8,274	12,855	11,848	27,686	2,147	31,738
2002	-1,239	4,420	6,785	2,459	7,043	12,189	10,904	27,267	2,411	31,992
2003	626	4,115	6,411	2,816	7,683	13,664	11,205	29,940	2,055	33,316
2004	2,140	3,516	6,275	3,005	7,189	16,024	12,825	36,358	1,895	39,507
2005	4,188	3,237	6,002	5,602	7,013	17,436	13,718	39,767	2,198	43,888
2006	7,349	4,412	7,442	8,420	9,205	19,185	14,657	43,319	2,493	47,155
2007	4,604	3,868	7,257	10,873	11,369	21,107	17,580	50,286	2,418	55,970
2008	1,694	4,781	8,357	7,242	11,3375	24,016	19,763	57,383	2,495	64,125
2009	7,476	3,710	7,438	5,724	10,186	22,195	17,193	45,760		46,002

	Capital and financial account											
	Financial account										Capital account	
	Statistical discrepancies	Reserve assets net	Financial derivatives	Other investments			Portfolio Investments		Direct investments		Government	Private sector
				Liabilities		Assets	Abroad	In Israel	Abroad	In Israel		
				Total	Thereof long term	Total						
1995	154	-1,097	-56	3,185	556	-611	154	1,723	-820	1,351	200	609
1996	950	-3,531	92	1,303	773	955	276	3,774	-815	1,398	198	576
1997	2,292	-9,240	89	2,978	571	1,462	126	4,128	-923	1,635	176	552
1998	-1,126	-1,730	208	1,901	-441	-1,741	-102	2,388	-1,125	1,738	180	397
1999	-4,212	-1,011	0	6,232	1,042	-3,689	-1,301	2,439	-830	3,763	163	406
2000	-814	-937	0	3,255	1,048	-3,634	-3,312	4,603	-3,335	5,920	161	305
2001	-239	110	8	1,462	1,020	-2,527	-1,240	140	-687	4,181	162	559
2002	2,264	776	-10	-453	-847	-1,477	-2,645	1,648	-981	1,910	-120	328
2003	2,158	-1,068	14	-371	86	-1,962	-3,247	1,314	-2,086	4,088	191	344
2004	1,633	-301	50	384	496	-6,581	-2,853	6,864	-4,533	2,529	173	494
2005	5,426	-1,937	35	344	-626	-5,277	-7,975	3,142	-2,946	4,273	163	564
2006	-847	-433	-66	2,751	654	-10,449	-8,017	9,107	-14,944	14,763	203	584
2007	-1,801	1,681	20	3,325	427	-8,232	-3,938	1,479	-6,981	9,020	201	622
2008	2,145	-14,163	-156	-1,823	-115	10,054	-2,030	1,000	-7,210	9,876	145	964
2009	2,858	-16,823		3,095		9,342	7,609	2,483	1,152	3,771	664	-1,275

Source: CBS, *Statistical Abstract of Israel 2009* and Central Bureau of Statistics, *Current Account by Main Components 2000–2009.*

Appendix 5.2. *Foreign trade (excluding diamonds) by country of import or export destination, 1995–2008 (percent)*

Year	Total	European Union (27 countries)	Of which: Euro-bloc	Rest of Europe	USA	Rest of America	China	Japan	Rest of Asia	Africa	Other
					Destinations of exports						
1995	100.0	40.9	29.9	5.4	26.2	4.9	0.6	3.3	9.1	2.6	7.0
2000	100.0	35.0	25.5	4.3	29.7	5.2	1.0	2.3	12.9	2.1	7.5
2005	100.0	34.5	24.0	6.2	28.3	6.5	2.4	2.3	10.2	2.6	7.1
2008	100.0	33.3	23.7	7.2	28.0	7.5	2.6	1.9	11.7	3.2	4.6
					Sources of imports						
1995	100.0	50.1	38.6	6.2	21.6	1.9	0.6	4.0	6.4	1.8	7.5
2000	100.0	41.9	32.5	5.9	21.9	2.3	2.0	4.0	9.0	1.3	11.6
2005	100.0	37.3	29.7	8.7	14.9	3.7	5.3	3.5	9.3	0.9	16.4
2008	100.0	33.8	26.6	9.9	12.7	3.0	7.6	4.0	9.3	1.3	18.5

Source: Bank of Israel, *Annual Report 2008*, Table 7, p. A6.

Appendix 5.3. Output in the information and communications technology sectors, 2000–2006 (2005 prices, millions of NIS)

	Electronic components	Electronic communication equipment	Industrial equipment for control and supervision, medical and scientific equipment	ICT Manufacturing total	Tele-communications	Computer and related services, Research and development	Start-up companies	ICT Services total	ICT total
1990	1,416	2,809	9,369	13,055	3,696	4,817	-	8,424	21,986
1992	1,857	4,095	10,672	16,134	4,495	6,131	953	11,115	27,793
1995	3,453	7,061	11,186	21,521	10,529	10,209	830	22,318	43,856
1996	4,357	9,697	11,839	25,922	13,657	12,768	1,907	29,212	54,890
1997	4,725	10,868	13,219	28,848	14,042	14,129	1,900	30,763	59,493
1998	5,432	12,352	14,913	32,784	16,378	18,536	3,341	38,500	70,912
1999	7,046	13,785	15,673	36,621	17,778	19,601	4,230	41,867	78,133
2000	15,300	17,586	12,278	50,536	19,728	23,939	13,591	57,277	107,342
2001	10,980	15,410	18,638	45,285	21,605	25,665	9,303	56,628	101,563
2002	8,482	10,855	18,310	37,661	22,772	29,450	6,332	58,588	96,251
2003	8,378	10,475	17,720	36,594	23,061	29,485	4,384	56,993	93,588
2004	8,403	12,814	19,446	40,682	25,197	33,493	4,286	63,016	103,706
2005	8,471	13,636	20,755	42,862	26,071	35,940	5,069	67,079	109,941
2006	10,025	15,233	22,555	47,813	26,704	41,895	5,160	73,758	121,571

Source: Central Bureau of Statistics. 2008. Information and Communication Technologies (ICT) Sector 1995–2006. Jerusalem: Central Bureau of Statistics. Publication no. 1306, Table 2.

Appendix 5.4. *Output and employment in the construction sector, 1980–2008 (output in 1995 prices, NIS millions, and employment in thousands)*

	Output	Foreigners	Palestinians	Israelis	Total employment
1980	34,032.0		36.5	79.2	115.7
1981	34,347.6		39.8	78.5	118.3
1982	33,002.1		44.4	79.8	124.2
1983	32,164.1		45.6	86.2	131.8
1984	28,672.8		45.8	79.1	124.9
1985	25,824.6		44.3	72.2	116.5
1986	24,746.6		47.6	61.8	109.4
1987	27,253.6		49.7	67.7	117.4
1988	27,978.6		54.0	73.8	127.8
1989	29,408.5		56.0	71.6	127.6
1990	35,237.0		64.0	75.9	139.9
1991	50,902.2		66.9	96.2	163.1
1992	54,514.8		85.9	107.6	193.5
1993	51,845.8	6.0	61.0	118.3	185.3
1994	55,338.1	21.2	46.9	125.0	193.1
1995	65,094.5	45.5	38.0	144.1	227.6
1996	70,673.6	62.1	33.1	149.9	245.1
1997	71,971.1	68.4	42.4	146.7	257.5
1998	67,295.4	63.5	60.1	131.4	254.9
1999	60,269.2	59.0	63.9	120.4	243.3
2000	54,963.5	62.5	57.8	116.6	236.9
2001	52,830.2	79.1	23.4	117.0	219.5
2002	53,337.4	79.5	13.1	118.7	211.2
2003	50,326.9	60.1	18.0	129.8	207.9
2004	48,888.6	48.8	15.5	128.7	193.0
2005	48,239.0	36.8	19.4	127.1	183.4
2006	52,065.2	34.9	18.5	134.4	187.8
2007	55,018.0	33.0	22.5	150.2	205.6
2008	55,895.0	35.9	26.7	151.3	213.9

Sources: Bank of Israel, *Annual Report 2008*, Tables 2A.34 and 2A.35.

Appendix 6.1. *Budgetary and extra-budgetary defense spending, 2000–2005*
(shekels, millions, current prices)

	2000	2001	2002	2003	2004	2005
1. Grand total – direct	48,615	51,485	58,831	55,411	53,329	55,894
Expenditure and additional	26,757	28,431	30,082	28,702	28,452	28,536
Other expenditure – Net	21,858	23,054	28,749	26,709	24,877	27,358
2. Direct expenditure	39,587	41,788	48,957	46,350	43,988	46,239
Compensation of employees	18,006	18,969	20,436	19,888	19,398	19,341
Other expenditure	21,581	22,819	28,521	26,462	24,590	26,898
Thereof: Defense imports	9,370	10,795	13,704	11,321	10,150	11,724
Sales	−1,524	−1,542	−1,456	−1,256	−1,074	−1,094
3. Additional cost components-total	9,028	9,697	9,874	9,061	9,341	9,655
Additional cost of labor due to conscripted and reserve soldiers and risk premium (1)	8,189	8,918	9,065	8,149	8,335	8,522
Shelters construction and maintenance of emergency stocks	152	106	105	128	138	160
Defense expenditure of government civilian ministries	687	673	704	784	868	973
Thereof: Compensation of employees	562	544	581	665	719	673
As percent of GDP						
1. Grand total – direct	9.9	10.3	11.4	10.6	9.7	9.6
Labor cost	5.4	5.7	5.8	5.5	5.2	4.9
Other expenditure – Net	4.4	4.6	5.6	5.1	4.5	4.7
2. Direct expenditure	8.0	8.4	9.5	8.8	8.0	7.9
Compensation of employees	3.7	3.8	3.9	3.8	3.5	3.3
Other expenditure	4.4	4.6	5.5	5.0	4.5	4.6
Thereof: Defense imports	1.9	2.2	2.6	2.2	1.8	2.0
Sales	−0.3	−0.3	−0.3	−0.2	−0.2	−0.2
3. Additional cost components-total	1.8	1.9	1.9	1.7	1.7	1.7

(*continued*)

Appendix 6.1 *(continued)*

	2000	2001	2002	2003	2004	2005
Additional cost of labor due to conscripted and reserve soldiers and risk premium (1)	1.7	1.8	1.8	1.6	1.5	1.5
Shelters construction and maintenance of emergency stocks	0.0	0.0	0.0	0.0	0.0	0.0
Defense expenditure of government civilian ministries	0.1	0.1	0.1	0.1	0.2	0.2
Thereof: Compensation of employees	0.1	0.1	0.1	0.1	0.1	0.1

Current Statistics no. 10/2007, Table 6.
* imputed
Source: Central Bureau of Statistics, *Defence Expenditure in Israel 1950–2006.*

Appendix 10.1. *Crude birth rate and death rate, 1950–2010*

Period	Crude birth rate*	Crude death rate*
1950–1955	32.5	6.9
1955–1960	27.9	6.2
1960–1965	25.5	6.0
1965–1970	25.5	6.7
1970–1975	27.4	7.1
1975–1980	26.0	6.8
1980–1985	23.8	6.8
1985–1990	22.7	6.6
1990–1995	21.5	6.3
1995–2000	21.5	6.3
2000–2005	21.1	5.6
2005–2010	19.7	5.5

* per thousand of the population
Source: Population Division of the Department of Economic and Social Affairs of the United Nations Secretariat, *World Population Prospects: The 2006 Revision and World Urbanization Prospects: The 2005 Revision, Medium variant.* http://esa.un.org/unpp, Wednesday, September 24, 2008; 3:39:56 AM. http://esa.un.org/unpp/p2k0data.asp

Appendix 10.2. *Immigration by period and last place of residence, 1882–2007*

	Total	Asia	Africa	Europe	America and Oceania	Not Known
1882–1903	25,000					
1904–1914	37,500					
1919–1948	482,857	40,895	4,041	377,381	7,754	52,786
1948–1951	687,624	237,352	93,951	326,786	5,140	34,395
1952–1954	54,676	13,238	27,897	9,748	2,971	822
1955–1957	166,492	8,801	103,846	48,616	3,632	1,597
1958–1960	75,970	13,247	13,921	44,595	3,625	582
1961–1964	228,793	19,525	115,876	77,537	14,841	1,014
1965–1968	82,244	15,081	25,394	31,638	9,274	920
1969–1971	116,791	19,700	12,065	50,558	33,891	577
1972–1974	142,753	6,345	6,821	102,763	26,775	49
1975–1979	124,827	11,793	6,029	77,167	29,293	545
1980–1984	83,637	6,912	15,711	35,508	25,230	276
1985–1989	70,196	6,563	7,700	36,461	19,301	171
1990–1994	609,322	5,900	32,157	553,622	17,220	423
1995–1999	346,997	38,843	12,248	275,667	20,061	178
2000–2004	181,505	22,077	16,256	119,586	23,572	14
2005–2007	58,580	5,421	11,362	29,998	11,771	28
Total 1919–2007	3,513,264	471,693	595,275	2,197,631	2,465,797	84,377

Source: CBS, *Statistical Abstract of Israel, 2008.*

Appendix 10.3. *Number of families, people, and children* living in poverty before and after tax and benefits, 2002–2008 (including East Jerusalem)*

	Before tax and benefits	After tax and benefits	Before tax and benefits %	After tax and benefits %
2002				
Families	634,000	339,000	33.9	18.1
People	2,079,000	1,321,500	33.3	21.1
Children	828,000	617,600	39.7	29.6
2003				
Families	645,300	366,300	33.9	19.3
People	2,156,200	1,426,800	33.8	22.4
Children	862,200	652,400	40.7	30.8
2004				
Families	656,800	394,200	33.7	20.3
People	2,184,100	1,534,300	33.6	23.6
Children	881,600	713,600	41.0	33.2
2005				
Families	668,200	410,700	33.6	20.6
People	2,235,800	1,631,500	33.8	24.7
Children	899,600	768,800	41.1	35.2
2006				
Families	665,800	404,400	32.9	20.0
People	2,254,800	1,649,800	33.5	24.5
Children	921,900	764,500	41.5	35.8
2007				
Families	668,600	412,900	32.3	19.9
People	2,224,600	1,630,400	32.5	23.8
Children	901,000	773,900	39.9	34.2
2008				
Families	680,900	430,100	32.3	19.9
People	2,283,300	1,651,300	32.7	23.7
Children	931,300	783,600	40.4	24.0

* Children aged up to 17 years.

Source: National Insurance Institute, *Measures of Poverty and Social Gaps 2007 (Jerusalem, 2008)*; *Measures of Poverty and Social Gaps 2008 (Jerusalem, 2009)*; *Annual Surveys 2002–2003, 2005, 2006*.

Appendix 10.4. *Number and share of pupils entitled to a school leaving certificate and meeting university entrance requirements, 2000–2006*

	2000				2006			
	Met university entrance requirements		Entitled to a Certificate		Met university entrance requirements		Entitled to a Certificate	
	% of pupils in grade 12	Number	% of pupils in grade 12	Number	% of pupils in grade 12	Number	% of pupils in grade 12	Number
Total	41.4	36,779	50.6	44,923	45.9	45,237	53.4	52,650
Jewish	44.1	33,586	52.1	39,667	48.3	39,393	54.9	n.a.
Sex								
Boys	39.7	14,706	46.7	17,279	43.8	17,403	49.5	19,682
Girls	48.2	18,880	57.2	22,388	53.4	21,990	61.0	25,096
Origin								
Israel	46.6	17,199	53.7	19,833	49.6	21,390	56.2	24,217
Asia-Africa	35.5	6,221	46.8	8,207	41.2	6,099	50.9	7,536
Europe- America	51.7	8,946	58.3	10,091	54.6	9,389	59.3	10,197

(continued)

Appendix 10.4 *(continued)*

	2000				2006			
	Met university entrance requirements		Entitled to a Certificate		Met university entrance requirements		Entitled to a Certificate	
	% of pupils in grade 12	Number	% of pupils in grade 12	Number	% of pupils in grade 12	Number	% of pupils in grade 12	Number
Arab	25.4	3,193	41.8	5,256	34.4	5,844	46.3	7,872
Sex								
Boys	22.6	1,306	36.7	2,117	27.5	2,168	36.5	2,873
Girls	27.7	1,887	46.1	3,139	40.7	3,676	55.3	4,999
Religion								
Muslims	22.1	2,106	39.2	3,742	31.4	4,208	43.7	5,854
Christians	51.8	716	63.5	878	56.3	929	60.9	1,005
Druze	22.5	366	38.7	628	38.0	693	54.6	996

n.a. = not available

Source: Central Bureau of Statistics, *Statistical Abstract of Israel 2008*, Table 8.25; *Statistical Abstract of Israel 2002*, Table 8.20.

References

Amir, Shmuel. 2002. "Overseas Foreign Workers in Israel: Policy Aims and Labor Market Outcomes." *International Migration Review*. April.

Arieli, Shaul. 2008. Jewish Population over the Green Line. http://www.shaularieli.com

Arlozorov, Meirav. 2009. "Goshen: Giving Guarantees to Banks Does Not Require Limiting Salaries of Senior Managers." *Ha'aretz*. 9 February.

Arlozorov, Meirav. 2008. "Hard Look: Handing the Haredim a Noose." *Ha'aretz*. 10 April.

Arnon, A. and J. Weinblatt. 2001. "Sovereignty and Economic Development: The Case of Palestine." *Economic Journal*, Vol. 111. No. 472. F291–F308.

Arnon, Arie, Israel Luski, Avia Spivak and Jimmy Weinblatt. 1997. *The Palestinian Economy*. Leiden: Brill.

Arnon, Jacob. 1985. *Economy in Turmoil*. Tel Aviv: Kibbutz HaMeuchad.

Arnon, Jacob. 1988. "Forty Years of the Israeli Economy," *Economic Quarterly*. Vol. 39. No. 138.

Arrow, Kenneth J. 1962. "The Implications of Learning by Doing." *The Review of Economic Studies*. Vol. 29. No. 3.

Asali, Muhammad. 2006. Why Do Arabs Earn Less than Jews in Israel. *The Maurice Falk Institute for Economic Research in Israel*, http://pluto.huji.ac.il/~msfalkin/pdfs/paper%2006–3.pdf

A Survey of Palestine. 1946. Prepared in December 1945 and January 1946 for the information of the Anglo-American Committee of Inquiry, Vol. I. Government Printer, Palestine.

Avnimelech, Gil and Morris Teubal. 2002. Israel's Venture Capital (VC) Industry: Emergence, Operation and Impact. Hebrew University, Economics Department. http://economics.huji.ac.il/facultye/teubal/VCPaper1%20-%20Dilek%20Book.pdf

Bank of Israel. 1975. *Annual Report 1974*. Jerusalem: Bank of Israel.

Bank of Israel. 1978. *Annual Report 1977*. Jerusalem: Bank of Israel.

Bank of Israel. 1982. *Annual Report 1981*. Jerusalem: Bank of Israel.

Bank of Israel. 1983. *Annual Report 1982*. Jerusalem: Bank of Israel.

Bank of Israel. 1985. *Annual Report 1984*. Jerusalem: Bank of Israel.

Bank of Israel. 1985. *Recent Economic Developments*. Jerusalem: Bank of Israel, No. 38.

Bank of Israel. 2000. *Annual Report 1999.* Jerusalem, Bank of Israel.

Bank of Israel. 2004. *Annual Report 2003.* Jerusalem, Bank of Israel.

Bank of Israel. 2005. Annual Report 2004. *Jerusalem, Bank of Israel,* http://www.bankisrael.gov.il/deptdata/mehkar/doch04/heb/p1_5.pdf

Bank of Israel. 2006. Recent Economic Developments. *Jerusalem, Bank of Israel,* http://www.bankisrael.gov.il/develeng/develeng115/develeng.pdf

Bank of Israel. 2007. Annual Report 2006. *Jerusalem, Bank of Israel,* http://www.bankisrael.gov.il/deptdata/mehkar/doch06/eng/pe_8.pdf

Bank of Israel. 2008. Annual Report 2007. *Jerusalem, Bank of Israel,* http://www.bankisrael.gov.il/deptdata/mehkar/doch07/eng/pe_2.pdf

Bank of Israel. 2008. Recent Economic Developments. *Jerusalem, Bank of Israel,* http://www.bankisrael.gov.il/develeng/develeng123/develeng.pdf

Bank of Israel. 2009. Annual Report 2008. *Jerusalem, Bank of Israel,* http://www.bankisrael.gov.il/deptdata/mehkar/doch08/eng/pe_8.pdf

Bank of Israel. 2009. Inflation Report July–September 2009. *Jerusalem, Bank of Israel,* No. 28, http://www.bankisrael.gov.il/deptdata/general/infrep/eng/inf-09-3e.pdf

Bank of Israel. Israel's External Financial Transactions. *Jerusalem, Bank of Israel,* http://www.bankisrael.gov.il/deptdata/pik_mth/pikmth_e.htm

Bard, Mitchell. The Jewish Virtual Library. http://www.jewishvirtuallibrary.org/jsource/History/histadrut.html. Accessed 23 June 2010.

Barkai, Haim. 1986. "Reflections on the Economic Cost of the Lebanon War." *The Jerusalem Quarterly.* No. 37. 95–106.

Barkai, Haim. 1987. *Kibbutz Efficiency and the Incentive Conundrum.* Jerusalem: Falk Institute.

Barkai, Haim. 1995. *The Lessons of Israel's Great Inflation.* Boulder, CO: Praeger.

Becker, Gary. 1971. *The Economics of Discrimination.* Chicago: University of Chicago Press.

Ben Bassat, Avi and Momi Dahan. 2004. Social Rights in the Constitution and in Economic Policy. The Israel Democracy Institute Working Paper no. 41, Jerusalem.

Ben Bassat, Avi. 2002. "The Obstacle Course to a Market Economy in Israel," in Avi Ben Bassat ed. *The Israeli Economy, 1985–1998: From Government Intervention to Market Economy.* Cambridge, MA and London: MIT Press.

Ben Porath, Yoram. 1986. *Patterns and Peculiarities of Economic Growth and Structure.* Jerusalem: Falk Institute.

Bendelac, Jacques. 1998. Average Salaries and Earnings by Settlement and by Other Economic Variables, 1994–1995. Jerusalem: National Insurance Institute, Periodic Report no. 154.

Bendelac, Jacques. 2003. Average Wages and Incomes and Their Distribution by Various Economic Variables, 2000–2001. Jerusalem: National Insurance Institute, Periodic Report no. 189.

Bendelac, Jacques. 2007. Average Wages and Incomes and Their Distribution by Various Economic Variables, 2004–2005. Jerusalem: National Insurance Institute, Periodic Report no. 210.

Bendelac, Jacques. 2008. Average Wage and Income by Locality and by Various Economic Variables, 2006. Jerusalem: National Insurance Institute, Periodic Report no. 219.

Ben-Rafael, Eliezer. 2007. "Mizrachi and Russian Challenges to Israel's Dominant Culture: Divergencies and Convergencies." *Israel Studies*. Vol. 12. No. 3.

Berglas, Eitan. 1983. *Defense and the Economy: The Israeli Experience.* Jerusalem: Falk Institute for Economic Research in Israel.

Berman, Eli. 2000. "Sect, Subsidy and Sacrifice: An Economist's View of Ultra-Orthodox Jews." *Quarterly Journal of Economics*. Vol. 115. No. 3.

Berman, Eli and Ruth Klinov. 1995. Human Capital Investment and Nonparticipation: Evidence from a Sample with Infinite Horizons. Jerusalem: The Maurice Falk Institute for Economic Research in Israel, Discussion Paper Series no. 97.

Bialer, Uri. 2007. "Fuel Bridge across the Middle East-Israel, Iran, and the Eilat-Ashkelon Oil Pipeline". *Israel Studies*. Vol. 12. No. 3.

Bregman, Arie. 1974. Economic Growth in the Administered Areas 1968–1973. Bank of Israel Research Department.

Breznitz, Dan. 2007. *Innovation and the State*. New Haven, CT and London: Yale University Press.

Bruno, Michael. 1971. "Economic Development Problems of Israel," in C. A. Cooper and S. A. Alexander, eds. *Economic Development and Population Growth in the Middle East*. New York: American Elsevier, 92–156.

Bruno, Michael. 1985. "Economic Stabilization: The Emergency Plan in Its Early Phases." *Economic Quarterly*. Vol. 31. No. 126.

Bruno, Michael. 1986. "External Shocks and Domestic Responses: Israel's Macro-Economic Performance 1965–1982," in Yoram Ben Porat, ed. *The Israeli Economy through Crisis*. Cambridge, MA: Harvard University Press.

Bruno, Michael. 1993. *Crisis, Stabilisation and Economic Reform: Therapy by Consensus.* Oxford: Clarendon Press.

Central Bureau of Statistics. 1974. Statistical Abstract of Israel 1974.

Central Bureau of Statistics. 1986. Statistical Abstract of Israel 1986. Publication No.37.

Central Bureau of Statistics. 1996. Current Briefings in Statistics. Publication No. 15.

Central Bureau of Statistics. 1999. Statistical Abstract of Israel 1999. Publication No. 50.

Central Bureau of Statistics. 2000. Productivity, Compensation of Employees and Capital Return 1995–1999, Current Statistics. Publication No. 23.

Central Bureau of Statistics. 2003. The Arab Population in Israel 2003.

Central Bureau of Statistics. 2007. Construction in Israel 2007. http://cbs.gov.il/publications/build2007/pdf/t09.pdf

Central Bureau of Statistics. 2007. Defence Expenditure in Israel 1950–2006. Current Statistics. Publication No. 10. http://www.cbs.gov.il/webpub/pub/text_page_eng.html?publ=7&CYear=2006&CMonth=1

Central Bureau of Statistics. 2007. Statistical Abstract of Israel 2007. Publication No. 58. http://www.cbs.gov.il/reader/shnaton/shnatone_new.htm?CYear=2007&Vol=58&CSubject=2

Central Bureau of Statistics. 2008. Information and Communication Technologies (ICT) Sector 1995–2006. Publication no. 1306.

Central Bureau of Statistics. 2008. Information and Communications Technologies (ICT) Sector 1995–2006, p. XXV. http://www.cbs.gov.il/publications/ict_06/pdf/e_print.pdf

Central Bureau of Statistics. 2008. Labor Force Survey 2007. http://www.cbs.gov.il/

Central Bureau of Statistics. 2008. Labor Force Survey. Publication No. 1377. http://www.cbs.gov.il/reader/y_labor/yearm_e_new.htm#11

Central Bureau of Statistics. 2008. Macro-Economic Statistics Quarterly. October–December. http://www.cbs.gov.il/www/publications09/macro0109/pdf/t1_1.pdf

Central Bureau of Statistics. 2008. Monthly Bulletin of Statistics. Publication No. 8. http://www.cbs.gov.il/reader/yarhon/yarmenu_e_new.html#15

Central Bureau of Statistics. 2008. Statistical Abstract of Israel 2008. Publication No. 59. http://www.cbs.gov.il/shnaton59/st20_12.pdf

Central Bureau of Statistics. 2009. Foreign Trade Statistics Monthly. January. http://www.cbs.gov.il/www/fr_trade/td1.htm

Central Bureau of Statistics. 2009. Israel's Balance of Payments, January–March 2009. Press Release. http://www.cbs.gov.il/hodaot2009n/09_09_116t1.pdf

Central Bureau of Statistics. 2009. Israel's Foreign Trade by Country. Press Release. 20 January.

Central Bureau of Statistics. 2009. Monthly Bulletin of Statistics. Publication No. 10. http://www.cbs.gov.il/reader/yarhon/yarmenu_e_new.html

Central Bureau of Statistics. 2009. Monthly Bulletin of Statistics Publication No. 11. http://www.cbs.gov.il/www/yarhon/k1_e.htm

Central Bureau of Statistics. 2009. Press Announcement. http://www.cbs.gov.il/reader/newhodaot/hodaa_template.html?hodaa=200819206

Central Bureau of Statistics. 2009. Productivity, Compensation of Employed Persons and Capital Return 2004–2007. Publication No. 1350. http://www.cbs.gov.il/publications09/prod_07/pdf/t04.pdf

Central Bureau of Statistics. 2009. Statistical Abstract of Israel 2009. Publication No. 60. http://cbs.gov.il/reader/shnatonenew_site.htm

Central Bureau of Statistics. 2010. Israel's National Accounts 2009. Press Release, 10 March. http://www.cbs.gov.il/reader/newhodaot/tables_template_eng.html?hodaa=201008049

Central Intelligence Agency. 2008. World Factbook. https://www.cia.gov/library/publications/the-world-factbook/geos/is.html#Military

Chiswick, Barry and Timothy Hatton. 2003. "International Migration and the Integration of Labor Markets," in M. Bordo, A. Taylor, and J. Williamson, eds. *Globalization in Historical Perspective*. NBER Conference Report. http://www.nber.org/chapters/c9586.pdf

Clifton, Eric. 1998. The Decline of Traditional Sectors in Israel: The Role of the Exchange Rate. International Monetary Fund, Working Paper no. WP/98/167.

Cohen, Alma, Rajeev Dehejia, and Dimitri Romanov. 2007. Do Financial Incentives Affect Fertility? *NBER Working Paper*, p. 19. http://www.nber.org/papers/w13700

Cooper, C. A. and S. A. Alexander. 1971. "Introduction," in C. A. Cooper and S. A. Alexander, eds. *Economic Development Population Growth in the Middle East*. New York: American Elsevier, 2–19.

Council for Higher Education, Planning and Budget Committee. 2005. Annual Report 2005/6. Publication No. 33. http://www.che.org.il

Degani, Avi and Rina Degani. 2004. Characteristics of the Housing Market in Beitar Elite and Recommendations for Marketing Land in the Settlement. *Geocartography Knowledge Group, for the Ministry of Housing.* http://www.moch.gov.il/NR/rdonlyres/

B5711295-153D-4A66-89FC-28D492D5BF89/1572/sekerYeshuvBeytar Elit.pdf

Della Pergola, Sergio. 2007. *Actual, Intended, and Appropriate Family Size in Israel: Trends, Attitudes and Policy Implications: A Preliminary Report.* New York: Population Association of America.

Doron, Avraham. 2007. "Multiculturalism and the Erosion of Support for the Universalistic Welfare State: The Israeli Experience." *Israel Studies.* Vol. 12. No. 3.

Dun and Bradstreet Israel. 2009. Annual Conclusions about Large Corporate Groups in the Economy. Press Announcement, 15 December. http://dundb.co.il/NewsShowHeb1.asp?idnum=475 Hebrew.

Easterlin, Richard A. 1961. "Israel's Development: Past Accomplishments and Future Problems." *The Quarterly Journal of Economics.* Vol. 75. No. 1.

Economist. 1988. 7 January. London.

Economist Intelligence Unit. 2005. The Occupied Territories Country Profile 2005. London.

Economist Intelligence Unit. 2008. The Occupied Territories Country Profile 2008. London.

Efrat, Elisha. 2006. *The West Bank and the Gaza Strip.* Abingdon, Oxon: Routledge.

Etzioni, Amir. 1998. The Israeli Cement Industry. *The Institute for Advanced Strategic and Political Studies.* http://www.israeleconomy.org/cement.htmfile

Federal Reserve Bank of New York. 2008. Taking the Pulse of the Technology Sector. August 13. http://www.newyorkfed.org/survey/TechPulse/tech_pulse_index.html

Feldman, Mark and Michal Abouganem. 2003. Development of High-Tech Industry in Israel 1995–1999: Labour Force and Wages. Central Bureau of Statistics, Working Paper Series no. 1, Table 7. http://www.cbs.gov.il/publications/hitech/xls_table/table7.pdf

Fershtman, Chaim and Neil Gandel, 1998. "The Effect of the Arab Boycott on Israel: The Automobile Market." *The Rand Journal of Economics.* Vol. 29. No. 1.

Fishbach, Michael R. 2008. *Jewish Property Claims against Arab Countries.* New York: Columbia University Press.

Flug, Karnit and Michel Strawczynski. 2007. Persistent Growth Episodes and Macroeconomic Policy Performance in Israel. Bank of Israel Research Department Discussion Paper no. 2007/08. Jerusalem: Bank of Israel.

Foreign Policy. 2006. The Global Top 20 November–December 2006. http://www.atkearney.com/shared_res/pdf/Globalization-Index_FP_Nov-Dec-06_S.pdf

Gabbay, Yoram. 2009. *Political Economy.* Tel Aviv: Hakibbutz Hameuohad.

Gabbay, Yoram and Rafael Rob. 2002. "Trade Liberalization and the Unification of the Exchange Rates: Implications for the National Economy," in Avi Ben Bassat, ed. *The Israeli Economy, 1985–1998: From Government Intervention to Market Economics.* Cambridge, MA: MIT Press.

Galbraith, James. 2008. *The Predator State.* New York: The Free Press.

Gansler, Jacques. 1980. *The Defense Industry.* Cambridge, MA: MIT Press.

Gazit, Shlomo. 2003. *Trapped Fools: Thirty Years of Israeli Policy in the Territories.* London and Portland, OR: Frank Cass.

Gerschenkron, A. 1962. *Economic Backwardness in Historical Perspective.* Cambridge, MA: Harvard University Press.

Goldstein, Tani. 2007. "Arabs Out of Israeli Hi-tech." *YNet News.com.* 9 August. http://www.ynet.co.il/english/articles/0,7340,L-3447252,00.html

Gorenberg, Gershom. 2008. "The Etzion Illusion." *Ha'aretz.* 29 September.

Gottheil, Fred. 2003. The Smoking Gun: Arab Immigration into Palestine, 1922–1931. *Middle East Quarterly.* http://www.meforum.org/article/522

Gottlieb, Daniel. 2007. *Poverty and Labor Market Behaviour in the Ultra-Orthodox Population in Israel.* Jerusalem: The Van Leer Jerusalem Institute.

Greenaway, David and Douglas Nelson. 2000. "The Assessment: Globalization and the Labour Market." *Oxford Review of Economic Policy.* Vol. 16. No. 3.

Greenwald, Carol Schwartz. 1972. *Recession as a Policy Instrument: Israel 1965–69.* London: C. Hurst & Co.

Grief, Avner. 1993. "Contract Enforceability and Economic Institutions in Early Trade: The Magrhribi Trader's Coalition." *American Economic Review.* Vol. 83. No. 3.

Grinberg, Lev Luis and Gershon Shafir. 2000. "Economic Liberalization and the Breakup of the Histadrut's Domain," in Gershon Shafir and Yoav Peled, eds. *The New Israel.* Boulder: Westview.

Grinber, Mijal. 2007. "IDF: Nearly 28% of Israeli {Jewish} Males Avoided Conscription in 2007." *Ha'aretz.* 6 December.

Ha'aretz. 2005. The Marker. 1 November.

Ha'aretz. 1999. Tel Aviv. 21 June.

Haider, Ali, ed. 2008. The Sikkuy Report 2007 Haifa and Jerusalem. *Sikkuy: The Association for the Advancement of Civic Equality in Israel.* http://www.sikkuy.org.il/english/en2007/sikkuy2007.pdf

Halevi, Nadav. A Brief Economic History of Modern Israel. *EH.Net Encyclopedia.* http://eh.net/encyclopedia/article/halevi.israel

Halevi Nadav and Ruth Klinov-Malul. 1968. *The Economic Development of Israel.* New York, Washington, London: Frederik A. Praeger Publishers.

Halperin, Ariel. 1986. Military Build-up and Economic Growth in Israel. Jerusalem: Maurice Falk Institute Conference Paper, June.

Helpman, Elhanan. 2003. "Israel's Economic Growth: An International Comparison." *Israel Economic Review.* Vol. 1. No. 1. 1–10. http://www.bankisrael.gov.il/publeng/publeslf.php?misg_id=22&publ_num=Vol%201,No.1.

Harel, Amos. 2008. Israel Wastes 250 Million Shekels on Settlement Roads to Nowhere. *Ha'aretz.* 21 November. http://www.haaretz.com/hasen/spages/1039508.html

Honig, Benson, Miri Lerner and Yoel Rabin. 2006. "Social Capital and the Linkages of High-Tech Companies to the Military Defense System: Is There a Signaling Mechanism?" *Small Business Economics.* Vol. 27. No. 4–5.

Horowitz, Dan and Moshe Lissak. 1978. *Origins of the Israeli Polity.* Chicago and London: University of Chicago Press.

Horowitz, David. 1945. Jewish Colonization and Arab Development in Palestine. Jerusalem: Central Archives, Record Group S90/File 76. 4 October. http://www.ismi.emory.edu/PrimarySource/CZAcolanddevOct45.pdf

Institute for National Security Studies. 2008. Middle East Military Balance Database. http://www.inss.org.il/upload/(FILE)1206270841.pdf

International Monetary Fund. 2009. Israel: 2008 Article IV Consultation-Staff Report. Washington DC: Country Report No. 09/57.

Ishak, Saporta, Salem Abo Zaid and Dotan Leshem. 2006. Inequality in the Distribution of Income among Household and Wage Earners in Israel 1967–2003. Jerusalem: The Van Leer Institute, Economics and Society Program Policy Research Paper no. 2.

Israel Military Industries. 2009. Profile. http://www.imiisrael.com/Company/Profile.aspx?FolderID=25

Israel, Ministry of Foreign Affairs Website. 2005. http://www.mfa.gov.il, accessed 14 September.

Israel National Council for the Child. 2008. http://www.children.org.il/information.asp?id=30

Israel National Council for the Child. 2008. Selection of Statistics from the Yearbook: Children in Israel 2008. http://www.children.org.il/Files/File/leket2009.doc

Israel-U.S. Binational Industrial Research and Development (BIRD). 2007. 2007 Annual Report http://www.birdf.com/_Uploads/193BIRD_AR2007.pdf

Ivry, David. 2003. Privatization of Military Services and Its Implications. *The Fisher Brothers Institute for Air and Space Strategic Studies.* http://www.fisherinstitute.org.il/Eng/_Articles/Article.asp?ArticleID=37&CategoryID=25

Kanafani, Nu'man. 2004. "Economic Foundations for Peace," in Hassan Hakimian and Jeffrey B. Nugent, eds. *Trade Policy and Economic Integration in the Middle East and North Africa.* London: Routledge Curzon.

Karnit, Flug and Nitsa Kasir (Kaliner). 2003. "Poverty and Employment, and the Gulf between Them." *Israel Economic Review.* Vol. 1. No. 1.

Khenen, Dov. 2000. "From 'Eretz Yisrael Haovedet' to 'Yisrael Hashniah': The Social Discourse and Social Policy of Mapai in the 1950s," in Gershon Shafir and Yoav Peled, eds. *The New Israel.* Boulder: Westview.

Kin, George. 2003. Low Labor-Input Technology Utilization in the Construction Industry. *Central Bureau of Statistics.* http://www.cbs.gov.il/publications/singapore.pdf

Kleinman, Ephraim. 1985. *The Indexation of Public Sector Debt in Israel.* Jerusalem: Falk Institute.

Kleinman, Ephraim. 1987. "The Histadrut Economy of Israel: In Search of Criteria." *Jerusalem Quarterly.* No. 41.

Kleinman, Ephraim. 1998. "The Waning of Israeli Etatism." *Israel Studies.* Vol. 2. No. 2.

Klieman, Aaron. 1985. *Israel's Global Reach.* London: Pergamon Brassey's.

Knesset Research and Information Center. 2002. Report and Survey of the Development of the Social Gaps in Israel in the Last Twenty Years. http://www.knesset.gov.il/mmm/eng/doc_eng.asp?doc=me00416&type=pdf

Knesset Research and Information Center. 2003. The Core Curriculum. http://www.knesset.gov.il/mmm/data/pdf/m00557.pdf

Knesset Research and Information Center. 2008. Encouraging Employment of Haredi Women. http://www.knesset.gov.il/mmm/data/pdf/m02006.pdf

Kosenko, Konstantin. 2007. Concentration of Business Ownership. *Israel Economic Review.* Vol. 5. No. 2. http://www.bankisrael.gov.il/deptdata/mehkar/iser/10/iser_3.pdf

Kosenko, Konstantin. 2008. Evolution of Business Groups in Israel: Their Impact at the Level of the Firm and the Economy. Bank of Israel, Research Department Discussion Paper Series no. 2008.02. http://www.bankisrael.gov.il/deptdata/mehkar/papers/dp0802e.htm16.4

Kuran, Timur. 1998. *Islam and Mammon: The Economic Predicaments of Islamism.* Princeton, NJ: Princeton University Press.

Lal, Deepak. 2004. *Unintended Consequences.* Cambridge, MA: MIT Press.

Landes, David. 1998. *The Wealth and Poverty of Nations.* New York and London: W.W. Norton.

Levanon, Gad and Yaron Raviv. 2007. "Decomposing Wage Gaps between Ethnic Groups: The Case of Israel." *Southern Economic Journal.* Vol. 73. No. 4.

Lewin-Epstein, Noah. 1990. The Arab Economy in Israel: Growing Population Mismatch. Pinchas Sapir Center for Development, TAU, Discussion Paper 014–90.

Lewin-Epstein, Noah and Moshe Semyonov. 1993. *The Arab Minority in Israel's Economy.* Boulder: Westview Press.

Lifshitz, Yaacov. 2003. *The Economics of Producing Defense Illustrated by the Israeli Case.* Boston, Dordrecht, New York, London: Kluwer Academic Publishers.

Madrick, Jeff. 2008. *The Case for Big Government.* Princeton, NJ: Princeton University Press.

Ma'ariv. 1985. Tel Aviv. 2 August.

Mahler, Gregory S. 2004. *Politics and Government in Israel.* Lanham, Boulder, New York, Toronto, Oxford: Rowman & Littlefield Publishers Inc.

Mark, Clyde R. 2005. Israel: US Foreign Assistance. *CRS Issue Brief for Congress. Order Code IB85066, Congressional Research Service, The Library of Congress.* http://www.fas.org/sgp/crs/mideast/IB85066.pdf

Mathias, Peter. 1999. "How Do Minorities Become Elites," in Elise S. Brezis and Peter Temin, eds. *Elites, Minorities, and Economic Growth.* Amsterdam: Elsevier.

Mekorot: Israel National Water Company. 2009. Israel's Water Supply System. http://www.mekorot.co.il/Eng/Mekorot/Pages/IsraelsWaterSupplySystem.aspx

Meltzer, Jacob. 1998. *The Divided Economy of Mandatory Palestine.* Cambridge: Cambridge University Press.

Metzer, Jacob and Oded Kaplan. 1985. Jointly but Severally: Arab-Jewish Dualism and Economic Growth in Mandatory Palestine. The Maurice Falk Institute for Economic Research in Israel, Research Paper 180.

Ministry of Construction and Housing. 2008. Press Notice, 5 August. http://www.moch.gov.il/NR/exeres/6CAED619–3D14–4914-B9A9-C2E9EDFAD1D0.htm

Ministry of Defense. 2007. Report in Accordance with the Law for the Freedom of Information. http://www.mod.gov.il/pages/about_office/pdfs/2007.pdf

Ministry of Finance. 1986. The Budget 1986/87.

Ministry of Finance. 1990. Main Points of the Budget 1991.

Ministry of Finance. 1999. Ministry of Education Budget 2000. http://www.mof.gov.il/budget2007/fbudget.htm

Ministry of Finance. 2000. Economic Outlook, November. http://147.237.72.111/research_e/mainpage.htm

Ministry of Finance. 2001. Economic Outlook. February.

Ministry of Finance. 2001. Economic Outlook, June. http://147.237.72.111/research_e/mainpage.htm

Ministry of Finance. 2008. Appendix to the National Budget 2009. http://www.mof.gov.il/research_e/2009/stateBudget2009.pdf

Ministry of Finance. 2008. Ministry of Education Budget, pp. 34 and 173. http://www.mof.gov.il/budget2007/docs2009/hinuch.pdf

Ministry of Finance. 2008. The Budget in Brief. http://www.mof.gov.il/budget2007/docs2008/301.pdf

Ministry of Finance. 2009. Budget in Brief, p. 83. http://www.mof.gov.il/budget2007/docs2009/c01.pdf

Ministry of Finance. 2009. Budget, Office of the Prime Minister. http://www.mof.gov.il/budget2007/fbudget.htm

Ministry of Finance. 2009. Main Points of the Budget. http://www.mof.gov.il/budget2007/docs2009/c01.pdf

Ministry of Finance. 2009. Ministry of Defense Budget. http://mof.gov.il/BudgetSite/StateBudget/Budget2009/MinisteriesBudget/Safety/Lists/List/Attachments/1/safety1.pdf

Ministry of Finance. 2009. Ministry of Education Budget. http://www.mof.gov.il/BudgetSite/StateBudget/Budget2009/MinisteriesBudget/socialBudget/Lists/List/Attachments/2/education%202.pdf

Ministry of Finance. 2009. Non-Classified Items in the Defense Budget. http://www.mof.gov.il/BudgetSite/StateBudget/Budget2009/MinisteriesBudget/Safety/Lists/List/Attachments/2/safety2.pdf

Ministry of Finance. 2009. The Non-Classified Defense Budget, p. 38. http://www.mof.gov.il/budget2007/docs2009/bitachonLoMesuvag.pdf

Ministry of Interior. 2006. Local Authorities in Israel. Publication No. 1315. http://www.moin.gov.il/Apps/PubWebSite/publications.nsf/All/7EDFB6D72D07F81FC22574B30031F767/$FILE/Publications.pdf

Ministry of Trade, Industry and Employment. Intel Israel – Thirty Years of Successful Growth. http://www.moital.gov.il/NR/exeres/49CA1B09–31FC-4D88-A603-FFD3D78A973C.htm, accessed 23 June 2010.

Morck, Randall, Daniel Wolfenzon, and Bernard Yeung. 2005. "Corporate Governance, Economic Entrenchment, and Growth." *Journal of Economic Literature*. Vol. XLIII. No. 3.

Morris, Benny. 2004. *The Birth of the Palestinian Refugee Problem Revisited*. Cambridge: Cambridge University Press.

National Insurance Institute. 2008. Measures of Poverty and Social Gaps 2007. Jerusalem: National Insurance Institute.

National Insurance Institute. 2008. Poverty and Social Gaps in 2007. *Research and Planning Administration Annual Report*. http://www.btl.gov.il/English%20Homepage/Publications/Poverty_Report/Documents/oni2007-E.pdf

Official Summary of the Or Commission. 2008. *Ha'aretz*. 27 January. http://www.haaretz.com/hasen/pages/ShArt.jhtml?itemNo=335594

Olson, Mancur. 1982. *The Rise and Decline of Nations*. New Haven and London: Yale University Press.

Organisation for Economic Cooperation and Development (OECD). 2007. Roadmap for the Accession of Israel to the OECD Convention. Document no. C(20007)102/Final 3. http://www.olis.oecd.org/olis/2007doc.nsf/LinkTo/NT00004872/$FILE/JT03237381.PDF

Organisation for Economic Cooperation and Development (OECD). 2010. OECD Economic Surveys: Israel 2009. Vol. 2009/21, Supplement 3.

Pack, Howard. 1971. *Structural Change and Economic Policy in Israel*. New Haven, CT: Yale University Press.

Palestinian Monetary Authority. Department of Research and Monetary Policies. 1997. Monthly Statistical Bulletin. Ramallah: Palestinian Monetary Authority.

Passerman, Daniele. 2007. Do High Skilled Immigrants Raise Productivity? Evidence from Israel, 1990–1999. Samuel Neaman Institute, Technion-Israel Institute of Technology. Science, Technology and the Economy Program series. STE-WP-26–2007.

Patinkin, Don. 1967. *The Israeli Economy: The First Decade.* Jerusalem: Maurice Falk Institute for Economic Research in Israel.

Pavin, Avraham. 2006. The Kibbutz Movement: Facts and Figures 2006. Ramat Efal, Yad Tabenkin: Research and Documentation Center of the Kibbutz Movement. *Peace Now.* http://www.peace.now

Peled Dan. 2001. Defense R&D and Economic Growth in Israel: A Research Agenda. *Samuel Neaman Institute, The Technion.* http://econ.haifa.ac.il/~dpeled/papers/ste-wp4.pdf

Pepperman, Beni. 2006. Increasing Employment for Israeli Arabs. *Ministry of Industry, Trade and Employment, Research and Economics Authority.* http://www.moital. gov.il/NR/rdonlyres/FF6BBCA2-B2F9-4452-9EB6-CEC4DECC957A/0/taasukaarvim.pdf

Peri, Yoram and Amnon Neubach. 1985. The Military Industrial Complex in Israel: A Pilot Study. Tel Aviv: International Center for Peace in the Middle East.

Pomfret, Richard. 1976. *Trade Policies and Industrialization in a Small Country: The Case of Israel.* Tubingen: JCB Mohr Paul Siebert.

Porter, Michael. 1980. *Competitive Strategy: Techniques for Analyzing Industries and Competitors.* New York: Free Press.

Prime Minister's Office. 2007. National Economic Council Overview. Jerusalem: Prime Minister's Office. http://www.pmo.gov.il/NR/rdonlyres/93120D40-2790-4C14-A45E-80457D758FEB/0/NationalEconomicCounciloverview.pdf

Prime Minister's Office. 2007. Socio-Economic Agenda for Israel, 2008–2010. Jerusalem: Prime Minister's Office. National Economic Council. http://www.pmo. gov.il/PMO/PM+Office/Departments/econ20082010.htm.

Prime Minister's Office. 2008. The Arab Population and the State of Israel: Economic Integration Strategy. *Agency for the Development of the Arab Sector in Israel.* http://www.pmo.gov.il/NR/rdonlyres/76DFC487-D52D-4A4F-919D-166BDF0476FC/0/ecopaper.pdf

Prime Minister's Office. 2008. The Prime Minister's Conference on Arab Local Authorities, ppt#316, 18. http://www.pmo.gov.il/NR/rdonlyres/F071E419-6643-4A2C-8F32-337CD628EAB9/0/int

Radom, M. 1968. "Military Officers and Business Leaders: An Israeli Study in Contrasts." *Columbia Journal of World Business.* Vol. 3. No. 2.

Rafael Advanced Defense Systems Ltd. Welcome to Rafael. http://www.rafael.co.il/marketing/cor0porate.aspx?FolderID=197

Ribon, Sigal, Karnit Flug, and Nitsa Kasir. 2000 "Unemployment and Education in Israel: Business Cycles, Structural Change, and Technological Change, 1986–98." *Economic Quarterly.* Vol. 47. No. 3.

Report of the Commission of Enquiry into the Clash between Security Forces and Israeli Citizens October 2000. Jerusalem: The High Court of Justice 2003. http://elyon1. court.gov.il/heb/veadot/or/inside_index.htm

Rivlin, Paul. 1992. *The Israeli Economy.* Boulder, CO: Westview.

Rivlin, Paul. 2001. *Economic Policy and Performance in the Arab World*. Boulder, CO: Lynne Rienner.

Rivlin, Paul. 2009. *Arab Economies in the Twenty First Century*. Cambridge and New York: Cambridge University Press.

Rivlin-Tsur, Goni and Emad Zoabi. 2005. The State of Infant Education in the Arab Sector in Israel: Characteristics, Data and Conclusions. *The Abraham Fund Initiatives and The Citizens Accord Forum between Jews and Arabs in Israel, Newe Ilan*. http://www.abrahamfund.org/main/siteNew/index.php?page=4#

Sadan, Ezra. 2006. The Share of the Arab Sector in the Economy. *The Abraham Fund Initiatives*. http://www.abrahamfund.org

Sadeh, Sharon. 2001. Israel's Beleaguered Defense Industry. *Middle East Review of International Affairs*. Vol. 5. No.1. http://meria.idc.ac.il/journal/2001/issue1/sadeh.pdf

Sandler, Neal. 2006. Buffet Takes a Cut Out of Iscar. *Businessweek*, 8 May. http://www.businessweek.com/globalbiz/content/may2006/gb20060508_953503.htm

Saporta, Ishak, Salem Abo Zaid, and Dotan Leshem. 2006. Inequality in the Distribution of Income among Household and Wage Earners in Israel 1967–2003. The Van Leer Institute, Economics and Society Program Policy Research Paper no. 2.

Sason, Talya. Summary of Opinion Concerning Unauthorized Outposts. http://www.mfa.gov.il/MFA/Government/Law/Legal+Issues+and+Rulings/Summary+of+Opinion+Concerning+Unauthorized+Outposts+-+Talya+Sason+Adv.htm

Schmuel, Avi. 2001. "Hi-Tech Prosperity Does Not Reach Periphery." *Ha'aretz*. 6 June.

Schnell, Izhak, Michael Sofer and Israel Drori. 1995. *Arab Industrialization in Israel: Ethnic Entrepreneurship in the Periphery*. Westport, CT: Westview.

Schubert, Avi. 1990. "Koor Loses $303 Million." *Ha'aretz*. 21 June.

Schulman, Sofi. 2000. "Galileo Sold to Merval." *Ha'aretz*. 18 October.

Semyonov, Moshe and Ephraim Yuchtman-Yaar. 1988. Ethnicity and Occupational Inequality: Jews and Arabs in Israel. The Pinchas Sapir Center for Development. TAU Discussion Paper no. 16.

Senor, Dan and Saul Singer. 2009. *Start Up Nation: The Story of Israel's Economic Miracle*. New York: The Hachette Book Group.

Shahar, Ilan. 2008. "Record Yeshiva Enrollment Predicted to Cost Economy NIS 5 Billion." *Ha'aretz*. 28 August.

Shahar, Ilan. 2008. "State Saves NIS 19 Billion Due to Cut in Child Allowances Since 2002." *Ha'aretz*. 11 August.

Shahar, Ilan. 2009. "The Knesset Is Evading the Draft." *Ha'aretz*. 17 September.

Shahar, Ilan and Zvi Zrahiya. 2008. "Knesset Makes It Legal: Yeshivas Don't Need to Teach Math and English." *Ha'aretz*. 25 July.

Shiffer, Varda. 1999. *The Haredi Educational in Israel: Allocation, Regulation and Control*. Jerusalem: The Floersheimer Institute for Policy Studies. http//www.floershiemer.org.il

Shiffer, Zalman. 1982. "Money and Inflation in Israel: The Transition of an Economy to High Inflation." *Federal Reserve Board of St. Louis Review*. Vol. 64. No. 7. 28–41.

Shiffer, Zalman. 2007. "The Debate over the Defense Budget in Israel." *Israel Studies*. Vol. 12. No. 1.

Shmuel, Amir. 2000. Overseas Foreign Workers in Israel: Policy Aims and Labor Market Outcomes. Falk Institute Discussion Paper no. 2000.01.

Shragai, Nadav. 2008. "Open Element and Ultra-Orthodox Jews Deliver a Population Boom to the West Bank." *Ha'aretz*. 14 August.

Sinai, Ruth. 2008. "Poverty Report: The Many Faces of Destitution." *Ha'aretz*. 24 November.

Slaughter, Matthew J. 1999. "Globalization and Wages: A Tale of Two Perspectives." *The World Economy*. Vol. 22. No. 5.

Smith, Barbara J. 1993. *The Roots of Separation in Palestine 1920–1929*. London and New York: I.B. Tauris & Co Ltd.

State Comptroller. 1984. Report of the State Comptroller, no. 35 Jerusalem: State Comptroller's Office, 1984.

Stockholm International Peace Research Institute. 2008. *SIPRI Yearbook 2008*. Oxford: Oxford University Press.

Stolberg, Sheryl Gay and Stephen Labaton. 2009. Obama Calls Wall Street Bonuses "Shameful." *International Herald Tribune*. 29 January. http://www.iht.com/articles/2009/01/29/business/30obama.php

Sussman, Zvi. 1986. *Israel's Economy: Performance, Problems and Policies*. London: Institute for Jewish Affairs and The Jacob Levinson Center of the Israel-Diaspora Institute for Jewish Affairs.

Swirski, Shlomo. 2008. The Cost of Occupation, The Burden of the Israeli-Palestinian Conflict. Adva Center Report. http://www.adva.org/view.asp?lang=en&articleID=509

Swirski, Shlomo, Etty Konor-Attias and Ehud Dahan. 2008. Government Preferences in Financing Local Authorities 2000–2006. Adva Center Report. http://www.adva.org/UserFiles/File/settlements%202000–2006%20final

Szereszewski, Robert. 1968. *Essays on the Structure of the Jewish Economy in Palestine and Israel*. Jerusalem: The Maurice Falk Institute for Economic Research in Israel.

Tov, Imri. 2005. "The Disengagement Price Tag." *Strategic Assessment*. Vol. 8. No. 3. http://www.inss.org.il/publications.php?cat=21&incat=&read=194

Trajtenberg Manuel. 2000. R&D Policy in Israel: An Overview and Reassessment. National Bureau of Economic Research, Working Paper no. 7930.

Tzimuki, Tova and Aries Arad. 1987. "Answer on the Lavi at the End of the Month." *Davar*. 8 March.

United Nations. 1947. General Assembly Resolution 181 (II) The Future Government of Palestine, 29 November. http://unispal.un.org/unispal.nsf/0/7F0AF2BD897689B785256C330061D253

United Nations. 2005. Population Division of the Department of Economic and Social Affairs of the United Nations Secretariat, World Population Prospects: The 2006 Revision and World Urbanization Prospects: The 2005 Revision, Medium variant. http://esa.un.org/unpp/p2k0data.asp

United Nations. 2006. World Population Prospects. The 2006 Revision. http://esa.un.org/unpp/index.asp?panel=2

United States. 2008. Budget of the United States Government: Browse Fiscal Year 2008, Summary tables. *Government Printing Office*. http://www.gpoaccess.gov/usbudget/fy08/pdf/budget/tables.pdf

Van Arkadie, Brian. 1977. *Benefits and Burdens: A Report on the West Bank and Gaza Strip Economies since 1967*. New York and Washington DC: Carnegie Endowment for Peace.

Weber, Max. 1930. *The Protestant Ethic and the Spirit of Capitalism*. London: George Allen and Unwin.

Weinshall, Theodore D. 1972. "The Industrialization of a Rapidly Developing Country – Israel," in Robert Dubin, ed. *Handbook of Work, Organization and Society.* Chicago: Rand McNally College Publishing Co.

World Bank. 2002. Long Term Policy Options for the Palestinian Economy. http://www-wds.worldbank.org/external/default/WDSContentServer/WDSP/IB/2003/08/14/00 0160016_20030814165921/Rendered/PDF/263360PAPER0GZ0News0Update0.pdf

World Bank. 2005. The Palestinian Economy and the Prospects for Its Recovery. Economic Monitoring Report to the Ad Hoc Liaison Committee, no. 1.

World Bank. 2006. West Bank and Gaza Country Economic Memorandum. Vol. 1 Report no. 36320 WBG. Washington DC: World Bank.

Yotav-Solberg, Idit. ed. 2008. *The Appointment and Reward of Senior Managers in Public Companies and Authorities.* Bank of Israel Survey, January, 19. http://www.bank-israel.gov.il/deptdata/mehkar/seker81/surv81_1.pdf

Zrahiya, Zvi. 2009. "Netanyahu Agrees to Raise Child Allowances." *Ha'aretz.* 23 March.

Zussman, Noam and Amit Friedman. 2008. The Quality of the Labor Force in Israel. Bank of Israel Research Department Discussion Paper no. 2008.01.

Zussman, Noam and Shay Tsur. 2008. The Effect of Students' Socioeconomic Background on Their Achievements in Matriculation Examinations. Bank of Israel, Research Department Discussion Paper no. 2008.11. http://www.bankisrael.gov.il/deptdata/mehkar/papers/dp0811e.pdf

Index

Agriculture, i, 4, 8–9, 14, 18, 20–21, 24–25,
  29, 33, 37–38, 43–44, 60, 109–110, 114, 130,
  155, 193–194, 198, 240
Arab boycott, 39, 47, 98
Arabs, x, 7, 10, 14, 17, 24, 27, 31, 33–35, 42,
  106, 116, 123, 155, 164, 176, 187, 189–191,
  193–199, 203–206, 212, 214, 223–225,
  232–233, 238, 244, 246, 271, 275, 280–281
arms, 46, 120, 131, 134, 141
austerity, 3, 8, 35, 48, 52–53, 95

balance of payments, 4–9, 20, 36–37, 41, 43,
  46, 49, 52, 54, 56–57, 59–60, 62, 64, 67–69,
  71, 74, 88–91, 93, 104, 106, 116, 240–242
Bank Hapoalim, 25
Bank of Israel, 5–7, 44, 50–52, 54–55, 61, 64,
  66, 70–71, 73–77, 80–82, 85, 89–92, 99–100,
  105, 107, 111, 113, 120, 124, 129–131,
  153–154, 164, 166, 174, 176–177, 195, 203,
  218, 220–223, 225, 227–229, 231, 234, 237,
  252, 258, 262, 264, 271–273, 275, 277, 281,
  283
Banks, 28–29, 35, 56, 67, 84, 115, 140,
  161, 271
Begin, Menachem, 49–50, 143, 247
Ben Gurion, David, 23, 118, 213, 246, 281
Bonds, 3
Bruno, Michael, 43, 56, 59, 61, 63–66, 273
Budget, ix, xi, 54, 61, 70, 81, 83, 116, 118–119,
  121, 123, 125, 127, 130, 137, 148, 172, 178,
  180, 182, 196, 220, 230, 232, 252, 274,
  278–279, 281–282

Capital, i, xi, xiii–1, 3–4, 6–8, 16, 18–23,
  25, 29, 37–39, 41–45, 49, 52–53, 59, 61,
  66–67, 69–75, 77–78, 88–91, 93, 96, 98–101,
  104–105, 108, 113–116, 134–136, 139–140,
  150–151, 171–172, 188, 206, 220, 223, 230,
  236–237, 240–242, 253, 255, 261, 271,
  273–274, 276
Child allowances, 168, 174, 176–177, 184–185,
  191, 203, 220, 227, 235, 238, 243, 281, 283
China, i, 9, 71, 97–99, 262
Citrus, 4, 22, 45
Conscription, 9, 118, 123–125, 138, 171,
  245, 276
Conscripts, 124–125
Construction, 9, 18, 24–26, 28, 38–40, 51–52,
  84–85, 95, 109, 111–114, 116, 129–131,
  145, 148, 151–154, 165, 183, 198, 244–245,
  265–266
Consumption, 4, 30, 41, 46, 48–49, 51–52, 55,
  65, 72, 78, 83, 96, 102, 114, 117, 120, 123,
  129–130, 141, 180, 188, 228, 253
Credit, 52, 60–61, 66, 83–84, 89, 115, 230
Current account, 6, 41, 43–44, 46, 60, 63–64,
  71, 88–90, 93, 242
Customs duties, 51

Debt, v, 5–6, 8–9, 46, 48, 56, 67–69, 78, 80–83,
  90, 93–94, 122, 127–129, 141, 149, 228, 242,
  245, 247, 252, 258
Defense, i, xvi, 2, 8–9, 16, 24, 30, 41–44, 46–49,
  51–52, 54–55, 61, 64, 78, 81, 83, 102–104, -
  118–138, 140–142, 153, 160, 165, 180–181,
  243, 245–246, 248
Demobilization, 124–125
Devaluation, 3, 41, 49, 51–57, 62–63
Diamonds, 4, 45
Discrimination, 77, 186–187, 189, 194–198,
  207, 211, 213, 228, 238
Dollarization, 5, 56

Education, x, 106, 150, 177–179, 182, 184, 196, 199, 202, 204, 206, 221, 227, 231–233, 274, 278–280

Egypt, i, 5, 40, 47, 51, 65, 98, 108, 127, 129, 138, 145, 149, 155, 158, 160–161, 164, 190, 206

Elections, 27, 49, 53, 161, 246

Emigration, 13, 129, 155, 157, 210, 213, 231, 250

Employment, 3–4, 7, 13–16, 21, 23–27, 36, 38, 41, 45, 54, 87–88, 95, 101–102, 104, 106–110, 113–114, 116–117, 124–125, 153–155, 157–158, 162, 177, 184, 187, 189, 192–199, 201–205, 207, 222–225, 227–228, 230–231, 238, 240–241, 244, 250, 252, 264

European Community, 4, 9, 41, 45, 94–95

European Economic Community, 241

European Union, 99–100, 163, 262

Exports, i, xi–4, 9, 18–20, 26, 36, 41, 43–46, 51–52, 57, 62, 71–72, 74, 88–89, 91, 93, 95–97, 100–101, 104–106, 114–115, 117, 130, 134–135, 137, 141, 158, 164, 262

Fiscal policy, 81–82, 115, 247

Free trade agreement (FTA), 4, 160, 241

Fuel, 25, 48, 125, 129

Galilee, 36, 38–39, 50, 145, 148, 193

Gaza, x, xi, 9, 24, 31, 49–50, 70, 109, 128, 131, 138, 143–147, 149–165, 190, 192, 244–245, 247–248, 275, 282–283

Germany, 17, 37, 39, 41, 77, 140, 241, 254, 256–257, 259

Golan Heights, 143, 145–146

Government expenditure, 47, 50–51, 57

Government expenditures, 43, 122

Government revenues, 60

Gross domestic product, 1–3, 41, 43, 119, 125

Gross national product, 1, 54, 120, 126, 155

Health, 15, 21, 26–28, 74, 118, 160, 239

Herut, 49–50

Hevrat Ovdim, 25, 28, 53

High technology, i, 4, 6, 9, 28, 69–70, 72, 74, 78, 81, 84–87, 89, 91, 94–97, 99–109, 112, 116, 133, 138–139, 198, 220–221, 231, 242

Histadrut, 8, 12, 14, 16, 22–28, 37, 44, 49, 53, 57–58, 64, 109, 132, 194, 276–277

Holocaust, 13, 23, 37

Housing, 20, 25–26, 32, 34, 36, 85, 109, 115, 144, 148, 154, 169–170, 212, 240

Ideology, i, 7, 21–24, 35, 138, 143, 145

Immigrants, xv, 2–4, 6–8, 10, 12–18, 20, 23–24, 26, 30–31, 33–35, 37–39, 42–43, 51, 70–71, 73–75, 77, 80, 98, 106, 113, 145, 208, 210, 212–214, 218, 223–224, 234, 240–242, 246, 249

Immigration, i–4, 6–7, 10, 13, 15–18, 20, 22, 34, 36, 39, 42, 69–70, 72–73, 75–78, 93, 98, 109, 112–113, 129, 190, 194, 206, 208, 210, 212–213, 216, 234, 238, 242, 249

Imports, xi–1, 3–4, 6, 9, 18–20, 36, 38, 41, 43–48, 51–52, 57, 62, 64, 69, 71–72, 74, 88–89, 91, 93, 95–99, 106–107, 112, 116–117, 128–129, 134, 141, 153, 158, 160, 164, 205, 237, 241, 260, 262, 265

Indexation, 3814n, 52, 59, 63, 65

Industrialization, i, 14, 29, 33, 37, 95, 165, 240–241

Industry, 4, 8–9, 14, 19, 21, 24–25, 29, 38, 48, 60–61, 84–85, 103, 105–106, 109, 112–114, 116, 129, 131, 133–137, 139–140, 145, 163, 165, 198–199, 236, 240

Inflation, 5–6, 8, 25, 28, 35–36, 46–48, 51–60, 62–68, 71, 73, 115, 142

Intifada (Palestinian Uprising), 6, 70, 78, 81, 120, 128, 130, 138, 156, 165, 197, 207

Investment, 1, 4, 6–8, 19–20, 23, 26, 36–37, 39, 41, 45, 51–52, 71–75, 77–78, 83, 88–91, 93–97, 99–100, 105–106, 108–109, 130, 135, 140–141, 145, 151, 154–155, 181, 186, 188, 196–197, 236, 249, 258

Israel Aircraft Industries, 120, 132, 134, 137

Israel Defense Forces (IDF), 23, 103, 117, 119–120, 159–160

Israel Military Industries (IMI), 132, 276

Jerusalem, 3, 7, 22, 25, 29, 37–38, 42, 46, 51, 54–55, 61, 64–65, 74, 86–87, 99, 101, 107, 116, 120–121, 126, 129–130, 132, 141, 144, 147, 155, 159–160, 163–166, 169, 171, 173, 175, 178, 183–185, 189, 199, 202, 204, 211, 218–219, 221, 225–226, 228, 230–231, 239, 243, 251, 263, 268, 271–273, 275–283

Jewish National Fund, 23, 31–32, 194

Jews, 1, 12–17, 20, 23–24, 31–32, 34–35, 37, 39, 49, 116, 143, 147–148, 166–167, 170, 177, 180, 183, 187, 190–191, 193, 195–199, 201–202, 204, 210–212, 214–216, 223–225, 232–233, 240, 243, 247, 249, 271, 273, 280–281

Jordan, 71, 97–98, 108, 143, 155, 161, 190, 206

Kibbutz, 12, 29–30, 50, 212, 271–272, 280
Koor, 26, 28, 132, 281
Kupat Holim Clalit, 26, 28

Labor, ix, x, xi, xiii, 4–5, 8, 13–14, 16, 21–25,
    27–30, 34–35, 38, 48–50, 57, 64, 71, 74–77,
    109–112, 124, 143, 146, 152, 156, 166–167,
    173, 182–183, 185, 194, 197, 199, 212,
    236–237, 241, 246, 248, 254, 258, 265, 271,
    273–274, 276–277, 281, 283
Lavi (aircraft), 61, 120, 133–134, 138, 282
Lebanon, 5, 55, 64, 120, 128–130, 137–138,
    190, 206, 245–246, 272
Liberalism, 53
Likud, 5, 28, 49–50, 53, 56–57, 64, 67, 70–71,
    143, 182, 246–247
Linkage, 58–59, 63, 65, 111
Loans, 3, 45–46, 61, 67, 89, 120, 126–128

Mandate, i, xiii, 12, 18, 21, 32, 34, 36, 103, 163,
    167, 187, 190, 251
Ministry of Defense, 104, 119–120, 125, 131,
    133, 142, 180, 278–279
Ministry of Finance, 44, 50, 54, 66, 70, 82–83,
    110, 112, 115–116, 119, 121, 123, 125, 127,
    130, 137, 148, 178, 180, 182, 196, 220, 230,
    278–279
Ministry of Industry and Trade, 44
Monetary policy, 52, 62, 66, 84, 115
Monopoly, 136
Moshavim, 23, 30–31, 146

National Insurance Institute, 124, 175–176,
    184, 201–202, 204, 217, 219–220, 222, 228,
    268, 272, 279
Negev, i, 33, 36, 38–39, 50–51, 118, 145,
    148, 193, 281
Netanyahu, Benjamin, 174, 283

OECD, ix, xiii, 7, 43, 47, 82–84, 97, 221, 226,
    231, 237, 249, 256–259, 279
Oil, 5, 39–40, 46–48, 60, 64–65, 98,
    100, 117, 129

Palestine Liberation Organization (PLO), 159
Palestinian Authority, 156, 159–161
Palestinians, i, vii, 2, 9, 24, 31, 71, 76, 97, 99,
    109–111, 113–114, 130, 143, 146–147, 149,
    151–153, 156–157, 159–162, 164–165, 195,
    218, 223, 243–245, 249, 264
Pensions, 119–120, 123, 125, 174, 227

Population, xvi–2, 6–7, 10, 13–14, 16–18,
    20–21, 23–24, 26, 29–31, 34–37, 39, 42, 49,
    75–76, 81, 97–98, 109, 117, 130, 144–148,
    151, 153, 155–158, 166, 168–170, 172, 174,
    176–178, 180–181, 183–187, 189–194,
    196–197, 200–208, 210–211, 213–218,
    221–225, 228–233, 240, 242–245, 249, 252,
    258, 266, 281
Populism, 53
Poverty, 7, 10–11, 177, 179, 181, 184, 186, 197,
    202–204, 207–208, 221–230, 232, 237–238,
    242–244, 249
Privatization, 82, 137
Productivity, 9, 20–21, 24, 26, 29, 38, 43,
    72–75, 77–78, 87, 93, 95, 111–113,
    125, 237, 249
Profitability, 26, 45, 116

Quotas, 9, 16, 96, 99, 112, 161

Rabin, Yitzhak, 48, 64, 71, 139, 144–145, 152,
    159, 174, 276
Rafael (Weapons Development Authority),
    112, 132, 137, 214, 272, 275, 280
Reparations, 37, 41, 45, 241
Russia, 12–13, 15–17, 97, 140, 160

Sadat, Anwar, 51
Sinai, 5, 40, 47, 51, 129, 143, 145, 149,
    164, 167, 226, 281
Six Day War, 4, 8, 67, 109, 121–122,
    143–144, 146, 241
Solel Boneh, 25–26, 28
Soviet Union, xv, 4, 6, 14, 17, 69–70, 73, 98,
    106, 109, 112–113, 197, 210–211, 213–214,
    216, 218, 234, 242, 249

Tariffs, 45, 96, 99, 112, 160, 248
Taxes, 9, 51, 53, 55, 60, 66, 124, 177, 179, 184,
    186, 202–205, 216–217, 219, 224–226,
    228, 242
Tel Aviv, i, iii, 8, 13, 16, 26, 43, 50, 56, 90, 106,
    108–109, 133–134, 151–152, 166, 193, 231,
    248, 271, 273, 275–276, 278, 280–282
Tourism, 114, 129–130, 155, 160
Trade, i, 3–4, 6, 8–10, 14, 18, 21–22, 25–28,
    34, 36, 41, 45–48, 50–51, 57, 71, 74, 86,
    88, 93–101, 105, 107, 109–110, 112, 117,
    136, 141, 155–156, 160–164, 192,
    199, 241, 274
Transport, 40, 84, 86, 98, 100, 126, 192, 204

Ultra-Orthodox Jews, 76, 123, 147–148,
166–172, 174, 176–180, 182–186, 191, 196,
203, 210, 214, 216, 218, 223–225, 229, 234,
236, 238, 243–244, 247, 249
Underemployment, 250
Unemployment, 3, 35–36, 41, 70, 75, 106, 110,
112, 116, 158, 169, 171, 197, 203, 207–208,
217–218, 220–221, 223, 227, 231
United Kingdom, 12, 84, 119, 140, 254,
256–257, 259
United States of America, i, v, ix, 3–6, 9, 12–13,
16–17, 20, 37, 46–47, 51, 59, 63, 66, 70,
83–84, 86–88, 94, 96–97, 99–102, 105, 108,
115–116, 119–120, 122, 126–129, 131–136,
141, 152, 160, 226, 239, 241–242, 248–249,
254, 256–259, 282
Universities, i, 17, 103–104, 233, 244

Venture capitalists, 105

Wages, 24, 26, 28–29, 52, 58–59, 62, 65, 71, 87,
102, 107, 110–111, 116, 153, 195, 201, 218,
223, 227–228, 230, 272
Water, 29, 39, 48, 85, 153, 163, 204, 228
Welfare, 5, 10, 14–15, 23, 26, 50, 68, 80–81, 94,
112, 149–150, 153, 160, 165, 170–171, 174,
177, 179, 181, 184–186, 195, 199, 203, 214,
216, 223–224, 242–244, 249, 275

Yishuv, vii, xiii–1, 12–14, 16, 18–23, 25, 27,
31–34, 39, 98, 167, 240, 251
Yom Kippur War, 5, 8, 46, 48, 54, 64–65, 67,
119, 122, 127–128, 142, 241

Zionists, 13, 15, 24, 30, 167